D0861536

BEHIND CLOSED DOORS

'In history . . . the study of homes and home life has undergone a revolution in the past few decades. One of the leading figures in that revolution is Amanda Vickery. Who can resist a book that describes one diarist as a confirmed grumbletonian. One would have to be a confirmed grumbletonian indeed not to find enlightenment – and pleasure – on every page of this book.'

Judith Flanders, *Sunday Telegraph*

'Vickery's prose is a model of its kind: as elegant and as bracing as a brisk rub-down in a gilt bath with carbolic soap. Some of the considerable achievements of this important book are Vickery's sheer mastery of the sources, the originality of her materials and methodology, and the provocations contained in her seductive prose.'

Helen Berry, University of Newcastle, Institute of Historical Research, *Reviews in History*

'Vickery's great skill lies in combining a sharp forensic eye with the ability to spot and tell stories, moving between different scales so smoothly that you can't see the joins. And then there is the wit of the thing. Few academic historians manage to be so funny without compromising the seriousness of their work. She did it 10 years ago in *The Gentleman's Daughter* and she has done it again here. It was worth the wait.'

Kathryn Hughes, *Guardian*

'Men and women were both under the illusion that they were in charge of the Georgian home. Amanda Vickery makes a delightful study of these roles and homes and draws from a huge range of period sources as she delves into the lives both of the rich and of the everyday Georgian.'

Nicola Sanders, *House and Garden*

'[Vickery] describes Enlightenment domesticity and the growth of elegant taste with wonderful aplomb and infectious enthusiasm . . . [*Behind Closed Doors*] is especially gorgeous in unusual and telling illustrations.'

Christina Hardyment, *History Today*

'What Vickery illuminates, often brilliantly, always entertainingly and through a myriad of examples from many different people, are the ways in which family and gender relations were played out in Georgian England.'

Stella Tillyard, *Times Literary Supplement*

'Professor Vickery is a thorough and disciplined academic who has trawled through many often obscure archives and tapped unusual or long neglected reservoirs of information. But not for a moment is she overwhelmed by the mighty volume of her research. She weaves it all into a compelling narrative packed with anecdote, strange characters and all manner of weird and wonderful details about Georgian home life.'

Dan Cruickshank, *Country Life*

'Comparison between Vickery and Jane Austen is irresistible. In a sense, this is history on the scale of the famous square of ivory on which Austen claimed the ideal novel should be created: graceful, delicate, sparkling with sprezzatura. As with Austen's novels, though, Vickery's research into the landscapes of Georgian domestic politics reveals a great deal more than embroidery going on in the drawing-room. . . . This book is almost too pleasurable, in that Vickery's style and delicious nosiness conceal some seriously weighty scholarship.'

Lisa Hilton, *Independent*

'[Vickery] opens resolutely shut doors and peeps into the private lives of servants, aristocrats and the "polite and middling sorts". . . Ms. Vickery's greatest achievement is to upend the notion that the home was divided into separate spheres in which men were responsible for brick and stone while women ruled over domestic life. . . Few writers have such a talent for transforming the driest historical source into a gripping narrative.'

Andrea Wulf, *International Herald Tribune*

'In supple, elegant prose [Vickery] repeatedly shows that domestic routines and choices were intertwined with political and public participation. Home life could be content or cruel, run smoothly or lurch through disasters, but it was the perennial obsession of every Georgian man and woman. A book full of fascinating discoveries – and radically important conclusions.'

Kate Williams, 'Historians' Favourites', *History Today*

ABCDEF GHIJK LMNOPQ RSTUVWXY Z&123456789 J

Aabcdefghijklmnopqrstuvwxyz z123456789101112

Exonerate your Mind from Earthly Cares
Spend each Lords day in Spiritual Affairs
Such wretched Souls who squander that away
Repent it sorely at their dying Day

Sarah   Stuart

1798

her   work

AMANDA VICKERY

Behind Closed Doors

At Home in Georgian England

Yale University Press

New Haven & London

For Hester, Rosamond and Dinah

PUBLISHED WITH ASSISTANCE FROM THE ANNIE BURR LEWIS FUND

Designed by Sarah Faulks

Printed in Great Britain

Library of Congress Cataloging-in-Publication Data

Vickery, Amanda.
Behind closed doors: At home in Georgian England / Amanda Vickery.
p. cm.
Includes bibliographical references and index.
ISBN 978-0-300-15453-5 (cl : alk. paper)
ISBN 978-0-300-16896-9 (pbk)

1. Households–England–History–18th century. 2. Great
Britain–History–1714–1837. 3. Social status–England–History–18th
century. 4. Sex role–England–History–18th century. 5. Social
contro–England–History–18th century. 6. Material culture–Great
Britain–History–18th century. 7. England–Social conditions–18th
century. I. Title.

HQ615.V53 2009
306.810942'09033–dc22
                                2009018592

A catalogue record for this book is available from The British Library

Frontispiece: Sarah Stuart, sampler, 1798, wool embroidered with silks, detail.
Fitzwilliam Museum, Cambridge, T.46–1938. © Fitzwilliam Museum, University of Cambridge.

CONTENTS

ACKNOWLEDGEMENTS

This book would simply not have been possible without the miraculous generosity of the Leverhulme Trust. Before I tore open the award letter in 2003, I would never have imagined a historian could be so grateful for the invention of Sunlight soap. The Leverhulme Research Readership, 2004–7, gave me the time to take a large project from scratch to completion, and the travel expenses to truffle about in more than sixty archives, comparing the full English breakfasts of the great British Bed and Breakfast.

I conceived this project under the umbrella of the AHRC Centre for the Study of the Domestic Interior, which ran between 2001 and 2006, of which I was an assistant director. The Centre was a collaboration between three partner institutions in London – Royal Holloway, University of London, the Royal College of Art and the Victoria and Albert Museum. Its aim was to develop new histories of the home, its contents and its depiction, staging seventeen international conferences, symposia and events, the V&A exhibition *The Renaissance at Home*, the collection *Gender, Taste and Material Culture in Britain and North America* (Yale, 2006) and a free online database, www.rca.ac.uk/csdi/didb/, an analytical survey of the ways in which the interior has been represented in text and image since the Renaissance in Europe and North America. The interdisciplinary encounter that the centre was built on and pursued in all its activities was a constant challenge to my training in social and economic history. I certainly had to fight for recognition of the Georgians, wedged between the glories of Renaissance and the frisson of 'Modernity'. My hearty thanks to all the fellows and associates: Marta Ajmar, Jeremy Aynsley, Helen Clifford, Quintin Colville, Flora Dennis, Jane Hamlett, Karen Harvey, Ann Matchette, Liz Miller, Giorgio Riello,

Carolyn Sargeantson and John Styles. I am especially grateful to Jane Hamlett who surveyed the advertisements in Yorkshire newspapers for me, and to Karen Harvey who reviewed a run of the *Ladies Magazine*.

I owe most, however, to Hannah Greig. Her intellectual energy, fiendish competence and (let's be honest) beautiful manners underpinned all the conferences with which I was involved. But do not be taken in by her company demeanour; she is a steely critic. It took me twenty-four hours to recover from her verdict on the first draft of my Introduction: 'I just don't care for it, Amanda.' Amidst an array of commitments at the CSDI, she offered me crucial research assistance, reconnoitring provincial archives in Aylesbury, Bedford, Birmingham, Chelmsford, Colchester, Doncaster, Hull, Keele and Matlock, ploughing through inventories in the Borthwick at York and Poor Law records in Leeds and Wakefield. We have snickered side by side in many a record office and debriefed over triumphs and disappointments: over sandwiches on stations, salads in LA and martinis in Manhattan – there have to be some perks, after all.

A supreme pleasure of the Centre and this project has been the hands-on encounter with museum objects. Although the material turn in historical studies is gaining popularity, meaningful research depends upon access and the generosity of curators swamped under their own timetables. Treve Rosomon took me through English Heritage's wallpaper archive in a garret in Kenwood; Sarah Medlam squirrelled out ladies' fancy work and shellwork in the V&A stores; while Lucy Wood unlocked the secrets of English cabinetwork. The great closets of the textile store at the V&A were opened for me and my students by Susan North and Clare Browne. Edwina Ehrman has been the soul of intellectual generosity, both at the Museum of London and now as a curator of textiles and dress at the V&A.

I must also acknowledge the exemplary service I have received from an army of archivists in the record offices of England, Wales and Scotland. I have lapped up the suggestions and research leads of Frances Harris at the British Library, Elisabeth Fairman at the Yale Center for British Art, Mary Robertson at the Huntington Library and Maggie Powell at the Lewis Walpole Library. And my thanks to the trustees of the Bowood Collection for allowing me to quote from Lady Shelburne's diaries. I am especially grateful to Andrea Wulf for allowing me access to the Grimes account book.

The work I have done in international archives was made possible by a Helen Bing Fellowship at the Huntington Library in San Marino, California, in 2003 and a fellowship at the Yale Center for British Art in 2008. My heartfelt thanks to Robert Ritchie of the Huntington and Amy Myers of the British Art Center for their public support of my projects and the warmth of their hospitality.

Earlier, briefer versions of chapters 1, 4 and 6 have already appeared in print: 'An Englishman's House is His Castle? Privacies, Boundaries and Thresholds in the Eighteenth-Century London House', *Past and Present*, 199 (2008), 147–73; 'Neat and Not too Showey: Words and Wallpaper in Regency England', in John Styles and Amanda Vickery (eds.), *Gender, Taste and Material Culture in Britain and North America, 1700–1830* (New Haven and London, 2007), 201–22; 'His and Hers: Gender, Consumption and Household Accounting in 18th century England', in Lyndal Roper and Ruth Harris (eds), *The Art of Survival: Essays in Honour of Olwen Hufton* (Oxford, 2006), 12–38. I thank Yale University Press and Oxford University Press for allowing me to republish some of that material here.

I have tested the ideas in this book on seminar audiences at Harvard, Yale, MIT, Princeton, Bard Institute, New York, Groningen, Turku and the Ludwig Maximilian University, Munich, and closer to home at the universities of Cambridge, Central Lancashire, East Anglia, Edinburgh, Oxford, Royal Holloway and Queen Mary, London, the Institute of Historical Research and the V&A.

My own institution, Royal Holloway, has furnished me with some of my toughest critics: Caroline Barron, Daniel Beer, Sandra Cavallo, Justin Champion, Penelope Corfield, Felix Driver, David Gilbert, Zoë Laidlaw and Alex Windscheffel, as well as the sceptical, but eventually triumphant, students on my undergraduate special subject 'Behind Closed Doors: House, Home and Private Life in England, 1660–1850', which ran in the years 2007–9. (See, I told you it would be all right!) For references, improvements and critical readings, I am obliged to Amy Barnett, Polly Bull, Clarissa Campbell Orr, Martin Daunton, Zoë Dyndor, Amy Erickson, Silvia Evangelisti, Martin Francis, Anne Goldgar, Laura Gowing, Michael Hatt, Tim Hitchcock, Olwen Hufton, Joanna Innes, Lisa Jardine, Ludmilla Jordanova, Susan Juster, Peter King, Lawrence Klein, Charlotte Mitchell, Miles Ogborn, Giorgio Riello, Beth Robinson, Lyndal Roper, Charles Saumarez Smith, Susie Steinbach, Naomi Tadmor, Wiebke Thormahlen and Susan Whyman. Mark Overton checked my findings on widows and spinsters against his own mighty database. John Mullan gave me a pained tutorial on historians' abuse of fiction. Michèle Cohen read the entire manuscript with patient rigour; perhaps it takes a non-native speaker to champion the perfections of grammar.

My agent Clare Alexander has been a beacon of calm and good counsel. I only hope I have lived up to her love of words and stories. I could not imagine publishing this book anywhere but Yale University Press. There can be few editors with the visual brilliance of Gillian Malpass. I knew she would labour to make *Behind Closed Doors* an object of beauty, ably abetted by Sarah Faulks. The pains of the copy-editor, Delia Gaze, along with the enthusiasm of the publicity, marketing and sales departments are fully appreciated by this cash-strapped author. 'Thank you' also to the three anonymous readers who assessed the manuscript.

Their comments made me sharpen up my conclusions, but also made me smile: 'Amanda surpasses even Richard Dawkins in spelling God with a small g.'

My love to all my friends – you know who you are – and my thanks to Gregory Battle, ever ready to treat a desperate woman to a bit of West End glamour. I hope my forensic interest in and detailed advice on your love life will make some reckoning in our accounts.

Last but also first, I must find a way to acknowledge John Styles without breaching the codes we were both trained up in. His understanding of history, archives, databases and images is impressive enough, but what he doesn't know now about strict phonics, ballet lessons and guinea pigs, Guerlain perfumes and white burgundy isn't worth knowing. Clever historians are ten a penny, but a talent for marriage and fatherhood is much rarer coin.

ILLUSTRATIONS

Figure References

Facing page: detail of pl. 34

Plate Sections

Plates 1–19 (between pp. 94 and 95)

3 John Wilks, 'detector' lock, made in Birmingham, *circa* 1680, brass and engraved steel, h. 11.3 cm., w. 15.5 cm. Victoria and Albert Museum, London, M.109–1926. V&A Images / Victoria and Albert Museum, London.

4 A padlock and a key left by mothers who had entrusted their babies to the care of the London Foundling Hospital, 1741–60. © Foundling Museum, London.

5 *The Dinner-Locust; or, Advantages of a Keen Scent* (detail), 1826, printed etching and aquatint. Lewis Walpole Library, Farmington, CT, 826.0.35. Courtesy of the Lewis Walpole Library, Yale University.

6 *A Common Council Man of Candlestick Ward and his Wife on a Visit to Mr Deputy at his Modern Built Villa near Clapham*, 1771, coloured engraving. Lewis Walpole Library, Farmington, CT, 771.11.1.2. Courtesy of the Lewis Walpole Library, Yale University.

7 *The Good House-wife*, n.d., mezzotint. Colonial Williamsburg Foundation, 1958–357. The Colonial Williamsburg Foundation.

8 Figure of a shepherd, *circa* 1754, Bow porcelain factory, London, soft-paste porcelain, painted in enamels and gilt. Victoria and Albert Museum, London, C.144–1931. V&A Images / Victoria and Albert Museum, London.

9 Teapot, *circa* 1750, Staffordshire, black earthenware with white decoration. Victoria and Albert Museum, London, C.95&A–1938. V&A Images / Victoria and Albert Museum, London.

10 Argand Lamp, by Matthew Boulton Company, Birmingham, 1814–23, Sheffield plate with glass funnels. Victoria and Albert Museum, London, M.14–1987. V&A Images / Victoria and Albert Museum, London.

11 Tea urn, *circa* 1780, Sheffield plate. Victoria and Albert Museum, London, M.237–1920. V&A Images / Victoria and Albert Museum, London.

12 Joshua Reynolds, *Anne, Duchess of Grafton*, 1761, oil on canvas. Private collection.

13 Pompeo Batoni, *Augustus Henry Fitzroy, 3rd Duke of Grafton*, 1762, oil on canvas. National Portrait Gallery, London, NPG 4899.

14 Katherine Read, *Lady Shelburne and her Son Viscount Fitzmaurice*, 1766, pastel. The Trustees of the Bowood Collection.

15 Joshua Reynolds, *William Petty, 1st Marquess of Lansdowne (Lord Shelburne)*, 1765, oil on canvas. National Portrait Gallery, London, NPG 43.

16 Robert Adam's Etruscan Dressing Room at Osterley Park, Middlesex, *circa* 1775–6. National Trust 132456. © NTPL / Bill Batten.

17 Trellis wallpaper and foliage border from the ground-floor front room of 50 Manchester Street, Marylebone, London, *circa* 1800, block printed. English Heritage, EH ASC 88082031/1. © English Heritage Photographic Library.

18 Geranium-leaf wallpaper and chain border from the ground-floor front room of 48 Manchester Street, Marylebone, London, *circa* 1790, block printed. English Heritage, EH ASC 88082030. © English Heritage Photographic Library. Photo: Jeremy Richards.

19 Oak-leaf wallpaper and Neoclassical border from the ground-floor front room of 50 Manchester Street, Marylebone, London, *circa* 1795, block printed. English Heritage, EH ASC 88082031/2. © English Heritage Photographic Library. Photo: Jeremy Richards.

Plates 20–39 (between pp. 190 and 191)

20 Joseph van Aken, *Saying Grace, circa* 1720, oil on canvas. Ashmolean Museum, Oxford, WA1962.17.4. Ashmolean Museum, University of Oxford.

21 Cream silk apron (detail) embroidered with English garden flowers by Miss Rossier for Miss Rachel Pain on her marriage to her brother, *circa* 1736. Museum of London 37.178/2. © Museum of London.

22 *Bodice-Coat Flannel the bottom worked*, 1759, flannel embroidered with worsted yarn. London Metropolitan Archives, A/FH/A/9/1/143, Foundling no. 12843.

23 Ribbon embroidery on the inside of the lid of a decorated wooden box , n.d. Museum of London, NN18716. © Museum of London.

24 Workbox, 1808, marquetry in exotic woods. Judges Lodgings Museum, Lancaster, LANMS. 2006.8. Judges Lodgings Museum (Lancashire County Museums Service).

25 *Lady Jane Mathew and her Daughters, circa* 1790, oil on canvas. Yale Center for British Art, New Haven, CT, B1981.25.268. Yale Center for British Art, Paul Mellon Collection.

26 Shellwork vase, 1779–81, probably made at Pelling Place, Old Windsor, Berkshire, by Mrs and Miss Bonnell. Victoria and Albert Museum, London, W.70–1981. V&A Images / Victoria and Albert Museum, London.

27 A shell-encrusted surround to a window in the Shell Gallery at A La Ronde, Devon, made by the spinster cousins Jane and Mary Parminter, 1790s. National Trust 113317. © NTPL / Geoffrey Ford.

28 Henry Walton, *Sir Robert and Lady Buxton and their Daughter Anne, circa* 1786, oil on canvas. Norwich Castle Museum and Art Gallery, NWHCM: 1963.268.9: F.

29 Settee seat cover, 1728–40, embroidery on canvas in wool and silk, mostly in tent and cross stitch, Victoria and Albert Museum, London, T.473-1970. V&A Images / Victoria and Albert Museum, London.

30 A frieze of feathers in the drawing room at A La Ronde, Devon, made by the spinster cousins Jane and Mary Parminter, using the feathers of game birds and chickens, 1790s. National Trust 146003. © NTPL / David Garner.

31 Crewelwork bed curtain (detail), 1700–15. Victoria and Albert Museum, London, 353 to I–1907. V&A Images / Victoria and Albert Museum, London.

32   Chimneypiece (detail) in the Chinese Room at Claydon House, Buckinghamshire, 1760s. National Trust 66889. © NTPL / Andreas von Einsiedel.

33   James Gillray, *Very Slippy Weather*, 1808, printed, coloured engraving. Lewis Walpole Library, Farmington, CT, 808.2.10.6. Courtesy of the Lewis Walpole Library, Yale University.

34   Anon, *A Family Being Served with Tea*, circa 1740–5, oil on canvas, Yale Center for British Art, New Haven, CT, B.1981.25.271. Yale Center for British Art, Paul Mellon Collection.

35   Embroidered casket or workbox, 1671, wood covered with panels of satin, embroidered with coloured silks. Victoria and Albert Museum, London, T.432–1990. V&A Images / Victoria and Albert Museum, London.

36   Workbox in the shape of a cottage, 1790–1800, wood veneered with ivory, made in Vizagapatam, India, for the English market. Victoria and Albert Museum, London, W.20–1951. V&A Images / Victoria and Albert Museum, London.

37   An 'elegant bookcase', 1772, mahogany. Judges Lodgings Museum, Lancaster, LANMS.2008.3. Judges Lodgings Museum (Lancashire County Museums Service).

38   Joseph Wright, *Sarah Clayton*, 1769, oil on canvas. Fitchburg Art Museum, Fitchburg, MA, Gift of Louise I. Doyle (1953.1).

39   Charlotte Augusta Sneyd, *Drawing Room at Cheverells, Hertfordshire*, circa 1835, watercolour. Keele University Library.

INTRODUCTION

O N A SPRING AFTERNOON IN ENGLAND OF THE 1760s an elderly spinster of decayed gentility dusts her chimney ornaments and sets out her well-polished mahogany tea tray to receive her female neighbours in her two-room lodgings in York. Meanwhile, a Liverpool merchant's widow throned in her drawing room leafs through an architect's plans for the refashioning of her town house in correct Palladian. A few streets away, a hard-pressed matron is setting her rented house to rights after a plague of bed bugs and family illness. At the other end of the country, a countess is painting botanical pictures in the dressing room of her Wiltshire mansion, while the earl reads aloud the latest aesthetic philosophy. In London, a bachelor student grows restless at his desk in his scanty chamber, and decamps to read the paper in a chop house. A Shropshire surgeon and father of five emerges from his consulting room, calls his wife from her sewing and prepares to lead his household in their daily prayers. Upstairs, the maid of all work is loitering to rearrange her treasures in a box, which sits under her bed in the room she shares with the children. In Essex, a middle-aged couple sit by the kitchen fire snatching a moment's ease after dinner. The farmer must now return to the fields. And in Bedfordshire, a timid schoolgirl is hiding from visitors, squirrelled away in the closet of her father's parsonage. All are at home in Georgian England.

Shelter is an animal need. Homes promise security, retreat, rest, warmth, food and the basis for both a family life and for full participation in social life. Home is a toddler's cosmos. A drawing of a recognisable house with strong walls and curling smoke is a sign for psychologists of a secure childhood, while the emotion freighted to the word 'home' testifies to our continued longing for a place of supreme safety and emotional sustenance. Home-made, home-grown, home-cooked are all promises of true satisfaction. The pangs of longing felt by Mole for his 'dulce domum' in Kenneth Grahame's *Wind in the Willows* (1908) resonate with us still. Historians trained to record oral testimony begin with house and home. 'Walk me through your childhood home' – we say – for opening the creaky front door unlocks the library of memory.

That we define ourselves in our aesthetic choices at home is now an inescapable cliché of advertising and the interiors industry. Nevertheless, domesticity is not a word to conjure with in art, publishing and the media. Domestication suggests the death of the spirit, synonymous with the gelding of male animals, the breaking of rebels and the house training of men, women and pets. The artistic avant-garde has long imagined itself escaping the well-upholstered parlour and the pram in the hall, seen as the antithesis and enemy of high art, while modernist architects are notorious for their antipathy to domestic refuge, ritual and decoration, seeking rather 'a machine for living'. A hierarchy of critical value still prevails that devalues that which is associated with the cloying concerns of women – eighty years after Virginia Woolf exposed the systematic privileging of masculine interests over feminine ones: 'This is an important book, the critic assumes, because it deals with war. This is an insignificant book because it deals with the feelings of women in a drawing-room. A scene in a battle-field is more important than a scene in a shop – everywhere and much more subtly the difference of value persists.'[1]

Beyond the reach of critical fashion, however, the fascination with past homes blazes on regardless of the taint of femininity or the middlebrow. Visiting historic houses is often listed second only to gardening as the favourite leisure activity of the British. When the census of 1901 for England and Wales went online in 2002, allowing the curious to find out who had lived at their address a century ago, it had 30 million hits a day, every day for its first week, and the server crashed. Public interest in the way we lived then is intense. Perhaps it is this very middle English intensity that provokes the reflex fear that to read a history of home would be like being locked overnight in a National Trust shop – suffocating under lavender bags and heritage paint. It is far too easy to scorn the desire to add colour and texture to daily existence. Lavender bags hold no terrors for me. But certainly the history of home is as much a saga of power, labour, inequality and struggle, as of sanctuary and comfort, colour and pleasure. Chaos often reigns. Cruelty begins at home.

Universal but unexamined, homes are implicated in and backdrop to the history of power, gender, the family, privacy, consumerism, design and the decorative arts. Women's history has long viewed home as a container of women, especially of middle-class women – a doll's house, a gilded cage, a suffocating prison – while an emergent men's history seeks to reintroduce men to the fireside, though neither tradition has been much concerned with physical structures and spaces.[2] Family history has pioneered the analysis of the household, a framework for inhabitants to be counted and ranked, while homes are invariably the scenery for chronicles of domestic relations.[3] The home is the setting, though perhaps not always the subject, for most discussions of consumerism. Britain's emergence as Europe's most successful mercantile and manufacturing economy caused major changes in consumption that pre-dated the Victorian department store, the factory or the so-called consumer revolution of the late eighteenth century. Quantitative inventory study has done most to recreate the domestic interiors of the polite and middling sorts, led by the ground-breaking work of Lorna Weatherill.[4] Unfortunately, married women's choices are concealed in the sources, since only spinsters and widows fell under the jurisdiction of probate, and inventory data dwindles in most areas after 1740. Economic history has discussed the household as unit of production and consumption, but has made little attempt to differentiate the precise contributions and jurisdictions of men and women.[5] Architectural history prefers exteriors to interiors and architects to users. Decorative arts scholarship neglects the domestic interiors of all but a fabulously rich minority.[6] This book takes the experience of interiors as its subject, staking claim to an uncharted space *between* architectural history, family and gender history and economic history. It brings hazy background to the fore to examine the determining role of house and home in power and emotion, status and choices.

Interiors do not easily offer up their secrets. The backdrop of a life is rarely the fodder of diaries and letters, just as routines are less interesting to record than events. They were taken as read at the time, and so remain elusive in surviving written records today. To recapture the texture of the everyday requires some versatility of approach. Often it is only moments of crisis or transformation in the life of a household that generate commentary; late courtship was a period of strenuous negotiation around the creation and appointments of the marital home, while the death of a partner often led to its dismantling, frantic underpinning or wholesale restructuring. Married men have proved the tersest commentators on domesticities in my researches, but bachelors and widowers who

THE PLEASURES OF MATRIMONY

1   *The Pleasures of Matrimony*, 1772. Lewis Walpole Library, Farmington, CT, 773.3.20.2.

were forced to manage for themselves could be prolix about their needs and difficulties, casting a sidelight on the silent satisfactions of conjugality (figs 1 and 2).
Domestic tension inspired more remarks than happiness and the difficulties of
dependence are more amply reported than the complacencies of power – but
structural tensions are themselves suggestive. Similarly, criminal records report
the transgression of social norms. Nevertheless, they can be used quantitatively
to chart the pans, teapots and boxes ordinary people had in their possession to
begin with, and they can be read against the grain to rebuild boundaries that
Georgian people, rich and poor alike, sought to defend.

Scores of lists, inventories and account-books enabled me to recreate the universe of possessions with which individuals lived, but precisely what those objects looked like and how they were arrayed in rooms often remains intangible.
It is only in a handful of surviving interiors belonging to the most exalted families that curators have been able to reassign named objects to their original lo-
cations. The possessions of the middling have long vanished, but I have
ransacked personal letters and diaries for discussions to supplement the bare labels in account-books and inventories, and endeavoured to match named objects

THE PLEASURES OF A SINGLE LIFE

2   *The Pleasures of a Single Life*, 1773. Lewis Walpole Library, Farmington, CT, 773.3.20.1. The wages of sin beleaguer the gouty old bachelor. Perhaps he should have married after all.

to their counterparts in manufacturers' pattern books or to comparable surviving objects in the research collections of museums. Individual householders are studied through personal account-books, which are plentiful in British archives, but it was the lucky discovery of three rare sets of matching accounts for both husbands and wives that allowed me to map the material jurisdictions of the sexes, and to weigh their interdependence. Married women's choices are actively concealed behind the names of their men in most shopkeepers' accounts and manufacturers' ledgers because women's debts were hard to recover in common law, but where business correspondence survives a less distorted story can be told. Manufacturers' letter-books are proof of trade, but they can also be read in new ways to recover the categories and criteria that informed the aesthetic judgements of a middling consumer public. In letters to the wallpaperman, consumers both prosperous and modest offer a word map of their homes.

This book draws on manuscripts in over sixty archives to explore the homes of English men and women during the period historians term the 'long' eighteenth century – loosely the years from the 'Glorious Revolution' of 1688 to the Great Reform Act of 1832. More precisely, it looks behind the closed doors of homes dating from the Oxfordshire mansion of the unhappy gentlewoman Anne Dormer in the 1680s to the dreary London lodgings of the bachelor clerk and future novelist Anthony Trollope in the 1830s. It embraces, therefore, not just a distinct period in political history, but one that was also culturally distinctive, an era dubbed 'the century of taste', when classicism was the dominant style in architecture and design, and the issue of taste – what it was, who had it, who should judge it, which artefacts partook of it – loomed large in cultural debate.[7]

Middling and genteel homes in London and the provinces take centre stage in this book, especially the homes of those who wrote letters and kept household accounts. Positioned below the nobility in the social hierarchy but above the vulgar, the assorted and growing ranks of the genteel and the middling included lesser gentry, distressed gentlewomen, doctors, surgeons, lawyers, clerics, schoolmasters, governesses, architects and stone masons, farmers, shopkeepers and manufacturers. Georgian architectural history has tended to focus on the grand, architect-designed houses of the nobility. Yet nobles comprised an astonishingly narrow elite, only 350 families out of a population of 18 million by 1832. I venture into their mansions to deal with debates around fashion, style and gender because most received theories derive from the exceptionally well-documented experience of aristocracy. At the same time, *Behind Closed Doors* does not ignore the domestic experience of the poorer majority of the population, those living in one- or two-roomed country cottages and city lodgings who rarely recorded their personal histories. The book uses court records, advertisements, wills, inventories and Poor Law records to reach down into the domestic lives of labouring people, identifying the vestigial elements of home.

The word 'home' derives from the Anglo-Saxon *ham* and is shared across the northern European languages – *heim* in German, Swedish and Norwegian. House and household are fused in its meaning. The peoples of north-western Europe attached a unique significance to the marital home. In Britain and northern France, marriage meant the construction of a separate household, unlike southern Europe or China, where a married couple were absorbed within the parental unit, or eastern Europe, where multiple families lived together. 'When thou art married', advised William Whately in 1624, 'live of thy self with thy wife, in a family of thine own.' Residential independence was natural – 'as the young Bees do seek unto themselves another Hive'. The need for a discrete establishment accounts for the late age of marriage in pre-industrial Britain, over 27 for men and 26 for women, dropping to 26.4 for men and 24.9 for women by 1750–99, when couples had saved sufficient or felt confident enough about cash flow to set up an independent home.[8] A home of one's own was proof of adulthood, and no respectable marriage could go forward without one. The English also placed an unusual premium on retaining a clearly defined home of one's own as long as possible into extreme old age. Residential independence was central to social respect and personal autonomy – an independence that the elderly were not eager to relinquish. Foreign visitors, especially Germans, perceived a 'long-cherished principle of separation and retirement, lying at the very foundation of the national character', believing it to be a deep instinct that the Saxons had carried with them from the Teutonic forests. Tourists were struck that even the labouring poor did their best to avoid communal living. (Note that the very terms for units in shared building were foreign, 'apartment' being French and 'flat' Scottish.) The English 'prefer the most miserable cottage hired in their own name, to more convenient apartments in another house', Von Archenholz noted in 1791. 'The national character is discovered in this very circumstance.'[9]

The home was crucial to traditional political theory, since the household was taken to be a microcosm of the state, revealing the hierarchical ordering of society in miniature.[10] It remained the founding social and spiritual unit in society. The Georgian family was still defined as all those living in the same house – the hierarchically ordered household of master, mistress, servants, apprentices and resident kin.[11] Neither the development of a contract theory of government, nor the spread of politeness, nor the fashion for domestic sensibility made much impact on the *structures* of authority in the family and household organisation. Indeed, the model was exported to the British colonies as an instrument of civilisation. Hanoverian kings ruled by the consent of Parliament, not divine right, yet hierarchy, rank, dependence and independence remained the categories used to make sense of the household and an individual's role within it. These were not spatial metaphors in themselves, but position in the pecking order had long been expressed spatially, through size of bed and place at the dinner table. Degree of power brought with it a corresponding ability or inability to govern the use of space.[12] As the eighteenth century advanced, however, these structural certainties were tested in ways unpredicted by political theory. The triumph of a unisex language of taste, the publicising of the interior through the increasingly formalised practice of visiting, and the commercial construction of the discriminating female consumer and artistic beautifier of the home redefined the genteel and middling home as an arena of social campaign and exhibition. Female agency and discernment were fundamental to this reorientation, as we shall see.

Myriad social privileges attached to occupying a house, but, contrary to modern assumptions, it was not necessary to own the house to benefit. Probably nine out of ten houses were rented in Georgian England. Even the obscenely rich were happy to live in leased apartments for the season.[13] The history of home is not a saga of home ownership. The *Oxford English Dictionary* defined the householder as 'one who occupies his house as his own dwelling'. A householder paid rates and taxes and thus had a financial stake in the administration of the community, qualifying him for influence and office. Householder status was one of the building blocks of local government and legal administration. The vestry and the jury were both imagined as fraternities of responsible householders. Hobbes, Locke and Rousseau all assumed that the political nation was made up of heads of the households who represented the interests of their entourage.

Membership of the polity rested in many towns on the occupation of a house. Of the 217 parliamentary boroughs, 53 had some sort of residential qualification. In the thirty-seven Scot and Lot boroughs (like Chichester, Leicester, Reading, Warwick and Westminster), all resident male householders who paid rates could vote, though it was sufficient to inhabit, not to own a house to qualify. In the thirteen Potwalloper boroughs (like Bedford, Hertford, Northampton and Pontefract), anyone who had a hearth on which to boil (wallop) a pot could vote, even if they were tenants. Houses were used as a commodity to gain the franchise in Northampton, finds Zoë Dyndor. Election minutes for 1768 reveal landladies swapping their status as home owner with their male lodgers to allow them to vote during the election, often in exchange for a cash consideration. Other matrons, however, were jealous of their householder status, contesting the tenants' claims to represent the house at the hustings. These women, usually widows, insisted that the voter was only a lodger, and so should be ineligible. Nevertheless, renting rooms delivered householder status to men, as long as they had a separate hearth and access to their property from the street, not via another property. The nature of one's housing was reinscribed as a determining feature of the male franchise across the nineteenth century, and dictated which women could vote in 1919.[14]

For most bachelors, marriage coincided with setting up home, and was synonymous with the onset of housekeeping. A boy took up the burdens along with the dividends of patriarchy, and became a man. The authority that marriage conferred was not the least of its satisfactions, promised *The Batchelor's Directory* in 1694: 'One finds nothing so sweet as the power of commanding others.'[15] With his responsible maturity in flower, a husband was entitled to community respect and a stake in local government. Did not a wife make a man 'a much more Useful and Considerable member of the common wealth than he was before? And advance proportionately his Credit and Reputation', enquired *The Ladies Advocate* in 1741.[16] Biblical authority underscored the domestic authority of the patriarch, of course. A sincere attempt to live up to the model of Joshua ('as for me and my house, we will serve the Lord')[17] was manifest in leadership of family prayers for many a Georgian paterfamilias. Nor was this moral superintendence necessarily at odds with the secular politeness for which the century is known. The Pelhams of Stanmer were model nobles in the opinion of starry-eyed visitor Parson Woodward at mid-century. Their pretty Sussex mansion was elegantly furnished, surrounded by a stylish landscape park with one of the new fashionable shrubberies. The couple were remarkable for both their 'courteous affability' and their insistence on daily household prayers, led by Mr Pelham when the gouty local clergyman could not hobble over to dinner.[18]

The married housewife was a pillar of wisdom and worth, with a prominent position in the hierarchical institution that society recognised as both normal and fundamental to social order, the male-headed conjugal unit.[19] There was, however, disagreement in print about the value and character of female government indoors; opinions ranged from stereotypical condemnations of female meddling and extravagance, to explicit advocacy of female administration, alongside implicit acknowledgements of a comprehensive managerial role in the detailed instructions that stuffed the many manuals directed at housewives. The pride that women took in their status is obvious in the frequency with which they claimed the label 'housekeeper' in court, and the regret with which widows deposed that while once housekeepers, they were now only lodgers.[20] Women did not see themselves as passing guests in the houses of men, but as house-holders in their own right.

Wives were subject to their husband's authority, yet they were equal souls in the marriage, often fond bedfellows and domestic allies.[21] A matron who had lain twenty years or more on her husband's breast, borne his children, carried his battles, made and mended his shirts and soothed his frailties, fully expected to be a partner in the government of the family. 'Therefore shall a man leave his father and mother, and shall be joined unto his wife; and they two shall be one flesh' proclaimed the *Book of Common Prayer* read at the solemnisation of most legal marriages. There is no reason to suppose that these injunctions rang false in the ears of the congregation. Expression of an indivisibility of interest is usual in the letters of the happily married – 'My Dearest Life' a routine address. When 39-year-old Elizabeth Platt lost her husband, a Rotherham stonemason and architect, to diabetes in 1743, she was left alone with seven children, unhinged by her grief. Fortunately, the widow's faith in her husband's continuing love was fathomless, and so in her unconscious moments George Platt returned to her, materialising in their old bed, urging her to carry on; 'when she obtained a few hours slumber she dreamed her husband [was] beside her, and used every tender argument to console and comfort her.'[22] One need not be a sentimentalist to appreciate the years of trust that conjured such comforting phantoms: the long habit of mutually dependent intimacy. Georgian men and women were not cardboard illustrations of sociological theories, but flesh and blood individuals capable of mixed feelings and contradictory reactions. Even authoritarian husbands who wanted women to be ultra-obedient also needed them to be competent to govern.[23]

Married women were at once deferential wives and powerful mistresses, a conceptual inconsistency that women often manipulated to their advantage and a contradiction from which men often profited. Even if polite magazines and sermons often idealised the melting qualities of modern femininity, the gentry and the middling sort despised the weak and wishy-washy in a mistress. In fact, a sexy battleaxe was what many busy men liked in practice – nimble, capable and commanding – to free them to pursue their own affairs without distraction. A wife of whom a man could be proud was handsome and decisive, mistress of any occasion, equal to any emergency. Yet where husbands and wives did not see eye to eye, the contradiction on which household organisation hinged made the home the obvious battleground (pl. 1). The paradox at the heart of marriage increased the likelihood of skirmishes over domestic space. Equally, the patriarchal edifice could easily be toppled by illness, death and financial crisis or undermined by treachery and insubordination. The widower's characteristic frenzy to find a replacement housekeeper and apparent inability to maintain a household alone expose just how much shoring up went on behind closed doors (fig. 3). In the ordinary jog-trot of domestic routine in harmonious families, patriarchal imperatives were quietly offset by the exigencies of life, husbands typically resigning the field to wives for the day, who themselves had no choice but to delegate to servants, apprentices and even lodgers as the need arose.[24] A general cannot run an army without lieutenants. A head without limbs has no grip on the levers of power. And access to the levers is no mean opportunity.

A trusted household manager was indispensable to genteel and middling men for their dignity, their comfort and their convenience. Mobility was the mark of an independent man. Even gentlemen of no obvious occupation liked to range widely in pursuit of sport, and were expected to assume administrative obligations appropriate to their property, on the bench, the jury and the turnpike commission, most of which carried them miles from home. Officers of the militia were called away on annual manoeuvres, and after 1688 MPs were obliged to be in London up to half the year. Country doctors and surgeons had to have their horses ready and baited, while Assize lawyers could be away on circuit for weeks at a time. Successful merchants and manufacturers rode the new turnpikes in pursuit of new markets and ideas. While Somerset MP Edward Clarke hobnobbed in Westminster in the 1690s, his wife Mary was left behind in Taunton, run ragged by their boisterous brood and 'mannageing your concerns heare . . . letting getting bying selling, receiving and paying to the best of my poore under-

The lazy, the proud Prelate's fed,
This Curate, eats no idle Bread:
Each Faculty and Limb beside,
Eyes, Ears, Hands, Feet, are all employ'd.

THE
WELCH CURATE.

His Wife at Washing...'Tis his Lot.
To pare the Turnips, watch the Pot
He reads, and hears his Son read out
And rocks the Cradle with his Feet

Printed for Carington Bowles, at his Map & Print Warehouse, N.°69 in S.t Paul's Church Yard, London.

Published as the Act directs 1 June 1775.

3   *The Welch Curate*, 1775, mezzotint. Lewis Walpole Library, Farmington, CT, 775.6.2.1.1. Welsh clergy, especially lowly curates, were notoriously impoverished. According to the accompanying verses, the print shows a curate so poor that his wife has to earn money by going out to wash. Unusually for a man, therefore, he is left responsible for the duties of housekeeping, which turn out to be onerous: 'Each Faculty and Limb beside, Eyes, Ears, Hands, Feet, are all employ'd.'

standing'. He had forgotten 'the incombrance of a wife and family children', she insinuated. When Edward complained that he was too busy to perform some errands, Mary's exasperation got the better of her: 'I phancey I am as much Imployed in the Care of my 6 children as you are with all your Business in Parliament and else where'.[25] Mary Clarke captured their division of labour with dry concision. It was the proficient housekeeper posted on the threshold who gave a gentleman peace of mind as he rode away, the axis around which his freedom revolved. Even the Scottish architect Robert Adam, who blazed the family name in pastels across the smartest interiors in England, felt the management of his London household to be a burden, not an opportunity for mastery:

> I can think of no other way of removing the Plague of it than by calling to my aid Some of our Females, Two of whom transporting themselves to London by the time I arrive, will with Judgment & Aeconomy aid me in Domestic determinations, & leave me more time to transact my Worldly interests.[26]

A desire for a housekeeper of one's own was not confined to the gentry and professions. Almost any man who went out to work liked to leave a woman behind on garrison duty. A Colchester silk weaver, John Castle, was worn down by his sole charge of household cares in 1843:

> I became a widower at the age of 24 . . . I could not get on without a woman in the house. I hired a woman as housekeeper at 1s per week and food and lodging. I soon found everything going to ruin – bad washing, bad bread. I consulted Mr Herrick [Minister of Congregational chapel] and he advised me, if I found anyone suitable, the best thing would be to marry again.

The need for a trustworthy domestic administrator had long driven men to the altar, and husbands could be querulous when left to administer households on their own. 'We go on tolerably well in housekeeping', fretted the Hampshire gentleman Richard Jervoise to his convalescent wife Anne in July 1756, 'but are in want of a head of superior judgement & things will never be right till we are so happy to be under your direction and management, which I heartily pray for the good of the family and my own happiness and comfort.' What the Lancashire curate Thomas Brockbank called 'ye many footed Monster house-keeping' in 1703 was not a beast that men felt equipped to wrestle single-handed.[27]

None of which is to say that women alone presided over the interior in all its aspects. In emergent economic theory, the household as a unit of accounting mirrored the checks and balances of a successful economy. A sexual division of consumer responsibilities is a feature of household accounting among the provincial gentry, a partition echoed in middling correspondence. Expensive household refurbishment, annuities, rents, taxes and tithes, men's wages, wines, exotic produce, gadgets, tailoring, wigs and accoutrements, coach and horses and all the multifarious tackle associated with transport are usually inked in the male account, while women's wages, expenditure on children, china and glass, groceries, meat, cottons, millinery, haberdashery and the great empire of linens all fell to the distaff. A matter of masonry and textiles, furniture and china, interior decorating thus straddled male and female domains, and indeed was supremely matrimonial in its connotations. Ledgers tend to record only heads of households, but unctuous letters from suppliers routinely address couples. 'Mr Walter Baghot's compliments to Mr & Mrs Sneyd & begs the favour of their acceptance of a Mah[o]gany side-board table.'[28] When Chippendale and Haig refurnished Sir Edward Knatchbull's house at Mersham-le-Hatch in Kent in the 1770s, Lady Knatchbull's commands were often on their lips: 'Sir Edward Your Chairs, Glasses, Table, etc is all ready to be sent away but as Lady Knatchbull seemed to want 4 larger Chairs . . . they must be made in the meantime . . . if all or any of the above designs [for Girandoles] meet with your and My Lady's approbation we shall be happy in being favoured with your orders.'[29] From first to last, the company truckled to my lady's taste even as they secured his master's bank drafts. A finely tuned interest in feminine taste and a diplomatic appreciation of the matrimonial quality of decision-making in interior decoration are trademarks of flourishing businesses from Chippendale and Adam to Boulton and Wedgwood.

Meanwhile, the balance of production and consumption at home was shifting over the eighteenth century. Large Stuart rural households enjoyed a marked degree of self-sufficiency in linen – growing and spinning the flax, though sending it out to a weaver to be made up. Equivalent Georgian establishments were much less likely to manufacture textiles at home, resorting instead to the linen draper, though as products diversified the expertise involved in equipping and provisioning a household by retail purchases should not be underestimated.[30] The moral panic around the decline of homespun virtue and the rise of frenetic shopping masks a more complicated story. Recent inventory study has discovered that it was better-off households that were most likely to sustain a sophisticated domestic economy of production as well as consumption – buying Caribbean mahogany but still brewing beer.[31]

The Georgian home remained the pre-eminent centre of servicing. It is easy to forget how astonishingly time-consuming and labour-intensive activities like cooking and laundry were (pl. 2). Decency of appearance for men, for instance, demanded a minimum of seven clean shirts a week – for pure white linen was the universal mark of self-respect. Even the working poor hoped to have one shirt on and one in the wash. Laundering those linen shirts required a good fire, copious boiling hot water, cauldrons and coppers, drying space, mangle and irons, as well as soap, bleach and starch, not to mention the woman-hours involved, a day's steamy toil at a minimum. A married Berkshire parson dreaded having his stepmother and sister for the summer in 1753 because of the burden of extra washing:

> for though she offered to hire washerwomen, and pay for soap; yet coals (especially with us) is a very great article . . . besides the continual fuss and stir there would be with wet clothes, for what between the washing of our family and hers too, which could not possibly be at the same time, the house would be continually full of this sort of business.[32]

Meals and laundry had long been organised in households, so making shift for oneself outside was weary work. Hence the appeal of full-service residential institutions like colleges to bachelors, amenities that were not available to lone women.

The late seventeenth century saw the rise of a new mode of sociability that had a transforming impact on domestic behaviour. The emergence of the urban culture of visiting revolutionised the uses of interior space, publicising the middling home to a degree unimaginable in the 1500s. Of course, the manors of the rich had long been settings for formal hospitality, while informal calls at home must be as old as urban settlement, but observers noted an altogether more ritualised and demanding form gathering strength in London from the mid-seventeenth century. The consolidation of the parliamentary calendar after the Glorious Revolution and the elaboration of the metropolitan season intensified social traffic. Lady Pomfret averaged only two or three fashionable visits a week when based on her Midlands estate, but from her London house on Brook Street she made or received almost ninety visits in May 1747. This contrast between town and country patterns of visiting was not restricted to fashionable noblewomen. Anna Larpent, a civil servant's wife, divided her time in the 1790s between London and Ashtead, a village in Surrey. She made and received far more visits when resident at her London house than when living in the country.

The provincial urban renaissance carried the contagion to the regional capitals. Fanny Burney believed the 'perpetual Round of constrained Civilities' tiresome everywhere, but absolutely 'unavoidable in a Country Town, where every body is known'.[33]

Visiting pre-dated the arrival of exotic hot drinks, but tea super-fuelled the activity and became synonymous with it (fig. 4). Visiting was a mixed-sex activity under female jurisdiction, a fashionable institution of inclusion and exclusion

A MORNING VISIT___or the FASHIONABLE DRESSES for the YEAR 1777.

Printed for & sold by CARINGTON BOWLES, at his Map & Print Warehouse, N°69 in S.Pauls Church Yard, LONDON. Published as the Act directs, 1 Jan. 1778.

4   *A Morning Visit; or, The Fashionable Dresses for the Year 1777*, 1778, mezzotint. British Museum, London, J,5.108. Two wealthy women greet each other in a well-appointed parlour. A tea kettle boils on the fire and a well-dressed servant carries a tea tray into the room. Hostess and guest show off the latest, most exaggerated fashions in headgear, despite the convention that dress for morning visits was usually informal. The visitor sports an enormous calash or hood over a muslin and lace cap. The hostess flaunts a large hat tilted forward to display a huge bunch of feathers at the back. In the background, very much on the margin, a man dressed for country sport sits on a sofa holding a gun erect, quizzically regarding the visitor's headgear.

governed by matrons. Visiting routinely exposed the domestic interior and authorised female congregation, disturbing misanthropic husbands with 'the Din of Visiting day', introducing aliens to judge arrangements. The only way to put a stop to female longing for 'China, Silks, Ribbans, Fanns, Laces, Powder, Patches, Jessimin Gloves and Ratafia', claimed Sir Testy Dolt in *The Ladies Visiting Day* of 1701, 'must be to bar up my Door' and 'keep out all visitors'. Yet the commerce of female visiting generated profit for men too. The courtier Sir Charles Cottrell demanded that his widowed daughter Anne Dormer come to London in 1689, embark on 'visits and visiting', despite her hatred of town, 'to have me live as he says for his credit'.[34]

Conduct literature expected a man to select the bride most likely to lisp 'I know nothing of town and its wicked ways', but in practice most elite, upwardly mobile men desired wives varnished with sophistication. In 1757 the Hampshire gentleman Richard Jervoise recommended 'a very agreeable young lady' of 21 as a match for his son. The redhead 'dressed very genteely' and though no great beauty had manners to match her fortune. 'She conducted at the heads of the table extremely proper & genteel, has had a very good education' with an up-to-date metropolitan gloss acquired 'in town two months every spring'. She had polish enough for a Hampshire office-holder 'not at all in very high taste, nor too much on the reserve, but very sociable & familiar'. Rural innocence was all very well in a maid, but could be a handicap in the wife of a man of parts. Provincial maids were often sent to metropolitan relatives and exposed to visiting to burn off their bashfulness. A chatty bride was far more use than a wallflower. After all, one of the benefits of matrimony for men was the acquisition of a hostess to carry one's campaigns on the domestic front. A vulgar partner hampered a man's social ascent. The tone of a newly rich Liverpool family was spoilt by the accent and manners of the wife, noted Maria Edgeworth in 1813. 'In short though it is in the power of a father's genius to drag a whole family up in the world, yet unless the mother be a woman of education and good manners it seems impossible to give an air of gentility to the family.'[35]

The entrance of a wife transformed a man's house. Wedding bells announced the coming of the harpsichord, the backgammon set and sewing table to the affluent parlour, to jolly along the endless winter evenings of married love. When the Reading distiller Edward Belson bought new printed paper hangings and bed curtains, to refurbish his old bedroom to receive a wife in 1710, and the Lincolnshire surgeon Matthew Flinders 'got the best Chamber papered, 2 new hearth Stones, & Fire screens & c & c and some lesser improvements previous to my intended nuptials' in 1778, their efforts were typical.[36] In his gently tongue-in-cheek book, *The Pleasures and Felicity of Marriage* (1745), Lemuel Gulliver alerts the

5 'Madam goes to buy Household-Furniture', 1745, Plate 2 from Lemuel Gulliver, *The Pleasures and Felicity of Marriage* (London, 1745), Book 2. A recently married wife and her female companions process home with new furniture.

newly wedded husband that the bright morning of marriage has to be reflected in renewed furniture (fig. 5):

> You will be delighted to hear your Spouse every Moment talk of going with her Sister and Aunt, to order in such Furniture as may reflect Dignity and Grandeur upon the Owner. What Pleasure will you receive and how will you applaud the happy Choice you have made, when your Darling gives you a Specimen of the delicacy of her Taste in *Down-Beds, Rich-Counterpanes, costly Hangings,* Venetian *Looking-Glasses, enamel'd China, Velvet Chairs,* Turkey *Carpets, Capital Painting, Side-board of wrought Plate, curious in-laid Cabinets, rich Child-bed Linen,* Flanders *Lace,* and many other valuable Particulars. Certainly, the Joy of your Heart will far exceed the Chinking of your Purse, when your House, by the indefatigable Pains of your Spouse, is thus grandly adorn'd.

Such purchases were necessary, as Gulliver went on to emphasise, because married couples were expected to socialise in ways bachelors were not: 'Your prudent Spouse, to your great Satisfaction, will inform you, that [these purchases], and many others, are no more than what's needful, both for Use and Credit, unless you design to banish all reputable Company from your House.'[37] Worthy husbands were ready to grant their wives a leading say in the staging of domestic life, a concession which bespeaks the benefits that accrued to men from successful domesticity and an inviting, congenial interior.

The idea that the architecture, decoration and contents of a house projected the culture and learning of its occupants is not an eighteenth-century invention, yet the triumph of 'taste' as a means of assessing interiors, objects and behaviour belongs to the Georgians. Taste is a word of such bland good manners today that it takes an effort to remember that the concept was once fresh as paint, offering a thoroughly new way of understanding culture. 'Of all our favourite Words lately,' noted one London publication in 1747, 'none has been more in Vogue, nor so long held its Esteem, as that of TASTE.'[38] Taste, as we define it, meaning the faculty of discerning and enjoying beauty and perfection, first gained currency in seventeenth-century France. Le 'Goût' came to mean more than the physical sense of taste, but a whole field of discrimination. It emerged in the literary debate between the ancients and the moderns, proposed as a mode of discernment that was courtly, *mondain* and often female, which could be demonstrated without academic education or steeping in the classics. For taste was the antithesis of academic pedantry. In British philosophical debate, taste came to have some different associations, grounded in the critique of luxury. The idea that luxury was a fundamental danger to society derived from a civic humanism rooted in the republican political thought of ancient Rome. Luxury was deplored as corrupting and effeminising. Its dangers were as much courtly and French as commercial and opulent.[39]

Wedded to ideas of good breeding, and built on the rule of decorum, good taste had an affinity with rank, and was supremely exclusive in conception. Knowledge of the rules of design and thorough practice of their application were the essence of taste, an ineffable gift and a lofty vantage from which to disparage the vulgar ostentation and ignorant choices of upstart nabobs, merchants and shopkeepers. Yet insistence on the innate capacities of the well bred in conduct literature handed the laurel to ladies as well as gentlemen. In refined women, *The Polite Companion* claimed in 1749, 'the study of good taste . . . appears with a delicate lustre, not only in their air, conversation and epistolary correspondence but in the lowest articles of economy and dress'.[40] Some authors went even further, endowing women with a gift for regulating claims to culture in a com-

6 William Hogarth, *Taste in High Life*, 1746, printed engraving. British Museum, London, 1868, 0822.1555. Hogarth suggests the notion of taste was often an excuse for indulging in Frenchified furnishings, food, dress and manners.

mercial society. Virtuous women, by making consumer choices that were moderate and reasonable, could moralise commercial society, protecting it from its own depravity. Thus male extravagance would be tempered and domesticated by female refinement.[41]

The mystery surrounding the faculty of taste lent it versatility, and its adjectival usefulness to retailers, entrepreneurs and cultural impresarios hastened the spread beyond the patrician elite. The dire implication of this was that 'scarce a grave Matron at Covent garden or a jolly Dame at Stocks Market, but what is elegant enough to have a Taste for Things' (fig. 6).[42] The super-rich nobility, those whom Josiah Wedgwood called the 'legislators in taste', certainly had disproportionate power to hallmark 'good taste' and disparage the bad. Which is not to argue that the hegemony of patrician sophistication went uncontested. When a righteous 49-year-old Shrewsbury china shopkeeper, Thomas Brocas, went on an errand to Condover Hall in 1805 he was disgusted by the interior decoration:

The abundance of rich paintings are amazing . . . but oh what lewd indecent pictures, one figure large as life, a beautiful, full breasted woman, lying on her back stark naked, this in one of the best bed rooms. Had I not seen it I would scarce have believed it. In other rooms several small figures of women nearly naked, in fact everything to inflame the pasions [*sic*] and ruin souls.

Brocas was 'Methodist to the backbone', and in deliberate cultural revolt.[43]

Within the framework of classical decorum, the middling and genteel found a distinctive idiom in 'neatness', a low-key elegance that refrained from glitter and unseemly show. Josiah Wedgwood had an intuition for the sensibilities of this market, trying out his 'chaste' designs on circles of Quakers in the Midlands. By 1770 he was displaying 'various Table & dessert services . . . *to do the needful* with the Ladys in the neatest, genteelest & best method'.[44] Neat but not too showy was the established stylistic register of the sober middle ranks by 1790.

Complaints about women's impact on the way interiors looked were widespread in the eighteenth century. The principal stereotypes about female taste and aesthetic allegiance were minted in this period. Fussiness of ornament, greater delicacy or even fragility in furniture, and a yen for lighter colours were all associated with women in the male literature on architecture – clichés that abound in marketing and design circles to this day. Orthodox classicists, like Isaac Ware (1704–1766), the distinguished professional architect and translator of Palladio, invariably stamped Roman uniformity as male and despised any subversion of 'the noble manly orders'. The ignorance or merry abandonment of symmetry, perspective and proportion apparent in Chinese wallpaper and porcelain, Indian chintz, French curlicues and Gothic decoration aroused the disgust of purists, who wanted to purge British taste of any elements that were primitive, alien or exotic. True believers took diversions from strict classicism as unerring signs of meagre education and vulgarity, or effeminacy and female dominion. Chinoiserie decoration was fit only for pretty fellows 'of delicate make and silky constitution', according to *The Connoisseur* in 1755, who 'have a natural tendency to the refinements and softnesses of females'. The well-reported association of women with tea, china, wallpaper, chintz, silk and shellwork reinforced the suspicion that the rebellion against uniformity was female-led. In fact, the convention that Palladianism incarnated the nobility of British masculinity while the Rococo expressed the insouciance of a chic *mademoiselle* was belied in practice by elite patronage of both. Besides, there were plenty of antiquarian men who resented the Palladian assault, counterparts of those fictional gentlemen of the old school who revered country hospitality and Gothic gloom. Sir Fumbler Oldmode hankered after an Elizabethan

7   Thomas Chippendale, *Chinese Chairs*, Plate 27 from *The Gentleman and Cabinet-Maker's Director* (3rd edn, London, 1762).

golden age in the play *The Old Mode and the New* (1703). To humour him in his 'antique formalities', Lady Oldmode was prepared to don farthingale and ruff, the rousing sight of his wife in 'that provoking dress' being enough to take Fumbler's mind off the gout.[45]

Nevertheless, the myth that classicism was strictly masculine and diversions feminine settled into a formula that shaped the grammar of design. Hence Thomas Chippendale suggested that his delicate, fret-back Chinese chairs would be 'very proper for a ladies dressing room' (fig. 7). Furniture design manuals were a major new source of an explicitly gendered language around domestic objects. The rise of advertisements and other kinds of printed commercial propaganda provided manufacturers with new opportunities to manipulate gender as a marketing tool. From the 1750s London cabinetmakers, led by Chippendale, started to publish books of designs for furniture. Catalogues required that furniture be categorised in ways that made sense to their readers and attracted them. The principal categories the cabinetmakers employed were functional and stylistic, but 'lady's' and 'gentleman's' soon came to be used to differentiate certain specific types of furniture, principally writing tables, desks and dressing tables.[46] They differed most in scale – men's furniture tending to the massive and impressive, ladies' furniture to the petite and compact.[47] Hence, the furniture presumed that women's writing was a dainty drawing-room performance, while men's business was altogether more important. The diminutive became a design expression of femininity.

No Georgian house was yet a home without a sedimentary stratum of objects and furnishings crafted by women, yet no female activity has been so disparaged by both male critics and feminist commentators as domestic handicrafts. The contemporary importance of craft is dispensed with and a crucial layer of the household is torn away. Yet female handicrafts were endorsed by God, exemplified by the virtuous woman of Proverbs, who clothed her children and ornamented her house to the credit of her husband. Those who affirmed the femininity of Proverbs extended from the arch-Tory Sir Robert Filmer, the staunch Whig Richard Steele to the Reverend James Fordyce, who added a modern discrimination to archaic virtue: 'In every thing she makes, whether for sale or for use, she displays a just taste of what is both beautiful and splendid.'[48] For Fordyce, in other words, the Bible authorized the exercise of female taste in the home (fig. 8).

Not that taste was static. Massive needlework seemed as antique to the Regency commentator as seaweed landscapes and hair jewellery appear to us. 'Our great grandmothers distinguished themselves by truly substantial tent-work, chairs and carpets, by needlework-pictures of Solomon and the queen of Sheba', which were now all consigned to the garret, remembered Maria Edgeworth in 1798. 'Cloth-work, crape-work, chenille-work, ribbon-work, wafer work . . . have all passed away in our own memory.'[49] Fashions in craft changed dramatically between the Stuarts and the Victorians, excited by the efflorescent commerce in craft materials, manuals and education. In 1810 Rudolph Ackermann smugly congratulated ladies of refined taste 'on the revolution which has of late years taken place', fuelling his art materials business such that 'drawing and fancy work of endless variety have been raised on the ruins of that unhealthy, and stupefying occupation, needlework'.[50] The elaborate edifice of artistic novelty rested on biblical foundations, though the virtuous woman now had myriad talents to exhibit.

Cottage or lodging, town house or farmhouse, it is hard to overstate the importance of the Georgian home to its inhabitants. Yet it is important to recognise that homes came in a variety of forms besides the stable patriarchal household of master, mistress, children, servants, apprentices and other dependants on which so much attention was lavished by theorists at the time. Take the humble Hutton clan in Derbyshire in the 1730s. At the death of William Hutton's mother in 1733, his wool-comber father, quite forlorn, sold up their Derby house and moved the children into lodgings with a widow who had four children of her own. Meanwhile, Hutton also 'had an uncle who was a Grocer, and a bachelor; also a grandmother who kept his house', and two miles away 'three crabbed aunts, all single, who resided together as Grocers, Milliners, Mercers and School-

8   *The Seamstress*, 1765, mezzotint. Lewis Walpole Library, Farmington, CT, 765.0.89.

mistresses'.[51] Not one of the Huttons lived in the nuclear family household of biblical injunctions. Nevertheless, the obsession with the normalcy of marriage and the fitness of patriarchal structures was pervasive and painful for underlings and outsiders. Marthae Taylor was an 'old maid' who set 'a high value on herself', refusing several offers of marriage. Yet in the 1730s she cautioned her niece who looked set to follow in her footsteps: 'you see how lightly regarded I am by kindred, how I have been tossed from wig to wall as ye phrase is, how distressed for a Home, when years and Infirmitys made it necessary'.[52] Few spinsters sighed aloud for the lost opportunity of marriage, or for plump babies they would never hold, but lament for a safe haven was recurrent.

The difficulties of those who fell outside the family household emphasises its signal importance to a successful existence. When Ellen Weeton's marriage failed and she reverted to spinster mode in scanty lodgings in Lancashire in 1825, she felt her marginalisation most sorely: 'I have been passing my time in almost total solitude . . . So it is with all females of small incomes who have no families and few relations; if forced to live in lodgings, they are shut out from domestic comforts and a social fireside.' Ellen was spurned even by the butcher when she asked for a tiny cut of veal.[53] A bitter choice between domestic humiliation and social isolation faced many lone women.

The possession of a home of one's own was a universal goal. If her prayers for her future life were answered, versified the single poet Mary Chandler, then she would be the happy holder of 'A Fortune from Incumbrance clear, About a Hundred Pounds of year; A House not small, built warm and neat, Above a Hut, below a Seat'.[54] Independence was a pipe dream for most spinsters who were forced to shelter under the roof of a kinsman, carving out a corner to roost in, and to arrange their small stock of personal treasures. Failing the possession of a room of one's own, then a locking box to preserve the things of one's own was often the last redoubt of individuality. Some measure of control over space and time, however minimal, was necessary to make a house a home. All too readily, a house lost the warmth of home, generating only cold discomfort, petty trials and humiliations, and in extreme cases tyranny and psychological torture. Utter powerlessness invariably meant that the victim felt their subordination always and everywhere, leading them to seek out a corner to cower in, and to long for 'a little Cott' to call their own, or even 'a cabin' if it were 'exempt from the Domination of a man'.[55] A house where an inmate has nil autonomy is a prison. What then is home? Is home the household of birth, or the place you chose for yourself, or the citadel for which you long? For the powerless and marginal, home had to be a locking box, a collection of treasures and a consoling dream.

1

THRESHOLDS AND BOUNDARIES AT HOME

T HE DUSK SPREADS FROM THE RIVER. Candles are being lit all over London. The clatter of shuttering echoes and answers as every house in the Georgian metropolis fortifies itself against the advancing dark. The November gloom hastens lodgers home; they scurry back with sausages, oysters and a pennyworth of tea. At a house at the corner of Shoe Lane in the City, the landlord, a carpenter, is still away at his workshop, and the landlady is seeing her tenants in, unlocking the street door and the individual rooms for her three newest inmates, a laundress, a fruit-seller and a journeyman cabinetmaker. They exchange words on the cold stairs: she has changed their linen today. (Has she snooped through their things again? Almost certainly.) In the second-floor front chamber, the journeyman lights his fire, and then scuttles next door to the alehouse to fetch his dinner on a tray. Loosening his breeches, he empties his pockets and stashes the coin in the hiding place he has carved in the leg of the oak bed. Unusually, the landlady's linen press stands open in the corner. She must have forgotten to relock it. The journeyman runs his hands over the second-best sheets, all initialled and numbered with red embroidery silk. Tempting, but he wants a quiet life, and he has had worse quarters than these. The fruit-seller heats her sausages over the hearth in the second-floor back chamber. Warmer, she idly unlocks her box (she carries the key always in her pocket), checking over her shifts, Sunday-best gown and handkerchiefs. Her small stock of valuables – cash, a watch, a silver teaspoon and a ring – she keeps always on her person. In the draughty front garret, the young laundress eats her oysters, locks away some ribbons in her box and hides some coins in a hole in the wainscot. Sometimes she has to share her bed with passing girls and she is no fool. Presently, the maid of all work leaves by arrangement to visit a relative, and because the landlady must pop out to the alehouse for beer, she leaves the street-door key in the custody of her trusty, a mature needlewoman and widow who rents the first-floor back chamber. The widow can't complain: she holds her own room key and just now she is making her supper in the family kitchen, as she has done at this hour every night for the past seven years. Errand accomplished, the landlady takes back her keys, locks the kitchen and retreats to the ground-floor parlour to await her husband. By 9 o'clock everyone is gathered back in. The apprentice beds down in the back garret with the two little boys of the house, the maid in the warm back kitchen on a truckle bed, her bulging tie-on pockets stuffed under her pillow. At 10 o'clock the landlady locks the tenants, servants and children in their rooms for the night. The landlord hefts the iron bar across the street door, padlocks the door to the back lane and double-checks the window shutters. Only streetwalkers and housebreakers are lurking about now, he tells his wife as he lights her to the first-floor front chamber. In their curtained conjugal bed, in shift and shirt, husband and wife rehearse the details of their day. The landlady puts the keys under her pillow and settles to sleep, just as the watch calls out the hour of eleven.[1]

Where in this story does personal privacy reside? The very idea of private life is a creation of the early modern period, according to Philippe Ariès, and England is the birthplace of privacy. Between 1500 and 1800 the family changed from an economic institution that suppressed the individual, to an introspective emotional unit built round children, a haven from snooping strangers. These psychological shifts were inscribed in the fabric of houses, in the introduction of small rooms for withdrawal and solitude, and the provision of corridors and multiple staircases to separate personal quarters from circulating traffic. Privacy was entrenched in western Europe by the late eighteenth century, reaching its apotheosis in the Victorian home. However a unilinear advance of privacy from early glimmerings to modern conquest has long been contested by historians of the family. Homes may be havens in a heartless world, but they are also nurseries of conflict, so privacy is not necessarily a higher goal of civilisation. Early modernists argue that a notion of privacy in family life pre-dates the Georgians. Privacy may have been harder to obtain in the early modern period, argues Linda Pollock, but it is wrong to assume that it was not sought after. The Stuart gentry were spied on and gossiped about, yet they had 'a well developed sense of privacy', based on a 'desire for concealment and a predisposition towards secrecy'. In this reading, then, privacy is increasingly equated with the hidden. In parallel, feminists have long been concerned with what might be concealed within families, such as violence against women, and there is some debate about how far an alleged privatisation of the family drove abuse indoors and out of sight.[2]

The discussion of privacy in family history runs in parallel, but not quite in dialogue with, the reassessment of the public and private that has gone on in eighteenth-century gender and cultural history in the wake of a reassessment of Habermas (who identified an emergent public sphere of political debate and opinion in Georgian print and clubs). Though the public/private conceptual dichotomy was invoked in many discursive contexts in the long eighteenth century, it was rarely deployed to characterise an inside/outside, female/male division of space. In fact, what writers designated as belonging to the private sphere tended to vary according to the particular public they were counterposing. Consequently, privacy for eighteenth-century historians is a moveable feast, rather different from both Ariès' private life, and Pollock's secrecy.[3]

Nevertheless, the issue of privacy still haunts the history of space. Architectural history has furnished a story of advancing physical privacy for the most privileged. 'Servants no longer bedded down in the drawing room, or outside their master's door or in a truckle bed at his feet but in attics and separate annexes', Mark Girouard explained. The introduction of back stairs from the later seventeenth century meant that 'the gentry walking up stairs no longer met their last night's faeces coming down'. The Stones concluded that the architecture and equipment of segregation, from staff staircases to bell pulls linked by wires to the servants' halls, expressed a growing elite longing for privacy. For Christoph Heyl, post-Fire terrace architecture combined with polite protocols like the visiting card saw the 'creation of the middle class private sphere' in Georgian London. Yet a demand for privacy or distance from servants 'cannot be read straight from the fabric of contemporary buildings', warns Tim Meldrum. 'Is it not possible . . . that the advent of bells to summon servants may have simply originated with a fashionable distaste for shouting . . . ?'[4] Meldrum also poses the important question of exactly whose privacy is under discussion here: patently not that of the servant.

This chapter returns to the issue of privacy in a domestic context, by recreating the interior for ordinary householders in London. Not that London was typical of national experience, but it was immensely significant. London households were larger and more complex than their provincial counterparts because of the co-residence of servants, lodgers and apprentices. On the other hand, at least one in six adults, half the entire *urban* population, experienced London life in the period.[5] And immigrants needed housing. Wealth and taste (largely Palladian) were the foundation stones of the great Georgian building boom, decreed Sir John Summerson in his landmark celebration of the elegant terraces and squares of Georgian London. Architectural history, however, now seeks to move beyond the celebration of Georgian uniformity to retrieve diversity. Smaller London houses have been overlooked, argues Peter Guillery, an omission that reinforces a misleading picture of fashionable innovation and neat standardisation. Even the new brick-built terrace with its smooth façade could conceal irregularity. Where houses were let in tenements, and a room was available on the same floor in a next-door house, sometimes a door could be knocked into the party wall.[6] Yet for all the internal confusion, the integrity of the perimeter remained a keystone of legal, customary and spiritual understandings of home, as we shall see.

This chapter opens the door of the London house to consider how internal space was conceptualised, demarcated and policed, using the records of the Old Bailey, the principal criminal court in London. Witnesses rich and poor alike invoked an understanding of personal territories in their use of terms like 'private house' as opposed to public house or inn, 'private gardens' as opposed to communal turf, 'private door of my house', 'little private boxes' and 'private shop mark', as well as psychological individuality and introversion in concepts like 'private doubts', 'private information', to 'be private', that is, to keep one's own counsel, or to act 'as private as possible', that is, unobserved.[7] This is not, however, an exercise in semantic mapping, nor does it enlarge on privacy as a conceptual abstraction. It is an exploration of some of the lived meanings, practices and technologies of privacy broadly defined. I am revisiting 'the private' in some of its simplest dictionary definitions, looking at the claim and defence of private property and personal possession, but also the capacity and mechanisms to achieve seclusion and withdrawal, refuge, security and secrecy – some of the less concrete associations of privacy in the *Oxford English Dictionary*.[8] This chapter translates metaphysical abstractions like the public and the private into everyday rituals and physical objects, though revealing that these procedures were themselves freighted with conceptual meaning for the protagonists. The concrete way in which boundaries were materialised was replete with metaphorical resonance.

The threshold of the house was an ideological boundary of great power, yet the domestic interior was no haven. Nevertheless, it was the place where an individual might expect to defend his or her personal property and most 'private matters' with a battery of devices, from locks and keys to personal boxes and secret drawers. In the final analysis, access to a small place of privacy held out a promise of some autonomy and independence. Existing discussions of spatial privacy, with their allusions to back stairs, bell pulls and visiting cards, are predicated on the experiences of a narrow elite, yet a concern with personal space can be found throughout the social pyramid, even if its enjoyment was unequally distributed. Life with no vestiges of privacy was understood to be a most sorry degradation, which stripped away the defences of the spirit.

The external perimeter of the house was a frontier in custom and law. The house had long been a universal metaphor for the person and the body. The weak points of the house were its orifices: the doorway, the windows, the chimney and hearth, but without them a house was an airless prison. Around 1600, when Lauderdale House was built in the London suburban village of Highgate, a basket containing two shoes, a candlestick, a goblet, two strangled chickens and two live chickens was walled up behind the hearth on the first floor. This bundle was discovered only in 1963 and its context is obscure, but the offering evokes the mystical meanings of home and the centrality of hearths to the sustenance and safety of a family. Surely these gifts had a talismanic power and were sacrificed as a propitiation of the supernatural? In folk tales, fires were said to cackle and blaze when a wizard passed over because the soul of the house was in peril. The hearth became a metonym for domesticity, encapsulating both a sense of emotional core and life-sustaining warmth. The analogy between the house and the body was ancient and widespread. Unglazed holes in the earliest primitive houses were known as the wind eye, the origin of our window. If windows were eyes, the doors represented the mouth, vagina or anus, and the hearth the breast, heart, soul or womb. Apertures symbolised points of human vulnerability. Ink thrown on windows and excrement daubed on the door were visceral attacks on the person, and were read as such. In popular belief, witches attacked the house through the windows, doorways, keyholes, chimneys and hearth, just as demons entered the body through its orifices (fig. 9).[9] And while the offence of witchcraft was abolished in England in 1736, superstitious counter-magic survived for centuries. Londoners buried 'witch bottles' under the threshold or behind the hearth well into the 1700s, and horseshoes nailed 'on the threshold of doors . . . to hinder the power of Witches that enter the house' were still to be seen in Monmouth Street in the 1790s. House-shaming customs persisted long into the 1800s and beyond.[10] The house/body analogy was not expunged by the Enlightenment.

The new-built metropolitan brick house gave onto the street in ways that emphasised the importance of the boundary; the basement area was seen as domestic moat, defended with iron railing. Travellers claimed that London house fronts vied with those of the Netherlands for cleanliness, 'even the large hammers and locks on the door are rubbed and shine brightly', and of course the whitened doorstep was a lodestone of working-class respectability till at least 1945. The

9   Frontispiece (detail) from Joseph Glanvil, *Saducismus Triumphatus; or, Full and Plain Evidence Concerning Witches and Apparitions* (London, 1681), Part 2. Houses under supernatural attack, from a book that claimed to prove 'the real existence of apparitions, spirits and witches'.

doorway was the archetypal liminal boundary, where servants loitered and respectable housewives took up post.[11] The open door was universally understood as an invitation. National celebrations were often marked by a collective illumination, and patriots were required to show a candle or risk the consequences. A light glowing in the window of the house announced a vigil, the eye of the house sleeplessly searching for its lost inhabitant.

'The Englishman's home is his castle' was already a hoary cliché of English Common Law by 1700.[12] The Westmorland Justice of the Peace Richard Burn, author of the most authoritative eighteenth-century manual for magistrates, was stirring on the protections offered the house in criminal law:

Man's home or habitation is so far protected by the law, that if any person attempts to break open a house in the night time, and shall be killed in such attempt, the slayer shall be acquitted and discharged. And so tender is the law in respect of the immunity of a man's house, that it will never suffer it to be violated with impunity.

Breaking and entering a house in the night-time constituted the hanging offence of burglary, even if the burglar failed in the attempt to steal. House-breaking in the daytime where any inhabitant was put in fear, even if nothing was taken, was still a capital felony. Eavesdroppers and nuisances could be prosecuted, such as a neighbour blocking, damaging or removing sewers and gutters, and blocking light to one's rooms, and a householder was entitled to gather up to eleven fellows for the defence of his or her home. 'For a man's house is his castle, for safety and repose to himself and his family.'[13]

The law recognised the customary inviolability of the domestic threshold. Property in private possession was under private control, so an owner was permitted to use, alienate and control the land as they saw fit. If private property was invaded an owner had recourse to the civil law action of trespass for damages. Then again, the government, the church, the courts and parish constables were empowered to enter privately controlled properties under specific circumstances. Constables could gain a warrant to enter a private house without a householder's consent, if they were in breach of the law. Officers in a civil suit could not break an outer door or window, 'if he doth he is a trespasser', but if they found these open, or was let in, 'he may break open inward doors if he find that necessary to execute his process'. Officers of the excise could inspect the houses of brewers. Ecclesiastical jurisdiction empowered the church courts to monitor the goings on in a household where sin was suspected. Even the implementation of building regulations could involve a visitation from parish officials. Nevertheless, all these intrusions required a warrant or legislation to authorise public entrance into private houses. 'Concerning the breaking open of the doors of the house in order to apprehend offenders . . . that law never allows of such extremities, but in cases of necessity.'[14] English law recognised that in principle the domestic threshold was sacrosanct; in fact, the law had erected a fortification around it.

It was the classic responsibility of the head of household to patrol the boundaries and lock up fast at night. 'Shutting in' was a universally recognised hour, after sunset, but before bedtime, a fateful moment that set in motion a ritual ceremony of fortification. The street door could be locked with an integral lock, padlocks, internal bolts, iron bars and wrought-iron chains. Sir John Fielding recommended that windows be fitted with bars in the shape of a cross. Bells, trip wires, servants sleeping across the doorway and nasty guard dogs were all expected to rouse the household. Defensive weapons including firearms were common. But even the cheerful window boxes and garden pots were a barrier of sorts, crashing down in warning when intruders blundered through. Robert Southey was bemused to find that a battery of defences lay behind the elaborate festoon curtains and Venetian blinds of the ground-floor front parlour of the London house where he lodged in 1807: 'at night you might perceive you are in a land of housebreakers, by the contrivances of barring them, and the bells which are fixed on to alarm the family, in case the house should be attacked'.[15]

The external boundaries of the London house and the security of its access points were of obsessive concern to the judges of the Old Bailey. Criminal cases offer a pessimistic version of the functioning of households, but of course social codes are exposed as much in the breach as in the honouring. Moreover, due process demanded the gathering of a wealth of supporting evidence about domestic traffic to substantiate a charge or exonerate an accused. Houses could be invaded through front doors, but also via back doors from back lanes, courts and even water, through hatches and area stairs into cellars, through windows and even from the roof via trapdoors. The Old Bailey allows us to visualise a three-dimensional city of houses connected by streets, yards and water, but also by another network over the rooftops, called the leads. By accretion, the court proceedings offer an atlas of the metropolis, perhaps not far removed from the mental relief maps of citizens, in a period before house numbers (introduced only in the 1760s), when addresses were understood by an ensemble of juxtapositions: 'At Shakespeare's Head, Over Against Catherine Street in the Strand'.[16]

The Old Bailey Proceedings provide a unique source on locking. Since burglary had to involve a break in, by extension a house had to be seen to be secure for a robbed victim to bring a successful case: 'As if the door of the mansion stand open, and a thief enter this is not breaking.' Even if a thief 'with a hook or an engine draweth out some of the goods of the owner, this is no burglary, for there is no actual breaking of the house'. The onus was on the victim to have secured the perimeter. Prisoners in the dock were well aware of the technicalities. Charged with robbing a house in Scotland Yard in 1793, William Lacy interjected in court: 'I would wish to ask him whether the place was broke open or not, as I am indicted for a burglary.' In the same year, another defendant tried to throw doubt on the nature of the lock: 'Please to ask her whether it is not a spring lock, that the lock naturally flies open?' Hence most aggrieved householders were primed to assert the regularity of their bedtime routines and testify to the integrity of their frontiers. 'The house was secured in every part of it', insisted Thomas Wallis of Monkwell Street, '. . . I make a practice of examining it myself; I went to bed about eleven, I am always last up.' Early bedtimes were a sign of decency. There had been no curfew in London since the sixteenth century, but vagrancy statutes made wandering the streets at night grounds for suspicion. After the watch was set, around 11 o'clock, dubious pedestrians ran the risk of apprehension and detention, and latecomers could easily find themselves locked out. By midnight, the watch houses were known to be full of 'young fellows shut out of their apartments'.[17]

The common law drew a distinction between burglary and housebreaking – housebreaking being a lesser offence committed in daytime.[18] Securing a conviction for housebreaking was not straightforward, because houses were far less barricaded in daylight. Morning, of necessity, involved an opening up of the house. Doubts about an open window ensured that Sarah Hall was found only part guilty of housebreaking in September 1784. Rebecca Phillips claimed that when she went out at three in the afternoon, she locked her door, padlocked it, shut her kitchen windows, but left the shutters open. 'Why in that hot weather were none of your windows open?' she was asked. Though Phillips insisted she shut them all as she was going out, a neighbour testified that 'Mrs Phillips had had her windows cleaned, and left her window open, or else I could not have seen.' The court advised the jury that where 'there is a deficiency in the proof of breaking and entering, that makes an alteration in the charge, for unless the house is broke and entered, stealing therein to the value of five shillings in the day time is not a capital offence'.[19] The jury found the lesser charge of simple theft.

The perimeter of 'the private house' represented a sacred frontier, but it was emphatically not the case that once over the domestic threshold all was secluded. Living cheek by jowl with comparative strangers robbed the London house of any automatic association with privacy as we understand it. Indeed, more solitude and anonymity was probably found outside the house than in. The capital was so overwhelmed with population that teeming, multi-occupied houses were commonplace. Estimates based on the Poll Tax returns for the City of London of 1692 suggest that 47 per cent of houses contained subsidiary lodger households. In short, most Londoners, both rich and poor, lived in rented accommodation where space was at a premium, though the history of the lodger has been overlooked until recently.[20] In fact, the pressures of congestion, and the feelings of vulnerability they provoked in property owners, gave rise to new capital statutes in the 1690s, addressing theft by servants and theft from lodgings. Before 1691 a tenant making off with her landlord's furnishings was not committing a felony, since technically she had gained legal control of them when she agreed the rent. Meanwhile, servants might be the enemy within, in league with burglars, housebreakers and receivers, willing to allow strangers into the house to steal, especially at night.[21] Theft by servants, theft from lodgings and shoplifting were all new capital offences prompted by concern that London was facing new forms of criminality as a consequence of physical and commercial expansion, although their enactments also reflected the fact that passing legislation of all kinds was easier after 1689. Notoriously, the so-called Bloody Code defended the rights of property owners above all. Tenants were far less able to defend their privacy and property than householders. The type of tenancy arrangement was crucial to the integrity of their domestic space. Some landlords relinquished the right of possession to their tenant, endowing them with the right to defend the space through recourse to the legal action of trespass. Landlords were legally permitted to cross the threshold and inspect for waste just twice a year. If rent was outstanding, however, the law allowed a landlord to go into the lodging and seize any chattels against the arrears. The leases of short-term lodgers offered even less protection. Single-room lodgers might share food and servants with the landlord, so had to resign themselves to continuous traffic through their rooms. Moreover, the landlord or landlady who was in residence among the lodgers always maintained the right of possession. Consequently, lodgers had scanty legal recourse if they felt their living spaces were violated.[22]

Where were lodgers in the house? Conventional architectural hierarchies decreed that the first-floor rooms were the most impressive, the front rooms better than the back, the ground floor the most accessible and work-a-day, and the damp cellars and draughty garrets the least desirable spaces in the house. Probably the owning family kept the ground floor; the smarter tenant secured the lighter first floor, with the least pretentious lodgers consigned to the higher and nether regions. Certain rooms became synonymous with small incomes and struggle. 'Who turns his attention to the second-floors, the garrets, the backrooms and the cellars of this metropolis?' asked one anecdotalist in 1808. The hack and the poet proverbially starved under the rafters, in their 'sky parlours', sacred to the Muses (fig. 10). More prosperous landlords lived apart from their lodgers in a separate establishment. Some buildings were given over entirely to lodgers – it was in such 'lodging houses' that the most degraded rooms were to be found, where a bed could be had for as little as a penny a night in every nook in the house. Meaner still were 'the tenants of sheds, stalls and cellars' attached to houses they never entered.[23]

Disputes amongst lodgers were a common currency of the Old Bailey, while the co-residence of family and multiple lodgers was often inherently problematic. Observers remarked on the 'discontent and altercations . . . between the landlord's family and the lodger' that were a common consequence of shared space.[24] Busy metropolitan lodging houses were low-trust environments, and inmates sought valiantly to control access and flows. This control turned on the existence of locks and the custody of the keys. Locks and keys were not the focus of forensic attention as in burglary cases, because a lodger had no need to break

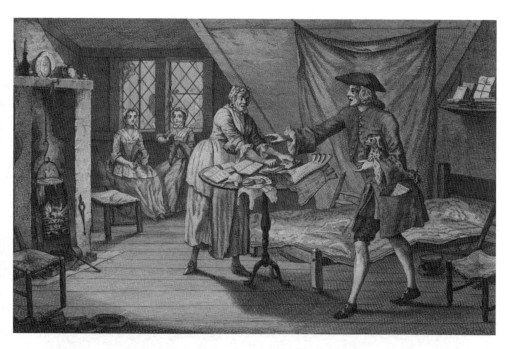

10 'A Description of the Miseries of a Garreteer Poet' (detail), from Francis Coventry, *The History of Pompey the Little; or, The Life and Adventures of a Lap Dog* (London, 1751). Lewis Walpole Library, Farmington, CT, 751.5.20.1. An impoverished poet's family is portrayed in a miserable garret lodging. A large cooking pot hangs by a chain over the fire. At the window, the poet's daughters darn their father's stockings. A teapot sits on the mantelpiece and under the bed a chamber pot, described in the book as 'a green Jordan'.

and enter to steal. Violence at the threshold was not the deciding drama of the narrative. Nevertheless, witnesses and defendants tended to report entry and traffic, if only to widen the pool of potential culprits. From my examination of 265 cases from the 1750s and '90s, under the Act of 1691 making theft from lodgings a felony, it emerges that ninety refer to locking. In sixty-eight of these cases the lodgings were locked, whereas in just twenty-two they were unlocked and automatically accessible to the landlady.[25] Thus in more than three-quarters of the cases where locks are mentioned, the rooms were internally locked, suggesting that most lodging rooms could be secured (fig. 11). Behind this generalisation, however, an array of permutations emerges. The lodging room might not have a locking door, allowing the landlady to come and go about her daily business, ensuring that the lodging room functioned as an extension of her family house. The lodging might have a locking door, but the key would remain under the control of the landlady, who unlocked the room, as necessary, and in some cases

11   William Hogarth, *The Distressed Poet* (detail), 1736, printed engraving. British Museum, London, 1868,0822.1541. A milkmaid demanding payment crosses the threshold of a sparsely furnished garret lodging room, to the surprise of the poet's wife, who is sewing a pair of breeches. The door lock is not visible, but the staple for a rim lock can be seen on the door frame behind the milkmaid. A teapot stands on the mantelpiece.

even locked her tenants in for the night. The lodging room might lock, with the key shared by landlady and lodger, or very rarely both might carry a key. Finally, only the tenant might hold the room key, perhaps supplemented by further padlocks and barricades.

The outer defences of the house raised yet another set of combinations. The lodging house might be left unlocked all day, so the tenants could enter and exit without fuss. Where the outer door was habitually locked, however, a privileged tenant might have custody of both her room key and the key to the street door. Less trusted lodgers might share a street-door key with their fellows, or knock and shout for admittance. Where the street door was habitually left on the latch, family rooms tended to be locked.[26] Again, however, a trusty might have controlled access at certain times to the family kitchen or parlour. When master and mistress both went out, they might delegate authority over the street door to a faithful servant, apprentice or lodger, who stayed at home guarding the bundle of keys. The person who carried the keys was in a position to manage access to the house and its internal compartments. The privileges of access were finely calibrated.

Monitoring the comings and goings in the rooms was second nature to many landladies, but it also appears that often lodgers came and went with only the minimum surveillance. Householders who suspected thefts of their property from furnished rooms often demanded admittance to check for losses, and many a skirmish in the doorway is reported at the Old Bailey.[27] Nevertheless, an officious breach in a tenant's boundaries could be aggravating. The tenants in George Court resented the landlady, Mary Dickerson, who had 'false keys to go into all her lodgers rooms'. And indeed the jurors seem to have frowned on her interference too, for they overturned her prosecution. Other landlords broadcast a nicer sense of the lodger's right to privacy. When a Holborn silk-dyer had some gowns stolen from his shop in 1779, he abstained from a full search of the house, despite the open door between the shop and the common stairs, and seemed in no haste to get a warrant. 'I asked [Watson] why her master did not search the house; she said she advised him to search it, but her master said he was a poor man, and could not afford to lose his lodgers.'[28] Landlords could be at pains to demonstrate a proper respect for the lodger's threshold.

Smashing an internal lock in one's own house was not a criminal act, but it was still a momentous gesture, so householders sought to show the Old Bailey that they had not acted lightly. When Mary Howard's first-floor lodgers 'went to gather elder berries, and said they'd pay me on their return' in 1752, she waited a full month and then took legal action: 'I broke open the room-door, with a warrant'. By the 1790s a victim could call in the support of the patrol, a forerunner of the police, to add authority to their incursions. Resort to the services of a locksmith defused the violence of forced entry, and lessened the damage to the doorway. Some proprietors invoked a public recognition of landlords' rights as a justification for their incursions. The presence of friends and witnesses at an internal breaking and entering added a whiff of formality. Typically, grounds for suspicion were cited as the prelude to break-in. 'I look'd through the crack of the door and missed the looking glass that fronted the door', Catherine Freelove admitted in 1757, 'then I went in'. Although breaching a threshold uninvited required justification, peering through cracks was routine, and even invasive spying was not objectionable to the court. 'I then went and got a gimblet, and bored a hole in the wainscot', divulged a mistrustful landlord in 1753, 'thro' which we saw the quilt was gone.'[29] 'Key holes' were mentioned in at least 280 cases at the Old Bailey.

Given the bustle of the congested London house, where might individual privacy reside? Servants and apprentices had the least personal privacy in the London household. Architectural treatises assumed that servants generally slept in the garrets, with any overflow in the basement. Early modern church court records, however, reveal that servants slept all over the house, even on temporary truckle beds in passages or public rooms, and rarely enjoyed anything approaching a personal room. Inventories imply that sleeping arrangements were directly proportional to status, the pecking order expressed in the size and permanence of beds.[30] Old Bailey depositions agree that the possession of a fixed, individual and secluded bed was still a rare privilege. A Harp Alley brazier placed his journeyman's bed 'in the Shop . . . it lies so near the Doors that 'tis impossible for any one to make the least Noise without waking the Person who lies in that Bed'. Ad hoc sleeping arrangements survived well into the nineteenth century. A servant of John Camplin, a surgeon, 'slept on the ground-floor behind the shop, in the surgery' in Finsbury Square in 1833, on a bed that he put away first thing every morning.[31] Where servants had a bedroom, it was invariably shared, often with children, and their own movements indoors were subject to control. The average London servant had no settled space to call their own, let alone a place of withdrawal and solitude. However, almost all had a locking box.

Church court papers suggest the importance of locked trunks, boxes, closets and chests for the preservation of personal things and secrets in rooms trafficked by other members of the household and even the general public (so when a locked box sat in a victualling room, public and private coexisted in the same chamber),[32] a finding confirmed by the Old Bailey. Householders tended not to have one centralised safe for all treasures, but an array of hiding places dispersed about the house. The robbed surgeon John Camplin testified in 1833 that his assistant stored 'his private matters' in one of the drawers of the shop in Finsbury Square, while he himself kept money and jewellery in a locking desk and escritoire in the dining room, and his wife kept a gold seal in her own desk. It was surprisingly common for a householder to leave personal possessions in locked storage in the room of a lodger. Conversely, locked storage was a means by which lodgers preserved their valuables and secrets from the inquisitiveness of the landlady herself, other inhabitants and intrusive strangers. Even rich lodgers seemed resigned to traffic through their rooms, locking away choice provisions like tea and sugar to put them beyond the reach of temptation. Yet the lock could ensure illicit secrecy as well as legitimate security. Thieves often kept their booty hidden in locking closets, or secret drawers hidden within other pieces of furniture, or secret cupboards concealed behind the wainscot known as 'plants'.[33]

The Old Bailey conjures a world of habitual, often ingenious concealment. Secret drawers were an expression of a cabinetmaker's virtuosity. French masterpiece desks and toilet tables often contained secure compartments, protected by locks and activated by springs and other triggers. With its complex inner spatial arrangements and hidden routes known only to the maker and client, the desk housed an interior within an interior. The interstices protected possessions from intruders, but also secrets from other householders.[34] While only the wealthiest could afford exquisite cabinetwork, mundane secrecies could still be engineered. In 1810 when naval officer Charles Maitland was lodging at the Cannon Coffee-house, he hid his guineas in 'a secret drawer of a small dressing case' that he locked inside his trunk in his bedroom, keeping the key in his pocket. In 1823 a Guards officer kept jewellery in 'a Kingswood box' in his house in Berkeley Square: 'it usually stood in my wife's dressing-room'. Luckily, the stolen box contained a hidden drawer, and when it was retrieved some of the captain's property was still secreted within it. In 1817 a 91-year-old Hillingdon farmer 'used to put the money into a private drawer in his bureau, and keep the key in his purse in his right hand breeches pocket'. The existence of a secret drawer was not discovered till after the owner was killed by a burglar, the bureau stolen, retrieved and sold on. As in burglary cases, prosecutors often dramatised the brutal smashing of the lock, the breaking open of the receptacle and the violation of their personal belongings.[35] The legal implication of breaking open a box is vague, yet the violence done to these internal boundaries was an insistent theme of the victims' narratives, probably to confirm malicious intent, but also to invoke a customary taboo.

Secure storage was a necessity for any respectable individual who had no room of their own. Some valuables could be carried on the body, in pockets, pouches and lockets. Beggars and the destitute hung onto their personal bundles of rags and resented any interference in them, but they had no safe place to leave them. In Renaissance Italy, the working population could leave valuables in the custody of the church, but there was no comparable safe deposit system in Georgian London. The rich might store valuables with a goldsmith or even the Bank of England by special arrangement.[36] The only demotic institution that potentially offered anything approaching a deposit system was the pawnbroker. For urban workers in possession of more than a single set of clothes, safe but accessible storage was crucial. Having things of one's own put one in need of a locker.

The portable box was especially used by single, mobile workers, above all by servants. The box itself became a symbol of service, appearing in the first print of Hogarth's *Harlot's Progress* (1732), when Moll Hackabout arrives in London from the country; it is also ransacked in the last scene as she lies dying (figs 12,

12   William Hogarth, 'A Harlot's Progress', 1733, Plate 1, printed etching and engraving. British Museum, London, s,2.21. Moll Hackabout has just arrived in London on the wagon from York. Her luggage is shown in the bottom right of the print, consisting of a parcel, a basket and her trunk, marked MH.

13). Moll's box is the size of a large trunk, but some were small enough for a woman to carry. Boxes stolen from servants were valued at between sixpence and a shilling. They were commonly made of deal (i.e., pine, the cheapest wood), often named or initialled, and even decorated. Lucy Stockford's deal box, in which she kept her clothes and money in 1795, was 'covered with flowered paper'.[37] Without a room of their own and the defence of a locking door, servants had to put their faith in the lock to their box, though these could be forced too, as they often complained.[38] The lack of even a box was a sign of the meanest status. Suspicions about a servant's collusion in a theft at a surgeon's house in 1785 were dismissed when it became clear he had nowhere to hide the haul: 'Have you ever searched for the things that were lost in his places? – No, the maid makes his bed constantly, he has no place, he has no box.'[39] Those without a box

13 William Hogarth, 'A Harlot's Progress', 1732, Plate 5, printed etching and engraving. British Museum, London, 1858,0417.548. Moll Hackabout is dying of venereal disease in a run-down garret lodging. On the left, a woman is shown rifling through the clothes in her trunk.

slept with their valuables under their heads at night. William Droyre and his wife survived by selling cabbage nets and rags in 1787. At their lodgings in Hampshire Hog Yard there was

> neither a bolt nor yet a latch to the door; the last that goes out, takes a bit of padlock, and locks the door, and takes the key down, and hands it in the kitchen; several people lodge in the same room; there are three beds all occupied, and there was one woman drunk in bed when they came there . . .[40]

The bit of padlock is the crown of squalor. Access to privacy was an index of power.

My evidence derives from a particular source. Perhaps the low-trust atmosphere that pervades the Old Bailey is a distortion; doubtless longer-term tenants had more relaxed relations with the landlady and each other. The legal records, however, chime with folkloric understandings of the proper boundaries of a house, customary prohibitions around breaching internal thresholds, and personal commentary on anxiety and concealment at home.[41] A comprehensive test of the metropolitan findings would require a comparative study in provincial Assize and church court records. Nevertheless, even sporadic evidence from letters, diaries and reportage confirms that Londoners were not unique in their obsessions. It is possible that rural householders were even more inclined to make their house a fortress at night, for isolation brought its own terrors. Mary Clarke, the wife of the Somerset MP Edward Clarke, was left alone with the children and servants in Taunton for months at a time in the 1690s, while her husband was attending Parliament. Having heard that a miscreant had broken out of gaol, and considering 'our house being but poorly guarde', extra measures were called for. The solution she devised was fiendish: 'the way I take now is to tye up one of the Mastfes a days and lett [him] losse about the House a nights', a deterrent 'which I phancey as good as a Man'. The signal importance attached to a fastened house was more than a piece of legal pedantry. Provincial diarists worried about minor breaches in their defences even if they did not go to law.[42] Account-books document that renewing door locks and fixing new internal locks to cupboards, boxes and bureaux were common measures taken by inheriting sons, new householders and lodgers (fig. 14)[43] There is no evidence to suppose that keys were a metropolitan fetish: 'Barricaded, bolted, barred and double lock'd fast', as the playwright David Ogborne described an Essex home in the country in 1765, 'both public and private, backside and foreside, top and bottom.'[44]

An infinity of devices could be had from an ingenious locksmith. A London ironmonger supplied brass locks, iron rimmed locks, spring locks, spring plate locks, stock locks, drawback locks, closet locks, hatch locks, pew locks, cupboard locks and box locks in 1686 (pl. 3).[45] The lock and key, however, was no foolproof system. The inventor Joseph Bramah suspected that most locks delivered a false confidence, warning that 'no invention for security of property hath yet been offered to the world, which the ingenuity of wickedness has not found means to defeat'. Even the Chubb detector lock patented in 1818, or the burglar-resisting safe of 1835, were only as reliable as their owner. 'No lock whatever will guard against culpable negligence with regard to its key, or . . . the treachery of supposed trustworthy servants.' Householders usually possessed only one set of keys. When a 'terrible fire' swept through Brook Street in 1763 'one great misfortune was that Lady Molesworth always had the key of the street Door carried up in her room, which could not be got at, and the door being very stiff could not be forced open' to relieve the twenty-one inhabitants. The pos-

14 'Design of Furniture for the Locks of Doors', for the Duke of Northumberland at Sion House, Middlesex, 1770, from Plate 8 in Robert and James Adam, *The Works in Architecture*, vol. 2, no. 4 (London, 1779). This and other lock designs shown in the same plate are described as 'Designs of various pieces of Furniture, which were first invented for particular persons, but are since brought into general use'. A central handle is flanked by pendant swags and scrolling foliage. The escutcheon below conceals the keyhole. It was created to operate and decorate a mortice lock whose mechanism was built into the fabric of the door. Mortice locks were introduced in the first half of the eighteenth century, increasingly replacing rim locks attached to doors, of the kind show in pl. 3.

session of only a single set of keys per household looks perversely inefficient, but this restriction was deliberate. What was at stake was controlling access to the house and its recesses, and monitoring the flows within it, not ease of admission and speed of circulation. A single set of keys guaranteed a monopoly of control. Automatic suspicion fell on 'false keys' or 'pick-lock keys'. The custodian of the keys was accountable, negligent in the case of breaches and liable in the event of losses. '"Guard your keys" is a sound motto for everyone', warned the mighty house of Chubb.[46]

Keys were emblems of authority. Church court cases suggest that ownership of the keys of the house lay with the male head of household; despotic husbands liked to play the gaoler, locking women in or out in campaigns of abuse. In ordinary marriages, however, even while the master was technically the owner of the keys, the wife carried them. In fact, without these delegations of authority the work and rituals of the household would grind to a halt.[47] The Old Bailey Proceedings confirm that the paterfamilias was seen to be the ultimate key holder, his bedtime security rounds emphasising his role as protector of the family. But even this ceremony could be entrusted to a kinswoman or trusted servant, and was performed *faute de mieux* by a woman in the many female-headed households. Patrolling the territory by day, opening and locking rooms, closets, cupboards, presses, meat safes, caddies and boxes, was part of the customary performance of housekeeping, which fell to the mistress and her acolytes. Responsibility for the keys was a mark of trust, but it assumed accountability too, so could be experienced as a burden, and even refused.[48] In an echo of the respective domestic roles of men and women, the rules of the general hospital at Bath in 1749 obliged the house steward to patrol the perimeter and check the locks, but to return the keys to the matron who kept them.[49]

Keys are an ancient instrument of civilisation. Christ delivered the keys to heaven to Peter the apostle, and thus 'the power of the keys' descended to the popes. In England, keys were badges of office at court, often an elaborate accessory of formal dress. Museum collections boast fine early modern keys bearing royal monograms, or the engraved name of the owner, fashionable Rococo and Neoclassical locks, ingenious masterpieces, as well as humble late eighteenth-century latchkeys. The association of keys with women is archaeological. Anglo-Saxon women were buried with keys. A collection of keys hanging from a belt at the waist was a female ornament from at least the Renaissance. Eighteenth-century pick-pocketing trials reveal that keys were commonly found along with money, teaspoons, thimbles and scissors, pieces of jewellery and handkerchiefs in women's tie-on pockets. Small padlocks can be found amongst the tokens vouchsafed by desperate mothers (probably servants) when they surrendered their infants to the London Foundling Hospital in the mid-eighteenth century (pl. 4).[50] In paintings, the bundle of keys was the attribute of Martha, the patroness of housewives. Trial responsibility for the keys was part of female training: 'By taking the trouble of the Keys . . . a young Lady may learn how to go through her domestic Offices.' The passing of household power was also ritualised in ceremonial renunciation, as when a Lancashire merchant's wife, Elizabeth Shackleton, handed to her inheriting son in 1778 'the keys of the Buroe where he wo'd find all the keys'. A Shropshire servant, Thomas Brocas, was exultant when his master's malicious housekeeper was sacked in 1786, and he was told to withdraw all the keys, hence she 'had the mortification of delivering up her authority to me'. The keys were both instrument and emblem of the housekeeper's office. She 'had compleat controul over the house; she had the key' was a convincing statement at the Old Bailey.[51]

The emergent individuality of children could be expressed in personal storage. Sea captain's wife Tidy Russel informed her clergyman brother that his motherless daughter should be so provided when she was seven in 1759: 'A very little trunk will be necessary for her to put her work in and book every night; most girls have them besides drawers.'[52] This is not to argue, however, that the strongbox was the sole refuge of authentic identity, or that individuality was forged only in seclusion and solitude. It is a Romantic fallacy that only alone in the closet or on an isolated peak does the self truly know itself. Social interaction and public performance were crucial to the building and enactment of identity, especially in a century that had a much more developed belief in the naturalness of communal and hierarchical systems of being and belonging than we do today. All the same, some separation of private from communal property was an indication of individuality, and props were vital to the ability to perform one's decency, propriety, religious commitment, social values, family ties or even sexual availability; and only a secure place to deposit one's chattels preserved the equipment for future performances. If you were a mobile, single worker, the locking box was the only sure protection for the things of your own. And personal things were, and remain, important building blocks of identity. A secure space was a valuable privilege, read by contemporaries as an unambiguous mark of status. Even a faulty lock asserted that here was a personal boundary.

This study recreates a particular historical moment, between the enactment of new criminal legislation in the 1690s and the proliferation of the latchkey in the early nineteenth century. A recognition of the power of keys is older than Pompeii, but the elaborate use they were put to in Georgian interiors was a response to galloping urbanisation and dense over-crowding. Doubtless the devouring metropolis led the way, for London 'may truly be said, like the Sea and Gallows to refuse none',[53] but the provincial towns grew faster than London in the 1700s, especially in the Midlands and the north, facing the same problems of multiple occupation, though on a larger architectural footprint. In Ludlow, one in seven households contained lodgers. In nearby Shrewsbury an estimated 12 per cent of the population were lodgers.[54] A flow of comparative strangers through the house was not unique to London.

We cannot blame the quantity of locks on the terms of contents insurance against theft (possessions could be insured only for fire), but it is conceivable that the spread of legal understandings of burglary drove locking practices. For instance, locked doors became general amongst the gentry and nobility of the Scottish Highlands only after 1740, following the employment of legally trained factors, it was claimed.[55] Part of the legitimacy of the law, however, lay in its mirroring of vintage and visceral concerns about securing the boundaries of the house against invaders.

It is not assumed here that a desire for personal privacy was a biological given or a cultural and temporal constant, though an appreciation of the multiple meanings of privacy appears well developed at all social levels in the 1600s, if not before. But rather than searching for epistemic shifts in the conceptualisation of elite private space, this chapter has looked at the mundane tools and everyday tactics used by ordinary Londoners to draw physical and psychological boundaries within doors, and to control access to space and possessions. Many, probably most, houses in the Georgian metropolis enveloped a subdivided interior made up of multiple households, trafficked by all sorts, interlaced with internal boundaries and protecting dispersed pockets of privacy. A comparable Victorian study remains to be done, but the censuses do not suggest that households became more streamlined: one or two servants, multiple lodgings, domestic workshops and family retail posing the same spatial and personal challenges to householders, lodgers, apprentices and servants. Privacy in this worldview involved the safety of one's defences, the separateness of one's concerns and the preservation of the things of one's own. The safeguarding of all three turned on the possession of a key.

One cut above the beggar's bundle and bulging pocket was the portable locking box or trunk. Those without a house, room or even bed of their own might still have a compartment that was sacrosanct. Some institutions recognised the provision of a secure personal compartment as a basic decency. Scores of tiny keys found on the site of a medieval London hospital have led archaeologists to posit the existence of lockers for the patients.[56] Personal receptacles stood proxy for individuality, so the taboo around violating them was powerful. The forcing of the boxes is presented as a theatrical act of mutiny and misrule in Tobias Smollett's *Roderick Random* (1748) as a ship founders: 'The sailors . . . according to custom broke up the chests belonging the officers, dressed themselves in their clothes, drank their liquors without ceremony.'[57] Even institutions like the workhouse sometimes acknowledged the importance of spatial autonomy and props to the preservation of self-respect. Physical separation, basic furniture and personal equipment were understood to mimic 'the comforts of a private fireside', the reward of deserving old age. Witness the commentator Frederick Eden on the Liverpool workhouse in 1797:

> The old people, in particular, are provided with lodgings in a most judicious manner: each apartment consists of three small rooms, in which there are one fire-place and four beds, chairs and other little articles of domestic use, that the inmates may possess: who thus being detached from the rest of the Poor,

15   *The Sequel to Maria, The Unfortunate Fair* (detail) n.d. [1790s], printed engraving.
Washington State University Library, Pullman, WA, PN1376.S53. This illustration to a broadside
ballad is a rare depiction of the interior of a parish workhouse. The workhouse master and
mistress stand to the right. A pair of keys hangs prominently at the mistress's waist, one
labeled 'Bread', the other 'Small Beer'.

may consider themselves as comfortably lodged in a secluded cottage; and thus
enjoy to some degree even in a workhouse, the comforts of a private fireside.[58]

Punitive institutions, however, were not in the business of protecting the dignity of the undeserving, indeed quite the reverse (fig. 15). In 1775 the Wimbledon
vestry decreed not only that all inmates of the workhouse were to wear a badge
at all times marking their degradation (as the law had required since 1697), but
also that none was allowed a lock to their box:

They are not to have any box, drawer or other receptacle under lock and key, but may each of them receive from the matron a proper box belonging to the workhouse with a lid thereto for holding their linen and wearing apparel, which boxes are to be continually open to the inspection of the matron whenever she sees proper.[59]

The feckless were allowed no barrier against officious intrusion. Quite deliberately, the Wimbledon workhouse tore the last vestige of privacy away from its hapless inmates, as a degradation and form of control. Plainly, the locked box was the lowest common denominator of respectable independence, almost of personhood itself. Some veil of privacy was essential to human integrity in eighteenth-century England, a covering the destitute had little choice but to regret and renounce.

2

MEN ALONE: HOW BACHELORS LIVED

SOFT-EYED, DARK-HAIRED AND AMIABLE, Susanna Flinders was reckoned 'clever in housekeeping and managing children' (fig. 16).[1] Just as well,
because she was married to a striving Lincolnshire surgeon, who rode out
with his forceps at all hours to establish his midwifery practice in the 1770s and
'80s. Matthew Flinders could be abruptly summoned across the county for two
days at a stretch: 'I had not been in bed or my boots off for 40 hours.' Annually
totting up his life savings, Flinders was fixated on the burdens he hefted – 'we
have nought . . . but my industry to depend on'. When in November 1776 'death
made his first approach in our little family, taking from us our second son –
Jackey', Flinders remained practical: 'We ought to think of the non increase of our
family as a blessing.' The following July, when Flinders delivered his wife of still-
born twin daughters, he was relieved: 'How kind is providence of God thus to
free us from the expense and care of a numerous family, for had all our young
ones lived with us, we should scarce have known what to have done with them.'
Twin boys born prematurely in May 1778 survived barely two days and were in-
terred in the same coffin, but again Flinders acknowledged God's mercy 'for not
burdening me with additional care of more children'. He was not a sentimental
man. However, a catastrophe loomed that would tax his strange equanimity.

16   The house at Donington, Lincolnshire, where Matthew Flinders, surgeon, lived during the later eighteenth century, photographed about 1920, subsequently demolished. State Library of South Australia, SLSA: B 1785.

After a gruelling 'fatal lying' in the winter of 1782, Susanna failed to rally, and died in the spring of 1783. 'My tears are plentifully shed each day', Matthew reported in his diary, 'and when I regain my peace I cannot tell.' His household was tottering: 'My situation is truly deplorable and unhappy on my own account, and my comfit being gone, but doubly so on account of my 5 children, two very small and one at nurse.' How was he to attend to his patients and support his motherless offspring? 'There appears nothing for me but care and trouble', or so Flinders bewailed.[2]

In alarm, Flinders looked to the old remedy of drafting in any available female kin, writing post-haste to his brother 'desiring to have Henny's assistance which I hope may be of use to me'. At last in May, 'after long expectation', his niece arrived, and Flinders prayed she would be 'some consolation to me under my great distress', but the makeshift was insufficient. By July 1783, not four months after 'losing the dearest & most valued friend I had on Earth', Flinders was looking about him for a substitute wife, contriving the necessary with such dispatch that he blushed to report developments even to his diary: 'I have now to Note a circumstance [which] will perhaps appear somewhat odd in my records, after the real and extraordinary Grief which I have manifested for my late valuable partner & whom I shall regret to my latest hour.' Pragmatic, however, he decided that it was futile to repine: 'As a continual grieving can be of no avail, but injurious to me, I begin to be not without thoughts of a 2nd marriage.' He wasted no time in contemplation: 'Accordingly I have pitched on the amiable Mrs E late Miss EW of this place.' A few letters and three visits were sufficient to secure a date for the wedding. In demonstration of his good faith, he papered the best chamber to receive a bride. In truth, Flinders worried that he could be judged heartless. 'By noting these things I would by no means have it understood that I have forgot my ever dear departed friend and wife. God knows I have yet many bitter hours on her account, and am, not without some fears, that it will be impossible for me to be so happy as I have been, but what can I do?' Professional life and fatherhood were simply impossible without a mistress of his family, and he was too lonely without 'the society of an agreable woman'. By New Year's Eve, he thanked God for 'having again the comfort of a kind and bosom friend', and merciful providence for enabling him to lay by £56 15s. 8d., despite the year's extraordinary expenses.[3] Home and family restored to order, Flinders was back on course.

Fifty years later, in the same county, another widower household was compromised by the want of a mistress. Lincolnshire solicitor Benjamin Smith was a childless widower of prominent local standing, but a cold bed. He was a rich householder, employer and office-holder, but for the thirteen years of his survivorhood, this churchwarden and governor of the Bridewell hospital pursued a liaison with his servant Mary Newbat that tortured his conscience. Each sexual encounter was crowned with a froth of guilt: 'Newbat came in the Eve & sat with me – may I from this day earnestly resolve to be different & better & correct in my conduct to Her – O God that I was married.' But when she rejected him he was frustrated, morose and still ashamed: 'In Eve: Newbat went Bed without Coming to me tho she knew I wanted Her – O God that might be well married.' Every Sunday, after church, the solicitor was especially depressed that he could not resist temptation at home: 'O God that I was but married to some good woman.' The discrepancy between his secret shame and his religious observance was scalding and his longing for guiltless companionship deep. One summer Sunday in 1819, two local misses sat in his pew. Afterwards, he walked with another family of daughters, calling on them to read his bible: 'I have been much depressed all Day by the want of a female companion O god grant my want.' The solicitor was unusual in the length of his widowerhood. He had 'for some years past wished to be married again' but 'ill health & other consideration have prevented me seeking in Earnest to be so'. At last, in the winter of 1819, he proposed to a Miss Graves, and his servant gave notice: 'I confess I think it will be best she should before I am married.'[4]

Behind Closed Doors puts men back by the fireside. The history of men and masculinity has bloomed in the wake of women's history, recreating *inter alia* the preoccupations of Victorian fathers and sons, Georgian gentlemen and rakes, and Stuart patriarchs and rebels. Fitting the existing pieces of the men's history jigsaw together, one can discern the rudiments of a narrative of very old standing. Crudely summarising, the story might run thus. Early modern husbands and fathers laboured to engineer patriarchal authority over their households, for the home was the anvil on which adult manhood was forged, and the household a little commonwealth. However, the home was not the first space of masculine performance for the Georgians, who proved themselves in the burgeoning public sphere of coffee shops, debating societies and drinking clubs. Early Victorian middle-class men renounced the alehouse for *Gemütlichkeit*, reigning over a Christian family from the well-upholstered parlour. Then again the late Victorian period saw a flight from bourgeois domesticity, the petticoats and the piano-playing, the aspidistras and the antimacassars, to club land, the smoking room and the billiard room, Boy's Own militarism and even the empire, a jingoistic mode of no-ties masculinity that met its nemesis on the first day of the Somme. Interwar masculinities were rewritten in a minor key: suburban, domesticated and withdrawn, complete with pipe and slippers, knitting wife and wireless. 'Just Molly and Me and Baby makes three, We're happy in My Blue Heaven', as a popular song put it in 1927.[5] Men's relationship to household, home and domesticity is a critical element in what it means to be a man, and is a crucial measure for historians of the changing culture of masculinity over time.

A history of Georgian men at home remains to be written. While architectural histories and decorative arts studies have rarely been anything but accounts of male patronage, they have neither been concerned with masculinity per se, nor in dialogue with the social and cultural history of gender. Domesticity and the private sphere have long been leading themes in the history of women and gender, though men's investment in domestic life has not been the primary focus. Georgian masculinity has been seen to flower in the club and the coffee house, the debating society and the political crowd. Some historians, however, regret the accent on the new public theatres of masculine performance and the modish secular cult of politeness, urging instead a recognition of the persistence of the household as the principal site and religion as the pre-eminent code in the construction of Georgian manhood.[6] Nevertheless, the polite gentleman was not a breed apart from the Christian householder; he was often one and the same person. Politeness, as expounded by Addison and Steele, meshed particularly easily with an unenthusiastic religion and a vernacular stoicism. If Jesus Christ could be acclaimed the first true gentleman and Samuel Richardson's Sir Charles

Grandison the ideal man, then Christian politeness was no oxymoron.[7] Nor was the trading worldview intrinsically antithetical to politeness, which was less an all-encompassing identity than a repertoire of manners that could be performed when circumstances demanded it, over the counter in the shop or across a makeshift tea tray at home.[8] Polite rituals added a little elegance to the routines of the patriarchal household, but did not constitute a direct assault on hierarchy. Since politeness was built on the rule of decorum, which held that all should behave strictly according to their rank, station, age, gender and occasion, polite manners could be read as an elaboration and reinforcement of preordained power structures. In fostering a graceful interaction of unequals, politeness introduced a little flexibility to patriarchal frameworks and a patina of modern glamour that assisted their survival in a changing commercial world. On the other hand, politeness powered the expansion of domestic sociability, which encouraged traffic and ornamental decoration at home, increasing the asset value of the gracious domestic hostess.

This chapter places gentry and middling men in the context of home, and asks what domesticity meant to them. The 'domestic' is a baggy category, its primary dictionary definition embracing and eliding 'home, household or family affairs', while 'domesticity' is even more nebulous, invoking 'home life or privacy' or 'homeliness'.[9] For most men, 'homeliness' was synonymous with marriage and with women. Once the ideal bride donned her apron, the matter was taken care of and required no further worry or reflection. Men's written remarks on life at home rarely approach the comprehensive commentary that a historian might wish. Herefordshire farmer Charles Bennet jotted only memoranda about hops and livestock sold, and agricultural day wages, with the odd riddle, in 'his book' for 1740, while Richard Partridge's invitingly named 'personal diary' for the years 1763–1806 turns out to be a miscellany of lists. 'At home & nothing particular' was a typical diary entry for the Nottinghamshire land agent John Jowett in 1789.[10] Reticence about all but the outlines of home life is characteristic of the majority of male diaries that survive in the record offices of England and Wales. Given male reserve on paper, men's diaries as a genre require some introduction.

Six linked genres shape the forms taken by personal life writing by men: the diary of conscience – the fruit of a Protestant obligation to cast up spiritual accounts; the commonplace book urged by Locke but around since the fourteenth century; the secular progress report encouraged by Georgian conduct literature promising social improvement; the account-book, which translated the chaos of life into orderly calculations and rhythms; the appointments diary; and the professional record.[11] Of these, only the diary that served as a public record was an exclusively masculine genre: official diaries were first produced by MPs and JPs in the sixteenth century, and required of excise men from the late seventeenth century (which had to be handed in to be checked by superiors), while professional day-books such as the physician's casebook and the ship captain's log are all diaries of a sort. All six distinct genres persist, though diarists often combined several forms. The London-based upholsterer Jonathan Hall of Elland kept the accounts of his furniture business and an intermittent spiritual diary in the same notebook from 1707 to 1724.[12] Self-scrutiny in words and in numbers were fused in hybrid form in a new commercial production – the pocket-sized diary, or memorandum book.

Pocket-books were printed by canny publishers and stationers, mostly in London. Small and handy, pocket diaries had a basic format, flourishing an exemplary illustration on the frontispiece, a miscellany of printed frontmatter, followed by space for daily notes and accounts. It is the commonest surviving form and invited the scantiest entries. A note of where one had been, whom one had met and what one had spent, seldom more than fifteen words, constituted lavish reportage for many diarists. The clergyman John Ogle used his pocket diary 'the Yorkshire Memorandum Book for 1784' as a terse appointment diary covering six years. Most entries were barely a sentence, often a memo of his letters, visits to the club and his children's births. Occasionally, events overwhelmed the dry record, but even then Ogle was not prolix: 'February 6 1786 Our lovely Dau[ghte]r Eliz died this E'ning after a struggle of 18 hours of ye Hooping cough.'[13] The Shrewsbury surgeon and bachelor Thomas Jeffreys made concise but inconsistent note of activities and expenditure in his Kearsley's Gentleman and Tradesman's Pocket Ledger for the year 1797. On Saturday, 13 May he was 'At home all day but supped at Mr H. Had from Mr Bush some wine and spirits'. Almost invariably, being 'at home' was shorthand for nothing interesting to report.[14]

The Welsh Methodist Reverend David Jones of Llangan recorded his routines for 1807 in the *Christian Gentleman & Preacher's Diary* (fig. 17). As an itinerant preacher with few ties (he was a widowed father of grown children), David Jones's life was built around his religious peregrinations, and when not journeying to Fishguard and Caerphilly, Woodstock and even Newcastle, his week was structured around the climax of his Sunday sermon. Monday, 12 January saw him 'At home, with my accounts & having some rest'; Tuesday, 'At home, in the morning took a walk in the fields'; Wednesday, 'At home, all day with my books'; Thursday, 'At home, doing but little'; and Friday, 'At home, preparing for Sunday'.[15] Home was where he geared up for and recovered from his round, wrote his sermons and letters, did minimal business and was ill; the burning purpose of his life lay elsewhere. Lest he forget, his printed pocket diary boasted an image of a missionary on the frontispiece and a bolstering motto for every day of the week: from the

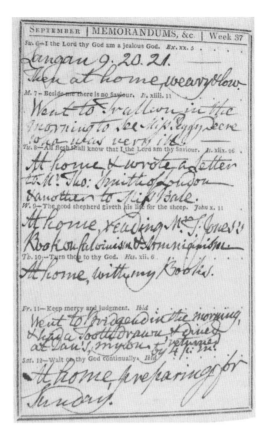

17 Reverend David Jones of Llangan, Glamorgan, Wales, diary entries for a week in September 1807 made in *The Christian Gentleman and Preacher's Diary for 1807* (London, 1807). Glamorgan Record Office, D/D X 223/1. 'At home' was an entry that required little elaboration for this Welsh preacher.

hopeful 'seek and ye shall find' to the unbending 'all unrighteousness is sin'. Home was where Jones marked time, the better to take the Methodist fight across the valleys. The content of domestic life was worth barely a mention.

Male silence on the home is of a piece with broader assumptions about that which was significant to report and seemly to broadcast about a man's life. Action could be in tension with reflection. 'I have neglected my Journal for an immense time' reported merchant and landowner John Biddulph in 1787. 'Indeed my various and active occupations will not allow me to continue it.' On the other hand, serenity could be just as unproductive. Marriage reduced the fodder for a journal, believed the attorney and composer John Marsh. 'Being now quietly settled at Romsey, living a domestic life & being but little from home, the events of the succeeding . . . will probably be comprised in a much shorter compass than those of the 2 or 3 preceding years.'[16] Jane Hamlett had to read twice as many male as female autobiographies to garner an equal amount of commentary on Victorian domestic life. From her study of eighty autobiographies, she concluded that most male memoirs were built around the central narrative of career, to which accounts of home served as sparse prelude: only wordsmiths and hacks told of childhood homes.[17] Of course, the most revealing diaries and autobiographies in the language were often penned by men, some in code, others with an eye on classical models and the judgement of posterity – think of Pepys, Evelyn and Boswell. The rank and file, however, usually presented home as an unremarkable backdrop, even offstage altogether while the dramatic action went on somewhere else.

It could take a catastrophe to make men reflect on what home had been to them: Joseph Priestley was flattened by the violent destruction of his domestic library and laboratory in the Birmingham riot against dissenters in 1791, and never lived again in the Midlands.[18] But placid routine and complacency inspire few chroniclers. Only when men had to manage for themselves did questions of household organisation, servicing and comfort loom into focus. Bachelors and widowers are a useful case in point, for they had the burden of creating their own domesticity and had to search out what they could not take for granted, allowing the identification of the crucial ingredients of domesticity for men.

This chapter is built round the personal testimonies of a range of literate lone men from a variety of confessions (Nonconformist, dry Anglican, Latitudinarian, Catholic and republican deist) and occupations (law student, medical student, solicitor, surgeon, cleric, clerk and small gentlemen), spanning the 1710s to the 1830s. Although most felt strapped for funds, all were drawn from the wealthiest 10 per cent of the population. The memoirs of Dudley Ryder (1691–1756), John Courtney (1734–1806), Sylas Neville (1741–1840) and John Egerton (1796–1876) all partake of the careerist *Bildungsroman*; developing a plumed and preening persona on the page, with varying degrees of assurance and mortification. An older merger of spiritual and financial bookkeeping frames the writing of George Hilton (1673–1725); his annual casting of accounts erupts like a savage *cri de cœur*. Hilton is unusual amongst diarists in his extreme drunkenness, and unusual amongst drunkards in managing to keep a diary. The autobiography of Anthony Trollope (1815–1882) is an exquisite publication, a rollicking narrative driven by the wonderful engine of his comedy. Trollope's account of his awkward age in the 1830s is as crafted as any of his fictions, and it triumphs in presenting the misadventures of a callow but endearing character, while skating over details, and entirely omitting the particulars of his own romances. With a dash of *David Copperfield* and the vim of *Tom Jones*, Trollope heightens the young man's predicament to hilarious effect. Nevertheless, his sketch encapsulates the dilemma of the bachelor across our period. Between his desk and his scanty lodgings, where was a chap to find some domestic cheer? Six bachelor testimonies spanning 120

Mr. *Forth's*	Bill for the		
Qr ending at *Xtmas 1783.*	l.	s.	d.
Tuition	0	15	0
Cash lent			
Steward	0	17	3¼
Lecturer	0	0	6
Coals and Coal-porter	1	11	10
Butler	2	5	1
Cook	1	3	2
Bedmaker	0	12	0
Laundress	1	2	0
Barber	1	4	3
Grocer	1	6	0
Bookseller			
Milliner			
Draper			
Taylor			
Shoemaker	0	2	9
Shoeblacker	0	4	0
Glazier			
Smith	0	8	7
Apothecary			
Glover			
Joyner			
Brazier	0	5	0
Milkman	0	4	5½
	11	19	9¾
Dedt. Fenwtr Schl. 2.3.9¼ Deans Stip. 1.0.0 Horn Schl. 2.10.0	5	13	3¾
	6	6	6½
Balance in favour of Mr. Forth at Michs.	6	5	7¼
Balance due to Mr. Gifford	0	0	11¼

18 John Forth's quarterly bill as a student at Jesus College, Cambridge, Christmas 1783. York City Archives 54: 20. The printed list prices the many domestic services a young, unmarried man might expect to enjoy at home for nothing.

years cannot claim an Everyman typicality. Moreover, the memoirs performed different functions for the authors. On the other hand, important similarities emerge in the routine details of their accounts – in their daily concerns, their reliance on non-domestic provision, their recourse to the domesticity of others – similarities that are confirmed in scattered letters and diaries and remarks in court. Above all, they share a preoccupation with the costs and benefits of marital domesticity. Together they document an urgent literate point of view.

A makeshift quality characterised most bachelor accommodation. Doctors, lawyers and clerics underwent a long professional apprenticeship during which time they expected to be mobile and versatile, poised to seize opportunities as they arose, striking camp as and when. There were venerable institutions that provided domestic services for lone men: the colleges of universities, the Inns of Court, the Army barracks (fig. 18). Commercially serviced rooms wherein the

A CHOP-HOUSE.

19   Henry William Bunbury, *A Chop House*, 1781, etching. British Museum, London J, 6.66. All-male company and little ceremony at a chop house.

landlady and her minions cleaned and changed the linen could be found, though many lodgers had no meals, or laundry provided in-house.[19] The proceedings of the Old Bailey attest that some lodgers had access to the landlady's kitchen at certain hours, while others cooked or heated up their victuals on a fire in their room. Personal cooking equipment was stolen in 38 per cent of thefts of furnishings from lodgings in the 1750s.[20]

A thriving service industry catered to the needs of unattached urban men. London was a humming hive of working women ever ready to clean, launder, mend and tend to men with cash. Washing, charring, nursing and the making and mending of clothes were the four leading female occupations in towns from 1200 to 1850. We might add the ancient livelihood of whoring, for though few ever admitted this occupation, sex was not the least of the domestic services for which most bachelors were forced to pay. London taverns, pie shops, coffee,

THE COFFEE·HOUSE.

20   Henry William Bunbury, *The Coffee-House*, 1781, etching. British Museum, London, 1893,0731.61. A man eats his dinner in all-male company.

bun and chop houses, breakfast huts and food hawkers were the talk of travellers (figs 19 and 20). By 1700 the commercial provision of food probably constituted the second largest occupational sector in the metropolis.[21] Canny customers came to an understanding with local inns to provide them daily hot meals on a take-away basis. The footman John Macdonald recalled his master who lodged at Pall Mall Court in 1773, ate breakfast at home, but 'had his dinners from the Star and Garter'. In 1807 Southey noted one of the sights of the London morning was 'the porter-house boy [coming] for the pewter-pots which had been sent out for supper the preceding night'. London was a paradise for bachelors with ready money: 'there every sort of necessity is to be had in the smallest quantities; and provided a man has a clean shirt and three pence in his pocket, he may talk as loud in the coffee house as the squire of ten thousand pounds a year. No one asks how he lives or where he dined'.[22] As Dr Johnson was advised in 1737, 'A man might live in a garret at eighteen pence a week, few people would enquire where he lodged and if they did it was easy to say, "Sir I am to be found at such a place".'[23] Coffee houses and taverns offered a home away from home, more than a century before the flowering of Victorian club life. How then did our three London lodgers fare?

Dudley Ryder was the son of a Cheapside linen draper, who rose to become a judge. Ryder's early diary records in shorthand his bachelor routine as a law student at the Middle Temple in 1715 and 1716, but only an uncannily prescient observer could have foreseen middle-aged success for the aimless *flâneur* of the journal. Educated at a Nonconformist academy in Hackney, finished in Edinburgh and Leiden, and with two years of legal training under his belt, Ryder at 24 was the pride of his draper father. He flew free on a guy rope of family money, though the £80 a year from which he was 'to find clothes and everything' was predictably seen as too meagre an allowance. Ryder lodged in the Temple itself, and from 1716 began attending the formal dinners there that were an essential element of the professional apprenticeship. He had access to the services of a maid at certain mealtimes. Unusually, he mended his own clothes, but linens were the family trade, so the handling of fabric held few mysteries. Probably the maids did his laundry and cleaned his rooms, for they trafficked freely across his threshold. Discovering some women's linen scattered about his room, he suspected that one of them had slept there in his absence, though when his enquiries met blank denial, he let the matter drop. Too dependent on maid service or too lazy to instigate further investigation, he 'said no more about it'.[24]

The diary reveals what has been described as an 'unstructured regime' of desultory reading and observation in court, combined with 'the extra-curricular activities typical of young men who aspired to politeness but were tempted by the pleasures of the town'.[25] Daily closet devotions and serious reading were interspersed with hours of lethargy, leafing idly through his *Tatler*s and yawning.[26] Yet for all his loafing, Ryder was still a young man of his moment. He has figured in an anthology of courtship, a history of the middling sort, and of polite society, as a staunch Whig, who fretted about his dignity, gentility, deportment and conversation, as well as the tension between refinement, tearful sensibility and true masculine understanding.[27] Ryder collected prints, played the flute and bass-viol and employed a dancing master. He decried the 'extravagance and the folly and the ridiculousness' of his brother's penchant for fripperies like lace ruffles, but himself refused a sober calamanco nightgown from his father, because he fancied one in silk satin, and donned his 'best clothes and laced ruffles' for promenades about St James. Ryder could not help examining his new sword 'several times with a peculiar kind of pleasure', and noticed that he carried himself 'with a very genteel and becoming air' when he glimpsed his reflection in the shop mirrors of the New Exchange.[28] He was no stranger to the thrills of narcissism.

Domestic happiness for bachelors turned on easy access to regular meals and the warmth of familial hospitality. Of the three bachelor lodgers, Ryder was most advantageously placed. He had the wherewithal to orchestrate some modest hospitality, the ready money and wide acquaintance to make recourse to commercial outlets a convenience, not a burden, and above all an abundance of kin near at hand whose hearths were ever warm to him. In his own lodgings, he hosted his dancing master to tea, his brother over cards, and his cousin to play sonatas. Female guests, however, were rare and alarming: would his arrangements rise to the occasion? 'Was in some little concern about the providing for the breakfast of the ladies that were to come to see me. I was not so brisk and gay and full of spirit as I was last night.' The greater part of Ryder's socialising took place out of his own house. He was a member of two clubs, attended guild functions, and resorted to chop houses and coffee houses for solitary dinners, meetings with acquaintances and deliberate encounters with strangers in a campaign to work off his bashfulness. Occasionally, he took refreshments with married couples at their lodgings.[29] It was Ryder's kin, however, who beamed most helpfully in his social universe. He regularly met his male kin in coffee houses and taverns, but also returned to the Ryder headquarters in suburban Hackney and to his relatives for meals and celebrations, where he encountered respectable women of all ages. The Ryder cousinhood made a platform from which the young lodger launched his flirtations amongst the young and nice – though these affairs were inconclusive and humiliating, ending literally in Ryder's tears.[30]

The scion of an upstanding clan, Ryder was regarded as acceptable company for middling girls, but occasional suburban mothers resented his access. Gossips suggested that some Hackney dancing parties were 'designed on purpose to give me an opportunity of gaining one of the young ladies Greys and their mother did not think that proper, as I was only a student'. Since Ryder was in no position to support a wife, the mother felt his entrée should be curtailed: 'If I had been at the bar and had business indeed there might be something more said to it. And therefore she was not willing I should have any more of these opportunities.' Matrons bestirred themselves to make certain that no young fox was let loose in their dovecotes. Ryder's male friends had unhappy affairs with other tenants in lodging houses, but otherwise they were forced on the town to find women. Lambeth Wells, a haunt of 'wretched sad company', epitomised the dubious attractions of barely respectable commercial entertainment. It was heaving with bachelors on the loose, 'such as have nothing else to do but spend their time this way, as officers of the Guards or young fellows that are glad of every opportunity to gratify their pleasure, as attorney's clerks and the like'. Yet the chances of meeting a presentable girl were minute. Instead, the women 'seemed to be all whores and of the meanest sort, not one dressed like a gentlewoman'. Ryder himself was not above transactions with prostitutes.

Dudley Ryder had more opportunity than most to mingle with women of his own rank, but close encounters unnerved him. He was bashful in female company, often lacking full command of his arms and legs. His conversation failed to charm, and Ryder suspected that he made an idiot of himself in the effort, envying men 'that are successful in their address to the ladies'. Juvenile insecurities plagued him. He had a mind to ask his mother whether his 'breath smelt strong but could not tell how to bring it out'. He even fretted that he might prove impotent on the big night, and that any wife would be unsatisfied with him.[31] Ryder regarded women with a churning mixture of fascination, disapproval, desire and alarm.

Nevertheless, the domestic patriarch is discernible in embryo. Ryder liked to read the sermon to the family in Hackney, and disliked giving way to his father in this performance. Playing the senior role came naturally to him: 'spent all the day within doors, reading the History of the Reformation to the women'. Ryder cast a critical eye over the Hackney household, indicting both his father's management and his mother's anxious hospitality. Finding his mother weak-minded, he decided that his own wife must be a woman of judgement on whom he could rely. The balance of burden and benefit in marriage obsessed him. The 'miseries and inconveniences' of matrimony 'were much greater than the advantages of it'. And 'a man runs a cast hazard in entering upon it'. Still, Ryder could not imagine full content without a spouse. Only through lawful marriage could one make a claim on posterity: 'I cannot but be uneasy to think that my life shall terminate with myself. The having of children is a kind of continuance and prolonging life into future ages and generations.' So while Ryder wished he had the iron for perpetual bachelorhood, he harboured 'a strong inclination towards [marriage]', not, he claimed, 'from any principal of lust or desire to enjoy a women in bed, but from a natural tendency, a prepossession in favour of that married state'. That lawful sex was a minor benefit of wedlock is unconvincing, belied by Ryder's own recurring dreams of passionate wedding nights, followed by consternation and repentance the morning after. He woke from these fantasies of ecstasy and remorse in some perplexity, but also regret that he was a bachelor still. His sentimental and sexual hankering after conjugality was powerful, if shot through with panic and ambivalence. Ryder revered the happy state of matrimony as described in the *Spectator*, *Tatler* and *Guardian*, and was impressed when he heard of couples who regulated their lives upon their modern precepts. The concept of marriage was 'charming and moving', and he fell into transports at the thought of 'a pretty creature concerned in me, being my most intimate friend, constant companion and always ready to soothe me, take care of me and caress me'. For all his mutterings, Ryder longed for an 'excellent, prudent, discreet wife' to wipe his brow, share his bed and adore him.[32] Yet not till 1733, when he was 43, an MP and solicitor general did he finally marry the daughter of a rich West India merchant.

The residual domestic life of the clever young man about town is catalogued in the unpublished diaries of John Egerton (1796–1876). Egerton was the elder son of a Dorset vicar, schooled at Winchester, a fellow of New College, Oxford, who followed his father into the Anglican Church. When the diary opens he was still nomadic, deputising and sermonising for various incumbents around London and the south-east.[33] His alliances and sympathies were all dry Anglican, and he deplored 'enthusiastic, fantastic, I may say fanatic notions' in religion. He was supercilious about Catholics, contemptuous of Methodists, hostile to Evangelicals, and signed a petition against admitting Dissenters to the universities. He scribbled an attack on the writings of Lord Byron for the patriotic periodical *John Bull*. On his first Monday in the metropolis, in March 1823, Egerton chose furnishings for his study and went to an evening meeting of the Medical Society. He tutored a struggling student, practised his Latin, attended botany lectures and sampled the metropolitan churches, as well as touring the varied sights of the capital, from skeletons on the gibbet to the sulphurous fumigating baths. Through his younger brother, a trainee eye surgeon, Egerton became interested in surgery too, watching operations and post-mortems almost every day at Guy's Hospital. He rented a Broadwood piano, played the flute, had singing lessons and was learning the violoncello. Aged 26, the spectacle-wearing John Egerton was a cleric of parts and pretension, though hardly oozing with the milk of human kindness.[34]

With no mother and sister on hand to look to his linens and his dinner and no bevy of household maids to do for him, Egerton tried to make his way and sustain a basic level of housekeeping as a lodger with bought-in services. In the summer of 1823 Egerton took unfurnished rooms in chambers in Lincoln's Inn Fields, at the top of the house for 90 guineas a year. He commissioned the painting of the rooms, and bought a rug, carpet and bureau, ordered a bell to be hung, installed a clock and rented the piano. The Inns of Court, like colleges, were designed to meet the personal needs of single men. Egerton paid to have his rooms serviced by a maidservant, a married woman named Mrs Pitt who lived in the same building and did for the other lodgers. She changed his linen and made his dinner. However, reliance on the services of a stranger was nerve-wracking. In April Egerton had already had a lock put on his bureau. By the autumn Mr Egerton began to suspect Mrs Pitt of dishonesty, accusing her 'of taking my sheets to her own use'. Hearing on 3 October 1823 that 'she have plundered the other lodgers of various things', he reported her to the Bow Street runners, where to his frustration he 'was told that she was not punishable by law'. There was no criminal case for theft when goods had not been removed from the house, though possibly Egerton could have made a weak case for 'conversion' of his goods and claimed for civil damages, but even then Mrs Pitt had been given his implied authority to take his linens out of the house to wash. Perhaps Mrs Pitt thought busy bachelors were inattentive, or that use of the linen was a legitimate perquisite of the job. Doubtless she had a shrewd idea of the scope of the grey area between taking a liberty and committing a crime. However, she had not reckoned with Egerton's tenacity. After dining at Johnson's coffee house on 7 October, he came home '& gave Mrs Pitt a good rowing for using my sheets. She vowed she never had touched them, but I saw them with my own eyes on the Bed.' Despite his chagrin, Egerton was still reliant on Pitt's services. At last, in March 1824, he 'had a proud row with Mrs Pitt who is the most impudent [servant] I ever heard & dismissed her from having anything more to do with my Rooms, or with me'. With a certain defiant bathos he added: 'Dined at a chop house'. Thereafter, Egerton tried to manage without a servant and was smug when he devised a means to eat a square meal at home without recourse to the conniving Pitt: 'Dined at home: tried the Experiment of sending out for cold Boiled Beef[.] had a beautiful Plate for six-pence: so find I can have my Potatoes cooked upstairs & need not dine at a Chop House.' When he had a bevy of medical men to dinner he had the event part catered by the local tavern, and 'a roasting Pig sent by Mrs Price', '& every thing went off capitally', he was gratified to report.[35]

Like most bachelors, Egerton was attentive to his stomach, and his diary abounds with lip-smacking descriptions of good meals taken out of his own house. Institutional dinners, such as those given by the Eye Infirmary, Guy's Hospital, Ironmongers' Hall, New College and the Wykehamists, were contrived for single men, providing one of the chief comforts of domesticity without any of the toil. Male guests need not concern themselves with the provisioning, the cooking, the tidying and polishing, the linens, the silverware, the candles, the setting and serving, or the clearing away, laundry, washing and cleaning. Nor did they have to coordinate a battalion of impudent servants, so were free from any of the managerial nuisance that beset most housekeepers. Conviviality in a quasi-domestic, but painless form was the *raison d'être* of the institutional dinner, providing a convenient context for the reunion of old friends and the gathering of professional acquaintances. Egerton was at ease with hale professionals like himself, praising gents who were 'friendly and hospitable', relishing their larders and cellars, conversation and curiosities. Egerton voiced none of the financial anxiety that plagued other young men on the make, but an air of self-congratulation still surrounds every good dinner he managed to strike off. The same hungry opportunism was apparent in his friends (pl. 5):

> Dennis called expected to be asked to dinner as he called when I was not at home, but said he would wait in the dining parlour. The Cloth & c was laid. But I never asked him to stay – so after a little hint or two, he took his departure, lamenting much poor Mr Chandler, or rather he meant I suppose Mr Chandler's dinners.[36]

Egerton was eligible and urbane, and his credentials were an open sesame to the family homes of his friends. It was an unusual bachelor who gave no thought to the charms of matrimony, or to the qualifications of his ideal bride. Egerton sized up every maiden who glided across his path, and with special scrutiny once he saw her white hands tripping across the piano keys. Characteristically, however, he also had a keen appreciation of the costs of marital housekeeping and presumably the bachelor freedoms he would have to renounce. After an afternoon stroll with a Miss Payne and her brother in July 1823, he reflected: 'He who can afford to treat himself to a wife should make up to Miss C Payne – very pretty, sensible & good humoured.' Wrily, he added, 'O Dear!'[37] To marry or not to marry, that was the question. At length, Egerton was snared by another daughter of the cloth, Ellen Gould, the 22-year-old sister of his good friend Philip Gould, another clergyman. Miss Gould first aroused his admiration at a domestic music recital in Hertfordshire in April 1823: 'Two of the Misses play on the harp only learners. One very pretty; plays on the Piano very well & would sing I am told, but for a dreadful cold which she at present possesses.' For more than eighteen months, he was intimate with the family, stood godfather to Gould's baby daughter, and saw his 'Pulcherrima!' often. He confided no plans to propose, and developed no inner struggle between love and freedom on the page. But in December 1824 he abruptly came to his resolution, and bustled up to Suffolk where his lovely was ensconced, his clumsy dawn entrance the only sign of impetuous emotion. 'On my arrival found nobody up. awakened the footman & on my Entrance the first thing I did was to break the Lamp in the Hall with my Portmanteau . . . Requested an audience tete at tete with Ellen[.] Every thing settled. Gave her a ring.'[38] They married in 1828 and settled in Cheshire the year after, Egerton succeeding his bachelor uncle to the post of preacher master at the grammar school at Bunbury. Egerton's man-about-town pageant was behind him.

The industrious and indefatigable novelist Anthony Trollope (1815–1882) inaugurated his manhood at a desk in the General Post Office in London in 1834.

Trollope's father was a failed lawyer who took on a farm that ruined him. It was Trollope's gallant mother who kept the family afloat through her frantic writing: 'A sadder household never was held together. They were all dying – except my mother, who would sit up night after night nursing the dying ones, and writing novels the while, so that there might be a decent roof for them to die under.' At the end of his erratic education at Winchester and Harrow and in languages in Bruges, young Anthony was still gauche and directionless: 'I was an idle, desolate hanger-on, the most hapless of human beings, a hobbledehoy of nineteen without an idea of a career, or a profession or a trade.' Though he was coming to appreciate the fullness of his father's failure, it was a young man's mission to quit the household and make shift for himself: 'I could do nothing but go and leave them. There was something that comforted me in the idea that I need no longer be a burden to them – fallacious idea, as it soon proved.'[39] The answer was the junior clerkship at the GPO.

The charm of family life for men, as well as the truly dreadful dinginess of domesticity on a budget, are carefully developed in Trollope's œuvre. His fiction is exquisitely attuned to the vulnerabilities and vacillations of young men on the make. 'He must give up his clubs, and his fashion and all that he had hitherto gained, and be content to live a plain, humdrum domestic life, with eight hundred a year in a small house full of babies', reflected one of his unworthiest lovers, the caddish civil servant Adolphus Crosbie on the verge of matrimony. 'Could he be happy in that small house, somewhere near the new road, with five children and horrid misgivings as to the baker's bill?'[40] Even Trollope's open-hearted heroes can be found hesitating on the brink. The promising barrister and MP Frank Greystock had chambers in the Temple, lived in luxurious rooms in a big hotel in the West End and dined at his club or Westminster, revelling in the company of countesses and rarely out of debt. Knowing that marriage to a mousy governess would interfere with his ambition, forcing him to renounce his 'Belgrave-cum-Pimlico life' for 'dim domestic security' somewhere north of Oxford Street, Greystock evaded the consequences of his promises for nearly 600 pages.[41] Trollope often made a comedy of those slippered bachelors who dodged matrimony altogether the better to husband their cigar fund. He warned of the dangers of growing old in selfishness amidst the fleshpots: 'He had seen what becomes of the man who is always dining out at sixty.'[42] Conversely, Trollope shed a little dignity on those dowdies who never had time to strut in a good suit before the bills or the babies came, and who lived monotonously thereafter on an unrelieved diet of fireside chat and scrag end of neck.[43] And Trollope was fondly sympathetic to the embarrassments entangling clerks in lodgings. But then he knew whereof he spoke.

'My salary was to be £90 a year, and on that I was to live in London, keep my character as a gentleman and be happy.' Looking back in 1873, in the fullness of 58, he considered the task an unfeasible one even in conception. It was all too easy for a young chap to come to grief on the rocks of his London expenses; in fact, Trollope considered shipwreck inevitable.[44] Keeping one's end up on the salary of a junior civil servant was a feat of domestic husbandry, requiring 'The courage of a hero, the self-denial of a martyr, and much more financial knowledge than generally falls to the share of a Chancellor of the Exchequer'.[45] Living 'a jolly life upon £90 per annum' proved impossible for Trollope in the 1830s at any rate, and for his entire post office career in London he was strangled by debt. He took rooms in a lodging house on Northumberland Street in Marylebone, looking out on the workhouse: 'a most dreary abode, at which I fancy I must have almost ruined the good natured lodging house keeper by my constant inability to pay her what I owed'. Apart from breakfast, which he got on credit, there were no meals provided at his lodgings, and he often lacked the cash for dinner. 'I had no friends upon who I could sponge regularly. Out on the Fulham road I had an uncle, but his house was four miles from the Post-office, and almost as far from my own lodgings.' Pursued by a moneylender and threatened with prison, he had to slink back to his mother to recoup. Young Anthony missed his ma and longed to be adopted at some surrogate fireside: 'I belonged to no club, and knew very few friends who would receive me into their houses . . . There was no house in which I could habitually see a lady's face and hear a lady's voice.' His companions seemed as bereft as himself, so even access to sisters of his friends was non-existent. The GPO itself unwittingly afforded some quasi-domestic, though risqué leisure to Trollope and the 'whole bevy of clerks' who lived in the building. Trollope fell in with the higher-paid officers of the foreign mail, who enjoyed free lodgings on site. 'There was a somewhat fast set in these apartments given to cards and tobacco who drank spirits and water in preference to tea. I was not one of them, but was a good deal with them.' Trollope and some of his racier colleagues would adjourn after lunch to the 'comfortable sitting room upstairs' devoted to the use of the live-in clerks, to 'play écarté for an hour or two', and for suppers and nocturnal card parties: 'great symposiums, with much smoking of tobacco'.[46]

Without the means of a man about town, or the compensations of a sisterly cosseting, Trollope shivered in a domestic vacuum. Trollope implied that he might not have erred if only he had gained a foothold in some respectable parlour, been plied with cakes and sympathy, lionised by the innocent daughters of the house, and taken to the ample bosom of its right-thinking matron. As it was, 'no allurement to decent respectability came my way'. The details of his rackety life ('entirely without control – without the influences of any decent household around me') are not disclosed, but unsavoury company, liaisons with tarts and reliance on a shady moneylender were acknowledged. Trollope's more autobiographical heroes had similar woes, like the raw clerk Johnny Eames who worshipped a graceful maiden back home but became embroiled with the landlady's vulgar daughter, blood running icy at the thought of discovery by his own mother. Trollope himself was 'always in trouble', most hilariously so, when he found himself engaged to be married against his will: 'The invitation had come from her, and I lacked the pluck to give it a decided negative.' Despite keeping his head down and ignoring the girl's love letters, he reaped the whirlwind in the shape of the mother, who bore down on him at the office, declaiming: 'Anthony Trollope when are you going to marry my daughter?' Seldom have a young man's troubles been captured with such economy. 'We have all had our worst moments and this is one of my worst', was Trollope's gloss. At length, aged 26 in 1841, he landed a better-paid job as an itinerant surveyor's clerk in Ireland. With his luck on the turn, and emerging from his protracted boyhood, he met and married the daughter of a Rotherham bank manager, in 1844, and, at last, his late-budding literary career began to bloom.[47] Only in his late twenties and through marriage did Trollope, by his own reckoning, grow into the full dimensions of a man.

Upon marriage, the lodger gave up his rooms, renounced the chop house and established his own household in either a rental or a freehold property. Some men, however, fronted households before marriage, particularly at higher social levels. Propertied bachelors might have already come into their inheritance, or been gifted an early independence if they were lucky enough to be first born. The bachelor householder had a stake in society that the lodger was seen to lack. What follows is a discussion of three single householders: George Hilton, John Courtney and Sylas Neville, all of whom drew consequence from keeping house, yearned for women's company, but varied in their attitude and access to feminised domesticity.

George Hilton (1673–1725) was a Westmorland Catholic and Jacobite. Heir to the mortgaged manors of Hilton and Murtin in Westmorland, he and his widowed mother hung on to two properties, the Parsonage house and the newly built Hilton House, after his father's death in 1691. Hilton had been dealt a poor hand. He could not take a university degree, pursue a profession or hold county office because of his Catholicism; and he was strapped for cash from the outset. In 1696, turning 21, he sold a large slice of his inheritance, including the heavily mortgaged manor of Hilton. In riposte, his outraged sister Mary Hilton launched a suit against him for her portion in the Court of Chancery in 1700. He was embroiled with the lawyers until February 1701, when the judgement went against him, and he was even arrested at her behest and taken into custody. Even more disastrously, he had married and lost a wife, all before the age of 26. The identity of the bride and the details of the breach are mysterious, though Hilton complained of 'unkindness' from his wife, and mentioned an attempt at reconciliation by letter. In his cups, Hilton had a ferocious temper. At Appleby in August 1701, 'being much in drinke', he struck a man so forcefully with his stick that the unfortunate man lost an eye, costing Hilton £50 in damages. Spirits were as firewater with him. Unsurprisingly, Hilton's wife never rematerialised, and he lived, to all intents and purposes, a bachelor for the rest of his disaffected life. When his diary opens in 1700, he was already, at age 26, galloping down the high road to ignominious ruin.

In an attempt to re-establish his standing and perhaps to entice back his errant spouse, he leased the medieval manor house of Beetham Hall in 1700, which he made his base for twelve years, whereupon he bought Park End, a late Stuart house typical of the local yeomanry. Hilton was also forced to take London lodgings to fight his Chancery suit, and rented rooms in Gray's Inn, where he could have his dinner sent in. From his post-mortem inventory, it emerges that his total personal property stood at £88. The list of his movables suggests a dignified, though conservative, material culture. There was a modest array of traditional furnishings, like table linen and bedding, and worthy equipment such as a little plate and pewter, brass and copperware, and even treen (woodenware). Although he had a little of the newer earthenware, he had none of the new specialist tableware, no paraphernalia for hot drinks, and no porcelain or any silver lighting gear. He was equipped for neither tea parties nor genteel dinners. In furniture worth mentioning, he had three beds, a cabinet and drawers, three glass cases and a great looking-glass, a cupboard, writing desk, a table and a screen, but he had no clocks or scientific instruments. For decoration, he had a manly assortment of maps, pictures and 'goods on the chimney', and a library, though nothing in the way of small china ornaments, which featured in the homes of merchants and aristocrats in this period. Most of his personal wealth lay in his cattle, two horses, saddlery, husbandry gear, gun, sword and pistols. The loss of more than £3 worth of property when paralytic in Kendal – 'hatt wigg & steele buckell & handchuchers . . . sword & coate[?] & bridle' – confirms that he carried all the usual masculine accoutrements.[48]

Hilton was a slave to strong liquor. He easily 'fell a-drinking' at any social or business encounter with men, and invariably proceeded to drink himself to oblivion, sometimes for two days together. 'Much fuddle', 'fuddled' and 'mortally fuddled', he was ashamed to report on countless occasions. In fact, Hilton asterisked his 'fuddle days' in his manuscript journal, though the editor of the published version has helpfully introduced a symbol of a bottle for these lost episodes. Some bouts ended in utter mortification, when he 'exposed' himself 'most miserably', and was easy prey to sharps and robbers, as well as careless loss and accidents. However disreputable, Hilton was no social outlaw. He was on easy terms with the men of the northern squirearchy. When he was arrested at the suit of his sister, Hilton caroused all night with the lawyers, and was immediately bailed. After a day in court, he 'dined at the Castle with the Judges at night at the Castle . . . all night dancing'. In London, he went on drinking binges with the vice-chancellor of the prerogative court of Lancaster. Cronies, elite or plebeian, were never lacking, but there is no evidence that the northern gentry made him a domestic guest. But then it would be one thing to shoot with such a rogue, and quite another to bring the wolf home to feast on one's daughters. Apart from dinners with his mother, Hilton had scanty interaction with ladies of his own rank. Women of lower rank were quite another matter, however. In October 1704 he boasted: 'Friday Saterday & Sonday last past I laid with my housekeeper all nights & did my utmost efforts to her &c', noting later with relief 'Grace had her flowers'. After carousing in London taverns, Hilton 'picked upp a couple of w-ores and gott a severe clapp'.[49] Following this, he was laid up a week with a nasty swelling in his groin. Hilton would never have lawful heirs, or any respectable domestic companionship. There were to be no elegant dinners, no polite ceremonies, no genteel domesticities, no grace and graciousness at Beetham Hall.

Like most male diarists, George Hilton recorded only sparse commentary on his routines. His daily entries were hardly ever more than a single sentence, noting where he was, and with whom, culminating in the amount spent each day. In few words, however, he could be extraordinarily self-revealing. Neither a fool nor self-deceiving, Hilton did not flinch from reporting sessions with whores, a dose of the clap or drunken humiliation. Once a year he felt moved to summarise the events of the preceding twelve months, and was forced to some reflection on his actions, lugubrious self-reproach and heartfelt, if unavailing, resolutions for the future. Looking back in 1722, he bravely calculated the financial costs of his drinking:

> Memorandum from the primo of April in anno 1714 till this present Monday the primo October in anno 1722 which is just 8 yeares & 6 moneths I've been 220 times drunke in which contained in number of dayes 629: which is 3 dayes per time one time & with another & in Moneys £376.10.0 which is almost £40 per time one time with another, & very near £50 per annum in drunken bootes . . .

Consumed with shame, he dreamt of reformation. In February 1702, 'being now 27 yeares & 3 months o[ld]', he set down a new list of resolutions at the beginning of his diary, first among which was to moderate his drinking:

I am most passionately resolved to have soe punctuall a guard over my in-
clynacions as never to loose my reason by immoderate drinking. In performance of which I hereby oblige myselfe to shun all ale houses as much as in me
lyes except called by businesse or some particular friend . . . neither will I (except detained for businesse) ever be out of my owne lodging after 12 at night
nor exceed my bottle for my owne share in any strong liquours as wine punch
& 6 d in brandy.

His next resolution was against whoring: 'Never will I knowe a woman carnaly
except in a lawfull state.' He further resolved against backbiting, lying, gaming,
swearing, laziness ('I will spend more time in my study than hithertoo I have
done'), and 'against remisness in religion'. Lastly, he implored the Almighty to
help him perform these 'moralityes', and to keep the fasting days of the churches
of England and Rome. He ended with a hopeless prayer: 'God the Father Sonn
and holy gost one perfect family blesse me and inable me to conquour stuborne
nature that I may be the last day happy Amen Amen.' Stubborn nature made
short work of his resolutions, as he admitted with impressive candour: 'broake
3 of my resolucions vizt eate flesh laid with a woman and up till 2 o'clocke in the
morning'.[50] From his mournful reckonings, it is clear that Hilton knew well
enough that between drink and fornication, he made disgrace his bedfellow and misery his companion.

John Courtney (1734–1806) was a minor Yorkshire gentleman, the son of a
senior administrator of the East India Company and a Beverley widow. Courtney was nothing if not a polite urban gentleman. His Cambridge law degree was
a mere ornament, because he came early into his money on the death of his father in 1756. Unlike our other bachelors, he was unequivocally a wealthy householder, with all the stake in genteel society that this entailed. Living on his rents
and investing money through a broker in London, Courtney was minimally occupied overseeing the family property. After the death of his uncle, he became
head of the family, handling the financial affairs of his mother and relatives.
Serving on committees for the local militia, drainage schemes and charities,
Courtney played an administrative role commensurate with his property. Beverley was the hub of the East Riding of Yorkshire, boasting a medieval minster,
the quarter sessions and new assembly rooms opened in 1763, to which Courtney subscribed. He was a leading mover of the genteel social round that the town
afforded, attending three private balls, an assembly and a play in a mere five days
in December 1761. He was enmeshed in the genteel networks of the town –
lawyers, medics, clerics and the military – and on a nodding terms with the Yorkshire aristocracy. Courtney jaunted to Scarborough, Harrogate and Bath for the

spa, York for the dancing and Hull for the races. He played the organ and the harpsichord, composed cantatas and country dances. A correct and natty dresser, he carried himself with a dapper formality.

In 1759, when the diary begins, his studies were behind him and his inheritance in his hands. Living with his widowed mother in a house in Walkergate, Beverley, his household arrangements were impeccable. No complaints about insubordinate servants, inadequate meals or sloppy housework made the pages of the diary. Courtney's co-resident mother ran the daily accounts, which he settled periodically. Probably Mrs Courtney also managed the maids, for no domestic details obtruded. Courtney was on tender and dutiful terms with his mother, and they socialised together. Their town house with its organ and space for dancing was adapted for parties and even balls.[51] All that was wanting for his drawing room was a fitting wife. Cumulatively, the diary brings to mind a mildly conceited, but thoroughly domesticated young gentleman, who could be trusted to sit demurely in the parlour with anyone's daughter, subjecting her to nothing more scandalous than a few verses of plaintive song. Nevertheless, he was a man on a mission.

The governing preoccupation of his twenties and thirties was the quest for an accomplished, well-endowed bride. Courtney spent almost a decade on this great task, having a go with almost every eligible maiden to whom he was introduced. His unimpeachable gentility gave him easy access to family groups, chaperoning marriageable young women at resorts and across the polite thresholds of the East Riding. His amours proceeded at racehorse speed; generally, the period from first glance to proposal barely covered a month. He was rejected on eight occasions. John Courtney's first love affair set the pattern. Turning 27, Courtney was passing the average age of marriage for men. In York on 3 February 1761 he heard a Miss Newsome's fine singing and playing at a domestic party. Two days later, he called on her at home to give her some music. That same evening, he sat behind her at the play, plied her with sweetmeats and 'handed her out'. When she sang at a tea party the next Saturday, 'I was confirmed in my resolution.' On Thursday, 19 February he repeated his officious little attentions at the theatre: 'I dare say the young lady may begin to guess that I like her.' On Friday he managed to dance with the maiden, and on Saturday 'handed her into the coach'. Given the conspicuousness of his manoeuvres, the Newsomes can have been in little doubt of Courtney's goal. On Wednesday, 26 February he declared his suit to the family, returning the next day by appointment to make his declaration. The family gave Courtney controlled opportunities for intimacy at home with Miss Newsome; he was left alone with her downstairs chaperoned only by a child running in and out, and was allowed an hour's private conversation in the best parlour while the aunts were at church. But on 1 March the aunts ambushed Courtney after a tea party and told him to desist. After the frankness of his embassy, the tacit approval of all parties, his welcome in their parlour and presumably the attractiveness of his credentials, Courtney found the refusal hard to credit. In short, 'I was thunderstruck.' The afterglow of the affair lingered another fortnight. Miss Newsome returned his music; the ladies reiterated that there was no hope; and Courtney had an opportunity to play one last bittersweet air, 'Ariadne and Soft Invader of my soul', to his lady love.

In the spring of 1762, turning 28, Courtney met 18-year-old Mary Smelt of Bedales at the Beverley assembly and was smitten. Thereafter, he encountered his 'Pulcerimma!' at local tea parties of young ladies, and delighted in her playing on the spinet. Their first *pas de deux* took place in March, when he wrote a country dance for her – 'she gives the name of Whim to the dance' – at a Sunday afternoon tea party in Beverley. After two more abortive courtships, Courtney reverted to the tuneful Miss Smelt, but his uncle disapproved of her small fortune and doused the suit. Courtney's next attempt took place in Harrogate, where he and his mother befriended a Newcastle family. On 3 September 1764 he danced with the daughter, Miss S., who 'made an entire conquest of my heart'. One dance at the Green Dragon was enough to reveal her 'a most amiable and accomplished woman', one more public ball sufficient for blatant courtship, 'I now show myself attached', and a ride *en famille* the only further preamble to a proposal of marriage made via the parents. On 10 September he was rejected. The whole skirmish had lasted a week. By his early thirties he had tried his practised gallantries on five more women to no effect.[52]

Few gentlemen of means are unable to marry, if only they have the humility to address themselves to a girl who will have them. Why Courtney was such a repeated failure on the marriage market is obscure. He always aimed high, pursuing youth and prettiness allied with birth and fortune. Possibly too high. His own recommendations may not have been as sterling as he imagined. His respectability was invincible, but was his fortune flashy enough to offset his smallpox scars? For all his decorousness, Courtney was deficient in savoir-faire. He made poor capital of his access to young women at home, remaining deaf to the subtleties of female communication. Though punctilious in addressing himself first to a young woman's guardians, a smoother suitor would have arrived at a better sense of how the ground lay with the girl herself before he broached the matter with her elders. Overall, Courtney's romantic exercises were characterised by an air of ponderous sentiment, which was intended to be debonair, but may have looked pompous and wooden. Possibly, he was a little ridiculous.

Eventually, his smarting eyes settled again on the musical Mary Smelt. At 34 years of age, Courtney showed more resolution. When he received a doubting letter from his sweetheart, he 'galloped to Hull in half an hour; had an interview with my dear Miss Smelt and made up all matters to our mutual satisfaction, and removed all her scruples'. At last, in June 1768, the couple were married, both in white, in Hull, returning to a wedding tea at home in Beverley: 'we used our best agate knives . . . reserved for my wedding day'. After supper the servants came in to watch the couple dance a minuet, and the new Mrs Courtney played on the harpsichord for some country dancing. 'Soon after the bride retired to bed, in the best chamber and I followed.' The couple embarked on married life in Walkergate, living with Mrs Courtney senior till her death in 1771. Courtney purchased handsome Newbigin House, set in its own grounds, where Mary Courtney bore him ten children. His prayers were answered in full.[53]

Of a different kidney altogether was Sylas Neville (1741–1840), a cynical life-long bachelor, who moved in and out of stable housekeeping for almost a century. Neville had embarked with 'an ample fortune sufficient for every purpose of life', but after the death of his father he steadily drained the pot dry: 'deprived of his protecting care and misled by company I lost the greater part of it at play and the turf'. Despite a legal training at the Temple, and an Edinburgh medical education, Neville never practised any profession. A passionate republican, Neville professed himself 'a true friend of Liberty' and criticised the laws of property, although his views did not preclude his hopes of various legacies from kin. His religious sympathies also inclined to the independent. Neville's crowning feature was a self-indulgent code of sexual morality, dressed in specious philosophy. Sexual lusts gratified 'without invading any man's right or any woman's virtue' were not sinful, but merely 'a venial offence arising from a most natural desire'. He excused his adventures with poorer women (possibly prostitutes) as exercises in moral reclamation – 'every connexion I have had with such women was accompanied by my earnest endeavours for their reformation' – presumably expressed in a post-coital lecture. It was to his ignominious entanglements that the editor of his papers sternly ascribed 'his failure to do anything useful in the world'. Political historians have read his 'phallic adventuring' as an endorsement of radical 'liberty' in sexual as well as religious matters, comparable to the heterosexist libertinism of John Wilkes.[54]

Neville's diary begins abruptly in 1767, when he was 26, lodging in London. For all his callow radicalism, Neville behaved much like any younger son of moderate fortune, as if the metropolis were a banquet laid out expressly for his delectation. He preened himself on his connoisseurship, attended the theatre three or four times a week, and took in oratorios, pleasure gardens, parliamentary debates, post-mortems, Newton's tomb and the dragoons' review. A spartan disdain for fashionable appearances would have been consistent with his radicalism, but in fact Neville was obsessed with the figure he cut in the world. In Norfolk, he sat for his portrait in oils, requesting an 'ancient sepulchral urn' in the foreground inscribed D.M.G.G., signalling his admiration for the Gracci, 'those noble Romans who made such generous efforts to establish the liberty of their country on a more equal & lasting foundation'. Incongruously, however, our hero was bedecked like a cavalier, 'in Vandyke dress, the colour dark grey, sleeves and breast slashed with crimson', a contradiction to which he seemed altogether blind, though later he commissioned a portrait miniature, hoping to be depicted in Roman dress 'as it was in the times of liberty'. Despite his ideological austerities, Neville was as nice in his regalia as any dandy – 'so clean & always look as if I had just come out of a box'. He took lessons in horsemanship and swordsmanship, and had a weakness for the raciest horse furniture, like a 'new bit made from Lord Pembroke's pattern and Hussar saddle', which he flaunted round Hyde Park like any beau. He carried an engraved gold watch belonging to a sailor uncle, and brandished a gold cane, engraved with an image of Brutus and his motto 'Causa ardens'. Neville delighted to display himself in his accoutrements on all possible occasions.[55]

His twirling performance was unsustainable, however: 'my expense so far exceeds my income; but a house is not to be furnished and horses bought every year'. He rented a second-floor room full of bugs, but out-sourced his domesticity, reading the papers and breakfasting at coffee houses, and dining at eating houses and taverns: 'a good deal of sweet-bread is almost a sufficient dinner', he noted. Neville was always gratified to be offered hospitality, since it meant he was not put to the trouble of finding a meal. He recorded few invitations to respectable homes, but became embroiled in a farcical affair with a married woman. Otherwise, he was dependent on the tavern and his landlady for company. Tainted by the 'sordid principles and low manner of living' of the landlady, he came to see his lodgings as most disagreeable.[56]

By 1768 Neville decided to go in for provincial 'housekeeping' to retrench. After a reconnoitring tour, he hired a house near Yarmouth, and embarked on country life as a would-be squire. Taking on the role of 'master of a house', he realised 'the utility of keeping a diary & copies of the letters I have occasion to write', because there was so much to remember. He also attempted some patronising hospitality: 'Every person ought to be civil to those in inferior ranks.' Neville even refused a bed to the brother of a friend with the sanctimonious observation 'it is dangerous to admit a man having no home & given to drinking'.[57] His attempt at decorous housekeeping, however, was compromised from the outset. In Eastbourne, on his tour, he had hired a pregnant girl, Sarah Bradford, as housekeeper. Though he flattered himself on his rescue of a seduced maiden – 'Some may be censorious; but my motive for this action, the taking the girl out of her native place where her reputation is blasted, is a benevolent one' – she soon became his mistress. Thereafter, Neville's household consisted of himself, his 'Sally', now re-named 'Mrs Russell', serving as housekeeper and lover, her child, a man and a boy. It was an inherently unstable ménage, simmering with resentment and cloaked in subterfuge. Quarrels were frequent, with Sally bridling whenever Sylas corrected the child, and complaining about her lack of finery, which was, after all, one of the traditional compensations of being a gentleman's kept mistress. Belatedly, Neville realised that he was sacrificing his chance to attract 'a virtuous and well educated wife'. Whenever the subject came up, Sally threatened to embezzle him, and slit her throat. 'Lord deliver me from this connexion! For it prevents me entering into every good one.' Neville had sacrificed 'real joys' for low company. 'How miserable is the situation of a bachelor', he sniffed.[58]

The final insult was that his finances were worse than before. In January 1771, aged 29, he cast up his accounts: 'found that I had spent very near 4 times my income . . . God have mercy upon me! I know not what I shall do.' One possibility was to share housekeeping with two other Norfolk gentlemen, though Neville dismissed the scheme on grounds of expense, because their house was north-facing and gloomy, and the gentlemen had Tory connections and a 'slovenly way & want of neatness, which would ill agree with me'. He told his landlord 'It is absolutely necessary for me to leave off housekeeping' and took himself off to Edinburgh to qualify as a doctor of medicine, and presumably to escape the complications of his ménage. After graduating with distinction, he travelled three years on the Continent, was disappointed in hopes of an early inheritance from a childless uncle, and of an appointment in the Foreign Office. Despite fathering at least two children with Sally, Neville refused to make an honest woman of her, and instead married her off to his young manservant John Read in 1783. In the same year, Neville finally settled in Norwich, where he intended to practise medicine at last. 'Slept for the first time at my own house, quod felix fautumque sit, have never been happy since I left off housekeeping.' Yet still he did not marry.[59] He ended his very long life subsisting on charity.

Domestic arrangements dictated the tenor of a man's life, setting the terms of his engagement with the world and colouring the sort of man he was understood to be. Nevertheless, many married householders were tight-lipped on domesticities in their commentary, though male silence is revealing of the degree to which domestic business was handled behind the scenes; only when men had to manage for themselves and were harassed by conflicting demands might household details obtrude, as was the case for the Lincolnshire widowers, the London lodgers, and the Yorkshire, Norfolk and Westmorland bachelor householders discussed here. Between the leaving of the schoolroom and the reading of the banns, bachelorhood was seen as a natural phase – an era of adventure, exuberance and some expected licence. It is not a stage associated with domesticity. The unceasing pursuit of meals, company, comfort and sex, however, all expose the services complacently enjoyed by successfully married men behind closed doors. Young blades were expected to kick over the traces and skirt disaster, before they graduated to matrimonial housekeeping. The dyed-in-the-wool bachelor was another beast altogether, however, sometimes a figure of affectionate humour, but often seen as unrealised in his masculinity, at the mercy of his impulses, negligent in the government of society. Marriage was not the sole passport to adulthood for men as it was for women. There was no marital qualification for public office or occupational success. Nonetheless, the suspicion that never-married men were evading their proper share of the burden of domestic government and social provision surfaces in punitive form in proposals to levy a tax on bachelors. Perpetual bachelors were 'the vermin of the State' pronounced *The Women's Advocate* stonily.[60] 'They enjoy the benefits of Society, but Contribute not to its Charge and spunge upon the publick, without making the least return.' Unmarried men were never subject to the vicious ridicule heaped on old maids, but criticism of the selfishness of perpetual bachelors was quietly consistent, as was fear of the consequences if too many men refused to bed down in marriage and legitimate baby-making. 'I am for having every-body marry', declared Richardson's perfect Christian gentleman Sir Charles Grandison.[61]

The crucial factor that determined the life of a bachelor was the nature of his housing and tenure: was he a householder or a lodger? On this turned his standing in the community, his stake in local government, his relationship with servants, the furnishings and equipment of his home, his domestic sociability and, importantly, his access to women. The limitations of life in lodgings were an evergreen theme. Ryder and Egerton were aggravated by their maids, and Egerton liked to do without them altogether, preferring commercial and institutional provision wherever possible. Only Ryder entertained women in his lodgings, and then he made a nervous host. All three men were alert to where they might get a good dinner for free. Ryder was the most comfortably situated of the three, rising to some nervous hospitality, having funds for commercial mutton chops and a choice of family dinner tables at which he could pull up a chair. Egerton had no local kin, but thrived in the professional society of men, exploiting to the full his connections through school, college and his brother. Quasi-domestic, but bother-free, institutional dinners were custom-made for ambitious bachelors. At ease in the common room, practised with the brandy bottle, Egerton emerges as the archetypally 'clubbable' college man. With neither Ryder's vibrant kin network nor Egerton's professional resources, Trollope's circumstances were the least auspicious. His autobiography is vivid on his deprivations in his 'most dreary abode' behind the workhouse and his search for non-domestic but unsatisfactory solutions to his loneliness. All three lodgers sought female company and were on the watch for a wife. Their testimonies agree that budding brides were not to be happened upon in commercial venues, but had to be charmed in their nests. Sweethearts were discovered in the homes of relatives and family friends, the sisters of one's colleagues, the friends of one's cousins. Without a footing in a respectable household no proper courtship could prosper. Young Trollope had no friendly sofa to nestle on, no matron's workbasket to fidget with, and no young ladies to tease or admire him. He presented life without access to decent domesticity as a desert. Both Ryder and Trollope pined for feminine warmth. But in the meantime, in desperation, Ryder turned to tarts for comfort, to his crimson shame, and Trollope implied doing as much. Their yearnings, fretfulness and guilt were such that their bachelorhood reads less like a brief gaudy hour of buccaneering freedom than a mortifying sentence in purgatory.

The bachelor householder was not a rolling stone. He shouldered responsibilities that most lodgers evaded, and was inevitably a more prominent citizen. He was almost certainly an employer, with all the advantages and annoyances this entailed, a taxpayer and a ratepayer. The housekeeper was expected to be a man who paid scot and bore lot. Yet these responsibilities qualified a man for influence and office. Householder status was one of the building blocks of local government and legal administration. The householder probably had access to greater credit too.[62] The case studies of George Hilton, John Courtney and Sylas Neville demonstrate that some social position could be derived from housekeeping. Courtney was an acknowledged gentleman and office-holder who lived with his mother. His housekeeping was irreproachable and his gentility without blemish. No threshold was closed to him, but his desk organ waited ten years for a mistress. In contrast, the Catholic gentleman Hilton was a violent drunk who had scared off one wife and would never find another, which put a limit on his integration in gentry society. He performed to the hilt with poxy whores and his obliging housekeeper, but without a wife Hilton would never enjoy any creditable female companionship, or legitimate heirs, as he was only too aware. Lugubrious resignation to domestic emptiness is the keynote of his testimony. Similarly, Neville's wilfulness precluded the achievement of the reputable domestic life expected of a man of his fortune. 'How miserable is the situation of a bachelor, exposed to all the bad humours of low life, deprived of those real joys which a virtuous and well educated wife affords' was his supremely hypocritical conclusion.[63]

The contrast between life before and after marriage was starker for the bachelor lodger than for the gentleman householder. For most lodgers, marriage coincided with setting up home, and was synonymous with the onset of housekeeping. Grooms resigned their lodging keys and their fellowships, and supposedly bid farewell to the pie shop, the alehouse, the turf and the trinket shop. This was the moment when a young man took up the burdens along with the dividends of patriarchy. Naturally, weddings were momentous for householders too, many of whom had dreamt a decade or more of the love, sex, companionship, housekeeping, hostessing and potential mothering that a bride incarnated. However, the new wife entered into a pre-existing establishment. Marriage was not the residential revolution for Courtney as for Parson Egerton. When Courtney's diaries begin again after twenty years of matrimony, they find him with seven children, still attending oratorios and tea parties much as he had done with his mother, only now escorting his middle-aged wife and an assortment of his progeny. Courtney still pursued only a minimal social life in the exclusive company of men. When his son turned 21 in June 1790, Courtney broke out his vintage '65 port, donned a 'a New Suit of Clothes' and opened his doors for a dinner, ball and cold collation supper, gamely dancing every dance.[64] John Courtney's wedding marked no watershed in the arrangement of his social and domestic life. By contrast, marriage for John Egerton was a complete sea change. He exchanged compact metropolitan chambers for a Cheshire farm, stables, house and outbuildings requiring constant upkeep, and a staff of six servants. The evening lecture circuit was a thing of the past, yet Egerton was still busy and clubbable – attentive to the Grammar School, a moving force behind the Chester Conservative club, a subscriber to fifteen charities, excitedly taking advantage of the newly opened Crewe to Birmingham railway to shorten the pilgrimage back to Oxford and Winchester. The account-books and diaries for 1837 reveal a Victorian father of ten, hair glossy with Macassar oil, a grower of prize-winning dahlias, a dab with the magic lantern, for whom home was the hub of his operations.[65]

Nearly forty years after the sexual liberalisation of the 1970s, it is easy to forget that only marriage promised true sexual fulfilment for Christians, turning furtive or frustrated boys into fully realised men. Marriage was the only acceptable framework for children, through whom men made a claim on the future, but also confirmed their potency. Virility was one of the most celebrated masculine qualities, as the Georgian obsession with fertility and cults around sailors and naval potency make abundantly clear.[66] The father who led a handsome family into church radiated both an air of commanding respectability and a glow of unmistakeable sexual success. Marriage promised sexual excitement. Two days before his marriage in January 1754, 33-year-old Josiah Wedgwood positively

frothed with anticipation of 'the blissful day! When she will reward all my faithful services & take me to her arms! To her Nuptial bed! To – Pleasures which I
am yet ignorant of.' He took the precaution of working overtime the week before
his wedding to clear time to enjoy his bride uninterrupted.[67] Foreigners were
convinced that sex was inseparable from ideas of home for the Englishman. Even
adulterers paid oblique tribute to the importance of home, so entrenched was
domesticity in the national psyche. One of Madame de Staël's priggish English
heroes worried that there could be no love without 'domestic happiness'. British
adulterous liaisons 'are reflections of the married state', with lovers endeavour-
ing 'to find that happiness therein which they cannot experience at home, so that
even infidelity is more moral in England than marriage itself in Italy'. [68] There was
nothing bohemian about sexual intrigue in a cold climate. Five of the eight loners studied here admitted to fornication. Yet they were hardly blithe or brazen
Casanovas. Even Neville, the most shameless of our crew, concealed his philan-
dering from chance readers of his diary by means of a simple cipher. Guilt was
an incubus on their backs. 'Grant me the true circumcision of the spirit; that my
Heart & all my members being mortified from all worldly & carnal lusts I may
in all things obey thy blessed will' was the desperate preface to Benjamin Smith's
self-loathing diary for 1817. 'O God that I was married' was his repeated prayer.[69]
Only in marriage could a man satisfy both his desire and his conscience.

Sententious men could be prosy about the sentimental benefits of matrimony.
A Yorkshire clergyman and widower, John Ogle, hankered after 'Delight unknown to a single condition' in 1779, believing that 'the Employment a man is engaged in whether the Fatigues of a Camp the Confinement of Studies or
Embarrassment of Business tho ever so irksome ceases to harass and weary him'
once in possession of a spouse. There were no guarantees. Disgruntled husbands
are not far to seek. Benjamin Smith's second marriage was decidedly chilly after
all, especially once his new wife asked to preview his will. True domestic loyalty
came only from his dog Spark, 'an affectionate & faithful friend & companion',
whom he had stuffed in 1850.[70] The hurly-burly of the bachelor chaise longue
might look quite different from the vantage of the matrimonial double bed. As
babies and bills came thick and fast, the austerities of masculine companionship
could take on the allure of Sparta. Middle-aged Vicesimus Knox was a bachelor,
but 'disgusted at the noise of the servants, and the bustle of a family' used to
dream of 'the blissful region of the common-room fireside!' at St John's College,
Oxford: 'Delightful retreat, where never female shewed her head since the days
of the founder!'[71] Nor were all husbands fully house-broken, unsurprisingly. The
man who forsook the parlour for his old drinking cronies was a stock rogue of
female complaint.

21 *Dandies at Tea*, 1818, etching. Lewis Walpole Library, Farmington, CT, 818.11.0.1. Two exquisite dandies are shown taking tea in a ramshackle bachelor lodging room, where ragged garments are drying on a clothes-line. Despite their sartorial pretensions, their sordid linens demonstrate that they lack the wholesome domesticity that women provided.

When you are married will 'you spend your evenings at Home in reading and conversing with your wife, rather than spend them abroad in taverns or with other Company?' enquired a shrewd sweetheart of the New England patriot John Adams in 1759. Realising that much rode on a diplomatic answer, Adams temporised that he 'should prefer the Company of an agreeable wife to any other company for the most part', though qualified: 'not always, I should not like to be imprisoned at home'.[72] Middling men and gents were never tethered to home in the manner of their wives; their peripatetic business lives and public duties put them routinely in the way of extra-curricular leisure. The inventor and educationalist Richard Edgeworth insisted that he 'lived more at home than is usual with most men of my age' in the 1760s and '70s. Edgeworth was determined to re-energise his Irish estate by living amidst it, delighted in mechanical contrivances at home and developed an ideological commitment to the domestic education of his nineteen children. But even he could be absent for months. And going through four wives he could hardly complain of monotony on the home front.[73]

There are many male testimonies to the experience of marriage as apotheosis. When 29-year-old Thomas Hittingford, tutor and cleric, was at last able to marry and settle in 1812, he felt his life was about to begin at last. Nearly thirty years later, the glory of that moment remained an incandescent memory:

> Life was then fresh! My imagination was excited with pleasurable ideas of what was coming! Everything seemed to smile around me. The horizon had not a single cloud for me! Young, and in full health and vigour of mind and body, for there was no one thing upon earth which gave me the slightest feeling of anxiety or doubt! Nothing but a delightful anticipation of happiness and independence![74]

Independence did not mean rugged isolation and an escape from the petticoats, but the ability to found one's own household and fill it with underlings. This vision of responsible manly independence was deep-rooted and persistent, pursued as much by Victorian artisans as Stuart office-holders. By this view, a man achieved political adulthood when he could support his dependents and represent them, a conviction that found expression in the limited householder franchise of 1867.[75]

Settling down was suffused with possibility and glamour. Trading freedom for responsibility was not without its tensions, yet the intensity of men's longing for marriage and domesticity is the overriding impression their diaries convey, a desire not just for sex and services, but also for a continuity of female companionship and a centred domestic life. Domesticity for bachelors was fragmented and effortful, while their manhood remained in suspense. Bachelor dwellings were temporary encampments, more lair than headquarters, or dormant houses awaiting the female kiss of life, while widower households wobbled like the house of sticks. At home alone a man had no domesticity worth the title (fig. 21). Even those men who felt not a flicker of attraction to the opposite sex had to marry to benefit in full from housekeeping. A common male fantasy was a home with a woman in it, generating interior warmth and sociability, the cradle of personal happiness and a platform for social success. Far removed from twenty-first-century fears that settling down extinguishes virility, establishing a household was believed to give it full reign. In marital domesticity, bachelors expected to puff out their chests, lift up their heads and hit their stride.

3

SETTING UP HOME

/

Ⅰ<small>T WAS A TRUTH UNIVERSALLY ACKNOWLEDGED</small> that a Georgian house with a drawing room, French windows and lawn must be in want of a mistress. A man in possession of a comfortable house and a financial competence was a prime target of Cupid's arrows. Courting men were required to offer a suitable establishment before a couple could embark on married life, so a man's house and prospects were at issue when a young woman examined the small print of an offer of marriage.

When Jane Austen's Catherine Morland is shown around the parsonage of Henry Tilney, the gentleman that everyone expects her to marry in *Northanger Abbey*, the attractions of the house are revealed in a seductive tour. All eyes are on young Catherine to gauge her reactions to the 'new-built substantial stone house, with its semi circular sweep and green gates', Newfoundland puppy and witty bachelor on the threshold. Inside, Catherine registers that the parsonage is comfortable, the dining parlour 'commodious, well proportioned . . . and handsomely fitted up' and the manly study carefully tidied in honour of guests, but it is the charming drawing room, with French windows overlooking the meadows, still awaiting decoration, positively inviting a woman's touch, that clinches the deal. In the unfinished drawing room Catherine's reticence is overcome, and she betrays her ingenuous desires. 'Oh! Why do not you fit up this room, Mr Tilney? What a pity not to have it fitted up! It is the prettiest room I ever saw; – it is the prettiest room in the world!' Grasping his cue, the would-be father-in-law, still imagining that she is an heiress, insinuates that Catherine herself is the only thing wanting. '"I trust", said the General, with a most satisfied smile, "that it will very speedily be furnished: it waits only for a lady's taste!"' Catherine is even solicited for 'her choice of the prevailing colour of paper and hangings' by the importunate father-in-law.[1] The encounter is built on a misunderstanding, but the successful viewing of the house has become an implied contract of marriage.

Marianne Dashwood's unchaperoned tour of Willoughby's prospective house in *Sense and Sensibility* is one of the events that leads her sister to suppose them engaged, though Elinor is stunned by the impropriety of the undertaking. Predictably, Marianne is as delighted with the Devon mansion as she is enamoured of the dashing gentleman. '"There is one remarkably pretty sitting room up stairs; of a nice comfortable size for constant use, and with modern furniture it would be delightful."' In betraying her scheme to renovate, Marianne reveals the grand material assumptions that underscore her sensibility, as well as Willoughby's airy expensiveness, but also the firmness of her intentions – '"nothing could be more forlorn than the furniture, – but if it were newly fitted up – a couple of hundred pounds, Willoughby says, would make it one of the pleasantest summer-rooms in England."' Only betrothed couples mere weeks, sometimes days from the altar, have conversations of this practical intimacy, as we shall see from courtship correspondence, and as Mrs Jennings, an aficionado of the signs and symptoms of impending matrimony, points out later in the novel: '"No positive engagement indeed! After taking her all over Allenham and fixing on the very rooms they were to live in hereafter!"'[2]

[When a woman ex]plored a man's house she tried it on for size, thereby pro-[...]re. Upon examination of the apartments, she could substantiate a man's claims to consequence, but also study the materialisation of his character. Even Elizabeth Bennet, playful and knowing, jokingly dates her love of Mr Darcy from '"my first seeing his beautiful grounds at Pemberley"'. On her fateful tour, Elizabeth Bennet recognises Darcy's legitimate claims to status, the 'lofty and handsome' rooms, the 'furniture suitable to the fortune of their proprietor', and the true taste and elegance of the whole. It is his sister's personal sitting room, however, that offers material testimony of Darcy's unexpectedly sweet nature and domestic solicitude: 'they were shewn into a very pretty sitting-room, lately fitted up with greater elegance and lightness than the apartments below; and were informed that it was but just done to give pleasure to Miss Darcy, who had taken a liking to the room when last at Pemberley.'[3] The provision of a room where modern prettiness reigns, like the brotherly gift of a superb piano, functions as a demonstration of Darcy's generosity and readiness to care for the women nearest to him. Tender recesses of Fitzwilliam Darcy's character are thus revealed to the softening visitor, and by strong implication his potential kindness as a husband. Simultaneously, Austen reveals to us that female delight in stylish decorative schemes was taken as read, and that a dedicated feminine sitting room or drawing room was a standard feature of gentility.

Houses sprout architectural features in response to femininity in Austen's *Persuasion*, written in 1816. Upon the marriage of the young squire Charles Musgrove to the youngest daughter of a spendthrift baronet, a Somerset farmhouse is 'elevated into a cottage' complete with 'viranda, French windows and other prettinesses'. (Verandas were still new; one of the first in Britain was built on the Royal Crescent in Brighton in 1798.) Meanwhile, a quarter of a mile away at Uppercross, the great house is also 'in a state of alteration, perhaps of improvement'. Architecture and inhabitants are drolly discussed in the same terms. The house, like the old squire and his wife, is in the 'old English style', venerable in fabric, wainscoted, stately with family portraits and shiny with beeswax, but Augustan 'order and neatness' is giving way to Regency 'confusion'. The faintly ridiculous daughters of the house are superimposing a modern informality, 'a grand piano forte and a harp, flower-stands and little tables placed in every direction', on the antique fabric. Austen satirises the introduction of the sillier paraphernalia of fashion by the ill-educated Miss Musgroves: 'The portraits themselves seem to be staring in astonishment.'[4]

It was possible for modern feminine elegance to sympathise with a handsome structure, as Austen allows in *Pride and Prejudice*. Nevertheless, the female will to impress itself on houses is often unrealistic and pretentious. Barton Cottage, the Devon refuge of the disinherited Dashwoods in *Sense and Sensibility*, is comfortable and compact, but too small for the dreams of the mistress. Mrs Dashwood longs to give a 'greater elegance to the apartments', and has an eye to building work from the instant she take possession. 'The parlours are both too small' for the domestic sociability that a house of ladies ideally generated, but Mrs Dashwood will not be dictated to by mere walls. 'I have some thoughts of throwing the passage into one of them with perhaps a part of the other, and so leave the remainder of that other for an entrance; this with a new drawing room which may be easily added and a bed chamber and garret above, will make it a very snug little cottage.'[5] Of course, a cottage so opened up will be the opposite of 'snug'. Their straits make the improvements a pipe dream, but the fantasy also reveals Mrs Dashwood's failure to appreciate their reduced pretensions. The

Dashwoods are no longer the ladies of the manor, the cynosure of local sociability, but themselves clients of another big house.

The female drive to stamp personality on interiors is more sinister in *Mansfield Park*, but it is still automatic. As a woman of style and ambition, Mary Crawford admires the 'spacious modern-built house, so well placed and well screened as to deserve to be in any collection of engravings of gentleman's seats in the kingdom'. In fact, she finds Mansfield is 'wanting only to be completely new furnished' to be absolutely perfect. She is ruthlessly stylish, and the prospect of Edmund Bertram's mere parsonage is depressing to her, unsurprisingly, and only as 'the respectable, elegant, modernised and occasional residence of man of independent fortune' is the house acceptable at all. But Mary's dangerous London modernity is merely the counterpart of her brother's whimsy for irresponsible landscaping – forecasts of the emotional havoc both will wreak in Northamptonshire.

Renovation in itself was neither shallow nor vicious. The need for proper improvements to the parsonage at Thornton Lacey is recognised by the young clergyman Edmund Bertram, a pillar of rectitude, whose character and manners mark him out for domestic happiness. Only his heartbreak delays rebuilding. 'I want you home that I may have your opinion about Thornton Lacey', he appeals to Fanny Price. 'I have little heart for extensive improvements till I know that it will ever have a mistress.' [6] Building development is the reward of honour in *Sense and Sensibility*. Elinor Dashwood and Edward Ferrars both live by an exacting moral code, often at some personal cost. United at last, their unpretentious parsonage has to be remodelled before it will accommodate a marriage. Their patron, Colonel Brandon, pays for the repairs to the fabric, but to speed the completion of the details the newly weds 'superintend the progress of the Parsonage' together, chivvying the dilatory builders, choosing wallpapers, projecting shrubberies and curved drive in well-earned relief.[7] Their similarity of taste and feeling creates a home. We are left imagining that the improved parsonage will be the cradle of their matrimonial success.

To be mistress of a house was no paltry achievement. In *Pride and Prejudice*, the mature Charlotte Lucas is prepared to put up with a 'conceited, pompous, narrow-minded, silly' husband in return for 'a comfortable home'. She makes her trade with her eyes open, for marriage 'was the only honourable provision for well-educated women of small fortune'. Though Elizabeth Bennet scorns 'the sacrifice of every better feeling to worldly advantage', Austen allows that as the new Mrs Collins and mistress of an establishment, Charlotte has gained consequence and an arena for the demonstration of her skills. Through deft organisation of time and space in the Kent parsonage, conjugal intimacy is kept to a minimum, and Charlotte has liberty to enjoy her gains: 'her home and her housekeeping, her parish and her poultry, and their dependent concerns, had not lost their charms'. Even Elizabeth can see that Charlotte is managing with cleverness, and to the advantage of both stupid husband and modest house; 'everything was fitted up and arranged with a neatness and a consistency' that reveals the resourceful hand of the mistress.[8] Female ingenuity indoors is taken for granted by Austen, like letter writing and falling in love, a talent deployed by the worthy as well as the meretricious, expressive of characters both deep and shallow, sensible and sensitive, unselfish and opportunistic. Creating prettinesses at the parsonage next to Mansfield Park gives the vicar's wife a short-lived occupation: 'Having more than filled her favourite sitting room with pretty furniture, and made a choice collection of plants and poultry, was very much in want of variety at home.' A moral and intellectual lightweight, Mrs Grant is only running through 'the usual resources of ladies living in the country without family or children'.[9] Even Lucy Steele, perhaps the most cheerfully appalling of all Austen's female creations, a monster of cunning, quick as a lizard, though ignorant and illiterate, is imagined by Elinor Dashwood unleashing her fiendish cleverness behind the closed doors of Edward's parsonage. 'She saw . . . in Lucy, the active, contriving manager, uniting at once a desire of smart appearance, with the utmost frugality, and ashamed to be suspected of half her economical practices.' Though 'pursuing her own interest in every thought', Lucy expected to be judged on domestic performance and shiny front.[10] As a provincial solicitor opines in *Persuasion*, 'a house was never taken good care of . . . without a lady'.[11]

Austen assumed in her readers an elaborate sensitivity to the implications of taste and interior decoration. She relied on their ability to infer that domestic details signalled character and choices, and that even silly little tables had meaning. Beyond the symbolic and metaphorical significance attached to the finer points of interior decoration, Austen relied on the social, economic and emotional importance her readers would attach to the drama of setting up home. Her appraisal of home-making is consistent with genteel opinion across our entire period. The house was a demonstration of a would-be husband's financial strength. It was for a man to offer a suitable establishment to any miss he cared to marry, a stipulation that forced bachelors to postpone matrimony till they had the wherewithal to accommodate a bride, and some to shelve the matter altogether. The house itself was the major part of the offer on which a young lady took a view. Consequently, women's tours of young men's houses were pregnant with possibility for the key players – ' "And of this place", thought she, "I might have been mistress!" '[12] – and meaningful in the eyes of public opinion. Sweethearts and brides were expected to be keenly interested in all the appointments of the marital home. Derbyshire palaces apart, the characteristic bachelor house had scanty facilities for domestic entertainment and had to be overhauled before it made a genteel home – a pretty drawing room, modern furnishings, fresh wallpapers and elegant access to the garden were the features that gladdened the heart of an Austen bride. Floating in the ether is the further implication that a woman who could not like a pretty sitting room in a neat parsonage was not woman enough for marriage. Discussion of the improvements, wherein the couple projected their future life *en famille*, was part of the regular business of advanced courtship, integral to the consolidation of the match. Wedding bells announced the decorators. Honourable men, ripe for domestication, were ready with the sample book and their credit, but ladies' preferences carried the day. If a suitor was in earnest he had to show a willingness to spruce up the furnishings, and, if worthy, studied female preferences and promoted female comfort. A wife should have first claim on her husband's politeness. In truth, men of any sense would welcome female ministrations indoors, for Austen's wives could be shrewd and supportive in their domestic arrangements. The mistress of a house was a figure of respectability and power. In 'her house and her housekeeping' a woman experienced ownership. Interiors are plastic in the hands of Austen's women. Parsonages seem especially prone to transformation, but then this was the house form Austen knew inside and out. Petticoats trigger metamorphosis in full five fictional parsonages. (And perhaps six, for it is hard to believe that Mrs Elton would fail to give the vicarage a thorough going-over and impose some Bristol fashion in *Emma*.) Even the architectural fabric seems pregnant with the possibility of mutation to accommodate a lady: as General Tilney airily proposes for his son's bachelor vicarage: ' "a bow thrown out, perhaps" '.[13]

*   *   *

The need for a housekeeper drove many, if not most, bachelors into courtship, while desire for a house of their own was equally compelling for spinsters. So how far did male acceptance of female government at home shape the furnishing and decorating of the interior? The discussion that follows explores setting up home in middling and genteel families and the balance of decision-making between man and wife-to-be. The commencement of joint housekeeping was a climactic moment, which marked for most the achievement of full adulthood. Within most marriages, major interior decoration took place at the outset when couples first set up home together (fig. 22). In rich families, rebuilding and redecoration might take place on marriage, on inheritance, on sudden windfalls or social promotions, on expansions in the family, in response to damage, and when

Stakes were highest at marriage. When most people defined their look.

22   William Hogarth, *The Industrious 'Prentice Married and Furnishin[g]* and ink and grey wash, over graphite. British Museum, 1982,0227.1. A d[rawing for an] unused print, probably a discarded idea for Plate 8 of Hogarth's 'Industry and Idleness' (1747). A newly married couple supervise the furnishing of their new house. Refurbishment is the reward of industry and inaugurates a successful marriage.

taking new lodgings for the season, or to launch children on the marriage market. At lower social levels, however, major decoration occurred only at marriage. The Lathams were Lancashire smallholders, probably the humblest family for whom long-run personal account-books survive. Mr and Mrs Latham bought almost all their utensils and furniture in the twelve months after marriage in 1723; virtually no household goods were then bought till the late 1730s. And new iron pots, a looking-glass, upholstered chairs and window curtains came later still in the 1740s and '50s, when grown-up daughters were contributing to the family economy.[14] For most gentry and middling families, the wedding was the decisive moment for the look of the interior – when most of the couple's furniture was acquired, and any refurbishment contrived – before children arrived to drain the finances and take the shine off the chintz. For individuals who cared about appearances, this was when the stakes were at their highest. Eighteenth-century courtship is now understood to be a conciliation of strategy *and* emotion, prudence *and* affection, yet quite how much of that negotiation centred on the home has been unnoticed.[15] The letters of Ann Baker, the daughter of a Buckinghamshire linen draper in the first decade of the eighteenth century; George Gibbs, an Exeter physician in the 1740s; James Hewitt, a Coventry lawyer and aspirant career politician in 1749; Mary Martin, the daughter of a minor Essex gentleman in the 1760s and '70s; and Josiah Wedgwood junior, a fashionable manufacturer in the 1790s, all concern the creation of the marital home, epitomising the personal contract between man and wife at the very moment of its composition, and in four out of the five cases revealing the areas of household business over which women brought to bear a recognised expertise.

That women liked to have 'the whole management of the affairs of the family' and a leading say in the appointments of the marital home is clear from the surviving letters exchanged between most courting couples. Ann Baker was the eldest daughter of Daniel Baker of Penn in Buckinghamshire, a rich linen draper and brother to Elizabeth Verney, Lady Fermanagh of nearby Claydon Hall. When Ann Baker was courted by a Captain Mead in the second decade of the eighteenth century, she was gratified by her fiancé's detailed promises regarding the situation and manner of their future domestic life. As she reported to her father, her own wishes about the location of her future home were to be taken fully into account: 'He will take a House in any part of the Town that I like but is most inclined to the new Buildings near Ormond Street which are very hansome and airry.' The money she brought to the marriage would be translated into furnishing the social areas of the house, for her social credit and pleasure, not to shore up a struggling business or to pay off debts. Mead promised to 'lay out 200 pound in furnishing the first floor and parlour for he says he has furniture that will do for the other part of the House'. The captain's sensitivity to the accoutrements of feminine gentility and performance was manifest: 'says he has a good deal of Plate but will buy me a Silver Tea Kettle and lamp and . . . [?bone] Tea pot'. Appearances were given their due importance. He promised 'a present of Earrings' and 'to take a Man and put him in what Liverry I like'. Most winning of all, Mead guaranteed that 'I shall have the whole management of the Affairs of the family and that his Mother shant concern her self with any thing belonging to the house for indeed he says she is not capable of doing it and he shall like to live in a Hansomer manner.' Genial indulgence in a spouse, untrammelled household government, no mother-in-law to interfere and a determination to live in high style – the offer was irresistible. 'He seems to be very good natured and I hope if it is my Fortune to have Him I should live happy with him.'[16] They married and settled in London, maintaining cordial relations with both mercantile and gentry kin.

When the Exeter doctor George Gibbs courted Miss Ann Vicary in the 1740s, he took for granted that his future wife would have preferences about their first home, which he would do well to honour. After courting for some years, Gibbs was anxious to get established so they could marry: 'I have seen a house lately which I wish you & I were well settled in.' And though he wished to expedite matters – 'I have been to look at a House & am buying Furniture' – he hoped to carry his sweetheart's approval with him. 'Don't be surprized my Dearest, for I shall not make an absolute Bargain without your approbation, much less shall I pretend to fit up the Kitchen, or the Bed-chambers, you may think perhaps, that what I say upon this Subject is Spoken in jest but I must assure thee I am serious.' Gibbs's correspondence reveals him touring properties in Exeter and describing them at length to his fiancée. One possible house was 'situated just by Palace-gate in the Court, where the young Mr Williams the Attorney now lives'. Gibbs was continuing on paper a discussion they had had in person, 'but I imagine you can never have seen it, if you had, it would undoubtedly have occurred to you, among the others that we have thought on'. Dr Gibbs needed a house to suit his wife *and* his practice: 'The Situation of it cannot, to be sure, be call'd pleasant; but wth respect to my Business it is in the very part of the Town, that I shou'd desire it.' He was attentive to access: 'you come thro' the outer Door into a little square Court, which leads Immediately into the house, just within the second door, on the left hand, is a very small Room, [with] one sash'd window, which will do for a Surgery'. He was observant about layout, room size, light and aspect, as well as furnishings: 'beyond this, is a good Parlour (not large) wth two sash'd windows, wainscoted, & painted blue'. Above were two chambers 'tolerably good, & one of them, if I remember right, hung with paper'. On the right was 'a very good Kitchen, planck'd, & a Buttery or two', under it 'two pretty cellars, & over it two Chambers'. To the back were lumber room, coal house, brew house and a garden, 'just of the Bigness one shd chuse it of, wth a walk on the lower wall'. The staircase was 'a tolerable one, but not very light'. The first-floor dining room, usually the best room in a house, was deemed 'upon the whole pretty good with two sash'd windows looking into a Neighbours Garden and hung with yellow Harreteen'. It let into 'a very good lodging Room, but somewt dark'.[17]

Gibbs was kicking himself that his fiancée had not seen the house before she left. Receiving Vicary's approval by letter, he embarked on negotiations with the bishop's agent. The house was offered at £18 a year, though Gibbs hoped to get it for £16, but the bishop would not budge on the rent, and insisted on an immediate decision. Gibbs was forced to decide or lose the house. Gibbs was uneasy coming to a final decision about lodgings that his future wife had not examined herself. He even solicited the opinion of a kinswoman of Ann's but to no avail: 'I took Miss Vicary wth me to see it, but you know tis impossible to make her say any thing in such a case, for fear of being blamed for her advice.' Taking the house for three years, Gibbs swore he would undo all on Vicary's say so: 'if it shoud not be agreeable to thee, my Dearest, & I woud not give 20/ a year for it if you dislike it'. Any oversights subsequently discovered by Vicary could be rectified: 'Webber has promised that if I take the house every thing shall be done that is reasonable so that if you find after you return that I have not remembered all necessary matters, I dare believe he will not refuse to comply wth whatever is proper to be done afterwards.'

Gibbs's letters to his absent sweetheart expose the negotiations about setting up home that couples undertook on the threshold of matrimony. With some justice he admitted: 'I am quite weary my dearest Girl of writing to thee about Houses.' The letters are suggestive about the issues upon which a wife might have an expert opinion, from layout and dimensions, to light and aspect, to furniture and fittings. They also bespeak a man's concern to honour his wife's investment in the home. Gibbs set self-conscious store by the value of domestic life. As he told his daughter thirty years later, those 'who are well disposed will for ever take the greatest delight their own home; & indeed it is my opinion that those who are incapable of relishing domestic happiness, can never be really happy at all'.[18] That Gibbs was a man made for marriage, good-humoured, reasonable, anxious to give pleasure and reach agreement, could all be read from the outset in his letters about houses.

Not all professional men were so careful in building conjugal consent or so attentive to female tastes and fantasies for the future. Of the newly married Coventry couple, James (1709–1789) and Mary Hewitt (d. 1765), James was the dominant partner, whose domination extended unusually to the matter of decorating. Hewitt, however, was a man of singular ambition. The son of a mercer and draper who had become mayor of Coventry, he practised as a barrister and later a judge, rising to become Lord Chancellor of Ireland, in 1768, with an estimated income of £12,000 a year, ennobled as the first Viscount Lifford in 1781. His first wife, Mary, was the daughter of the Reverend Rice Williams, rector of Stapleford Abbots, Essex, prebendary of Worcester and archdeacon of Carmarthen. In her family's eyes, Mary was affectionate, but delicate in constitution, wanting in the spirited competence that became a woman of her background. Meanwhile, James Hewitt was a formidable spouse for any young woman, feeble or otherwise. A ripe 40 at the altar, Hewitt was said to be old-fashioned in outlook and formal in manner, though also patient, urbane and respected for his professionalism and the accuracy of his technical knowledge. In 1749, when the letters open, Hewitt was yet a Coventry alderman and barrister, though eyeing a potential political career as MP for Coventry.

The honeymoon bloom was still upon bride and groom, despite separations caused by his administrative obligations and her chronic ill health. Mary pined for letters, talked to his portrait, reflected longingly on the kisses she was missing, and wrote from her 'old bed chambere' where 'you & I have spend many agreable hour'. The new wife was not in a position to manage her husband's household business in Coventry, even had he wanted her to, since much of the time she was laid up with 'cholick', piles and later pregnancy, more than 100 miles away, at her father's house in Essex.

In the vacuum, James Hewitt directed the refurbishment of new lodgings himself without reference to his wife, while his brother Joseph, another attorney, acted as his foreman of works.

Dr Brother You tell me that my Parlours are painting. I am glad to hear it, provided that you mean the street parlour and garden parlour for as to the great parlour you know I don't propose meddling with it at present and if that is painting my money is throwing away. As to the Dutch tiles in the Chimney I leave it to do as you will.[19]

There was a limit to the money Hewitt was prepared to lay out on a rental property, but on the other hand he was determined to make a show. He desired 'paper for the staircase of a Stucoe pattern and for the upper part of the hall if there is enough left when the staircase is done'. Nonetheless, there was no point in papering areas that would not be seen by guests: 'I don't mean that any more of the Staircase should be papered than only what appears as you go up the stairs to the Front Rooms.' Hewitt was confidently conventional in his insistence that the first-floor front rooms should have the most impressive decoration:

There is also a Yellow paper made to the pattern of the Damask for the Bed chamber curtains & Chairs of the street rooms . . . I would have this Yellow Furniture in the room on the left hand over the street parlour, both because I think it rather hansomer than the other and because the Closit or Dressing Room is the best and looks towars ye street is more uniform.

The barrister was also familiar with the taste for matching curtains and wallpaper, and surprisingly adept at suggesting pattern and conveying visual effect: 'As to the other street room I have a new white flower'd Dimity . . . As the bed is white and the window Curtains so too the paper should be something light cool & airey. A white ground with small spriggs will suit it best. I leave it to you.' Hewitt was watchful about the manner of the work, insisting that the paper in the hall need not be hung on canvas, though 'the wall must be well scraped before it is put on', while the finer damask-effect papers on the first floor should be mounted, so they could be removed later. He was vigilant as well as frugal: 'Don't forget to have the water pump'd out of the Celler two or three times a week, to keep the House dry.' All the same, Hewitt was not entirely independent of female advice, directing queries about mundane household textiles to his mother.[20] In large part, he still acted like a bachelor.

Hewitt brought the same meticulousness to his management of household matters as to the technicalities of the common law. With its half-papered staircase and handsome 'street rooms', the Coventry house was decorated first and foremost for display. Probably it was designed for political sociability, a social headquarters for a promising alderman, who had a borough to win. (In 1754 he stood for Coventry, unsuccessfully, but eventually won the parliamentary seat at the General Election in 1761 for the Whigs.) By Georgian standards, Hewitt's career was meteoric, and it is hard to overstate the steel of his ambition. In his small way, Hewitt decorated his Coventry lodgings in the spirit that Sir Robert Walpole decorated Houghton, his Norfolk *palazzo*. Power, not domestic happiness, was Hewitt's primary object.

Yet for all his cleverness, he had miscalculated; young wives, like voters, needed some seducing. When it dawned on Mary Hewitt that she was to be mewed up alone in the showy terrace she had done nothing to create, while her lawyer husband went off on circuit, she revolted: 'I must live 8 months in a year without you or any father in a place where I have not one single friend of my own to speak to.' She could not and would not bear it – 'you will say I promest to go there & tis true [enough] I did so but not to live without you all ye year except 4 months'. This was not the bargain she had signed: 'I declear it I [married] you for yr company & conversation', while Hewitt, she suspected, would 'sooner have my fortune alone'. Passionate and aghast, she implied that death or divorce would be preferable to Coventry: 'I had much rather make room for your second wife who may make you happyer than I ever did'.[21] With a paradoxical combination of fragility and unbending will, Mary frustrated the lawyer's schemes. Isaac learned to his cost that there was more to setting up home than picking a house and telling a woman to live in it. At length, the Hewitts set up housekeeping under Mary's father's roof at Stapleford Abbots in Essex. It would be years before she would acclimatise to the alien soil of Coventry.

Competence in the management of household refurbishment, housekeeping, servants and even unruly family members hums through the seventy-three letters in the strong, legible hand Mary Martin of Alresford Hall, Essex, sent to her cousin and fiancé Isaac Martin Rebow in the 1760s and '70s. The Rebows were a

1 *The Comforts of Matrimony – A Smoky House and Scolding Wife*, 1790. British Museum, London, 1985,0119.115. The hearth, usually the source of life-giving heat and light, is here as unpleasant as the nagging wife.

2 Paul Sandby, *At Sandpit Gate: Washing Clothes*, n.d. [early 1750s], watercolour. Royal Collection RL 14330. Sandby portrays a woman hard at work over the wash tub in a genteel house near Windsor, Berkshire. A yoke for carrying heavy buckets of water leans against the wall.

3   John Wilks, 'detector' lock, made in Birmingham, *circa* 1680, brass and engraved steel, h. 11.3 cm.,
w. 15.5 cm. Victoria and Albert Museum, London, M.109–1926. This rim lock, which was attached to the
surface of a door, was designed to show how many times the door had been unlocked. The figure of a man
holds a pointer against the dial. Each time the key is turned in the lock, the engraved dial rotates and the
pointer indicates a number. The keyhole is concealed by the man's front leg, which operates on a pivot.
When a button is pressed, the leg swings forward to reveal the keyhole. The door-bolt is released by tilting
the man's hat. The verse indicates the lock's purpose: 'If I had ye gift of tongue, I would declare and do no
wrong, Who ye are ye come by stealth, To impare my Master's wealth'. It is the guardian of the threshold.

4 A padlock and a key left by mothers who had entrusted their babies to the care of the London Foundling Hospital, 1741–60. Foundling Museum, London. Left as tokens to identify the babies in case the mothers wished to retrieve them, they also symbolised the bond between mother and child. They suggest the kinds of padlocks and keys available to poor women.

5   *The Dinner-Locust; or, Advantages of a Keen Scent* (detail), 1826, printed etching and aquatint. Lewis Walpole Library, Farmington, CT, 826.0.35. The associated text emphasises the attractions of the domestic dinner table to the single man: '[Visitor] Egad, my Worthy Friend, it seems I have just hit your hour. [Host] Yes, you generally do.'

6 *A Common Council Man of Candlestick Ward and his Wife on a Visit to Mr Deputy at his Modern Built Villa near Clapham*, 1771, coloured engraving. Lewis Walpole Library, Farmington, CT, 771.11.1.2. Like the absurd suburban villa in Robert Lloyd's poem *The Cit's Country Box* (1756), Mr Deputy's villa is a ludicrous combination of classical, Chinese and Gothic architectural elements.

The GOOD HOUSE-WIFE.

Woman, when virtuous free from Sloth & Vice,   Heaven crowns her Labour with a plenteous Stores
Greater by far than Rubies is her price.   To feed her Household, and relieve the Poor.

Printed for Carington Bowles, Map & Printseller at N.º 69 in St Pauls Church Yard, London

7 *The Good House-wife*, n.d., mezzotint. Colonial Williamsburg Foundation, 1958–357. A well-off woman dressed for work in a plain bed gown sits at a table with pen and inkwell. She is doing household accounts, checking a sheet of paper against the book she holds on her lap. Around her on the floor lie bundles and a basket of bottles. The verse reads: 'Woman, when virtuous, free from Sloth & Vice, Greater by far, than Rubies is her price: Heaven crowns her Labour with a plenteous Store, To feed her Household, and relieve the Poor.'

8 (left) Figure of a shepherd, *circa* 1754, Bow porcelain factory, London, soft-paste porcelain, painted in enamels and gilt. Victoria and Albert Museum, London, C.144–1931. An English copy of a porcelain figure made at the Meissen porcelain factory in Germany.

9 (below) teapot, *circa* 1750, Staffordshire, black earthenware with white decoration. Victoria and Albert Museum, London, C.95&A–1938. Small, cheap earthenware teapots of this kind were made by many Staffordshire potteries in the mid-eighteenth century.

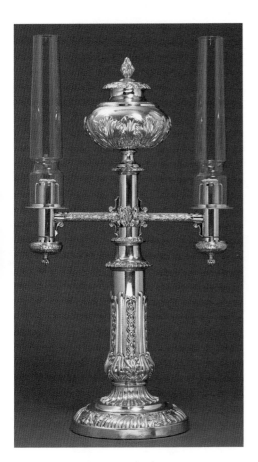

10 Argand Lamp, by Matthew Boulton Company, Birmingham, 1814–23, Sheffield plate with glass funnels. Victoria and Albert Museum, London, M.14–1987.

11 Tea urn, *circa* 1780, Sheffield plate. Victoria and Albert Museum, London, M.237–1920.

12 Joshua Reynolds, *Anne, Duchess of Grafton*, 1761, oil on canvas. Private collection. The proud duchess is robed for the coronation of George III.

13   Pompeo Batoni, *Augustus Henry Fitzroy, 3rd Duke of Grafton*, 1762, oil on canvas. National Portrait Gallery, London, NPG 4899.

14 Katherine Read, *Lady Shelburne and her Son Viscount Fitzmaurice*, 1766, pastel. The Trustees of the Bowood Collection. She is depicted in garter blue, reputedly her favourite colour.

15   Joshua Reynolds, *William Petty, 1st Marquess of Lansdowne (Lord Shelburne)*, 1765, oil on canvas. National Portrait Gallery, London, NPG 43.

16   (above) Robert Adam's Etruscan Dressing Room at Osterley Park, Middlesex, *circa* 1775–6. National Trust 132456. This is the kind of exquisitely decorated dressing room for which Adam became famous and which encouraged his characterisation as a ladies' architect.

17   (facing page top) Geranium-leaf wallpaper and chain border from the ground-floor front room of 48 Manchester Street, Marylebone, London, *circa* 1790, block printed. English Heritage, EH ASC 88082030.

18   (facing page bottom) Oak-leaf wallpaper and Neoclassical border from the ground-floor front room of 50 Manchester Street, Marylebone, London, *circa* 1795, block printed. English Heritage, EH ASC 88082031/2.

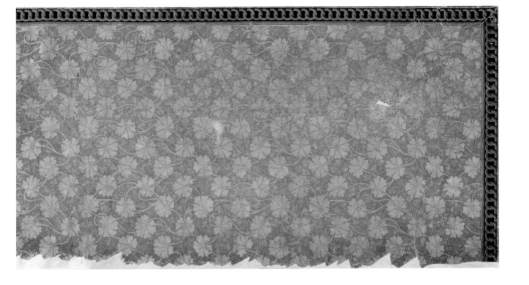

19   Trellis wallpaper and foliage border from the ground-floor front room of 50 Manchester Street, Marylebone, London, *circa* 1800, block printed. English Heritage, EH ASC 88082031/1.

military family of French Huguenot descent, who had settled in Colchester and made their fortune in the wool trade. When the letters open, Isaac Martin Rebow was installed with his aged mother in Wivenhoe Park, the house built for him to designs by Thomas Reynolds in 1758. The Rebow–Martin engagement lasted at least seven years, lengthened by the obstructive inertia of Isaac's mother. Mrs Rebow had been sole mistress of the house for an extraordinary forty-six years. Her husband, Isaac Lemyng, had died when young Isaac was only 4 years old, and her son was full 50 when he came to wed. While the letters report no outward opposition to the match, Mrs Rebow's actions display no enthusiasm for an early wedding. She may have disapproved of the marriage of cousins, for she was also Mary's aunt, but doubtless also did not welcome the passing of her authority. Mary always wryly referred to her aunt as 'Madam', and Mrs Rebow was mindful of her dignity. The widow proved difficult to dislodge from her son's house, despite, or perhaps because of, the fact that the marriage was not to go ahead until she was established elsewhere. Where Madam was to remove was a theme of several letters, with many prevarications and problems attending her transfer to the house in Wivenhoe, which she was offered by her brother Mr Martin, Mary's father. There were legal problems about the lease; the chintz bed must be re-hung, because the current drapes were a danger; Madam needed to break a new door out of the chintz bedchamber into the blue; her chamber needed repapering, but that could be done only in the summer time or it would not dry; her servant was threatening to leave because she refused to be confined all year round in the country, and 'because she will not live in a house that has bugs in any part of it'.

Mary Martin was a woman of self-possession and presence of mind. Her demeanour was ever that of a person of natural importance, who could do easily anything to which she put her hand. Ostensibly, her position was precarious, in '*anxious expectation*',[22] in limbo between her family home and her marital future, having refused to join in housekeeping with her father and new stepmother, but with the prospect of her wedding ever receding. Yet she remained composed in the face of her aunt's fussing delays and coolly critical of her father's clandestine second marriage. Martin may have been secure in the knowledge that she was indispensable to her future husband, or she may have been in the business of proving that she was more than a match for his mother. But whichever, acting as her fiancé's executive arm seemed to come altogether naturally to her, and in flexing it some of her managerial energy found an outlet. Superintending Rebow's renovations, keeping an eye on his workmen, chivvying his tradesmen, monitoring the fulfilment of his commissions as well as overseeing his provisioning, were all woven together in that 'multiplicity of business' she had ever on her hands. Isaac Rebow's letters have not survived, but Mary's letters take for granted his gratified acceptance of her energetic scrutiny of his undertakings.

Preoccupied with 'Military Business', as Colonel of the East Essex Militia, Isaac Rebow delegated business to his fiancée. Mary Martin functioned as project manager to the refurbishments going on in Rebow's London house on Duke Street, a role she had been asked to undertake: 'be pleas'd to know that according to my promise I have this Morning been to Superintend ye workmen at Duke Street'. Giving orders, finding fault and contradicting tradesmen raised no blushes, though Martin was emphatic that she was acting as Rebow's right arm, fulfilling his instructions to the letter.

> I sent for Mr Pickering who promis'd to send his Men in very early o' Monday morning but we have again differ'd in opinion a little; He says, you told him you would have nothing Painted, but ye Hall, & Front Stair Case, & I think you said, you wou'd likewise have ye Back Stair Case Painted as far as it was whitewashed, however Wednesday will be time enough for him to know for certain, so you will be so kind to send me word (which is right) by that time.

Martin bubbled with opinions. 'The painting goes on extremely well . . . it is *Amazing* smart but I wish you wou'd have had that little bit of ye back Stair Case Painted for it really looks very bad, now ye other is so nice.' She wrote like an oracle of common sense: 'The Smell of ye Paint is hardly any thing to signify but I think you had better not have ye Bed put up, till ye last Minute for ye Dust will be apt to Damage that & ye more air there is admitted into ye Room ye better.' In June 1772 she swooped on the workmen and frightened the decorator:

> Your Room was in a fair way of being finish'd to Night, but fortunately I went up this Morning to see how it look'd & behold they have Painted it Stone Color instead of Dead White, which I think was by no means your Intention as it looks so totally different from ye Dining Room & ye Cornish so I posted away to Mr Snow & have frighten'd him out of his Wits for he thinks he has certainly misunderstood . . . it shall be done White tomorrow & shall be finish'd quite tomorrow Night without fail.[23]

Martin represented herself as a diviner of Rebow's underlying intentions. 'I likewise have been with Mr Smith who has at last got ye Cloth quite ready, but it is so heavy that we all think you will *not* like it by any means, so he is to try another scheme.' There is no evidence that Rebow ever quarrelled with her interpretation of his will, so perhaps he took the happy view that she understood his true intentions better than he did himself, congratulating himself on the possession of such a formidable lieutenant in the battles of life.

Martin was the scourge of dilatory traders. Shopkeepers sprang to attention at her bustling approach. In the summer of 1770 she swept five times into Mr Neale's shop in St Paul's Churchyard in pursuit of Rebow's china: 'I cannot give you ye least account of your plates yet, though I have been after them both last week & this now', wringing explanations, apologies and assurances from the cringing retailer. Three weeks later, she was back on the prowl: 'I enquir'd again yesterday after ye plates & scholded Mr Neale well who assures me with a very melancholy face that if his life depended upon it he cannot help it, for he constantly writes about them every week.'[24] Martin ran errands for her aunt in London, paid off Isaac Rebow's maid, enquired into the references of prospective servants, hired them on Rebow's behalf, stored his new wig, took his socks to be dyed, checked his locks, planted his hyacinths, badgered the awning maker, paid his brewer and even sailed into the fishmonger's to complain about his turbot. Few particulars escaped her inspection. 'Betty has left ye House perfectly Clean & every thing *Exactly* right except two or three Glass & Knife cloth', she reported in June 1772. A week later she double checked: 'There is several little Trifles wanting such as a Brush, or two & two or three saucepans tin'd which if you will give me leave I will see about directly.' When she concluded 'I have dispatch'd all ye necessary business at Duke Street (without ye least assistance of Mr Fairborne)', the finality of her tone brooked no argument.[25]

Isaac and Mary finally married around 1775, and the remaining twenty-seven letters convey their intimacy and partnership, both practical and sexual. In the hot nights of one separation in July 1778, Mary did not sleep a wink until 3 or 4 a.m., but 'it is intirely owing to ye want of *my usual Method of going to Sleep*'. 'What do you think?' she added saucily. The new Mrs Rebow entered fully into the concerns of her 'dearest life', interested herself in the minutiae of his health and comforts, enquired into all his official proceedings, and insisted 'I have not a single secret from you.' In her husband's obligatory absences on militia manoeuvres, the young matron oversaw Wivenhoe Park with the watchfulness of a born administrator: 'Lupton has not done a stroke of work these two Saturdays I sent Beven yesterday to know ye reason & ye excuse is that he is gone to Colch[cheste]r for Change & is writing out his accounts. Shoud it be so, or wou'd you has me speak to him about it?' The birth of two little misses and a series of miscarriages had not weakened her surveillance: 'Pray shou'd ye Cart Horses & Mare & Filly be in ye Park? I saw them all there last night so I sent to ye Farmer to know if it ought to be so, as understood you wou'd not let ye coach horses be turn'd out till you had got some other Pasture for them.' Her gimlet eye for minutia was a point of pride: 'I am not surprised at your not finding ye cruet top, for I thought it was not possible many particulars cou'd pass & I not remember one; I dare say I am right in my first conjecture.' Colonel Rebow displayed no resentment of her bossiness, but then she was a superb deputy for a busy officer, and, better yet, she was as frisky in the bedroom as she was officious in the household. Charged with power, but earthed with loyalty, 'yours and only yours', Mary Rebow made a model partner, as her husband acknowledged. 'You really make me quite vain with your Praises on ye subject of farming; I am very glad you are pleased with ye Method of proceeding.'[26] Gentlemen needed wives who combined the virtues of Venus *and* Minerva, as the gentleman Matthew Robinson reflected in 1740: 'Happy the man, who in the widowhood & retirement of his life, meets united in one Companion those two amiable but almost incompatible characters, of Soft & complying mistress, but watchful & sollicitous Housekeeper.'[27] For Mary Rebow, the decoration of a house was simply one more terrain to monitor, just another aspect of the everyday business that engaged her time, and like worn saucepans, rotting fish and delayed plates called forth her genius for sorting things out.

As young middling men went, 23-year-old Josiah Wedgwood junior (Joss) was uncommonly expert in taste. Heir to the great pottery business at Etruria, fashionable objects were his stock in trade, and assessing colour, material and finish his very bread and butter. The continuing success of Wedgwood and Co. demanded that Wedgwood junior take a decisive view on new products, processes and decorative treatments. In a single letter to his brother Tom in 1790, Joss approved a set of vases depicting the *Life of Achilles*, delayed judgement on a 'red & black jasper vase' till he had examined it, and rejected 'black tea ware with lively colours' as too avant-garde for British taste, since 'we are not bold enough to adopt at once anything that is new and beautiful but require the sanction of fashion to give it value'. He had a canny appreciation of the distinction between intrinsic beauty and consumer appeal, but then Wedgwood & Sons was 'a business that depends almost entirely upon fashion'. Joss was as irritated as his brother with the whims of ill-informed customers. His realism, however, acknowledged that consumers needed humouring, for 'it has been in a great measure owing to the taking up hints given by customers and bringing them to perfection that this manufactory has established its character for Universality'.[28] His father, the celebrated potter Josiah Wedgwood, was assiduous in cultivating the patronage of those who led taste – the royal court and the nobility, architects and connoisseurs.[29] But they were not the only people to whose preferences Wedgwood senior deferred. He was convinced that the fortunes of his pottery also turned on women's preferences. 'I speak from experience in Female taste,' he wrote to his partner Thomas Bentley, 'without which I should have made but a poor figure amongst my Potts; not one of which of any consequence is finished without the Approbation of my Sally.' The Wedgwoods were famously devoted 'married lovers' and confidantes. Sarah Wedgwood was her husband's 'chief help-mate' who transcribed his experiments and helped with the business accounts and correspondence, as well as giving a trusted second opinion on his vases and teapots. It was Mrs Wedgwood who furnished Etruria Hall. A female visitor was struck in 1791 by her 'very elegant' drawing room, which featured a 'beautiful chimney piece of Mr Wedgwood's own composition the ornaments very chaste white on a blue or rather French grey ground'.[30] Female taste in domestic furnishing was as familiar as mother's milk to the Wedgwood boys.

Josiah Wedgwood had reared his sons in his own image. He had always intended them for 'genteel business, or manufacturers, but not for what are called the liberal professions of Law, Physic, Divinity or the army'. He soon settled that 'Joss and Tom to be potters, & partners in Trade. Tom to be the traveller, & negotiator, & Joss the manufacturer'. Nevertheless, business was not congenial to young Joss – especially serving in the Greek Street showrooms in London: 'I have been too long in the habit of looking upon myself as the equal of everybody to bear the haughty manners of those who come into the shop.'[31] In courtship, however, Joss Wedgwood was poised to bend the knee. Though his Pembrokeshire sweetheart the lovely Elizabeth Allen was 28 to his 23, the age gap did nothing to quell his protective ardour. Cuddling seems to have played a larger role than one might expect for the decorous couple of the 1790s. 'I hope to persuade you to put on my old friend your habit which I think I can contrive to spoil between Cresselly and London' wrote Joss in delicious anticipation of their first coach journey as a man and wife. 'If you wear a thin callico only I am afraid it will oblige me to take more than usual pains to keep you warm.' When apart, Joss wrote gratifying letters: 'I am sitting by the fireside, tired and sad, and if I had not this resource [corresponding] I should be very melancholy.' Every sign promised he would make a considerate spouse. Believing himself already 'your husband in heaven', he usurped 'part of the prerogatives of that character', sending a bank note to enable Miss Allen to 'make some little presents and gifts of charity' prior to her departure. This gesture was most carefully couched, auguring well for his thoughtfulness, his courteous appreciation of female dignity and his willingness to cede financial independence in small matters. 'Above all I beg you to take this offer in good part and to be assured that it is made as respectfully as it is affectionately.' Wedgwood was at pains to show his good nature and only on the request to delay the wedding was he inflexible, as behoved any red-blooded lover worth his salt: 'I trust you will in future find me accommodating and complying, but you must pardon me if I don't give way in the present instance.' Nonetheless, he did not want to play the tyrant, writing again: 'All the atonement I can offer for the impatience I expressed is to retract my views of heroic obstinacy and to say that I will do exactly what you please.'

The demonstration of Wedgwood's masculine complaisance was to the fore in the discussion of their future home in letters. It was for Wedgwood to find a fitting house, and though Allen made suggestions, he took the lead in decision-making: 'I have been revolving various plans of building in my mind . . . though I have not absolutely determined what to do.' Nevertheless, he expected to confer with his bride to be – 'we have time enough to consult upon the plan when we meet'. Keen to 'begin our housekeeping very soon', he toured the locality with his father, reporting back on the pros and cons of possible candidates: 'As I believe that an unreserved confidence is the basis of matrimonial happiness I am resolved to communicate both good and evil to you.' Wedgwood launched the proper improvements: 'I have been busy about our house and at length have fixed upon the alterations and repairs which are necessary. We shall be quite in the cottage style. Five small rooms on the ground floor and two spare bed rooms. We shall begin in a few days and I should expect the house to be ready for us in about three months.' Wedgwood, however, courted Allen's opinion over areas of traditional female expertise: 'my friends tell me that the kitchen I have . . . is too small. It is 18 feet square. As this [is] within your department I must beg your opinion upon it.' And while Wedgwood hired the male servants, his fiancée and mother found three females: all ugly. Wedgwood made a show of consulting Allen's preferences over details, writing to know whether she fancied yellow or light blue for their chaise: 'If you have any favourite colour for lining pray mention it and write immediately.' Allen's replies have not survived, but she must have waived the decision to her better-informed husband, for ten days later Wedgwood reported: 'I have desired John to order the carriage yellow which is the most fashionable and the most durable colour and I have left the lining all for his taste to decide upon.'[32] Allen prided herself on her frugality, and joked that Wedgwood knew nothing of the virtue. Perhaps fashion was a terrain she ceded to the Wedgwoods, and as a mature Pembrokeshire countrywoman took domestic economy and sensible housewifery to herself.

In four out of the five genteel and middling couples studied here the future husband anticipated strong female preferences about the look and layout of the marital home, to which he was prepared, within reason, to defer. Deep-seated tradition, at least medieval in origin, read men's intentions in the goods they offered and the material preparations they made. The church courts viewed men's gifts to maidens as tokens that they were in good earnest, the donation of a series of gifts being universal staging posts on the road to wedlock: indeed, if enough jewellery and pots had been handed over, a suitor could find that in the eyes of the church there was no turning back. Outside the courts, the material preparations men were prepared to make were also widely seen as an augury of future happiness for their wives. In 1708 Lady Barbara Arundell argued the wisdom of her choice in a new husband by explaining that 'he has furnished his House quite new he tells me, & by description it is very fine, & tho he made a new Coach this Spring yet would have had me bespoke another'. As early as 1724 Mrs Delany, then Mary Pendarves, noted that the new house of the young Lady Sutherland in Hanover Square was 'a very good one, and furnished with mighty good taste', a propitious omen for her marriage to the diplomat Sir Robert Sutton. The pink diamond wedding gifts and the sumptuous fittings bespoke the groom's goodwill, and promised well for Lady Sutton's future contentment: 'I hope she will be very happy; I think there is a great appearance of her being so: her house is charmingly furnished with pictures, glasses, tapestry, and damask all superfine of their kind.' The proposal she herself accepted in 1743 was less splendid but frank and practical, proffering a character 'fitted for all that is solid happiness in the wedded state', a clear income and 'a good house (as houses go in our part of the world), moderately furnished, a good many books, a pleasant garden'. The explicit discussion of housing is a striking feature of men's written proposals.[33] Georgian men and women looked square on at that which modern love glosses over, the determining role of financial competence and the nitty-gritty of housing in the making of marriage.

Failure to make special purchases could itself be read as a sign of bad faith. The Norfolk dowager Katherine Windham was determined in 1708 that her son make some decorative improvements in honour of his bride: 'if you design being here after marriage it is fit ye hangings should be put up & ye house in order'. Redecorating in and of itself could signal a willingness to marry. In 1764 the Yorkshire gentleman Thomas Wentworth was in the thick of refurbishment, supported by female advice in the matter of textiles for his bed. But the ladies could not resist teasing the bachelor about the implications of chintz and taffeta: 'Mrs Hustler & Miss Hodson tell me that I may soon get a Bedfellow for any Miss would be glad to partake of such a Fine Bed, so when it is finish'd I'll advertise.' Similarly, the sister of a Gloucestershire baronet, Sophia Blathwayte, gossiped in 1749 about bachelor schemes: 'We hear that Cupidon is likewise at Bath . . . & is about buying as he says one of the prettiest Houses in England & we presume will furnish it with a wife.'[34] Refurbishment was seen as a key to a woman's heart. It was a commonplace that women of the quality, the gentry and the middling sort put a high social and emotional value on interior furnishings.

Commentators both reactionary and progressive were apt to read modes of decoration as evidence of male or female agency, so varieties of furniture and fittings could stand proxy for power. A standing theme of misogynist humour was the spendthrift wife, who had her husband by the nose and in her excesses made a complete fool of him. One of the hoary jokes of the eighteenth-century luxury debate was the behaviour of those with more money than taste – Squire Mushroom, Citizen Sterling, Mrs Squander – upstart shopkeepers, farmers, merchants, servants, women. A classic of the genre is Robert Lloyd's poem *Cit's Country Box* of 1756, which sneered at Sir Thrifty and the pretensions of his wife. Their suburban villa is fitted out in glorious vulgarity, flaunting a muddle of architectural features and decorations that they lacked the education to understand and the discernment to harmonise. 'The traveller with amazement sees, A temple – Gothic or Chinese, With many a bell and a tawdry rag on. And crested with a sprawling dragon [pl. 6].' And predictably the author of all is Lady Thrifty: 'no doubt her arguments prevail. For Madam's taste can never fail.'[35]

Mining the same vein, Tobias Smollett's fictional ladies were often predatory consumers, 'vying in grandeur', driving their husbands 'at full speed, in the high road to bankruptcy and ruin'. In the *Expedition of Humphry Clinker* of 1771, Smollett's curmudgeon Matthew Bramble is appalled by the unbridled career of Mrs Baynard. Governed by 'vanity of a bastard and idiot nature, excited by shew and ostentation', she sold the family plate, spent money like water on tour in Europe and back in England felled the oak trees, laid waste the orchard and destroyed the façade of the house for the sake of fashion, which she affected to lead 'in every article of taste and connoisseurship'. Inevitably, when Mr Baynard finally shuffles on he is a cypher, 'so meagre, yellow and dejected', that Bramble first pities, then despises him for his feeble infatuation and unmanly submission to the tyranny of female taste. Where female connoisseurship is strong, masculine honour is weak, promising only 'misery, disgrace and despair'.[36]

The appeal of this sort of commentary lay in the fertile outrageousness of the extended joke; nevertheless, sometimes the vision of femininity run amok escaped the bounds of comedy to appear in jaundiced reportage. For John Byng (1742–1813), an embittered younger son and bureaucrat, frenchified or exotic interior decorating was disturbing proof of feminine mastery and male effeminacy. Wherever he went on his annual vacations from the Inland Revenue, Byng was on the look-out for signs and symptoms of the haemorrhage of traditional virtue in national life – forests in decline, the spread of London manners, 'milkmaids on the road, with the dress and looks of strand misses', housewifery and hospitality in decay. Calling on an old military comrade at his 'small white house' in the Forest of Dean in 1781, the upholstery warned him that any martial vigour was sadly fallen off. 'The parlour was (ill) furnish'd in the modern taste, with French chairs, festoon'd curtains, and puffed bell ropes; this and his keeping in bed informed me that the gentleman was not master of his own house.' The householder's eventual appearance 'in a loose bed gown' did nothing to lessen Byng's disquiet. Touring the Bishop's Palace at Farnham in Surrey the next year, the 'modern frippery' and tambour frames discovered in the long gallery confirmed 'that the petticoat rules the cassock'. Of course, Byng was not an impartial journalist, but a confirmed grumbletonian. He quoted approvingly from *Peregrine Pickle*, so in his 'description passion' fancied himself perhaps another Smollett, fighting a hopeless rear-guard action against modern life, 'wishing my descriptions to be, what most of my countrywomen are, elegant, neat and engaging; full of decency, simplicity and fancy; not tricked out with false taste, and French trimmings'. Byng had quite an axe to grind, and his Tory fulminations may have been an eccentric pose, but in linking the look of interiors to the dynamics of marriage Byng had hit upon a customary truth, recognised by men and women alike.[37]

Female commentators were awake to the implications of decorative choices. The denial of a woman's taste boded ill for her happiness and autonomy in marriage. One of the many insults delivered by the Hertfordshire baronet Sir William Cowper, as catalogued in his wife's indignant diary, was his impatient dismissal of her stylistic education and denial thereafter of any claim to arrange her interior. In 1706 'Sr W; intending to hang a Drawing Room with Damask Condescended to ask me Whither One or Two Coulers would Do best. But he hath Bred me so Ignorant in Such Matters that I cou'd not Resolve him till I have Enquir'd of the Skill full, yet after this he allows me not the prviliedg to place a Table or Stool but where he Fancies.' He even contested her right to remove 'a Table that Cumber'd up a Room', claiming 'I have spoil'd the Uniformity of it'. That Sarah, Lady Cowper, cited these episodes as yet more proof of William's perverse tyranny attests to the prevalence of the norms he outraged.

> Tis mervellous to hear him talk how much he is for Liberty . . . when at the same time there is not a more absolute Tyrant . . . He restrains me in all my due privileges . . . I just now mett with a Note that tells the difference between a wife and a Concubine. The wives administer'd the affairs of the Family, but the Concubines were not to meddle with them. Sure I have been kept as a Concubine not as a Wife.[38]

Material evidence of femininity in retreat could be distressing to observers. In Lady Portarlington's description of the Ardfert house in County Kerry in 1785, the wallpaper was one the few redeeming features, and its limited use a sign that

the wife, Lady Glandore, was at bay. Since Lord Glandore was 'so partial to everything that is old that he is determined not to alter it', the gloom was thick and the
scene almost unremittingly bleak:

> The house is also in the same style, small low rooms, wainscoted, and the
> drawing-room perfectly antique, which he won't let her alter. It is with diffi-
> culty he has let her fit up a little dressing room belonging to the apartment I
> am in, which indeed she has made a sweet little place. It is hung with white
> paper, to which she has made a border of pink silk, with white and gold flow-
> ers stuck upon it, and hung the room with all Mr. Bunbury's beautiful prints;
> the window curtains are pale pink linen with white silk fringe, the chairs pink
> linen with a border painted on paper, cut out and stuck on gauze, and then
> tacked on the linen. It does not sound well, but it has a very pretty effect, es-
> pecially for a little room.[39]

Hemmed in by wainscot, femininity is left to bloom in that archetypally female
space the dressing room. The brave prettiness of the little room is touching but
pitiful, pathetic in itself, but also dismal in what it represented for domestic life.
To Lady Portarlington the oppression of the wainscot implied the oppression of
the wife, suggesting the marriage was as gothic as the fittings were antique. Taken
as a whole, the marriage like the house looked soul-destroying.

The leading, perhaps even decisive, say in the look, arrangement and management of domestic life was something that honourable and happily married men
were prepared to cede to their wives. These were due female privileges authorised
by custom. That men acknowledged this authority despite the lamentable legal
status of women in marriage, an authority so precious that mothers-in-law were
highly reluctant to give it up, must speak of the importance to men of the benefits of successful domesticity. Marriage announced and confirmed men's adulthood (in ways that it is hard for us to credit, such is the gloom around
'commitment' today and the testosterone which infuses bachelor freedom in ad-
vertizing), admitting them to a confraternity of trustworthy husbands. A flourishing domestic life was both backdrop and platform for professional society and
business. But more than this, the consistency of men's efforts to please their
women and implicate them in a shared future bespeaks the depth and urgency of
men's need for the comforts of matrimony and delights of 'home', a masculine investment that has been thoroughly effaced in literary debate about the rise of the
eighteenth-century domestic woman. Once the happy home was made, most genteel and middling men needed to park a woman in it as domestic manager, the
better to prosecute their business affairs elsewhere. Common sense expected men
to resign the field to their women with relief; indeed, ordinary masculine con-

cerns prevented close attention to domestic arrangements. In fact, to a husband 'the Oeconomy of the House would be in some degree Indecent'.[40] Only little despots then would trespass so far on female prerogatives as to overrule on chintz, china, paper and prints, asserting their authority in every particular. Such petty tyranny was dishonourable and perverse, unbecoming in a husband and degrading to the dignity of his wife. Nine times out of ten, a man who failed to defer to a woman's tastes in material, colour, texture and finish was a scoundrel.

A personal relationship and a public institution, marriage was open to competing interpretations. In case law, older sermons and satires, marriage was an ugly institution built on female subjection, tempered somewhat by ecclesiastic teaching about equal souls and mutual comfort, romantic idealism and the immediate demands of living. Weddings were the gateway to both tyranny and domestic autonomy of women, and an array of circumstances in between. Neutral observation revealed that the spectrum of marital bargains was wide. The constraints of custom and religion, the viciousness of the common law and the mercies of equity, as well as the sugar of romance, created only the outer boundaries of a vast territory wherein couples imagined, negotiated and created their own practical contract. As Austen's Mary Crawford so rightly concluded on the basis of extensive observation in the best circles in Regency London, marriage was 'a manoeuvring business'.[41] How was a woman to predict the outcome for herself? She must try the metal and see if it rang true. Late courtship and very early marriage were formative periods for the marital dynamic, the era when the constitution of household authority and the division of powers was forged. A sensible maid had her eyes open when the furnishing of the interior was canvassed, since far more was at stake than the make of her breakfast set or the hang of the drapes.

4

HIS AND HERS: ACCOUNTING FOR THE HOUSEHOLD

Since Eve yearned for the apple, and so led Adam astray, Western women have been seen as more covetous than men. Classical philosophers and Christian moralists have long associated men with the rational world and women with the material. Western writers inherited Aristotle's contempt for feminine reasoning, and many saw fit to deride women for their mindless materialism and love of ostentation. Cleopatra, the Queen of Sheba, Pope's Belinda, Flaubert's Emma Bovary and George Eliot's Rosamond Vincy are all vain anti-heroines obsessed with self-adornment and competitive show. The woman who was blinded by the tinsel of the times, hypnotised by shop goods and thereby lost to sober housewifery and home production had already frozen into cliché in eighteenth-century print.

> Time was, when tradesmen laid up what they gain'd
> And frugally a family maintained.
> When they took stirring housewives for their spouses,
> To keep up prudent order in their house;
> Who thought no scorn, at night to sit them down
> And make their children's clothes and mend their own

Would Polly's coat to younger Bess transfer,
And make their caps without a milliner.
But now a shopping half the day they're gone,
To buy 500 things and pay for none.[1]

Flashy, extravagant, meretricious and avaricious, the female consumer is an archetypal villainess, while the male consumer is oddly invisible, somehow uncontaminated by the dirty business, his mind presumably on higher things.

History has done much to reinstate the skills, knowledge and practical power that women accrued as consumers. The efforts that campaigners made to engage women in consumer boycotts, the hysterical warnings to men about avoiding marriage to a spendthrift wife, the relentless advice to women on household economy and how to spot a rotten chicken, all attest to the control of the purse strings that custom and convenience ceded to women. 'It is the husband's duty to provide Money, and the Wives to lay it out providentially' was a keystone of ordinary conservative wisdom. Anti-slavery activists expressly targeted women because 'in the domestic department they are the chief controllers; they for the most part, provide the articles of family consumption'. Even within common law, the law of necessaries gave women control over the means of family consumption.[2] An emerging consensus agrees that women enjoyed some recognised independence as routine consumers. Female mastery of the language of goods has also been emphasised. Experts staged objects to convey a multitude of meanings, from fashion, taste and style, to wealth and status, history and lineage, from political and religious allegiance, to personality, relationships, mortality and memory. Possessions were crucial props in self-fashioning, the skilful creating an assemblage that came close to a self-portrait – a picture that could be shown off, rearranged or hidden as circumstances demanded. Material culture has thus emerged as an arena for the expression of considerable female eloquence.

It could be fairly argued, however, that fascination with women and the world of goods has overshadowed the role of men. Looking at the diaries of a shopkeeper, two clergyman and a schoolmaster, Margot Finn documents male consumption of a broad range of goods, both basic and luxurious. She reminds us that men were as highly acquisitive as women and rejects the assumption that women were the primary consumers for the family.[3] While Finn is surely right to lament historians' neglect of the male consumer (there is some important work on men's clothing but little else),[4] her sources and the situation of her subjects leave questions unanswered: it remains to be seen, for instance, whether Parson James Woodforde would have run the grocery accounts had he been in possession of a wife. To move forward in our understanding of gender and consumer practices, propensities and preferences, we need to study men and women in tandem, though in truth sources that simultaneously open out the customs of both are hard to find.

Looking at the consumption of men and women in relationship offsets a tendency in the more celebratory accounts of consumer behaviour to glorify the individual economic actor, wrenching him or her from their household and familial contexts. We should not forget the lessons of the history of poverty – that the consumption of one almost always affects or responds to the consumption of the others closest to her. No man or woman is an economic island. The individual consumer of economic rhetoric is often a beneficiary of a consumer collective, or even the material victim of other consumers in their household. The neglect of the household as a unit of consumption is especially odd for the Georgians when family and household loomed so large as living experience, organisational category and ideological trope. Jan de Vries has urged researchers to look behind the myth of patriarchy, whereby the household speaks with one voice (and that voice the master's), to get a sense of the choices made *within* households about market participation.[5] My discovery of three rare sets of accounts for both husband and wife permits the black box of the household to be prized open to let in a chink of light. The interweaving of men's and women's consumer responsibilities is hereby revealed.

The account-book is by no means a simple source, but is a special genre whose peculiarities warrant some elaboration before we proceed to haberdashery and horse furniture. Account-books assume literacy and numeracy, creditworthiness, a regular income stream and what we might term an accounting frame of mind. Double-entry bookkeeping famously arose in the counting houses of the city states of Renaissance Italy, and was quickly taken up by merchants and bankers in commercial centres across Europe. Household accounting seems to have been devised on the model of the stewardship of the large landed estate.[6] By the 1700s there were several published guides to household accounting that offered standardised models for the aspiring administrator to follow, such as those in Roger North's *Gentleman Accomptant* (1715), but most of these authors were prophets of double-entry bookkeeping, and simply laid out debt and credit on a month by month basis, offering advice to the novice on putting transactions in the right column. Few broke down the incomings and outgoings in any other way. Once the mysteries of double entry were grasped, the accounting system on offer looked deceptively simple, and easy to adapt. It could be borrowed, bowdlerised and elaborated. Domestic accountants often made do with single entry. By the late eighteenth century, printed account books could be purchased, providing a template for doing household accounting (figs 23 and 24).

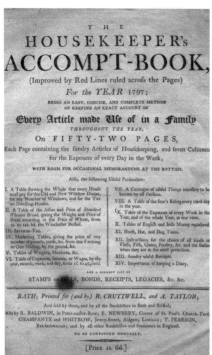

JANUARY, xxxi Days, 1797.																				
	Monday 9			Tuesday 10			Wednes. 11			Thursday 12			Friday 13			Saturday 14			Sunday 15		
	£.	s.	d.	£.	s.	d.	£.	s.	d.	£.	s.	d.	£.	s.	d.	£.	s.	d.	£.	s.	d.
Beer and Cyder																					
Bread and Flour																					
Candles · · · · ·																					
Cheese and Butter																					
Clothes · · · · · ·																					
Coals and Wood																					
Eggs and Milk ·																					
Fish · · · · · · · ·																					
Fruit · · · · · · ·																					
Garden-Stuff · ·																					
Malt and Hops ·																					
Meat · · · · · · ·																					
Oil, Vinegar, &c.																					
Pepper, Salt, &c.																					
Poultry · · · · ·																					
Rates and Taxes																					
Rum and Brandy																					
Servants Wages																					
Soap, Starch, &c.																					
Sugar · · · · · · ·																					
Tea, Coffee, &c.																					
Washing · · · ·																					
Wine · · · · · · ·																					
Sundries · · · ·																					
Each Day's Expence																					

Memorandums.

Monday · · · · · · · ·
Tuesday · · · · · · · ·
Wednesday · · · · ·
Thursday · · · · · ·
Friday · · · · · · · ·
Saturday · · · · · · ·
2d Week's Expences £.

23   *The Housekeeper's Accompt-Book* (Bath, 1797), title page. York City Archives, 69.1.1. By the end of the eighteenth century printed account-books kept track of 'the sundry Articles of Housekeeping' on a daily basis.

24   *The Housekeeper's Accompt-Book* (Bath, 1797), 10, page for the second week in January. York City Archives, 69.1.1.

Account-books were not written for the entertainment and instruction of posterity. They lack the emotional expansiveness of diaries and letters, and can give limited insight into attitudes. They are often, however, the only surviving document of family fortune, charting economic vicissitudes, family tensions, triumphs and disasters. The human story is belied by the terseness of the writing, yet the lists and numbers bear witness to drama nevertheless. What did practitioners think they were for? Their goal was financial security, according to contemporary exponents of the art: 'making inspection into that, that is to keep me and mine from ruine and poverty'. The dangers of the business world and the fear of utter ruination may have increased the appeal of accounts as a comfort and protection.[7] Margaret Hunt suggests that the promise of bookkeeping was even more profound: a method of predicting and controlling the future, a mysterious art on a par with divination and magic. Historians of management argue that for traders and manufacturers accounts could express a 'quest for order and regularity when dealing with overwhelming detail, perhaps without reliable managerial staff or settled routine'. It is in the very regularity of the system that bookkeeping assumes 'the colouring partly of a tool of management as well as a system of reckoning'.[8]

This tool was not a male preserve (pl. 7). While the husband was lord of all, the wife was to 'give account of all', asserted John Dod's and Robert Cleaver's *Household Government* of 1612. A century later, Richard Steele was conventional in his recommendation that daughters be trained up in accounting: 'tis good to accustom them from their very Childhood, to have something under their Government and Managery, to keep Accompts, to see the Manner of the Market to understand every thing that is bought'.[9] Financial proficiency and an air of household competence were winning qualities in middling and genteel brides, especially when coated with a patina of urban sophistication and domestic prettiness. Even titled ladies could be expected to manage accounts. The Duchess of Richmond tried to shield her husband from 'household affairs' in the 1740s, and personally ran the house accounts at Goodwood House in Sussex, her system spoilt, however, by minor orders made by servants on the duke's authority: 'I am always att a good deall of trouble in collecting all the little notes in the quarterly bill.' Some husbands were keen to hand over the whole burden of financial administration to a wife. When Margaret Blague married Sidney Godolphin in 1675, she was expected to run all major outgoing accounts, even paying her 'Husbands Cloaths, Stables & al, other House Expenses (except his pocket money)'. In the same decade, the widowed Surrey gentleman George Evelyn was infuriated that his lazy daughter refused to take on an executive role in the household. He even tried to bribe her into running the house accounts by offering her any savings as personal profit. In the end, Evelyn had to pay a woman in the village to run the accounts, a dismal defeat for a man with two daughters at home.[10] Domestic economy was a field many men were only too happy to resign.

Conversely, men sometimes confined the territory of the female accountant. Matrons who had considered themselves abreast of the family finances could be surprised by outstanding debts at the death of a spouse. Even painstaking accountants could be kept quite in the dark. When the Hampshire gentleman Lieutenant Colonel Jervoise was away with his regiment in the 1790s, his wife Eliza Jervoise managed the estate accounts with the advice of her father and a steward, supervising expensive renovations at Herriard House. 'The Furniture for the bed rooms is done but not put up . . . Fry desires me to inform you that Cash runs short; and an instalment of the assessed taxes; will come on to be paid. I have paid Attwoods bills for the months of July, August and September'. Yet for all her busyness, Eliza had no inkling that her husband was contemplating absconding because of 'the embarrassed state of my finances'. If his father would not bail him out then Lieutenant Colonel Jervoise would be forced 'to disclose the secret of my breast to the knowledge of my wife, whom I have hitherto kept ignorant of my distress' and to ask her to quit 'her native country to seek with me an Asylum'. Jervoise senior must have come through with the funds because the building went on. Not a breath of the difficulty ever ruffled the lieutenant colonel's correspondence with his wife, who continued to enthuse about her choice of paint for the stairs, 'not so dark, as to appear dismal by candlelight', and the erection of the cupola to the pigeon house.[11] Eliza Jervoise's blithe accounts were but a partial and wholly misleading representation of their finances: an island of knowledge on a larger map of which she was oblivious.

A woman's account-book could be read as a map of her jurisdiction, but it might also document a patriarch's surveillance of her time and spending. Fathers sometimes audited and signed off the account-books of daughters.[12] Anne Brockman, a Kent gentlewoman, was an assiduous accountant, running the household books for nearly twenty years, but she was married to an 'over busy' magistrate and Whig MP, notorious for the carefulness of his record keeping, who found time enough to check her calculations. In July 1719 Mrs Brockman was compelled to record: 'Miscounted in Mr Brockman's reckoning from London 0-10-0'.[13] Readers may remember the scene in Louisa Alcott's *Little Women*, of 1868, when the monthly checking of the housekeeping account and personal pocket-book forced the newly wed Meg to reveal to her hard-working husband the £50 she had spent on violet silk: 'When John got out his books that night, Meg's heart sank; and for the first time in her married life, she was afraid of her husband.[14] By one view, domestic accounting sustained the operation of patriarchy in the Victorian middle-class home. It was an instrument for controlling female consumption and containing women in domestic roles.[15]

An account-book was always and ever a tool of domestic control, though whose management exactly may sometimes remain moot. Modern sociology draws a distinction between the day-to-day management of family finances and overall control of financial decision-making. In this reading, day-to-day management is not seen as a site of much power. Female manipulation of limited resources where men have final say can be a dispiriting system in practice, incurring responsibilities but few privileges. Contemporary households where the wife controls the money and the husband manages it are rare; and in the even rarer cases where men both control and manage money there is a strong likelihood of extreme abuse.[16] This sociology, however, is too pessimistic about the possible benefits of accounting expertise and consumer management, even within a framework of masculine control. If the management of money were not a significant freedom, then abusive husbands would not seek to crush it. The accountant who massages the figures accrues practical power thereby, even if she presents the books to a higher authority. After all, fraud is a secret form of control. An unhappily married housekeeper at a Lincoln boarding school was salting away money to fund a new life in 1816, having resolved never to kiss her husband again. She assured her lover, William Pratt of Kegworth in Leicestershire, that her £10 goal was almost reached by stinting on the housekeeping: 'I heave not bought anny butter or shuager and very lettel met and less aill so I will leve you to juge what I have in my [power] at present.'[17] Men often had no choice but to trust to female knowledge, and knowledge, it scarcely needs repeating, is power.

Yet even where the ultimate control behind the account-book is hard to ascertain, we can still conclude that account-books are as much an active representation of domestic business as they were a record of it, and varied with the financial circumstances, business culture and emotional climate of different families. The account-books that survive are emphatically not a systematic sample. Account-books that were kept in attics and desks, to be deposited in local record offices, tend to belong to solvent, organised families who have managed to reproduce themselves and bequeath their property. Although some survivals seem to be entirely serendipitous, in general the records of feckless and disorganised householders have rotted away. When families went to the wall, the contents of houses were often brought to the hammer and the papers to the bonfire, although some account-books of the utterly insolvent fetched up in the courts of Chancery.

Household account-books were not designed to answer the questions this chapter sets. They are often either too broad or conversely too partial. The model estate account chronicles income from rents, investments, inheritance and allowances, loans, farm produce, sales alongside outgoings on rents, annuities, allowances, taxes, dues, interest on loans, wages, services (e.g., doctors, tutors), as well as the running expenses of house, farm, stable and estate, travel, pocket money and cash in hand. In practice, however, account-books are rarely utterly all encompassing either in conception or execution. Many ignored double entry altogether, and kept separate records of incoming and outgoings. Even keen accountants may have chosen to capture only one area of their lives in a record book. Two magistrates noted for their professional record keeping, William Brockman of Kent and William Hunt of Wiltshire, had no one with whom to share the duties of domestic accountant at certain points in their lives. Yet as a bachelor in the 1690s and a widower in the 1730s, Brockman and Hunt often recorded only livestock and produce sold, wages paid and large accounts settled. Brockman's accounts were roughly jotted into his old Latin exercise book.[18] Lord Chesterfield, who recommended that the young gentleman about town 'keep an account in a book', rose above petty detail: 'I do not mean that you should keep an account of the shillings and half-crowns which you may spend in chair-hire, operas, etc.: they are unworthy of the time, and of the ink that they would consume; leave such minutiae to dull, penny-wise fellows'.[19] Mathematical knowledge was uneven. Consumers with good memories and a flair for financial improvisation may have kept only sketchy accounts on paper, if they bothered at all. Defoe complained about merchants who believed they could carry the whole history and future of their businesses in their heads.[20] Written accounting was not for everyone.

On the rare occasions where manuscript accounts exist for both husbands and wives, the historian is offered a unique opportunity to examine the interrelationship of men's and women's consumer responsibilities, services and pleasures. This chapter is based on three unusual sets of single-entry gentry accounts that throw light on the distribution of consumer responsibility between women and men: those of the Cottons of Cambridgeshire, the Grimes of Warwickshire and the Ardernes of Cheshire. None of them provides perfectly symmetrical his and hers account-books, but each set reveals a distinctive form of accounting with common assumptions about male and female territories.

The Cottons of Madingley Hall, Cambridge, ran an accounting system that allowed female domestic management within a framework of male surveillance (fig. 25). The Cottons were rich greater gentry – baronets, but not nobles – capable of spending a huge £4,153 in a single year.[21] Sir John Hynde Cotton was MP for Cambridge in 1765 and 1771. He married Anne Parsons in 1745, spending a princely £1,209 on the wedding. Miss Parsons was the daughter of an alderman, twice Lord Mayor of London. Anne Cotton's personal account-books have not survived, but details from them were transferred into the master's book roughly every other month. This chapter analyses the account-books in detail for 1761, sixteen years into the marriage.[22] Seven times a year, Lady Cotton cast up the house accounts, and her husband recorded the transaction each time with a particular form of words: 'accounted with my wife viz. house book for May 30th to July 22nd £18.4.6'. In addition, Anne Cotton paid the annual wages of ten female servants, her daughter's allowance, the salary of the French master, the dancing master and the writing master, though Sir John Cotton paid his son's board at Westminster School. Lady Cotton also ran the account with butcher, confec-

25   Madingley Hall, Cambridgeshire, from John Britton, *Beauties of England & Wales; or, Delineations Topographical, Historical and Descriptive*, vol. 2 (London, 1801). The sixteenth-century house of the Cotton family.

tioner, tallow chandler and candle supplier, brazier, turner, china man and glass man. She was the queen of the textiles; dealing with the mantua maker, mercer, five different milliners, three haberdashers, two linen drapers, the coat woman, the hosier and a weaver, but she had no dealings whatsoever with the tailor. Lady Cotton's spending in 1761 amounted to £933, 22 per cent of expenditure recorded in her husband's account-book.

Account-books aim to record the financial life of a household and therefore have a much broader remit than shopping. Sir John Hynde Cotton was responsible for paying out on rents, annuities, taxes, tithes, fees, interests on loans, wages, estate supplies and so on. Nevertheless, Sir John was also a beau. His bills to his tailor amount to a splendid £435 in 1761. He also liked special provisions. His one-off purchases included oranges and lemons, venison and snipe, brawn and sturgeon, rabbits, oysters, cheese and a half hogshead of madeira. His biggest single outlay was to the wine merchant, known chummily as 'Charlie'; his bill for 1759 to 1760 was a cheerful £154. Unique to himself were accounts with the peruke maker, 'Pretorias', the hatter, the sword cutler, the saddler, horse dealers and the coach maker. Strikingly, Cotton's mandate allows personal consumer indulgence on the stable, travel, alcohol, luxury foodstuffs, newspapers, tailoring and

26 Coton House, Warwickshire, *circa* 1900, as rebuilt by Abraham Grimes in the late eighteenth century. Warwickshire County Record Office, PH 352/49/5.

masculine accoutrements. Yet his overall surveillance accommodates his wife's management of crucial areas – particularly household provisioning, linens, the equipping of children and the education of daughters.

My second case study suggests a much more restricted female financial mandate. The most formal, structured, legible and patriarchal accounting system I have encountered is that set out in the Grimes account-book.[23] The Grimes of Coton House, Warwickshire, were as rich as the Cottons, with an income of £4,851 in 1781, £4,397 in 1782 and £3,086 in 1783 (fig. 26). The household accounts of Abraham Grimes, Esq., for 1781–8 are internally divided by category: the annual account, the house, stable, rent and taxes, miscellaneous, the debtor account, and finally, in a cordoned off category of their own, Mrs Grimes's and the children's account. It is not clear who was running the house account on a daily basis (Abraham's house account often gives summary totals, not a breakdown on foodstuffs, which suggests that another detailed house book was in operation), but if it was Mrs Grimes, then her husband was not giving her written credit for the effort. Expenditure on children was always at the core of any matron's purchasing, but here mother and children are fused in a single category, as if both are dependants. Mrs Grimes's dispensation is reduced to its narrowest possible definition. The spending in this category of 'Mrs Grimes & children', or more often just 'Mrs Grimes &C', amounts to a relatively meagre £307 in 1781, £352 in 1782 and £242 in 1783, respectively 6 per cent, 8 per cent and 9 per cent of total recorded family expenditure in those years.

This accounting system, however, looks more formal and orderly than it actually is. The miscellaneous category is huge: miscellaneous spending in 1781 is £3,383 – 71 per cent of the whole. Buried in this category are some of the consumer services that Mrs Grimes performed for her husband. For instance, on 24 November 1782 Abraham records 'Pd by Mrs. G for cambrick & c for self £2 2 0' – a husband's shirts again.[24] On her own account, Mrs Grimes dealt with three different linen drapers, a woollen draper, glover, mercer, hosier, shoemaker, mantua maker, haberdasher, lace man, stay maker, breech maker, two milliners, a jeweller, a bookseller and a man she disdainfully calls a 'Mr Jew-tailor' for a coat for herself and the children. She also paid the children's writing master, music mistress, dancing master and later their schooling. Mrs Grimes is *credited* with a very limited terrain of consumer management – only that which pertains directly to herself and her children. Nevertheless, the Grimes household operated on a similar accounting system to the Cottons, that of discrete female accounting within a framework of masculine oversight, but interpreted much less advantageously to the wife. In fact, the account-book constructs her more like an eldest daughter than a wife and mistress of the household.

The final case study, that of the Ardernes of Cheshire, offers yet another financial model. John and Sarah Arderne were a gentry couple established at Harden Hall, near Stockport in Cheshire (fig. 27). Eleven notebooks document Sarah Arderne's personal and household expenditure over an eleven-year period between 1741 and 1752.[25] Unfortunately, her husband's account-books do not survive, although the bills have been kept, so it is possible to identify the gaps in Sarah's own accounting, in order to ascertain some of the major areas that lay outside her jurisdiction. Sarah Arderne's accounts record only outgoings; there is no record of income. Nevertheless, her annual expenditure in 1745, a year I have broken down by category, is a liberal £546, less than the annual spending recorded in Anne Cotton's account for 1756, but more than the annual spending assigned to Mrs Grimes in the early 1780s. The Ardernes came from north of England lesser gentry and were probably less well off than the Cottons and the Grimeses, but they were sufficiently prosperous to maintain a coach and horses. In 1745 the Ardernes were ten years into the marriage. John was a mature 36, but had still not yet come into his inheritance. Sarah was in the thick of childbearing; she already had three girls and two boys, and would go on to have four more babies. For nine months of this account-book, she was pregnant.

27 'View of Harden Hall', from John Aiken, *A Description of the Country from Thirty to Forty miles round Manchester* (London, 1795). The sixteenth-century house of the Arderne family.

Had they been a poor family, this would be a nadir in the family poverty cycle; and even for a rich family the outgoings are prodigious. The shoe bill for six months in 1745 runs to thirty-two items – and totals £2 14s. 6d., roughly equivalent to the annual wage of a scullery maid.[26] The expenses of running a large nursery are obvious. The apothecary's bill to Mr Thornley was an impressive £40. The vouchers reveal that Mr Thornley supplied 570 individual items: from orange-flower water, gripe water, purges and frankincense to 'A large pott of cataplasm for Mrs Arderne's breasts and a linament to dress it with'. With three children, a toddler and two infants, the washing bill alone is £33, equivalent to the yearly wage of ten maids.[27] The account-book is a drier ego document than the diary, but its details are still replete with concentrated emotion. The weeks leading up to the birth of Letitia in September were fraught with preparations. On 20 June 1745, for example, Sarah Cotton 'Pd for 14 yds of Diaper against my lying inn'.[28]

But what of the gender comparison? Mr Arderne's account-books do not survive, though there are seventy-five bills for the year 1744–5.[29] We cannot know whether all the bills survive, but there are enough to identify significant areas of personal and household consumption that lay beyond Mrs Arderne's jurisdiction. So how did Mr and Mrs Arderne manage their finances? Unusually, it appears that much family money flowed through the wife's account-book, probably because, as an heiress, married to a man who had not yet come into his property, the ready money was quite literally hers. John Arderne had to accept an allowance from both his father and his wife.[30] Mrs Arderne's single largest outgoing in 1745 was to her husband; she paid him a hefty £169 in cash, in regular instalments. Like the pattern wife of the conduct book, Sarah Arderne passed a dollop of her settlement straight into the hands of her husband. Yet still not the whole, so she remained in a position to give her 'dear lord' spending money, like the £40 she gave him 'for Cheltenham' in June 1745, when she was heavily pregnant, authorising his spree at the spa. She paid some of his bills, and supplied him with all his linens. In April she 'Pd Mary smith for making ten fine holland shirts for my Dear lord'. She sourced muslin for cravats and India handkerchiefs, and kept all his linens washed and mended. So in all Mr Arderne's personal needs accounted for an outlay on his wife's part of £195 in that year, 36 per cent of her annual expenditure.

Sarah Arderne's largest single category of expenditure in 1745, after her husband, was unsurprisingly the children: £47 4s. 8d. – 9 per cent.[31] After that, the next largest amount was £42 on servants' wages, and then £33 on washing. That which she designates as personal consumption ('for self') is very small in relative terms: £12, only 2 per cent. Arderne seems to have given herself up to her growing nursery, buying no new gowns, though she did have her christening gown re-trimmed. The gown was getting hard use in those years, so she 'Pd Miss Shallcross for 7 yards of Edgin for my christning suit at 7 pr yard', to freshen it up a little. Mrs Arderne seems to have gone hardly anywhere, not even Stockport. Though to the limitations of pregnancy must be added the disturbance of the Jacobite rebellion, which deterred many travellers in the north-west that autumn.

So what was Mr Arderne's province as a consumer? The vouchers that bear his name cover payments to odd-job men, the blacksmith, gunsmith, saddler, cobbler, linen draper, haberdasher, glover and his tailor. A huge category of consumption, with which Mrs Arderne has no direct engagement, is what we might loosely call men's tackle. There are sixty-eight items on saddler William Davenport's five-month bill to John Arderne, including dog collars, stirrups, bridles, halters, saddle straps, a martingale, curry comb and brush, whip cord, dog whip, cart whip, springs for the landau, as well as payment for the mending of a pillion, saddle, bridles and other household goods like a trunk and a footstool. The total came to £2 11s. 3½d. Effectively, he was spending the equivalent of an annual servant's wage on leather. Interestingly, however, in January 1745, when William Davenport put in a bill for a whopping £13 13s., cash must have been wanting, because Sarah Arderne covered the cost. Crucially, she did not settle the account herself, but gave her husband the money to pay the bill. Presumably for her to have settled directly would have been embarrassing and effeminising for her husband. It was for the man of the house to see to the horses, dogs, sport and vehicles, even if his wife's inheritance oiled the wheels. The only thing Mrs Arderne bought for the horses was medicine; potions for their legs and hooves are included in her huge bill to the apothecary Mr Thornley. But here it seems the feminine responsibility for family health and medicine has overwhelmed the masculine responsibility for the stable. Physic has trumped horses as a category. Despite Mrs Arderne's control and management of much of the family's ready cash, it was evidently important that her 'dear lord' appeared to the world as the uncontested master of their financial affairs, not a man who had to resort to his wife for spending money.

Mr Arderne was happy to have his wife provide his personal linens, but he commissioned his own stylish main garments, paying a dandyish £6 6s. for a Dresden work waistcoat. The tailor Daniel Downs made breeches, drawers and a coat for Mr Arderne, but also made coats and mended waistcoats for the coach-man and other male household servants. At first glance, it is surprising that Arderne paid a tailor, John Sudlow, for making the children's coats, and a cob-bler for their shoes. It seems that Mrs dealt exclusively with teams of seamstresses and laundresses, while Mr traded particularly with the male tailor, even in the feminine matter of children's clothes. Who dealt with who may be governed by conventions of propriety, as well as the convenience of drawing upon a pre-ex-isting relationship between supplier and customer.

So what can the account-books tell us about gender, accounting and goods? Eighteenth-century account-books are not a straightforward source for the his-tory of consumer practices. They are a representation of the way that the allo-cation of financial responsibility between master and mistress was conceptualised in these families. The key here is notional responsibility, because the accounts do not necessarily reveal who decided on a purchase, or who eventually made the payment, or even who physically went to a shop. The accounts of the Grimes, Cotton and Arderne couples disclose different ways of mapping financial re-sponsibility, yet consistent assumptions about the appropriate division of labour is apparent in all three cases. A deep-seated notion about what women and men should control emerges. This idea of female responsibility varied from marriage to marriage in what it embraced at its fullest, as we can see from the contrast be-tween Mrs Grimes and Sarah Arderne, but at its most circumscribed the female dispensation still covered personal dress, the clothing and education of children, especially girl children, and the provision of the family's personal linen.

The link between women and everyday textiles is strong and persistent. Female weakness for fine fabrics, especially silk, was a cliché of casual commentary, as was the hypnotic allure of haberdashery and the plethora of lady's linens. Witness Campbell in *The London Tradesman*, on millinery, 'no Male Trade':

> The milliner is concerned in making and providing the Ladies with Linnen of all sorts, fit for Wearing Apparel, from the Holland smock to the Tippet and Commode; but as we are got into the Lady's Articles, which are so very numerous, the Reader is not to expect that we are to give an exact List of everything belonging to them; let it suffice in general that the Milliner furnishes them with Holland, Cambrick, Lawn, and Lace of all sorts, and makes these Materials into smocks, Aprons, Tippits, Handkerchiefs, Neckaties, Ruffles, Mobs, Caps, Dressed-Heads, with as many *Etceteras* as would reach from *Charing-Cross* to the *Royal Exchange*.[32]

The mystery of femininity itself could be seen to inhere in the infinite variety of ladies' accoutrements, 'of which cost and profusion, no batchelor can, or shou'd have, the smallest idea', concluded the London bureaucrat John Byng, a beleaguered husband and father, in 1782.[33] Though such commentary emphasises a woman's fetishistic self-indulgence in linens, in stark contrast, the account-books chart a story of emotional responsibility and consumer service, not selfishness, through the ongoing provision of linen garments for others, especially men.

Mr Arderne's personal linen and cotton was Sarah Arderne's concern. It is clear that Mrs Cotton had batches of shirts made up for her husband, while Cotton's aunts kept him in linen and muslin in his bachelorhood. ('Pd my aunt Polly for linnen, lace & c 89-14-0.')[34] Even Mrs Grimes sourced some of the cambric for her husband's shirts and ruffles, and the muslin for his neckcloths. Making a husband's shirt was widely seen as a fundamental matrimonial duty. Women's plain sewing had a resonant emotional symbolism that carried over even when a mistress did not ply the needle with her own fingers. In gentry families, wives did not expect to make shirts and shifts in bulk themselves.[35] Yet *administering* the production of personal linens, from buying the Holland, sourcing the thread, to employing the neat seamstresses and overseeing the making up and washing, perhaps personally finishing them off and labelling them, was one of the crucial ways that women serviced the needs of their men. If you did not provide the shirts you were hardly a wife.

The link between women's and men's linen is confirmed by other sources. The Birmingham Unitarian Catherine Hutton remembered with pride that she became 'contriver and cutter of the family linen' from the age of 14.[36] 'Pray let me know what order your shirts are in?' is a leitmotif of women's letters to bachelor sons. The lawyer Thomas Greene had chambers in Gray's Inn by the 1770s, yet he continued to rely on his mother and then his sister (even after her own marriage) for the creation and overhaul of his personal linens. Greene must have found a laundress nearby, but he still sent his linen home 300 miles to Lancaster to be bleached and mended, and asked his sister to get him black silk stockings and to make his shirts: 'they fit extremely well except that the neck & wrists are a little too narrow but that you may easily alter when I come down'. But even men in metropolitan textile trades relied on their ageing mothers for personal linen.[37] The young scholar John Ogle, later an Evangelical clergyman, gave a full account of his personal needs at Jesus College, Cambridge, to his doting mother back in Yorkshire in 1799; in fact, some letters offered an inventory of such tedious detail that only a mother could have read them with eager interest.

> . . . I have got a pair of white cotton stockings which seem to be very nice but I am rather afraid they are too fine to last long I got Mrs Becket to buy me them. . . . I wish I had known before I could easily have brought towels with me. I think you had better not trouble yourself to buy me any stockings before I come home for all that I have bought must be either white Cotton or Silk I shall want another pair of breeches soon I think Do you think Nankeen would be dear wear? If not I think a pair of Nankeen Breeches would be the most suitable for summer. I don't think it will be advisable for me to save my best breeches as they will be too little for me.[38]

Household linens were a female province, and one that men never thought of exploring for themselves. The only matter on which the ambitious barrister James Hewitt sought female advice for his Coventry home in 1749 was ordinary textiles: 'Pray let me know what Bedding I must buy for those two beds and what for servts – ask Mother.' Even the brilliant Adam brothers who were to establish themselves as the most stylish architectural designers of their generation still bleated to their womenfolk after linens when they first struck camp in London in 1758. 'Linnens are what we want most', James Adam appealed to his sister Helen back in Edinburgh, '& coud wish you woud send by first Convoy a Box of those lately made consisting of 4 pairs of fine sheets 3 pairs of Course ones & half a dozen of course table cloaths for any thing passes down with batchelors.' In 1803 at Trinity College, Cambridge, the Dorset gentleman William Bankes thanked his grandmother for 'all the care & trouble you have taken in providing linen for me'.[39] One might imagine there was not a linen draper to be found in London, Cambridge and Coventry. Female responsibility for, expertise in and authority over linens are reiterated in a host of manuscripts. Only tyrannical or hen-pecked husbands carried the key to the linen cupboard. One of Lady Cowper's self-right-

eous grievances against her despotic Hertfordshire husband in 1701 was his refusal to give her the key to the linen cupboard, a symptom of his wider campaign to undermine her due authority as housekeeper.[40] And while linens may
sound a mundane province, it is a province that was ever enlarging in this century.[41]

Household linens were a *terra incognita* to the civilian adult male. Save authorising the occasional bank draft on the finest linens, a proud man had nothing to do with the selection, or spinning and weaving, making up, washing,
mending and monitoring of linens. Bewilderment is a common bachelor theme.
'I beg to be informed by my mother to what uses I must apply the napkins, and
to what the towels' appealed Oxford scholar John James in a letter to his father
in 1778. Basic matters were puzzling to him, needing mother to say 'how long a
pair of sheets must be used before they are washed; and what price I must set on
a stock if my laundress should lose one'.[42] Yet clean linen was the most ubiquitous statement of moral worth, a snowy cuff being a universal mark of personal
cleanliness, dignity and self-respect. The guardian of the whiteness, the insignia
of family honour, was always the mistress, perhaps because the making and
washing (if no longer the spinning) of the linens involved the orchestration of
an all-female workforce. Each weight of linen had its own washing requirements.
Male disinclination to involve themselves is so powerful as to argue that here
was a real taboo. Outside the sealed world of the Army and the Navy, male antipathy to laundry was extreme. A man who had to wash for himself was a pitiful spectacle – hands in the tub was a feature of the widower's desperation (fig.
28).[43]

If women were responsible for linen and cotton, it seems that men had most
oversight of wool, a point made in jocular fashion by *The London Tradesman*
when distinguishing between the mercer and the woollen draper: 'they are as
like one another as two eggs, only the Woollen draper deals chiefly with the Men,
and is the graver Animal of the two, and the Mercer trafficks most with the
Ladies, and has a small Dash of their Effeminacy in his Constitution'.[44] Gentlemen did not live by broadcloth alone, and there were occasions when they had
to strut in silk and velvet (in fact, men probably wore more velvet than women),
but for this they resorted to the tailor. Men almost invariably ran a separate account with the tailor, who was always a man. The relationship between a gentleman and the trader who had his measurements may already have been a
distinctive one. In the 1600s tailors made men's *and* women's clothes, but the
rise of the mantua maker led to a bifurcation of the trade by the sex of the customer.[45] A good tailor, according to *The London Tradesman* again, was able 'not
only to cut for the Handsome and Well-shaped, but to bestow a good Shape

28 George Cruikshank, illustration to 'A Distressed Father', in J. Wight, *Mornings at Bow Street* (London, 1824). In the accompanying text, the widower says: 'I was left alone with the children; and every night after I had done work I washed their faces, and put them to bed, and washed their little bits o' things, and hanged them o' the line to dry, myself – for I'd no money, your honour, and so I could not have a housekeeper.'

where Nature has not designed it'.[46] Therefore a tailor could achieve a position of considerable intimacy and trust. Nineteenth- and twentieth-century tailors made the shop a homosocial sanctum for urbane customers, discouraged female intervention and fostered a clubby, confidential relationship between consumer and supplier. The raw consumerism of male clothes shopping was thereby cloaked in a mantle of discretion, protecting the dignity of the male consumer. For all the caricatures of male customers ogling shop-girls, men may, in fact, have found it far more congenial to deal with other men. Indeed, the hyper-masculine decor of successful men's shops (from dark wood panelling to suspended biplanes) and the provision of men's side entrances to department stores in the twentieth century does suggest a certain reluctance on the part of the average male consumer to run the gauntlet of femininity.[47]

Tailors performed occasional services for women, often making a lady's riding habit or travelling dress, which echoed the lines of men's coats. Anne Lister, who wore riding habits every day, had habitual dealings with her Halifax tailor, but perhaps the mannish lesbian romantic is the exception that proves the rule. Some milliners specialised in riding habits and masquerade dress for ladies.[48] Mrs Grimes's disdain for 'Mr Jew-tailor' suggests that he was a less prestigious tradesman than her husband's regular tailor. Mr Arderne accounted with the tailor to make his children's coats, despite the assumption that clothing the children was a female concern. It was intercourse between a gentleman and his tailor that was customary.

A conspicuous object of male consumer desire, indeed *the* most flamboyant masculine accoutrement, was the coach. All three families studied here maintained one. The vehicle was always ultra-expensive in itself, but the running of it demanded coachmen, postilions, horses, stables, feed, farriers and so on, and could be ruinous. The full equipage ate up so much capital that in modern terms the coach's equivalent would be less the proverbial sports car than a helicopter. Abraham Grimes's stable account cost him £418 in 1781. More than £80 of this he laid out to the coach maker, more than £213 on new horses, and the rest on coach tax, feed, the farrier and the saddler. Which brings us to a major area of *repetitive* male shopping – tackle. Of course, one might guess that tackle for horses, dogs, sport and vehicles would be a significant male interest, but the multiplicity of this equipment and the regularity of men's visits to the saddler are remarkable (fig. 29). In fact, one can read John Arderne's bill from the saddler as a summary of many hours spent fingering an astounding array of whips, combs, collars and bits of horses' tack; so many etceteras, so oddly named, from norzel and sirsingle, to rowlers and cruppers. The month of September alone saw the purchase or mending of twenty-nine items, on seven different occasions. It seems that John Arderne comforted himself in an utterly masculine, dark brown territory of goods, while his wife laboured away to produce his sixth child.[49] If women adored the assortments on the haberdashery counter, then the multifariousness of horse furniture was probably equally magnetic for men. In fact, it was even known in some trade directories as horse millinery.[50] However, male handling of a plethora of leather and buckles was never satirised by critics or captured by cartoonists. Gentlemen were lucky that their fetishism could be presented to the world as an altogether practical concern with transportation.

Expensive household refurbishment also seems dominated, if not determined, by men. In two of the three accounts, major redecoration is itemised and in both cases it is listed under the male account. Abraham Grimes and John Hynde Cotton both employed an upholder on account. Whether gentleman and upholder consulted or perhaps even responded to the mistress's taste is not recorded for posterity.[51] Here, however, perhaps we come to the limits of account-books and

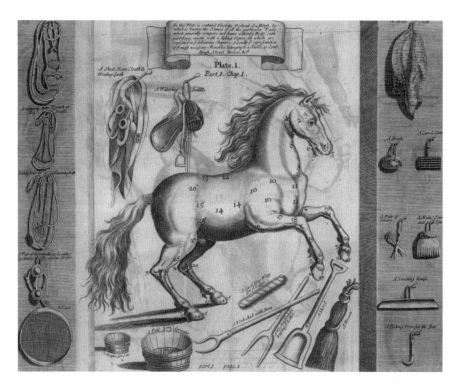

29   Jacques de Solleysel, *The Compleat Horseman or Perfect Farrier* (London, 1729), Plate 1. The plate shows the parts of a horse and 'the most necessary Movables belonging to a Stable; as Comb, Brush, Shovel, Broom, etc.'.

ledgers as sources for female agency. Theresa Parker masterminded the stylish interior decorations at Saltram House in Devon, and was admired by Sir Joshua Reynolds for her intuitive 'propriety of taste'. She was told in 1772: 'the Design of yr Bowl . . . is faultless', but you will not find her name in any ledger. Similarly, Lord Palmerston's letters tell a different story from his accounts. Witness his report to his wife in 1795 on the fulfilment of decisions they had made together for their Hanover Square house:

> I have been in the City and called at the two carpet warehouses. I see nothing better than the two patterns we chose . . . I suppose I shall keep the same sofas and chairs that I had before, only having them new repaired and covered, but with what and what are the curtains to be? . . . I think the sofa will be best in your dressing room and I find Ince has been altering it as to the stuffing and making cushions etc according to directions you left with him. The question now will be, will you have those eight chairs of his which will match very well

with the sofa or will you have new ones? . . . The fringe is a mixture of worsted and I believe cotton with some silk. If you think it better I can have cotton fringe but I thought when you was here you decided to have the fringe part worsted with silk head.[52]

Stereo conversations become mono decisions in accounts. The letters of manufacturers themselves bespeak the concertedness with which they wooed the patronage and good opinion of wives. 'I have to day been with Lady Bute, Lady Charlott Burgoin, Lady Charlott Seymore, the Honble Mr Granville, Lord Clan Brazil [sic] besides sundry other visits amongst Commons' boasted Birmingham inventor Matthew Boulton to his wife in 1776.[53]

In the account-books studied here, however, purchases of decorative household goods allocated to the wife's account are restricted to a handful of smaller items, like the two china dogs and the pair of china figures Mrs Cotton bought in 1756, probably either Meissen or, if English, Bow or Chelsea, and the black and gold teapot, probably Staffordshire, that Mrs Arderne bought in 1745 (pls 8 and 9). These are exactly the kind of new, small decorative wares that manufacturers and moralists alike regarded as 'feminine'. Poor Mrs Grimes, however, got to buy very little of this kind of thing on her own account, perhaps because her husband was particularly controlling, but probably because of his own personal interest in consumption. Abraham Grimes seems to have been obsessed with the gadgets and novelties of the 1780s. Unusually, he bought a Bramah water closet (patented in 1778) and Argand lamps (patented in 1784), as well as a regulator stove, an array of Wedgwood earthenware and plated silver candlesticks and tea urns (pls 10 and 11). It is perhaps significant that Grimes, the most adventurous individual consumer in the three account-books, was the one who formally accorded his wife the least financial room for manoeuvre. Men, like women, varied in their willingness and desire to engage with the new world of goods, as inventory data on the qualitatively different consumerism of yeomen, craftsmen, professionals and merchants make clear.[54]

This chapter has wrestled with the interrelationship of men's and women's consumer responsibilities and consumer pleasures, emphasising where men's hands were freed, and women's were tied. None of which is to suggest that these mistresses were materially deprived. Rather, their consumption should be seen as an element in a bigger system, locked in relationship with the consumption of their husbands and households. Married gentlemen were able to rise above daily dealings with the grocer and the butcher only because their wives handled these tedious accounts for them. A customary division of women's tasks and men's pleasures underlies the jokes in Jane Collier's sparkling satire *The Art of Ingeniously Tormenting* (1753). Collier advised husbands bent on torturing 'a very careful prudent wife . . . who by her good economy confines all the expenses under her inspection fairly within her appointment' to stint her funds: 'part with your money to her, like so many drops of your blood', lecturing her 'on extravagance for every necessary that is bought into the house', meanwhile 'sparing no expense for your own hounds, horses or claret'.[55] The explicit contract recorded in 1758 by Mary Delany, then wife of the dean of Down in Ireland, is suggestive of a common division of labour: 'The Dean has now settled my allowance for housekeeping at six hundred a-year, which I receive quarterly, and out of that pay everything but the men's wages, the liveries, the stables, wine cellar and garden, furniture and all repairs.'[56] Wives were unlikely to trespass on the masculine preserves of horse furniture and port.

A division of labour based on the sources of goods is specified in the papers of Susanna Whatman, the wife of a rich Kent paper manufacturer. Her note for servants written *circa* 1776 is precise about responsibilities: 'Mrs Whatman pays all her house bills weekly, including the Butcher's bills, and candles and flour when they are brought in. But soap, wax candles and grocery come down from London and are paid for by draft by Mr Whatman.'[57] While James Whatman authorised payment on high-quality metropolitan groceries, he was dissociated from petty local bills.

Geographical mobility is a factor that contoured male and female engagement with the world of goods. The nursery years were particularly immobilising for young matrons, while gentlemen led peripatetic lives as sportsmen and local administrators, easily combining a swift survey of the shops in a county town with a session on the local bench or a jaunt at the races. Of course, much could be acquired from a distance. This was an era when a high percentage of provisioning was done by order, and an array of goods could be commissioned by letter. Women were adept at describing the design, colour, pattern and ornament of luxury goods (particularly china, fabric and dresses) in words. Nevertheless, it took a seasoned hand to select the prettiest lawn, feel the quality and judge the newest pattern and one had to visit the showroom in person to discover the unexpected novelty sitting on the counter. Women's irritation with the inept choices of proxy consumers speaks to the frustrations of distance. Husbands often acted *faute de mieux* as their wives' consumer agents, and so again the account-books must underestimate the extent of women's procurement.

His and hers accounts tell a distinctive story. They offer a particular construction of financial allocation within households. It is striking that the precise allocation of financial responsibility varies in all three case studies. We should not find this too surprising; modern sociology on methods of money management within marriages reveals that today, despite potentially equal access to banking and credit, and public professions of total equality, there exist four major systems of managing household finances, each with different implications for power and personal spending.[58] Yet despite the variation from family to family, the account-books expose deeply held and consistent categorisations of material responsibility, propriety and expertise. Greater recourse to shopping did not undermine women's material obligations. Women had long been responsible for children's material needs, among which clothing loomed large. It would be a mistake to presume that the emotional investment diminished as the balance shifted away from domestic to retail provisioning. Recent anthropology reveals the extent to which modern wives and mothers see shopping for family as a practical exercise in caring.[59] Nor should we underestimate the expertise required by Georgian consumers as the range and quality of products like linens diversified.

Georgian retailers who targeted the male consumer as a desirous individual, and not just as the representative of his household, were plentiful. Wig makers, barbers, hat makers, watchmakers, tailors, tobacconists, stationers, wine merchants, saddlers, sword cutlers, horse dealers and coach makers, among many others, prospered by attending to the personal needs of both bachelors and patriarchs. While hooped petticoats fluttered in the doorway of the milliners, models of Scottish Highland soldiers standing to attention outside tobacconists and of naval officers guarding scientific instrument shops proclaimed the unambiguous manliness of the treasures within.[60] Men's ornaments and accoutrements were as varied as women's. 'A fool cannot withstand the charms of a toy-shop . . . ', Lord Chesterfield warned his son, 'snuff boxes, watches, heads of canes, etc are his destruction.'[61] It is an irony that the consumer self-indulgences of married men so often went unnoticed: the dandy and the fop singled out in satire are almost always young bachelors. Yet a wife's responsibility for basic provisioning exposed her to accusations of vanity, avarice, extravagance, materialism and even fetishism. It was the big spender Sir John Hynde Cotton who traded with 'Charlie' the wine merchant and 'Pretorias' the peruke maker, while his wife made him dutiful presents of full sets of Holland shirts. Women's consumer services remained deeply indebted to an older economy of virtuous, productive housewifery, despite the decline of manufacturing within the household, the proliferation of goods available for purchase and the multiplication of shops.

5

ROOMS AT THE TOP

Architecture was the most expensive Georgian taste. The history of style offers a chronological sequence of new houses – Baroque extravaganza to Palladian villa to Rococo folly to neo-Gothic cottage – promoting a glamorous narrative of fashion-driven change. An appetite for new buildings, or even substantial rebuilding, however, was far from universal, even among the peerage. Many innovators did not see their monument finished in their lifetime, and there were often changes in fashion, style and design philosophy between the inception and completion of an architectural project. 'Goodwood is another singular example of what is produced by a Duke being his own Architect' remarked William Bankes in 1811; 'it was left very unfinished at the time of his death, but enough is to done to be (I should think) a great load upon his heirs, who will not be very affluent.' Some tasks were deliberately bequeathed to the inheritors, to bind them to the house, and its improvement. At Malmesbury, Bankes found that Lord Suffolk's mansion was but a shell, the skeleton of an opulence long since decayed: 'Within it is all unfinished & scarcely half inhabited; a lord Suffolk who was much richer than the present had a design of making a most splendid suite within but left it incomplete & his successor lives in a poor corner of it almost as if by stealth.'[1] Few houses were designed, erected, decorated and furnished *de novo* in a single phase.

The abundance of country houses open to the public creates a deceptive picture of Georgian society. The nobility was a peculiar minority. In England and Wales, there were only 160 peers in 1688, a mere 220 by 1780 and still just 350 by 1832, in a population of about 14 million. The peerage remained small and rich because only eldest sons inherited titles, and new creations were few. The basic minimum of aristocratic lifestyle probably required an income of £5,000 or £6,000 a year in 1790; and it took an income of £10,000 to afford it in comfort, when pretenders to parish gentility managed on merely £300 per annum or less.[2] The peers, however, were only the generals of the serried ranks of the landed, running into the thousands, who all had to maintain, furbish and refurbish houses. Younger noble children all descended to the gentry, so a dense web of family connections unified the landed. New peers were almost invariably recruited from within the landed rich. For outsiders of new wealth, the typical ascent was laborious and could take generations.[3] The nouveaux riches were at liberty to erect pompous buildings, for there were no sumptuary laws in England, unlike in France, where flourishes like dovecotes were the preserve of nobility. Equally, there were always rich private gentlemen, like the fictional Mr Darcy, long in possession of impressive houses, while florid architectural statements about pedigree were often made by peers of very recent creation. Meanwhile, downward mobility is a forgotten fact of noble life. Some of the most ambitious Georgian gentlemen were trying to recover what they saw as lost rank. Both Clive of India and Warren Hastings bought back ancestral estates.[4]

The history of architecture is proudly masculine in subject matter and tenor. With the exception of Bess of Hardwick, Eleanor Coade, inventor of Coade stone, Alice Hepplewhite the cabinetmaker and Anna Maria Garthwaite the silk designer, most famous patrons and virtually all architects, designers, interior decorators and luxury producers were male. Yet if men were preoccupied with the architectural fabric, many curators and architectural historians believe that interior decoration fell to the distaff. Both Charles Saumarez Smith and John Cornforth note a feminisation of elite interiors, though they disagree slightly on chronology. Only from the 1760s, argues Saumarez Smith, did women emerge as arbiters of taste, while for Cornforth they made their mark on design forty years earlier.[5] Both experts, however, are reliant on the flowering of ladies' letter writing for their evidence of a new intervention in interiors, though it is rash to claim from silence that ladies were indifferent to decor before 1725. Given the fact that women had long been considered responsible for the daily management of the household in all its routine aspects, and that biblical authority demanded domestic decoration by good women, it is implausible that ladies did not exercise some control over the way that interiors were designed, furnished and beautified much earlier than this. Evidence of female designs and patronage dates from 1600 at least.[6] Nevertheless, the 1700s did see the flowering of the language of taste, which educated women were very quick to master, as we shall see.

The recuperation of women's role in building and interiors is hampered by the poverty of evidence. Even identifying women's commissions is difficult, acutely so in the case of married women. The ledger of the neo-Palladian architect Matthew Brettingham for the years 1746–53 lists only three female customers – Lady Litchfield, Lady Seabright and the Countess of Suffolk – to eleven male clients, though it is clear from his commentary that sometimes he considered himself working for couples: elsewhere, he notes costs to 'Mr Villiers and Lady Charlotte for a plan for altering their house at Grove'.[7] If a lady patron was married, convention decreed that all formal correspondence and bills be made out to her husband. Family letters document that the noblewoman Caroline Fox was primarily responsible for the new commissions in the gallery at Holland House in the early 1760s, but you would never know this from the family account-books, or the bills of the artist Joshua Reynolds. Ladies often colluded in the concealment of their activity even to their lords. Paying effusive lip service to marital subordination while pursuing one's own will was a vintage female device.[8] Only a goose or a monster of conceit would boast any independence abroad. The stylish Theresa Parker was careful to present the interior decorations at Saltram House in Devon in the early 1770s as driven by her socially inferior husband: 'I have some thoughts (that is) Mr Parker talks of having the little Boy put into the half length of Sir Joshua's.'[9] And where husbands and wives worked in concert to create their houses, posterity credits the husband with the entire achievement. Masculine ascendancy was the default assumption of tourists, even in the face of spectacular evidence to the contrary. It was Lady Leicester's inheritance that helped her husband to start work on Holkham in 1729, and her administration that ensured that work continued long after his death. But when Arthur Young visited in 1768, he saw Holkham as entirely the work of her husband: 'the celebrated house of the Countess of *Leicester*, built by the late Earl'.[10] Architecture was so quintessentially masculine a prerogative that if women built then another mantle had to be flourished – such as family loyalty or unusual refinement.

Given the subterfuges of wives, and the circumscribed nature of married women's property even in the more flexible courts of equity, it is unsurprising that the ladies who left an indelible architectural mark were heiresses or widows. Mary Blount (d. 1773), Duchess of Norfolk, wife of the ninth Duke, was a co-heiress, the moving force behind the building of Norfolk House and the unfinished palace of Worksop in Nottinghamshire. In a revealing quip General Conway reported that the duke and duchess were considering digging a lake:

'The Duke does not positively know whether he shall do it or not, but the Duchess does and says "My Lord Duke intends to do it very soon." I fancy she is in the right.'[11] The female patrons that do emerge in tourist guides and biographies are presented as peculiar: strong-minded, exquisite or eccentric. Given the vagaries of the Georgian demographic regime, however, heiresses and widows were common amongst the nobility. Perhaps as many as a third of all family seats came to women, or passed down the female line in the later eighteenth century, an era when the average nobleman married aged about 33 to a much younger bride, an age gap that tended to produce active widows and long minorities.[12] Hence Linda Colley regrets the connoisseurial close focus on one or two lady patrons as exempla of an unusual degree of aesthetic refinement. Instead, she urges that we register the broader context: that female access to family funds, ideas and autonomy was normal for a large minority of the patriciate.[13]

Unlike the French nobility, who saved their glare for Paris, the British placed political importance on the possession of an ancestral provincial seat. Nestled amidst lucrative broad acres, the country house was a hub of power in the county and a radiator of authority. Building activity peaked in the 1720s and '70s, but dwindled with the French wars, recovering in the 1820s.[14] Early eighteenth-century edifices were massive in scale and heroic in display. John Vanbrugh promised his clients 'a very Noble and Masculine Shew'. The mightiest Whig politicians like the Duke of Devonshire at Chatsworth and the Earl of Carlisle at Castle Howard proclaimed their hegemony in stone, though perhaps the most notorious declaration of power was Houghton in Norfolk, Sir Robert Walpole's Palladian pile, which had an interior of such ornate monumentalism by William Kent that even his contemporaries considered it gross. Themes of interior decoration included national glories, the power of a Protestant monarchy or the virtues of the Catholic pretenders; political affiliation; the antique and Neoclassicism, antiquarianism and olden times; allegories of the virtues, triumphs and personalities of the owners; and the history and lineage of the family. How far political allegiance was expressed in architectural style is obscure. The great Whig magnates favoured the Palladian, as did the Protestant ascendancy in Ireland, but whether Tory patronage of the Rococo was deliberate enough to constitute an opposition aesthetic is questionable. Possibly, romantic loyalty to the old Stuart cause inclined Tories towards the aesthetics of France, but evidence for a coherent stylistic agenda is lacking. Tories and even known Jacobites subscribed in numbers to the Palladian bible *Vitruvius Britannicus*; plenty of Palladian houses had interiors of riotous Rococo; and even actively Whig architects like John Carr of York worked for Tory customers.[15]

Diversions from classical orthodoxy were attacked by the doctrinaire as proof of effeminacy and ill breeding. The corresponding thesis that ladies were aller-

30   *Frederick Elegantly Furnishing a Large House*, 1786, printed engraving. Lewis Walpole
Library, Farmington, CT, 786.0.36. Dating from the period when George, Prince of Wales was
spending ruinously to furnish Carlton House, London, in a magnificent style, this engraving
portrays a young nobleman commanding the fitting out of a grand house, watched approvingly
by a fashionably dressed woman.

gic to classical formalism is unsubstantiated, however, though women were often
vocal on the freezing inconveniences of staterooms, whether Palladian or
Baroque. In any case, Chinese wallpaper, porcelain, Indian chintz and French
silks that ignored symmetry, proportion and perspective were all to be found
within classical mansions commissioned by men, while an irregular landscape
park of serpentine paths encircled many a Palladian box. At mid-century the
tide of architectural fashion was turning against the monumental 'houses of parade' in favour of exquisite villas, with a corresponding reduction in opulent
decor in favour of a more delicate, though no less costly, elegance in interiors.[16]

The creation and re-creation of great houses were tied to the fortunes of the dynasty, and the embellishing of interiors was understood as an exercise in family
prestige. The customers of leading gold and silversmiths Parker and Wakelin were
almost all rich noblemen with incomes of at least £10,000. Majority, marriage
and full inheritance were celebrated in big commissions. By contrast, only 37 of
the 321 clients in Parker and Wakelin's gentleman's ledger for 1766–76 were women,
buying mostly small tea wares.[17] Where the dynastic continuity of the family was
at stake, men were expected to consume lavishly (fig. 30). A preoccupation with

status and dynasty, however, was hardly uniquely male. Brides of rank were keen to boast of their own illustrious ancestors. Ladies who perpetuated the blood of the Plantagenets, the Howards or the Percys tended never to forget it. Wives were typically ferocious for the family onto which they were grafted, corporate loyalty made flesh, and there was scarce a matron alive who would not bestir herself to promote her progeny. Jane, Duchess of Gordon, who had married off her daughters to three dukes, a marquess and a baronet, had her son-in-laws' titles triumphantly carved into her tombstone. Nor was an obsession with lineage confined to parents. Childless nobles tended to groom a favourite nephew who was singled out to inherit. Marrying inheriting daughters off to second cousins and discovering distant nephews were routine strategies in the face of the elite demographic crisis. Only 'heroic measures of adoptive name-changing' sustained the fiction of uninterrupted descent. A study of the Nottinghamshire landed shows that investment in nieces, nephews and young cousins was customary for the childless, and consequently how common it was for younger children to receive a supplementary legacy from wider kin, offsetting the extreme imbalances of primogeniture. 'There is generally an uncle or a grandfather to leave a fortune to the second son', as Jane Austen's Mary Crawford calculated.[18]

Principal heiresses were proud that it was they who preserved the name and bloodline, and many were driven by filial duty and fierce pride to memorialise the lineage. Renewing medieval castles after the Civil War was a passionate declaration about the roots and survival of the dynasty for some Royalist women, and a defiant archaism when classical symmetry was in the ascendant. Affection for antique features such as stained glass survived in the teeth of the Palladian revolution. Lady Betty Germain was admired for the 'religion' with which she kept up the traditions at Drayton House, Northamptonshire, in 1763: 'It is covered with portraits, crammed with old china, furnished richly and not a rag in it under forty, fifty, or a thousand years old.'[19] Curator of house and family history was a role that many a châtelaine took on with messianic devotion – just as well, because the mistresses of great houses had no choice but to deal with a galaxy of heirlooms that they were obliged to convey intact to their sons and grandsons.

Katherine Windham (1652–1729) of Felbrigg in Norfolk was a doughty dowager who expected her son and heir Ashe (1673–1749) to follow her advice on most matters, from mohair to matrimony, despite his Eton and Cambridge schooling, French tutor, Grand Tour, academic studies and Whig politics. Heiress to a rich Twickenham merchant, Mrs Windham shared the cost and oversight of their new orangery, writing to Ashe in February 1705: 'I design to find sashes, workmanship, shutters, doors, pavement for the orange house, you to find bricke, lime, timber, tile and carriage', and noting in her account-book of 1707: 'My son laid out on my account for ye Orange House £261 16s 11d'. Mrs Windham was sturdy on women's duties, praising wives who kept 'a very regular orderly family'. She oversaw the improvements on the Jacobean house while her son enjoyed his London house in Soho Square. As Ashe prepared in 1708 to marry Hester Buckworth, the daughter of an opulent London merchant, Katherine tried to limit the diamonds he gave as betrothal gifts: 'Consider what expensive things you have to do, yr selfe is jewel enough.' She worried that Ashe was beggaring the patrimony to fund his gestures: 'you act a most improper part with a small fortune to make an unreasonable joynture, & too great presents, when your house will nesserarally need so much'. Nevertheless, Mrs Windham hired Braxted Lodge in Essex, 'a large new built house', as a dower house, to make way for her daughter-in-law. Hester's abrupt death from smallpox catapulted Ashe into a doomed marriage to the melancholy heiress of a Chancery lawyer. When they separated in 1717, old Mrs Windham returned to Felbrigg to run the house until her death in 1729.[20] The country seat was a badge of ancestry that women were proud to burnish.

Splendid aristocratic town houses were an early Stuart innovation, but after 1688 they became indispensable to noble status. The new regime saw longer sittings of Parliament; the increasing prominence of cultural venues rivalling the court in glamour, like the opera and the pleasure garden; the elaboration of the London season from November to May; the consolidation of a national aristocratic marriage market in the metropolis; and the materialisation of the world of high society, encapsulated in the nebulous, but compelling, idea of the 'beau monde', itself gaining currency from the 1690s. A palatial town house was an essential camp from which to mount an assault on the higher reaches of fashion. Ladies were to the fore in the status displays by which membership was confirmed, coruscating in diamonds and silks at court, and centre stage as hostess of lavish parties at home: town house ablaze with costly wax candles, curtains drawn back as across the proscenium arch to reveal the tableau to the street.[21]

The spatial demands of great receptions inspired the building of large saloons ('We see an addition of a great room now to almost every house of consequence', Isaac Ware warned aspiring architects in 1756) and hastened the decline of the enfilade – a hierarchical succession of staterooms that enforced status and was impossible to short circuit.[22] Mark Girouard charts the rise from the 1720s of 'the social house', where an elegant set of rooms circled around a central staircase, and a variety of entertainments could take place simultaneously. The new arrangement was epitomised by Norfolk House (1748–52) in St James's Square, London

31　*A View of St James's Square, London*, 1753, printed engraving. Guildhall Library, London, p5405581. Norfolk House, built between 1748 and 1752, dominates the square on the far right.

(fig. 31). The first floor housed the Duchess of Norfolk's state bedchamber and a dressing room, but also an ante-room, a music room, two reception rooms and a great room, creating a circuit around the grand stair. 'All the earth was there', crowed Horace Walpole about the opening assembly in 1756. The confident duchess greeted her guests in the dazzling white and gold music room at the front like a sentry, while her shyer spouse received guests in the panelled state-room at the back. Patriarchy and personality were both satisfied by this arrangement, though, as Lord Rockingham joked, 'Oh! There was all the company afraid of the Duchess, and the Duke afraid of all the company.'[23]

The *palazzi* of Georgian London came to rival those of Paris.[24] Nevertheless, the leased terraced house sufficed for a surprising number of peers, while up-market lodging for the season was a common solution for those without funds for two establishments. Meanwhile, some nobles chose to have their chief, even only, residence in London. Dowagers were expected to quit the seat on the majority of the heir, retreating to a dower house nearby, or a house in London. Among the first occupants of Grosvenor Square were six noble dowagers, and four in Grosvenor Street. Good manners dictated that if a widow wanted to create a showy new house, then she did so in town, to ensure no upstaging of the new mistress.[25]

The spectacular power of the great house is an ancient trope. Aristotle argued that it behoved the nobility to display a magnificence appropriate to their rank. Georgian architectural treatises were built on Vitruvius' rule of decorum that held that houses should be adapted to the roles of the different classes in society, and that surroundings should reflect status and function. If anything, Georgian pundits were even more insistent that decorum was intrinsic to decor, exhorting readers to furnish in ways that demonstrated rank to avoid any misconceptions.[26] Ladies were not to dress or decorate above their station, but nor were they to descend in manners or modes from their eminence, for in so doing they undermined respect for rank and brought the whole social edifice into jeopardy. They were fully implicated in what E. P. Thompson called 'the theatre of power', so crucial to the maintenance of a deferential society.[27] In Georgian terms, ladies were not exempt from the obligations of splendour. Having fewer supports to their status than their men, ladies could be even more preoccupied with ostentation. The material and spatial requirements of rank were issues of painful sensitivity to noblewomen who were downwardly mobile, strapped for cash or socially exposed.

The correspondence relating to the separation of the third Duke of Grafton from his first wife, Anne, in 1764–5, charts a frantic mission to create and equip an establishment appropriate to the dignity of an estranged duchess (pls 12 and 13). Only the Wilton carpets, the letters imply, will save Anne, Duchess of Grafton from social eclipse. After Westminster School, Peterhouse and the Grand Tour, Augustus Henry Fitzroy, Earl of Euston (1735–1811), entered Parliament for the Whigs in 1756 aged just 21. In the same year, he married the 18-year-old Hon. Anne Liddell (*circa* 1738–1804), daughter of the first Baron Ravensworth, who brought him £40,000 and the promise of her mother's fortune on the death of the Ravensworths. Fitzroy inherited the dukedom the following year, and took possession of Euston Hall, his Suffolk seat, recently remodelled in the Palladian manner by Matthew Brettingham (fig. 32). In 1768–70, in his early 30s, the duke would serve briefly as prime minister. An alliance of fortune and family, arranged by the fathers, the Grafton marriage was also reported to be a love match. The couple went on to have five children together, of whom three survived. But marital friction was a matter of society gossip by the 1760s: the duke was attached only to horse racing, fox-hunting and womanising, and already the father of a bastard, while the duchess solaced herself in parties and cards. Horace Walpole, their mutual friend, offered an astute account of the deterioration of their relationship: 'The Duchess, a woman of commanding figure, though no regular beauty, graceful. Full of dignity and of art too, passionate for admiration, unbending to the Duke's temper . . . had yet thought to govern him by spirit, and had lost him before she was aware.'[28] In the autumn of 1764, after nine years of

32 'Euston Hall', from John Preston Neale, *Views of the Seats of Noblemen and Gentlemen in England, Wales, Scotland, and Ireland*, vol. 4 (London, 1821). The Suffolk house of the Duke and Duchess of Grafton, as remodelled by Matthew Brettingham in the 1750s.

marriage, Anne, Duchess of Grafton fled Euston Hall, taking refuge with her parents in Northumberland, though whether she was absolutely driven out by her husband, or took flight in precipitate misery, is unclear. It was barely four months since the birth of her last son, but years of quarrelling preceded the breach. By her own admission, Anne had been an intolerant wife, but she was not the first to desert the hearth, she appealed, citing the duke's 'Gaming & going constantly to Arthur's', in consequence of which 'I found myself night after Night alone, this hurt me & I sought amusements abroad (a wrong step I acknowledge)'. The duchess was poised to renounce all public life if only the duke would relent: 'if I come *home* once more I shall be no longer a *Woman of the World*, but employ my whole thoughts at home'.[29] Her vow of domesticity was as unavailing as it was unconvincing.

At first the letters are a wailing record of the duchess's remorse and yearning for reconciliation, understandably so, because the outlook of an absconding spouse was dire: 'no *home* to go to, & not one Moments ease of mind, I cannot shed a Tear'. The Ravensworths insisted that Anne sought no separation, and her father was adamant: 'if lawyers are to be consulted it must be stressed that we do not part by mutual consent and that I am very willing to live with you and do my best'.[30] As rumours about the duke's ulterior motives began to circulate, the duchess grew more remonstrative, though her criticisms were reported as originating elsewhere: 'I have had a foolish letter to say *no Husband had a right to force his wife out of the House & that I was a fool to consent as no crime was alleged.*' As a fugitive, the Duchess of Grafton had compromised her reputation, drawing suspicion and opprobrium on herself. Anne's father was even more far-sighted, concluding: '*you have freed the D of G to turn you out of His House & to live with a Woman of the Town*'.[31] Sure enough, the serially unfaithful duke was soon living openly with Anne Parsons, alias Mrs Houghton, who was notorious for her liaisons. To add caustic insult to injury, the duke reportedly installed his gorgeous mistress in 'the Dutchesses rooms' freshly hung with damask, had her preside at 'the head of his table', 'fitted up her House in the Richest way', and took her about in society dripping with diamonds.[32]

Panicked and humiliated, the duchess scrambled to establish herself in a manner supportive of her dignity. This was no idle snobbery. Wits might joke about 'the great Inconveniency of being a Dutchess: the trouble of a Coach & six; the Emptyness of Pomp & the Vanity of a Coronet', but the title was nothing without the dazzle. 'Remember that Nobility stript of Means, makes no genteel Figure', warned instructions for noblemen, 'it cannot stand without golden Supporters.'[33] Ornaments of fortune and rank were esteemed to a degree that contemporary democrats might find impossible to credit. Credence was extended everywhere on the basis of external signs of rank. They were crucial to offset the calumny the duchess had drawn on herself, her children and especially her daughter, for the reputations of girls depended on the conduct of their parents. As Mrs Delany observed in another divorce case, 'it is injustice, but . . . who will venture on the daughter, when the mother has proved such a wife?'[34]

It was imperative that the duchess retain the appearance of her husband's protection. She appealed to his mercy and threw the question of her children's accommodation on his conscience: 'I don't know where I shall turn mine or my Poor Children's Steps when my Father orders me to Town.'[35] A financial settlement was vital. Her friends urged that her annuity should be equal to her jointure at £3,000 a year, with an additional allowance of '150 or 200 per annum' for the maintenance of the children, and a lump sum to enable her to 'provide an Equipage and furnish a house & c'. The duke's intermediary, Henry Seymour Conway, a celebrated general, statesman and family man, did not find the duchess's demands unreasonable, believing her party motivated by 'only a General Desire & Expectation of what is for her Honour & suit the rank she is in'. Even over her diamonds Anne was surprisingly negotiable:

The affair of her Jewels, what are called Paraphernalia & several little things that may be supposed to be particularly her own, or for her most immediate Convenience, were also mentioned between us as Allowances usual on such Occasions; but I think this Disposition was rather to leave such articles chiefly to your Grace's Arbitration & Inclination.

Conway acknowledged that £3,000 per annum was 'a great proportion of your Grace's income', but that 'anything less, unless any Charge had been laid [against] her Grace, would not be for her honour, nor I think for yours'.[36] Public opinion held that the duke behaved well, 'with the utmost decency and politeness', pronounced the *Town and Country Magazine*, though, in truth, he had no case against his wife, as Conway stressed. In his farewell to the duchess, the duke claimed: 'That you should not suffer in the opinion of the world had been my endeavour, whatever were my private sensations.'[37]

On 11 January 1765 the deed of private separation was signed. The duke ordered his eldest son (aged only four) to be sent to Anne's mother, Lady Ravensworth, but permitted her to keep the two youngest, a concession that Walpole thought 'noble and generous'.[38] The duke agreed the liberal annuity, as well as £150 per annum for the children, in return for his wife's jewels as security. The loss of her son was dreadful. The renunciation of her personal jewels was also a social defeat, given the importance of diamonds to elite readings of connection. Alliances were advertised in borrowed jewels, and family support in the blazoning of ancestral stones. Probably the duchess had left the Grafton jewels behind on quitting Euston, but to give up her own diamonds as well gave her little equipment with which to make a show. The lack of flash advertised her social exclusion and the deficiency reinforced the ostracism. When the Duke of Beaufort married one of Admiral Boscawen's daughters in 1766, his mother's disapproval was the talk of the town: 'The young duchess had no jewels but a pair of diamond earrings, presented to her by the Duke's uncle', reported the Duchess of Northumberland.[39] For Anne, Duchess of Grafton some bravery of trappings was necessary in the glare of the mistress's finery. Even Anne's grandmother heard the duke 'kept a mistress who was dressd much better & had more jewels than I had'.[40] Perhaps the Duke of Grafton hoped to rusticate his inconvenient wife. Certainly, he refused point blank to 'pay down 1,000 £ or more for equipage', preferring to give some of his own furniture, rather than part with more cash. Despite her plea, 'do not make me send a list of what I would wish to have', the duke refused to declare what he thought proper, so she was forced to itemise her wants, wheedling proper furnishings by letter in a humiliating inventory.[41]

Estranged and slighted, striking camp in London was a courageous step, provincial seclusion or exile being conventional responses. High-spirited and handsome (Walpole likened her to Marie-Antoinette in looks), the duchess had more self-importance than most, but her desire for a stylish separate establishment was not unparalleled. When Henrietta Knight was banished to Barrels, the Warwickshire estate, by her husband in the 1740s, she transformed the house and grounds into her 'Arcadia', drawing visitors to testify to her taste in exile. When the Duchess of Kent agreed with her husband's heirs to give up her house in St James's Square in 1742, she asked for an annual income and £1,000 'towards furnishing another house' in town.[42] A lack of conviction about what was owing to their birth and consequence is not something of which noblewomen could be accused.

The temporary base of the Duchess of Grafton was to be in St James's Square, until she took lodgings from another nobleman, for which she claimed she needed at least three live-in menservants, and eventually hired a housekeeper, cook, housemaid, laundry maid, kitchen and a chambermaid. She would forego a sedan chair and chairman, but insisted on a carriage and four horses, without it 'yr children will have no means of getting fresh air'. A crested carriage was a crucial status symbol. If the duke refused her the landau, but offered a post coach instead, she would 'have it new painted & spruced up immediately'. In a deceptively casual enquiry she asked whether she should 'give Liveries the same as yours' to her menservants, for 'some sort must be orderd on my coming to Town', yet again this was no detail. The Grafton livery, like the coach with the ducal coronet, was a patent proof that she was Her Grace, the Duchess of Grafton, still. Anne had no intention of divorcing herself from the family into which she had married. Once in London, the duchess promptly called on all the Grafton kin, reporting 'great marks of attention from them'. Discarded and yet dangling, she assiduously avoided antagonising the duke, all the while asserting that in matters of dignity and form she would not easily be turned aside.[43] Anne reported that her parents felt she might even go to court occasionally. All of which evidences the strenuousness of her effort to retain the duke's goodwill, but also her resolve to uphold her status and connections.

The Duchess of Grafton's rented house was 'neat & in an airy situation though small', yet still included a coach house and stables. She asked for nothing but servants, landau and horses from the ancestral seat, Euston Hall. However, she requested an array of 'furniture, plate and linen' from their London house on Bond Street to bolster her uncertain future. In one letter she asked for her dressing table, writing table, book shelves and harpsichord, a collection of objects associated with female elegance at home; in another, she requested 'a *Cabinet some Conveniences for Cloaths . . . two tables, the shelves for books, & the Clock*', as well as '7 dinner & 7 Breakfast cloths & two pr of sheets to each bed', though insisting 'I must buy 7 more of each'. Anne sent an inventory of the plate she wanted, hoped to have pewter from Cleveland court, and wondered whether she could have the chairs from the Blue Room in Bond Street, since the current set were 'most beastly'. Permission must have been refused, because she later ordered the chairs recovered. Having nothing but 'an old dirty Turkey' on the sitting-room floor, she hoped to have 'that which is ye India Paper room in Bond street, [if] it could be made to fit I shoud be glad to have it'. If not, then 'I will order a new Wilton one for that room.' Tea, 'China, Candles & c & other things for immediate use' she got off the old factotum Dutoit. In a naked bid for sympathy, she begged also 'to be allowed a print of you & your Picture which is in ye Blue room'.[44] The duchess was determined to retain tangible proofs that she still enjoyed the protection of the ducal mantle, the accoutrements of nobility (the coach and the liveries) and a town house furnished to demonstrate that she had not been degraded. The full regalia of rank were testimony that she had not sacrificed her honour by some criminal act, or derogated from the rank of duchess, but they were also crucial to the retention of her footing in fashionable society.

It was impossible that a rejected duchess should march out undiminished in the full pomp of rank. She was 'Her Grace' in limbo, reported out and about at balls, in her box at the opera, at the play and 'in ruge' at church, a scandal waiting to happen. ''Tis certain the Duchess likes lovers, tho' I don't believe she means to do anything wrong', noted society observers.[45] Purgatory was short-lived. Meeting the amiable 22-year-old Earl of Ossory at Brighton in the summer of 1767, she embarked on an affair, and falling pregnant gave the Duke of Grafton the grounds to divorce her at last. At the birth of a bastard, the duke removed his remaining children from their mother's custody, the duchess saying farewell from her lying-in bed. The marriage was declared null and void by Act of Parliament in March 1769, the duchess deciding not to recriminate with counter evidence of the duke's adulteries, in return for a settlement of £2,000 a year. The divorced couple returned each other's pictures. The duchess was stripped of title and coronet, a humiliation 'which is most grievous', 'a heartbreaking circumstance', and denied all access to her Grafton children, 'the loss of whom I can never forget'.[46] Her social limbo, however, was at end. Two weeks later, the divorcée married the Earl of Ossory. The Duke of Grafton became the first prime minister divorced while in office. He pensioned off his mistress, and married the daughter of a baronet.

Once she lost her children and withdrew to Ossory's mansion in Bedfordshire, the ex-duchess seemed to lose her energy for London society. In any case, doors were now closed against her. There was head-shaking over her 'bad conduct', annoyance that she 'never looked better', melancholy muttering from the king about whether adulterous ladies should be permitted to marry again, and even her friends 'had no thought of bringing her to court'.[47] Grafton carried his vengeance so far as to block Ossory's attempt to become ambassador to Spain, an embassy that would have given the couple a new lease on fashion abroad. Ampthill became Anne's base *faute de mieux*. From here, the countess presided over a new family, amateur theatricals and made a tambour-work waistcoat for a fawning Joshua Reynolds, who painted her daughters.[48] Having regained legitimate male protection, the security of a country mansion and an unequivocal importance, albeit much reduced, perhaps she felt no further need for metropolitan battle array. Buried in Bedfordshire in 1804, estranged from her parents, forbidden to see her three Grafton children, perhaps at last Anne lowered her proud head in shame.

Magnificence was a parade of wealth in support of the hierarchical order, but in its classical meaning magnificence was also understood as a visible demonstration of morality and nobility of mind. In the 1500s architecture was the exclusive preserve of a coterie of humanists. Elizabethan great houses made a show of greatness in portraits, fine tapestries, sculptures and natural curiosities – though heraldry and didacticism were the dominant themes of ornament. The 1600s saw a decline in the profusion of heraldic references; rooms once named for a noble ally came to be known by their decoration. Meanwhile, a handful of paintings expanded into full-blown collections: portraits of ancestors and monarchs, supplemented by mythical subjects and landscapes expressing the alliances, affinities and discrimination of the owner. For Nicholas Cooper this reflects 'a willingness to see the interior of the house as less the public expression of the owner's virtues than the personal indulgence of his taste'. By the 1670s the antique had become an altogether conventional interest of nobility, and a flair for architecture just another aspect of the erudition of the complete gentleman.[49]

Classical learning had long been the bedrock of the educational curriculum for noblemen, but it was the Grand Tour (the term was coined by Richard Lassels in 1670) that entrenched the cultural parameters of the English ruling classes between the Restoration and the Regency. The early tourists headed for Rome via France, guidebook and tutor on hand, some detouring to Germany and the Low Countries, though by the 1750s the freshly excavated sites of Herculaneum (discovered in 1738) and Pompeii (discovered in 1748) promised unmediated access to classical truth.[50] The institutionalised pilgrimage of the juvenile lords had no counterpart for young ladies, for whom an education in Latin and Greek was unusual. Modern languages, however, were the female forte, and Continental travel *en famille*, or with their young husbands, was common for the super-rich. The grammar of the inheritors was married to a lightly worn knowledge of classical myth and allusion in their wives, such that both could read at a glance the references of any ornamental interior scheme. Viewing each other's improvements and trophies became customary amongst the cognoscenti. Meanwhile, the practice of opening country houses to visitors enabled thousands of genteel domestic tourists to experience the tour at one remove. The country house tour became an exercise in the finishing of genteel girls, recorded in the inevitable travel journal. Prints of fine houses and illustrated architectural catalogues whetted the appetite, while county maps identified the seats of nobles and gentry, representing mansions as the ornaments of the county. At least twenty visitor guides to the nation's country houses were published between 1760 and 1840. All this created the conviction that great houses were temples to the superiorities of aristocratic taste and civilisation.

Taste was a compelling new concept that emerged in seventeenth-century France, but was reworked in English philosophy around 1700 to help defend aesthetic discernment from the swamping of luxury. Taste was taken up in courtesy literature as one of the defining attributes of the well born and well bred. The theory of good breeding was built on the classical rule of decorum, which decreed that behaviour should vary according to one's place in society. Polite manners also married with the Neoclassical aesthetic ideals of order, proportion and harmony, ideals that also took decorum as their touchstone. The concept, however, was not without its ambiguities for social hierarchy. Since taste was a faculty built on the absorption of underlying rules, in principle any good student could learn it, but only years of practice and cultivation could ensure a proper level of judiciousness. The mastery of taste depended on a proper education, good company, leisure, travel and wealth. 'No-one can be properly stil'd a gentleman, who takes not every opportunity to enrich his own capacity and settle the elements of taste.'[51] There would always be aristocrats who were dull students (George I was 'void of taste' according to Horace Walpole), outshone by pretenders who seemed to have conjured an expertise from thin air. Nevertheless, the capacity to claim good taste was built on the privileges of rank. In a circular argument, courtesy literature agreed that good taste confirmed the good breeding of the elite, who themselves set the canons of good taste; the 'standard of taste thus both was defined by and itself defined membership of a cultured social elite'.[52] Hence elite women were fully implicated in the project. The innate good taste of gentlewomen revealed their blue blood as unerringly as any pedigree, claimed Jeremy Collier. 'Indeed they have a great Delicacy and Exactness in their Fancy: They pitch upon nothing that is Tawdry or Mechanick, Staring or ill Matched. One may know a gentlewoman almost, as well by seeing her chuse a Mantua, or a Ribbon; as by going to *Garter*, or *Clarencieux*.'[53] Of course, there were some experts (like Joshua Reynolds) who would argue that women lacked the mental capacity to discriminate; but most courtesy writers stressed the equal faculties of the sexes based on their good breeding – thereby presenting women with a fresh rhetorical opportunity.

A case study of the brief marriage of the Earl and Countess of Shelburne, from 1765 to 1771, based on the countess's diaries, reveals the extent to which palatial houses functioned not only as demonstrations of social position, but also as platforms for an enlightened interest in nature, history, ingenuity and curiosity, and further how far their creation could be a development of matrimonial harmony. Lady Sophia Carteret (1745–1771) married William Petty (1737–1805), second Earl of Shelburne and later first Marquis of Lansdowne, in a small private ceremony in St James's Chapel in London, on 5 February 1765 (pls 14 and 15). The 28-year-old earl was an austerely impressive groom. Though hardly dashing, he had already distinguished himself as a soldier in the Seven Years War, had been elected MP for Wycombe, represented County Kerry for the Irish Parliament in 1761, and had been briefly a member of George III's Cabinet and President of the Board of Trade. Blessed with lucrative estates in Ireland, and an income reputed to be about £22,000 a year,[54] the aspiring earl was busy modernising Bowood, his Wiltshire seat, employing Capability Brown to remodel the park and Robert Adam to enlarge the house. A blue-blooded bride was the one thing needful to add the coping stone to his edifice. Grave, thoroughly concerned with Enlightenment debates and ambitious for political office, Shelburne allowed his mother to arrange the match with the grandmother of the orphaned heiress.[55] It was a propitious alliance: the bride was the daughter of an earl, connected at court, with a fortune of £30,000 and estates in and around Bath.

Miraculously, the marriage proved a supremely tender union, characterised by studied courtesies and shared projects, recorded at length in young Lady Shelburne's manuscript diaries. Lord Shelburne's childhood had been grim, an epoch of 'domestic brutality and ill-usage' at the hands of his tyrannical grandfather, the first Earl of Kerry, and his father, who had 'no notion of governing his children except by fear'.[56] Doubtless wretched memories of his 'detestable' home fuelled Shelburne's careful cultivation of affectionate manners. At Sophia's first lying-in, the relieved earl promised £1,000 to William Hunter's anatomical school, in gratitude for the delivery of his son and the safety of his wife. At her sudden death in January 1771, aged only 25, William was said to be crushed. Suspending building and abandoning Whig politics, the stricken earl left the country, going to Italy for seven months to get a grip on his grief. Sophia appears the gentle Roman matron in her monument by Carlini in Wycombe church, 'Her Price was far Above Rubies' carved in the marble.

33 *Lansdowne House, Berkeley Square*, 1808, printed engraving. Guildhall Library, London, p542329x. The London house of Lord and Lady Shelburne, designed by Robert Adam and built between 1762 and 1768.

For all the sweetness of the Shelburnes' brief marriage, their domestic life had an invincibly patrician character – ever on the move between Bowood, Wycombe and London with a train of servants, tutors and companions like an army on campaign, or a royal progress, their movements dictated by the earl's political obligations and the countess's court calendar, their household routines structured by formality and the demands of official entertainment. In 1763 Shelburne was First Lord of Trade, and between 1766 and 1768 Secretary of State for Southern affairs, under Grafton's premiership. Consequently, their houses were great political engine rooms thronging with flunkies and dignitaries, built for public life. Shelburne House on Berkeley Square, bought half-finished from Lord Bute in 1765, was conceived as a venue for state business (fig. 33). In 1768 Lady Shelburne noted that it was still too unfinished for the King of Denmark to be asked to dinner. In 1783, so legend has it, Lord Shelburne drafted the peace treaties with America in the round room there.[57] Their dining room, now reconstructed at the Metropolitan Museum in New York, is an austere Neoclassical chamber encircled by a praetorian guard of marble statues, befitting a conclave of the great Whig leaders of the new Rome.

Such palaces had a titanic social capacity. The *London Chronicle* noted 1,500 people of distinction at a reception at Northumberland House in 1764, while 700 guests enjoyed breakfast at Mrs Montagu's house on its gala opening. 'The croud was so great', found Lady Mary Coke at one of Lady Shelburne's assemblies in 1767, 'it wou'd have been disagreeable in Winter, & the fifteenth of May intolerable.'[58] Even in the same house, the Shelburnes often communicated by notes and messages delivered via the servants, and the countess reported the earl making her 'a visit' at various times of day. Aristocratic domestic life had little of the Darby and Joan cosiness conjured by the word 'domesticity'. In December 1766 Shelburne was hosting a state reception at home in London, while his wife was bedecking herself for the Birthday court: 'Just as I was dress'd my lord sent up to tell me the morocco Ambassador was with him & that if I chose to see him I might come into his room . . . As I was very fine in my beautiful stuffs & jewel my dress was a sight to them.' Conjugal intimacy was contrived in the midst of blinding publicity, as if in the West Wing of the contemporary White House. Many matrimonial gestures were performed before witnesses. Lady Shelburne noted episodes of seclusion or relaxations of ceremony as rare pleasures, as when they 'spent the whole evening Tete a Tete in my dressing room writing letters & talking', or when 'I was order'd to keep in bed the whole day & my Lord was so good to come to me perpetually & to do a great deal of his business in my room till seven oth clock at night when he went to a council.' Only once in the diary did she recount something approaching the married routine of the richer gentry, and this during the parliamentary recess and when pregnancy authorised a social retreat, in the summer of 1768 at Bowood: 'Nothing can be more comfortable than we have hitherto been My Lord & I are quite alone here.' With their first son back from the wet nurse and getting to know his parents, they enjoyed a regime of early nights, daily conjugal walks and occasional drives in the cabriolet, 'after which we separate & follow our own occupations till Meals or Candlelight when we sit together he reads and I work'.[59] In the interstices of aristocratic public life, they crafted a mannered but supremely tender domesticity.

While few noble families sired a prime minister (Shelburne's ministry lasted eight months in 1782–3), the Shelburnes were not freakishly formal in their life at home. The inhospitable grandeur of great houses, combined with the chilly ceremony and relentless exposure of the daily round within them, were routine complaints in the letters of ladies. Huge Palladian houses were believed to be especially difficult to live in; after all, what suited the sunshine of the Veneto was ill adapted to the damp of Albion. A search for a comfortable warmth with close family and friends, what Hester Hoare of Stourhead called 'snugitude', surfaces in a host of manuscripts.[60] The rise of the dressing room, bedroom and closet as venues for elegant relaxation was itself a response to the stiff-backed awfulness of staterooms, an antidote to a domestic life 'overcharged with ceremony' (figs 34 and 35).[61] In making her dressing room the venue for matrimonial privacies and social inti-

Dressing Room a l: Anglaise.

34   *Dressing Room à l'Anglaise*, 1789, printed engraving. Lewis Walpole Library, Farmington, CT, 789.4.7.1. The English dressing room is depicted as a site of intimate, but wholesome femininity. The neoclassical wallpaper of repeating stripes and twining foliage frames an unaffected but elegant informality.

Dreßing Room a la Françaiß

35 *Dressing Room à la Française*, 1789, printed engraving. Lewis Walpole Library, Farmington, CT, 789.4.7.2. The French dressing room is depicted as a place for flirtation. The laquerwork cabinet was a typical ornament of ladies' private rooms.

macies, Lady Shelburne was in a venerable tradition. Exquisite 'cabinets' off the main bedroom, exempt from the conventions that governed the principal apartments, were first seen in court circles in seventeenth-century France. These cabinets, or closets in English, were niches for the display of taste, perfect for staging choice novelties – oriental lacquer, shellwork, tea tables and so on. Catherine of Braganza used her closet in Restoration Whitehall as a venue for evening amusement with the king and close associates. By the 1730s well-read ladies, like the daughters of the Duke of Richmond, the Duchess of Portland, Elizabeth Montagu and Mary Delany, championed the dressing room as a deliciously private sitting room in the noble mansion and genteel town house.[62]

The dressing room was the place where earl and countess spent their private evenings at home, where Lord Shelburne withdrew when he felt under the weather, and where Lady Shelburne wrote her letters and read sermons, but it was also the room in which they entertained their closest associates, playing chess, cribbage, reading, showing prints, drawing and playing the guitar. This room was the scene of her first social dinner after the birth of their son, Lord Fitzmaurice, where the countess showed him off '& all his little dress & Cradle which is quilled green satin'.[63] Some ducal dressing rooms were rooms of parade, but in this circle the dressing room was emphatically not a formal room. Nevertheless, they tended to be exquisitely fitted up, often at vast expense. Exempt from the obligations of grandeur, the dressing room lent itself to fantasy and experiment in decoration. Mrs Montagu described her dressing room at Hill Street, London, in 1767 'as really wonderfully pretty . . . just the female of the great room for sweet attractive grace, for le je ne sais quoi it is incomparable'.[64] Lady Shelburne's dressing rooms were ornamented with her growing collection of watercolours, prints and drawings. The ladies' dressing room, as a gorgeous cabinet of curiosities, became a forte of Robert Adam in the 1770s, a specialism that encouraged his subsequent characterisation as a ladies' architect (pl. 16).

Unlike extrovert Whig duchesses or Tory grandees, Lady Shelburne displayed no interest in the scrimmage of electoral politics, though high office was certainly familiar to her. She had grown up at court. Her father, Earl Granville, had been a gentleman of the bedchamber to George I, and held office in successive governments under George II. Yet Lady Shelburne sought no career as a political wife, at least not at county level. While adoring 'My Lord' husband, appreciative of all kindnesses from him, an automatic supporter of all his manoeuvres and an equal sharer in his moral seriousness, she reported little political discussion in her diary and avoided the drudgery of electoral entertaining at Wycombe whenever she could. The countess also enjoyed a high-profile public life independent of her husband. In May 1767, for instance, she went alone to the queen's birthday court in silver stuff and sable, and then in the evening 'my Lord having like the rest of the Ministers a great dinner of Men I dined with Mr Penn & lady Juliana in Spring Garden & went afterwards to the Ball where I danced with the Duke of Bucclugh'. Uninterested in elections, and often independent of him for society, the terrain she occupied with her husband was that of enlightened learning and informed taste. When the couple toured the Surrey house, park and gardens of a Mr Webb in 1769, the owner produced 'some Books of parliamentary business for Lord Shelburne & of Natural History for me'.[65]

The Earl of Shelburne had a conventional interest in the antique, but was remarkable in his consistent patronage of Enlightenment philosophers, perhaps in an attempt to make good what he considered his inadequate education. On his Continental tour in 1771, Shelburne sought out the *philosophes*, and his later circle at Bowood included the young Jeremy Bentham, Joseph Priestley, the chemist and philosopher, and Richard Price, the radical dissenter. It has been suggested that his unformed bride tried to share her husband's intellectualism out of deferential loyalty; but this interpretation seriously underestimates the sophistication of Sophia Carteret's own education.[66] Carteret was raised by her open-minded grandmother Henrietta Louisa, Countess of Pomfret, who hired Mme Le Prince de Beaumont, a French educationalist and émigré governess, to form young Sophia in the 1750s. Conversation, puzzles and creative play were among Le Prince de Beaumont's innovative teaching methods, while her message was a lofty, rational feminism and the moral responsibilities of aristocrats, both female and male. Sophia Carteret appears in one of Le Prince de Beaumont's works as Lady Sensible, and the *Magasin des adolescentes* (*circa* 1759) is dedicated to her. Another formative influence was her aunt, Lady Charlotte Finch, royal governess to the fifteen children of George III, said to train up all connected to her in the path of duty and usefulness.[67] Carteret was no milkmaid; indeed, it may have been Lady Sensible's impeccable credentials along with her Bath estates that made her so winning a candidate in the first place.

Sophia's accomplishments were not just a means to marriage; self-improvement was to be a life-long project, rational domesticity her family mode. For two years, the bride learnt botanical drawing from Georg Ehret, a leading botanical illustrator, who had tutored the cream of aristocratic womanhood. Her careful book of flowers still survives. She collected hot-house plants, planned a suite of hot houses at Wycombe, established a menagerie of exotic birds, took lessons on the guitar, sketched classical details, drew designs for and practised all manner of needlework from tambour to chenille.

Improving leisure with like-minded companions is noted approvingly in her diary, like the spring visit spent 'very happily reading Stillingfleets Tracts', or the

October day at Bowood in 1765 when 'I read a sermon of Tillotsons in ye blue dressing room to Lady Louisa' and showed off her flower drawings. Botany sat easily with devout Anglicanism, and, since nature expressed God's perfect design, could be pursued as a path to piety.[68] A critic of 'superfluous luxury', Lady Shelburne always felt the need to occupy herself productively. 'Having nothing particular to do', she reported on Monday, 13 July 1767, 'I employ'd myself with my embroidery & wrote out the following Opinion of the Antiquarians concerning the spear found by the late lord Shelburne in digging up some ground at Wycombe.' When the Shelburnes found themselves together at home alone or with close companions, the earl read aloud from the likes of Burke's *Sublime and Beautiful* and Hume's *History of England*, while the women sewed, or husband and wife leafed through architectural plans and prints, from Piranesi to views of Herculaneum and Palmyra. Even when Sophia was in labour, as the pains increased and husband and wife nervously awaited the arrival of Dr Hunter, the fashionable *accoucheur*, they looked over their print collection together; architecture and contractions interspersed.[69]

The Shelburnes lived their domestic life as if it were a cultural project. They could be said to be practitioners of what Irene Brown calls Enlightenment domesticity, which esteemed family affection and female friendship, while assuming the equal rational capacities of men and women within a Christian framework. The countess could also be claimed for that which Clarissa Campbell Orr has dubbed the Christian Enlightenment, fostered especially at the court of George III and Queen Charlotte,[70] but apparent in many aristocratic households where domestic learning was encouraged, licentiousness disdained and the sacraments of the Church of England devoutly fulfilled. In fact, the cast of aristocratic characters overlaps in the two different accounts, so probably they are discussing the same phenomenon. Both accounts, however, emphasise the country house as centre and fountain of Enlightenment, though social histories of ideas have typically underplayed the role of noble patrons in a countervailing emphasis on coffee houses and clubs.

First among the aristocratic seats of the Enlightenment must be Bulstrode Park in Buckinghamshire, favourite residence of the scholarly Margaret Cavendish, Duchess of Portland (1715–1785), whose fortune and commitment created something between a museum and a university on her estate. Bulstrode Park boasted a botanic garden, aviary and zoo, while an outpost of her collection, the 'Portland museum', was on show in London. The duchess funded natural history expeditions and drew experts to work alongside her on the collections. Bulstrode was a 'hive', 'a philosophical cabinet' and a 'noble school for contemplations!', and claimed as a model for the bluestocking salons by Elizabeth Montagu. Lady Shelburne had some bluestocking affinities. She was on cordial terms with her father's cousin Mary Delany, whom she watched embroider cloth chair covers in chenille; with the Duchess of Portland, who gave her plants and verses; and with Elizabeth Montagu, who procured 'a Young Woman to teach me to Embroider flowers on Satin'. With its mild learning, constant self-improvement and rational domesticity, Bowood was a satellite of Enlightenment, a lesser moon to the planet Bulstrode.

As a 20-year-old bride, Sophia, Lady Shelburne found herself in building dust from the outset. Just two weeks after the wedding, Robert Adam arrived at Bowood with the plans for the town house that Shelburne intended to build at Hyde Park Corner, though within months he had abandoned this site, having acquired the deeds to the half-built hotel on Berkeley Square, which would become Shelburne House. The massive expenditure, at least £2,000 per annum, laid out on Bowood and Shelburne House ran through the estate account-books, apparently managed by the steward. Lady Shelburne ran only her own personal accounts for clothing, paraphernalia for the babies and small items, paid for directly out of her pin money, as she makes explicit in her diary: 'came to Arlington street with the pin money Lord Shelburne had paid me the day before there I met all my tradespeople & paid almost every bill I have then bespoke childbed Linnen of Mrs More & all the Millinery part of my old Milliner Mrs Quarrington'.[71]

A fragment of Lady Shelburne's account-book for the summer of 1770 reveals her spending on her own account on charity, millinery, gowns, the wages of female servants, children's clothes and some Worcester salad dishes.[72] She reported some personal shopping trips, like her first outing after her confinement to Pall Mall, where she bought a 'Gilt Coral with eight bells' for the baby, and some celebratory teacups and Chelsea coffee cups for herself. The countess is credited with no significant commissions for their three houses. The diaries, however, offer a different perspective on the ledgers and account-books, illuminating both Sophia's growing assertiveness about their decorative choices and the scrupulously matrimonial character of the couple's luxury consumerism.

Marital excursions to factories, workshops and architectural showpieces punctuated their sojourns at Bowood, while a tour à deux of the great London studios, auction houses and showrooms was a characteristic expression of matrimonial unity. As newly-weds, in the spring of 1765, they went on a series of outings to 'Mr West the American painters where we [saw] several portraits & some Historical paintings', 'to look at some Chimney pieces making for Bowood at Carters & to see Mrs Reed's pictures', to see Mr Duval's Collection of pictures where the earl bought a Murillo, to Margasses to see the Reynolds, and to Ince and Mayhew 'ye Cabinet Maker' to give 'plans from Herculaneum & Palmyra for ornaments for a Comode of Yew tree wood inlaid with Holly and Ebony'.[73] Shelburne frequently sent messages from Council asking his wife to meet him to view these prints, or give an opinion on that vase. He was comfortable with the idea of faultless female taste; his excellent grandmother 'furnished several houses', so keeping up their 'style of living' in Ireland, while his beloved aunt Arabella Denny was remarkable for the 'elegance of her house'.[74] By reputation, Shelburne was constitutionally indecisive. A political subordinate noted that 'he was never satisfied with what anyone did, or even with what he did himself but altered and changed without end'. Harris argues that Shelburne's vacillation extended to his building projects.[75] Possibly, then, the earl sought to know his own mind by conferring with his well-educated, adoring wife, or perhaps her opinions prevailed when he wavered. What is beyond question is that the life they were building together was to be beautified with objects they had selected in concert and discussed ad nauseam:

> . . . we went first to Zucchi's, where we saw some ornaments for our Ceilings, and a large Architecture painting for ye Ante-chamber, with wch however, my Lord is not particularly pleas'd – From thence to Mayhew and Inch [Ince] where is some beautiful Cabinet work and two pretty Glass cases for one of ye rooms in my Appartment & which tho they are only deal & to be painted white he charges £50 for. From thence to Cipriani's where we saw some beautifull drawings & where Lord Shelburne bespoke some to be copied for me, to compleat my dressing room wch I wish shoud be furnish'd with Drawings & Crayon *Pictures*. From thence to Zuccarelli's where we also saw some large pictures doing for us – & from thence home it being half past four.[76]

It is possible that the countess exaggerated her intimacy with the solemn statesman, yet independent commentary confirms the diary's portrait of courteous matrimony and a mutual interest in craftsmanship (fig. 36). Visiting Shelburne House with his wares in the early 1770s, the manufacturer Matthew Boulton sat an hour with Lord Shelburne in his library, when

> Lady Shelburne sent a message desireing that she might come down but as she was ill of a putrid soar throat my lord desired she would not & therefore wishd she could have a few of my pretty things in her room to amuse her. I therefore took Coach & fetched a Load for her & sat with her ladyship two hours explaining & hearing her Criticisms.[77]

Since leading craftsmen waited on aristocratic customers at home, deference to the opinions of their gracious hostess could not fail to be a customary part of the business.

36   Trade card of Christopher Gibson, upholsterer, St Paul's Churchyard, London, 1730–45, etching. Victoria and Albert Museum, London, 14435:60. The card depicts the interior of an upholsterer's shop, where a dressy man and two women are examining furniture together.

An interest in interiors was of a piece with Lady Shelburne's cultivation, a seamless extension of her amateur artistry and painstaking familiarity with aesthetic ideals. The cultivation of the countess also matched the deliberate learning of the earl, and was an ornament to her perfections as a wife. Not that she was a prodigy; her art is wooden and bears no comparison to Mrs Delany's flora. In truth, the countess was conventional, tracking the preceding generation, with whom she was on visiting terms, ladies like the aforementioned Duchess of Portland and Elizabeth Montagu, who had responded quickly to novelties in decoration, adopting improved or new materials such as wallpaper and papier mâché, and imaginative ideas such as print rooms; ladies who regarded building, decorating and gardening as among the consoling pleasures of life.[78] Lady Shelburne drew patterns for velvets 'to be wove in China for the furniture of two rooms in our new House'; selected costly silks for upholstery, a hundred yards of spotted satin in one order; had her London bedroom hung with 'very fine India paper';

and collected 'water collour Views of the Ruins of Ancient Rome' and such like 'to furnish my dressing room at Bowood park'.

Lord Shelburne patronised the Adam brothers well before the wedding, but his bride engaged fully in that relationship thereafter, though who was truly handling whom in her confidential encounters with the blisteringly ambitious Robert Adam must remain moot: 'with the latter I consulted on the furniture for our painted Antichamber & determined that it shou'd be a pea green Satin spotted with White & trimm'd with a pink & white fringe it was originally my own thought & met with his entire approbation'. She went out the very next day and ordered 100 yards of the said green satin from Buck and Swann.[79] It is important to note, however, that while pink and pea green may sound quintessentially feminine in their delicacy, far lighter than the monumental Palladian decorations of the 1710s and '20s, architectural historians stress that 'delicate taste' *was* the Adam style, which was not understood at the time as especially feminine or effeminate.[80] In any case, the question of the femininity or masculinity of the Shelburnes' decorations may be missing the point. Rather than measuring which of the Shelburnes carried most weight in design decisions, it is fitting to their own outlook to register their concord about aesthetic matters, in which agreement the Shelburnes expressed not only their shared enlightenment but also the unity of their fortuitously arranged marriage. They were as rich as German princes, high-ranking, powerful, young, fertile, well matched and seen to be in love. They radiated an unclouded harmony of tastes and attitudes. One can only imagine the happy importance of their marital processions, arm in arm, in and out of the shops of Soho and St James – wealth, discrimination and devotion on parade.

Thus far our discussion has favoured the exceptionally well-endowed and intellectually progressive vanguard – a minority, within a minority. Building projects were often made possible only by some special cash infusion, say a lucrative government office (e.g., Castle Howard, Dyrham, Houghton), a big inheritance (Uppark) or prize-money (Shugborough). But even a radical new design could take thirty years to complete. The slack pace of work is a proverbial grumble in the letters of patrons. In dying before the completion of the renovations, the countess was unlucky, but she was not unusual. Most families installed fittings from earlier houses, lived perforce with the builders for years, and accepted that some jobs would have to be left for the next generation to complete. The remodelling and partial alteration of mansions coexisted with new build, but almost a third of great seats were not remodelled after 1660. The strong thread of conservatism in country houses has been neglected, though it is apparent in the prominence still given to heraldry in interior decoration, argues Cornforth.[81]

Most noble families were not avant-garde in philosophy, accomplishments or consumer preferences. Nor were nobles and greater gentry uniformly rich. There was more to a family than first-born males, and there were always many members to house.

Take the Bruces of Ailesbury, wealthy and well-connected but unremarkable Wiltshire nobles, who have rarely graced the pages of architectural history. Rebuilding, decoration and refurbishment were forced on the family by fires, the requirements of younger sons, the demands of court appointments and the London marriage market. The Ailesbury wives were prominent in the overhauling of the decorations, which were discussed in highly practical terms. The appropriate furnishing of a house in Poland Street, London, in 1710 concerned Ann, Lady Bruce, wife to the future Marquis of Ailesbury. Though a Mr Woodroofe was charged with the refurbishment, he worked to her blueprint: 'I told him I did not desire anything fine and genteel as he calls it only decent and he has promised it shall be so . . . or else he is to take it again.' Still, Lady Bruce preserved the convention that her lord and master had final say: 'Mr Woodroofe having with his own hand sett down ye perticulars of our agreament he can't go from it but I wd not decide whether or no he should do anything till I knew yr opinion of it.' Nonetheless, Lady Bruce volunteered her own opinion without apology: 'upon ye whole matter I think it is a good deal of money to bestow but he fell lower than I thought he would have done'. And she seemed to be managing the fine details herself: '[The builder] has Glasses to dispose of for over Chimneys wch I am to see when I come to town'. It was she who had scrutinised Woodroofe's estimates and suggested economies – 'I've abated pritty much in ye price of ye servants beds but think there is enough allowed for ym' – and was the accountant: 'I send yu up Mr Fawkes Bill least yu should have a mind to compare notes I think Ive settled every thing as to ye price.' In a reversal of roles, Lady Bruce expected her husband to convey her commands when he was on the spot: 'if you see Woodroofe wch I suppose you will pray repeat to him yt ye beds up 2 pair of stairs is to be made without posts at the foot'. She ended by requesting that 'if you & Woodroofe agrees pray let him go to work wth all speed & I've given him directions wht he is to begin first'. Lady Bruce ordered the old green curtains from her husband's closet to be remade for the parlour at Poland Street, telling her husband to look out for new curtain material in Guildford, or to ask the decorator to find him something. She made a play of consulting her husband's preferences: 'I don't intend to meddle with those curtains till I either hear from him, or see yu'. Overall, it appears that she was the instigator, while he had powers of veto. Possibly he did not want to be bothered, and she was badgering him into taking an interest.[82]

The refurbishment was overwhelmingly a matter of textiles and upholstery in 1710, but seventy years later the redecoration of a London house was much more a matter of paint, though transferring old curtains from one room to another still featured. Lady Ailesbury ordered redecoration in the house she had taken in Fulham in 1781 to accommodate the social needs of her growing daughters. 'I forgot in my former directions to mention that ye new work done in my closets & ye young ladies last summer should be immediately painted of ye lightest stone colour in *oyl* that ye smell may be gone no time to be lost.' Lady Ailesbury did not flinch from minor rebuilding, which she ordered with breezy authority: 'What I mean by an additional door to ye young ladies dressing room next ye library is to make ye side of ye room more level, and not show ye thickness of ye wall on either side but ye 2 Doors must not clash together.' Contriving a passably elegant interior was Lady Ailesbury's mission – 'what is doing to ye staircase in ye acct of ye work? I never cod make anything neat out of it ye place was so miserably dark and ugly.'[83] Ladies of the family came to be known for their artistry; Lady Caroline Campbell, widow of the Earl of Ailesbury, copied paintings in chenille, while her daughter Anne Damer became a celebrated sculptor. Nevertheless, family letters that comment on interior decoration all frame it within the mundane routines of general household maintenance.

Even great riches could not altogether insulate aristocratic patrons from the unpleasant aspects of interior decoration. 'Here my painters are all going away and leave the work half done, half undone', grumbled the Countess of Kildare to her husband in 1759. 'I am plagued to death with them and poisoned into the bargain.'[84] On the fringes of nobility and beyond, project management was inescapable for the mistress of the house. 'I expected a great deal of business, but not so much as I find', complained Mary Delany at her new home in Ireland in 1744. 'I have workmen of all sorts in the house – upholsterers, joiners, glaziers, and carpenters – and am obliged to watch them all, or the work would be but ill-finished.'[85] The bulk of decoration in elite interiors was a dirty business devoid of glamour. 'With respect to the back drawing room', Lady Arden told her wall-paperer in 1804, 'be so good as to attend particularly to evening the top of the paper next the cornice to prevent the dirt from finding its lodg [*sic*] in there.'[86] When Palladian Cusworth Hall was rising on a hill overlooking Doncaster in the 1740s, the affluent Yorkshire gentleman William Wrightson liked to dangle off the scaffolding in a bosun's chair to monitor the construction. Wrightson employed the architect James Paine, the painter Francis Hayman and the virtuoso stuccoist Joseph Rose of York, but the refurbishments still had their mundane aspect. Keeping the house accounts for her father, the young heiress Isabella Wrightson recorded the £1 spent on dying the green and striped satin curtains for Cusworth, alongside the outlay on eggs, barley, butter, sugar, cakes and veal, for 17 November 1743.[87] The role of housekeeper, like that of curator of house and heirlooms, was quintessentially feminine.

Being born to the purple did not disqualify a countess from the office of housekeeper; indeed, writers of advice literature were at pains to prove that great ladies were not exempt from domestic administration, just as noblemen were exhorted not to trust the management of the estate entirely to stewards.[88] But high rank did make activity discretionary, for not even a dinosaur would expect to find a peeress with a dirty apron on. Some Georgian advice books ignored housekeeping as irrelevant to ladies. The great houses often boasted an agent and estate steward who ran the overall finances, a house steward who hired and disciplined the servants, a housekeeper who kept the house accounts, a clerk of the kitchen who bought provisions and served as guardian of supplies, a butler who oversaw the distribution of wine and plate, a groom of the chambers who was responsible for the maintenance of furniture and so on, ensuring that 'the great are placed above the little attentions and employments to which a private gentlewoman must dedicate much of her time'.[89]

There is no evidence that young Sophia was engaged in any time-consuming, hands-on management of house or servants, or, if she was so occupied, that she was interested enough to write about it; but she did report that they were possessed of 'a most faithful able & Zealous agent', so perhaps earl and countess both had the luxury of acting like non-executive directors.[90] On the other hand, the countess was engrossed in her husband, marriage, children, friends, her moral and aesthetic education, and her socialising in high-minded court circles. She reported barely a trip to the stillroom, the dairy, the kitchen, the laundries or the servants' hall. One of her few recorded interventions was to lecture a pregnant maid on the sin of abortion, offering to subscribe to the lying-in hospital on her behalf. Instead, the countess expressed her commitment to the household in her daily religious devotions, rational domesticity, nascent collections, her connoisseurial engagement with the luxury trades and in her personal decorative sewing. By contrast, Anne, Duchess of Grafton was obsessed with the financing, staffing, organisation, furnishing, equipping and provisioning of her London household. But this was a dire emergency; her establishment was a supremely unstable edifice, and the duchess was humiliated by the wrangling stance she was forced to take. The role of active housekeeper was taken up here only in extremis. The duchess set more store by the coronet and the ermine than the apron, unsurprisingly. Close attendance in the laundry could be seen as absurd for the best-educated patrician ladies, who invariably read French and Italian, perhaps even Latin and Greek, natural philosophy, educational theory and all the latest poetry, maintaining a wide correspondence with writers, politicians and philosophers. The young Elizabeth Robinson praised women in high life who made admirable housewives, but clearly believed that she herself was a cut above the pantry, reflecting on one bride in 1741: 'I hope she will be a good housewife for if ever nature made a woman for no other purpose it is her.'[91] A lady too absorbed in mundane housekeeping might be reputed '*a notable house-wife*, but not a woman of *fine taste*', Eliza Haywood warned.[92]

Nevertheless, the aristocratic châtelaine remained a figurehead and moral mother to an immense household family (the Duchess of Beaufort managed a staff of 200 at Badminton in Restoration Gloucestershire), and thus potentially had more in common with an army colonel than the hard-pressed mistress of a parsonage. There are battalions of fiendish managers lurking in country house guides and in older histories of housekeeping, counterparts of the fictional gorgon Lady Catherine De Burgh, who was 'a most active magistrate in her parish', relishing any 'occasion of dictating to others'. Lady Betty Germaine found exercise enough on wet days patrolling Drayton as mistress, she told Jonathan Swift in 1725.[93] Hand-written compendia of recipes for dishes, medicines and household preparations were preserved and often annotated in titled families, testifying to a breadth and continuity of female experience. That of Isabella, fourth Countess of Carlisle ran to tips on making varnish, japanning, 'washing old paintings' and removing the smell of paint from decorated rooms.[94] On the other hand, the degree to which fine ladies were hectored in print on their responsibilities in household management implies both that the office was ever open to those who relished a bit of government and that at least an annoying minority sought to evade boring administration. Still, it was quite possible to advertise one's virtues as a great châtelaine through a single charming specialism rather than a consistent, comprehensive managerialism, enjoying a reputation for virtuosity in, say, the production of marmalade or pot pourri, or else presiding over an ornamental dairy or menagerie of rare breeds. Virtuous domesticity and concern for household was more a self-conscious performance than an inescapable oppression for the ladies of the great Yorkshire houses.[95] The variety of responses argues that the duties of aristocratic housekeeping could be personally interpreted and creatively fulfilled, signalled in gestures as well as in grocery lists.

Household management was a very different exercise for a duchess, on the move between two or three houses with a train of attendants like a small court on progress, than for genteel and middling housewives, who were expected to stoke the home fires while their husbands travelled without them. Potentially, the routinely peripatetic quality of patrician existence weakened the association between ladies and their houses. Nevertheless, when the leading hostesses threw assemblies, however, home was normally identified as female: soirées were held at 'Lady Jersey's or Lady Palmerston's'. In fact, the Duchess of Devonshire even noted in her diary for 1788 that she 'saw Sheridan at Mrs Sheridan's'. New wives took possession of the marital house in the manner of part owners, not dependent visitors. Diaries and letters comment in the same breath on the prettiness of a lady's dress, curtains, china and decorative accomplishments – as if she was at one with her ensemble.[96] Ladies could not fail to be implicated in maintaining the look of the domestic interior, given the patrician preoccupation with the projection of refinement and the physical manifestations of nobility. 'The more magnificently a house is furnished', averred Hester Chapone, 'the more one is disgusted with that air of confusion which often prevails where attention is wanted in an owner.'[97] If dukes were seen to buy the great showpieces, then duchesses were expected to ensure their upkeep and arrangement.

Dynasty, splendour and magnificence, taste, enlightenment, matrimony and housekeeping were the crucial categories used to understand the decoration and redecoration of noble interiors in eighteenth-century England. The role of the sexes varied in each category. Decor that recorded the triumphs of the dynasty was seen as an archetypally masculine affair; the great commissions and renovations marked the life stages of the heir – majority, marriage, full inheritance, promotions. It would be naive to imagine that women did not share fully in the patrician obsession with rank, family and lineage. Elizabeth Montagu pitied one Howard wife lately dead because 'to go into a world where there is no Herald's office, nor any right of precedency must be terrible', unless she had taken the precaution of having the 'name done on her arm with Gunpowder in hopes of an honourable as well as joyfull resurrection'.[98] Managerial widows were common, but the late onset of a dowager's independence reduced the life events that might be commemorated in lavish purchases, while trustees and the notion of stewardship tied her hands. Nevertheless, the dower house to which the widowed mother of a married heir withdrew discreetly could be exquisite. Full heiresses to fortune and title might behave to all intents and purposes like men with the architect, though an heiress was often a thorn in the flesh of male relatives. Amongst the Nottinghamshire elite, for example, independent kinswomen rankled, and there was usually unremitting family pressure to relieve an heiress of her fortune. Indeed, Samuel Richardson's *Clarissa Harlowe* (1747–9) can be read as a chronicle of the chaos and chicanery that ensues when a great fortune falls to a girl.[99] Still, the fathers of brides often tried to protect a separate female estate distinct from the patrimony, which itself might be bequeathed to a second son or daughter. It was rare for a noblewoman to have no personal access to cash. Pin money, though sounding paltry, might amount to £300 a quarter, a handsome sum when the director of the British Museum received the same in annual salary. All this being said, however, noble families were typically belligerently patriarchal and obsessed with patrilineage. Men and women alike laboured to support the fiction of unbroken descent from father to son, and supported the appearance of masculine superiority in all things public. Even women who had taken a free hand with design and interior decoration, like Frances Boscawen at Hatchlands, whose husband was at sea, tended to trivialise her activities, describing herself 'adding some little ornaments and directing the furniture etc', so as not to trespass on masculine dignity.[100] Concern for the decor of the ancestral pile carried no taint of effeminacy, and where luxury consumption expressed the prestige and endurance of the dynasty it was indubitably the proper business of men. Ennobled gentlemen were rarely shy about having crests engraved on family silver or painted on the side of their coaches.

Magnificence was an obligation entailed on rank. Given their princely funds, most of the leading noble families had no problem in exhibiting the proper ornaments of their fortune. A great house on the ancestral acres, a palatial town house in London for the season, an art collection, a stash of silver and gold plate, the latest upholstery and mahogany, family jewels, rich dress, a crested coach and six, a retinue of liveried servants and a dazzling equipage constituted the lowest common denominators of noble magnificence. Every member of the noble family was implicated in this project, expected to carry their share of the burden of reputation. While feminine extravagance was an old accusation, the duty to make a proper exhibition was a quietly insistent theme also. The unseemliness of excessive frugality is one of the unnoticed arguments of conduct literature. It was better to err on the side of liberality than of meanness. Ostentation on the part of upstarts was disparaged, not female ostentation per se. In fact, a glittering female show could be functional for husbands who wanted to announce their fortune and family, all the while maintaining a personal disdain for trumpery and tinsel. And having fewer supports to their rank than their men, ladies could be even more preoccupied with ostentation as verification of status. They could not, after all, lead an army onto the battlefield, contest an election (as sons might do before they inherited the title), joust in a debate in the House of Lords, or even fight a duel to confirm or enhance their standing. Aristocratic women who were downwardly mobile or marginalised were hypersensitive to the material and spatial requirements of rank. Dignity in furnishings and equipage was vital for women who were socially exposed and threatened with exile, as the furnishing crusade of the Duchess of Grafton evidences at length. Though in the end it was her own lonely foolishness, not the lack of diamonds or dressing table, that lost 'Her Grace' the coronet.

The idea that the architecture and contents of a house projected the culture and learning of its occupants was deep-rooted, but it was only in the eighteenth century that interiors, objects and behaviour came to be viewed through the prism of 'taste'. Taste was an empire open to colony by men and women alike, though in the insistence on the innate capacities of the well bred the rise of a language of taste represented more of a rhetorical departure for women than for men, who had had a historic claim to culture through scholarship. Some argued that great ladies had a special duty to act as arbiters of taste, and hallmark that which was truly worthy for the benefit of the less discriminating.[101] It was certainly possible to claim taste as a higher feminine calling. Interior decorating and consummate consumerism for Lady Shelburne offered an arena within which to act on her aesthetic education and demonstrate her discernment. Shopping for interiors was one aspect of the cultivation of a Lady Sensible, just as her collecting and botanical drawing expressed her Enlightenment affinities.

The role of interior decoration in the creation and projection of matrimony is a neglected theme, but conjugality, both its fruition and its denial, emerges distinctly here. The comparison of the Shelburne and Grafton marriages is instructive. The men were contemporaries, scions of peerages of recent creation and both were to become Whig prime ministers; their wives even employed the same fashionable obstetrician; both marriages were short-lived. Nonetheless, their matrimonial experiences were diametrically opposed, and their homes were concrete testimony to the differences. For the Shelburnes, the pursuit of new furnishings was a project both public and domestic, intrinsic to the solidification of their arranged marriage. Their conversations about taste built a harmony of conjugal purpose, while their promenades about the shops demonstrated their prosperous love. For the Graftons, the unequal division of the spoils was an unavoidable consequence, and for the duchess a degrading proof, of the disintegration of their love match. Estranged from her husband and first-born son, with no access to country seat, Grafton silver or family diamonds, the humiliation of the duchess was patent; only the agitation of her friends and her own ceaseless lobbying staved off an even steeper social decline. Aristocratic marriage was made and unmade in household goods. Spencer House on Green Park in London, decorated as a Greek temple to Hymen, was a monument to a passionate love match, but division was unmissable at Castle Ward in County Down in the early 1760s, where marital disagreement over style resulted in clashing Gothic and classical wings. The Wards separated shortly after the building was completed – architectural incompatibility was prophetic.[102]

Architectural history has taken a disproportionate interest in new country houses, but the bulk of decoration in elite interiors was less a matter of princely commissions and miraculous architectural transformation than an undramatic business of preservation and alteration akin to the mundane routines of general household maintenance. Repair and alteration services, even domestic dry-cleaning, dyeing and house letting were an integral part of the business of most firms.[103] Domestic life at the top was not simply a matter of 'diamonds, gold and silver ornaments, rich necklaces, the old masters and alabaster statuary', as Anthony Trollope smiled in 1880: 'Dukes and Duchesses must sit upon chairs – or at any rate on sofas, as well as their poorer brethren'.[104]

Housekeeping was the most mundane category within which interior decorating fell. Every duke, earl, viscount and lord would consider himself the ultimate head of the household, but none expected to be called upon to bother with the cleanliness of the table linen, the shine on his crested plate, the niceness of his upholstery and the arrangement of his drawing-room tables. The idea was preposterous. Decorative designs may have been set in the sketchbook and show room, but they were confirmed in the domestic interior, whose upkeep belonged to the distaff, as it had done for centuries. Outside the nobility and greater gentry, interior decoration was usually a piecemeal process of adaptation of an old architectural fabric (see figs 25 and 27), or the one-off, but superficial, refurbishment of a rental property. Consequently, for the majority of polite consumers, decoration fell not within the sphere of architecture, high-design debate and fashionable patronage, but rather came within the capacious but commonplace remit of housekeeping.

If the major categories that shaped the understanding of noble interiors – dynasty, magnificence, taste, enlightenment, matrimony and housekeeping – are imagined as coloured threads in a tapestry, some strands were more associated with one sex than the other; their interweaving varied over time; and different yarns were more dominant in some periods than others. The idea of a dynastic nobility was at least 1,000 years old, built on male-preference patrilineage, reifying the fiction of unbroken descent from father to son. Women colluded in the smoke and mirrors needed to sustain the lineal story and might efface themselves for the group, while sole surviving heiresses could nurse a mystical sense of destiny. Yet while women could lay claim to dynasty, men never ever colonised its mundane partner housekeeping. Huswifery and good Christian stewardship were the terms on which the upkeep of interiors had been understood since at least the Middle Ages. To these ancient threads the Georgians introduced the secular concept of taste.

The learning of leading magnates had long been read in the architecture, decoration and contents of their prodigy houses; but the humanism that might underlie the performance tended towards the exclusive and scholarly, whereas 'taste' was promulgated in an array of periodicals in English, and claimed to be modern, non-pedantic, cosmopolitan and urbane. Taste was a roomy concept, incorporating art and architecture, design, interiors, objects, dress, manners and people, creating an elastic territory that ladies inhabited with ease. This is not to say that patrician men did not delight in the part of virtuoso or dilettante, but the role was essentially an elaboration of the part of scholar-gentleman that had long been open to them, whereas the woman of taste had far less precedent. Bess of Hardwick (*circa* 1527–1608) was a great builder, but kept only six books for her personal use, according to her inventory, and all of them sober works of Protestant devotion. Nor did her example excite the Georgians. 'Vast rooms, no taste' was Horace Walpole's crushing verdict on Hardwick. Seventeenth-century France offered more congenial models for stylish Georgians, like the Marquise de Rambouillet (1558–1665), arguably the first *salonnière*, who received guests in her 'chambre bleue' and reorganised her Parisian hotel in 1618 the better to accommodate conversation in small suites of rooms. The mysteries of taste also offered one answer to new wealth; after all, if magnificence alone supported status then what was to prevent nabobs and bankers from simply spending their way to the top? Subtleties of choice demonstrated true taste, not just plunder and cash. By the 1750s the march of taste had effected the toning down of glittering splendour and excessive finery in interiors in favour of a more restrained, albeit still luxurious elegance, just as 'taste' in manufactures, not just the raw cost of the material, became more prized.[105]

The rise of the language of taste was especially significant for female assertiveness, and this new thread should shine florescent in our tapestry. If, however, Georgian ladies claimed a self-conscious role as arbiters of taste, the expression of this capacity in interiors came very close to the performances of an earlier generation under the banner of housekeeping and family duty. Even so, a reputation for taste, sometimes tinged with enlightenment, and shared with a husband or a coterie, was much more flattering to the cosmopolitan pretensions of ladies than old-fashioned huswifery. After all, it was far more exciting to design the curtains than to make and clean them.

6

WALLPAPER AND TASTE

A PREOCCUPATION WITH TASTE WAS NOT CONFINED to the peerage. In August 1799 a Sussex cleric, Dr Thomas Ferris, visited the architect-designed mansion of a friend and noticed the new wallpapers. He promptly wrote to the London wallpaper and decorating firm Joseph Trollope and Sons for something similar:

> I saw the other Day at our Friend Mr Pigous some very pretty papers your Man was putting up and Mrs Pigou recommended me to your House. I am in want of a paper for a very small Room which must be paper'd immediately . . . Pray . . . send a few of the cheapest patterns proper for Halls, Staircases; & Passages for a Parsonage House I care nothing about fashion if they are neat & clean.[1]

Mr Ferris privileged the pretty, the neat and the clean over the modish, and was concerned to decorate in keeping with the solid dimensions but modest pretensions of a Sussex parsonage. Perhaps it did not become a clergyman to advertise too keen an interest in fashion, however developed his aesthetic appreciation. Note that it was the wife, Mrs Pigou, who seemed mistress of the facts of the commission. This is but one example among hundreds of opinionated letters transcribed by Trollope and Sons between June 1797 and May 1808. The letters provide rare access to the wants and anxieties of a heterogeneous group of consumers and the vocabulary they deployed to frame their concerns. En masse, they constitute a lexicon of the working vocabulary of non-aristocratic consumer taste.

Taste was a key word of Georgian cultural argument, a new way of seeing culture and society, though it was a heroically slippery concept. 'The Term taste', reflected Edmund Burke, 'like all other figurative terms is not extremely accurate ... and it is therefore liable to uncertainty and confusion.' The sovereign importance of taste was invoked again and again, by philosophers, moralists and satirists, but none nailed down its elements in ways that helped ordinary consumers to make their choices. Equally, while many historians have wrestled with the extensive debates about taste that preoccupied the likes of Alexander Pope, David Hume and Joshua Reynolds, no one has asked what taste might have meant on the ground for the perplexed consumer. Research effort has concentrated on one of the obsessions of the genre – luxury. Waves of anxiety about the moral, political, social and economic consequences of new wealth swept through print in the 1690s, in the 1750s, and again in the 1780s in the wake of the loss of the Americas. Concern about immoral profusion and meaningless glitter was still not a spent force in the early 1800s. How *could* wealth be reconciled with virtue? One popular answer was through the operation of taste. Philosophical treatises on aesthetics, moral diatribes, fiction and graphic satire all circled around the question of good taste and bad taste, often invoking objects as props in their argument, from chinoiserie, porcelain and Venetian windows, to French silks, coaches and liveries. There were, however, no attempts to differentiate between tasteful and tasteless teacups in ways that would inform and reassure a consumer. Nor have historians examined how consumers brought 'good taste' to bear in the marketplace. The beauty of the Trollope letter-book lies in the insight it gives into how a range of people, from the hard-pressed landlady and the pen-pushing bureaucrat to the marchioness, appreciated and discussed the same material – wallpaper.

Histories of wallpaper chronicle the rise of this new form of culture over roughly a century. The earliest known example of English patterned wallpaper dates from 1509 from Christ's College, Cambridge, but it was in the later seventeenth century that wallpaper came into significant use, as an alternative to tapestry and other textile hangings. Wallpaper established a foothold in the corners of the house most associated with the individual in undress – the dressing room, the bedroom and the closet. In 1713, 197,000 yards of wallpaper were bought in England. By 1785 its consumption had increased tenfold to more than two million yards.[3] At the top of the market, wallpaper could be commissioned at a cost equal to that of fine textiles, but it was to be had in many grades and prices. Curators estimate that it was possible to buy 11 yards of paper for the cost of a yard of damask.[4] The affordability of paper delighted commentators.[5] Unlike elaborate stucco or luxurious velvet, wallpaper came within the reach of middling consumers.

Why should we be interested in wallpaper? For some it is beneath the notice of a historian. 'Wallpaper has long been considered the poor relation of the decorative arts,' Gill Saunders concludes, 'fragile, ephemeral, easy to replace.' Wallpaper's career was essentially one of pretence, imitating other materials from wood, stucco and masonry, murals and tapestry hangings, to textiles such as silk, chintz and velvet. Deception, ephemerality and veneer were the literary connotations of wallpaper for the Victorians. Wallpapering became a device for revealing a meretricious concern with surface, and perhaps a false heart.[6] Wallpaper was cheap in the worst sense. It lacked integrity. What could be read as an inauthentic veneer, however, could also convey wholesome domesticity on a budget. New wallpaper advertised spotlessness and was greeted with fastidious relief by travellers.

Wallpaper was rarely expected to be an investment for a lifetime, but embraced as a decoration that, if not quite transitory, was relatively impermanent. Martha Dodson of Cookham, in Berkshire, the elderly widow of a wealthy tin-plate worker, had rooms papered in 1748, 1749, 1753, 1758 and 1760. The paper for her chamber cost £1 15s. 0d., and seven pieces of chintz paper for another room cost £1 13s. 0d.; not dirt cheap, but more affordable than the alternatives. Though she was in her 70s, one room was repapered twice within ten years.[7] Wallpaper was widely seen to deliver instant effects for modest outlay. Slapping up wallpaper was one way to make yourself quickly at home, even in lodgings. Horace Walpole complained in 1745: 'The moment I have smugged up [to fit up neatly or nicely] a closet or dressing room, I have always warning given me that my lease is out.'[8] Landladies resorted to Trollope again and again to freshen up a let for the season.

The effects of paper could be startling. Wallpaper could utterly transform the look of a room for a fraction of the cost of textiles, stucco or wainscot. Just as ribbons, lace and handkerchiefs allowed women to refashion a garment without spending a fortune,[9] so wallpaper offered an economical makeover, bringing experiment and fashion within reach of middling householders. Highly decorative both in terms of colour and ornament, and often bought repeatedly by the same person, wallpaper required a developed aesthetic vocabulary to describe its visual qualities. Modest wallpaper thus reveals how 'taste' was articulated in practice by a broad and expressive consumer public.

Joseph Trollope and Sons was based in London, the centre of the British wall-paper industry. Launching in 1778, Trollope made his reputation in exotic paper, especially Chinese painted paper, but by 1800, when he retired, the firm's spe-ciality was printed pattern, coloured to order, serving a broad heterogeneous market. In 1830 the firm became paper hangers to George IV, and in 1842 to Queen Victoria, but in the period of the letter-book titled patrons could be listed on the fingers of two hands. The bulk of their customers were drawn from the ranks of provincial gentility – clerics, doctors, lawyers, small gentry and merchants across the southern counties of England, and from the mighty upper-middling market in London. Based in Westminster, the company sup-plied both town and city, catering to the likes of banker Thomas Baring as he rose from city counting house to a baronetcy and a smart West End address, but also to squadrons of London's senior civil servants and commercial man-agers – papering the offices and apartments of the bureaucrats of the Customs House, General Post Office, the Penny Post Office, the Sun Fire Office and Doc-tors' Commons, though they failed in their attempt to get a foot in the door of the Mint. Trollope and Sons had standing relationships with a handful of up-holsterers (professional decorators), but also several lan...... landladies in the booming London rental sector. The Lon...... the letter-book, though the company sent papers cross-...... Cumberland, Yorkshire, Staffordshire, Lincolnshire, Hun...... Dorset, Somerset, Wiltshire, Buckinghamshire, Bedford...... Surrey, Kent, Hampshire and Dublin. They even sent pap...... ficers at the Cape of Good Hope, though they had no...... Americas.

The question of who chose the wallpaper for a family dwelling is not easy to answer. A number of wallpaper commissions were orchestrated by an interme-diary: at the top end of the market via an upholsterer, steward, agent or servant in a family of rank, and at the bottom end of the market by a landlord or land-lady. Yet the stylistic capital of Trollope and Sons themselves was a force to be reckoned with. Sheraton recognised the potential pretensions of the trade in 1803: 'paper hangings are a considerable article in the upholstery branch and being occasionally used for rooms of much elegance, it requires taste and skill rightly to conduct this branch of business'.[10]

The gender breakdown amongst Trollope's private customers is conventional. Unsurprisingly, men outnumbered women in the order letters. In the letter-book for 1798, for instance, of a total of forty-three customers and their agents, thirty-four were male, while only seven correspondents were female and two further fe-male customers were represented by upholsterers. Thus women accounted for

37   Trade card for James Wheeley's Paper Hanging Warehouse opposite the church in Little Britain and Aldersgate Street, London, *circa* 1754, printed engraving. British Museum, London, Heal 91.58. The card promises that 'All kind of furniture are exactly match'd'.

less than a quarter of correspondents, only nine out of forty-three letter-writers, 21 per cent. There are numerous single women in the letter-book, yet married men customarily represented their wives and families. Nevertheless, several women in addition to the landladies led the ordering process, and while it is not always clear whether they were married or widowed, their aesthetic confidence is impressive. MP's wife Lady Charlotte Smith was an exacting customer, blunt in her dealings with her tradesman: 'Lady Charlotte cannot say that she likes any of the patterns that Mr Trollope has enclosed.' Assertiveness about workmanship was not confined to the titled ladies either. Mrs Hale of Jermyn Street, Westminster, was crisp in July 1804: 'Mrs Hale expected Mr Trollope woud have called on her for the payment of his small account when she intended to shew him the staircase which was so very badly done that something must be tried this summer for it is not fit to be seen.'

38 Trade card for Richard Masefield's Manufactory in the Strand, London, *circa* 1760, printed engraving. British Museum, London, Heal 91.41.

Even where the correspondence was led by a husband, female choices or at very least final veto do surface. The Reverend Charles Johnson of Bath had to return his papers because 'Mrs Johnson does not like the one [that] I chose for her bedroom therefore I'll trouble you to send down a dozen more of the newest Patterns'. Several letters invoke the first person plural and imply the conjugal co-operation that underlay decorative choices.[11] And certainly trade cards for wallpaper retailers advertise well-appointed shops, with women in groups and coupled with men, examining papers (figs 37 and 38).[12] Choosing wallpaper *à deux* may even have signified marital harmony.

The letter-book of Trollope and Sons conjures the interiors of lodgings, offices, parsonages and cottages. It is a rare source for discussion of mundane patterns and the middle market, a useful counter to the distortions of surviving museum collections of wallpaper, which inevitably favour the fine, the costly and the unique.[13] Unfortunately, there is no accompanying book of patterns, or even one-off samples to demonstrate precisely what a customer meant by a neat and pretty trellis pattern, or a French red, or a bright blue. There is no sample book to rival that of Cowtan twenty years later.[14] What the Trollope letter-book offers is a glossary of terms. The analysis that follows explores the factors that affected Trollope's customers' choice of a particular paper, the conventions that governed the decoration of different rooms and the everyday aesthetic vocabulary they deployed.

Trollope's customers had a lively appreciation of the decorations of their acquaintances. A personal recommendation and/or a viewing of Trollope's wallpaper *in situ* were the commonest reasons these consumers gave for their patronage. They did not reveal why they had chosen wallpaper over other decorations, or Trollope over other manufacturers. Sir Thomas Anson of palatial Shugborough, however, aborted an order in 1803, when he discovered that another nobleman had something newer and better from another supplier.[15] They were vigilant and critical consumers.

The pursuit of an all-encompassing decorative scheme governed the customers' choice of paper. Because wallpaper was markedly cheaper than the textiles that accompanied it, consumers expected the paper to be specially coloured to correspond. Indeed, the ability to produce wallpapers to tone with fabrics was a crucial selling point. Wheeley's paper-hanging warehouse advertised in 1754: 'All kinds of Furniture are exactly matched.'[16] Mr and Mrs Thomas Baring of Broad Street, London, were eager to ensure that the papers for their drawing room and bedroom in the country agreed with their furniture. In April 1800 Mr Baring wrote: 'Mrs Baring spoke to you a few days ago respecting the colour of the yellow border to our drawing room at lee, but forgot to mention that it must be the same colour as the lining to our Curtains which is a very light yellow, almost a straw colour.' The wrong yellow had been sent and the Barings were adamant that Trollope should 'rectify the mistake'.[17]

A horror of mismatched decor shrieks from the letter-book. Lady Lumm of Cheltenham was incandescent when she heard from her housekeeper that Trollope's men had mixed up the hanging, such that everything clashed:

> . . . you must have made a great Mistake in having put up the Crimson and white border in the back Room, which was only intended to match the Curtains and furniture in the front Room; and the Curtains in the back Room being yellow I proposed having the border of the paper in the back room something of yellow and black which you sent me a pattern of in Flocks if you could not yourself choose me something more elegant; I am quite vex'd at this Mistake; as it will make the back Room frightful . . . you do not know how vexd I am at the Mistake.[18]

Mistaken, mistaken, three times mistaken! There was no question that the clash was vexing. Paper was expected to marry with curtains and other hangings, up-

holstery and even the colour of wood, though the 'match' was a similarity
hue, not juxtaposition with a contrasting complementary or a co
colour.[19]

Colour was the salient feature of wallpaper, although withou   ...ying
samples it is impossible to know exactly what shade a customer had in mind
when they used a term like 'crimson'. In colour theory, Newton's seven-colour
spectrum was displaced around 1800 by a six-colour system of the three primary
colours (red, yellow, blue) and their complementaries (green, violet, orange),
but in practice colour names could cover a variety of shades.[20] Trollope and his
customers may even have been at odds about what a particular colour name signified. In 1807 Mrs Marryat ordered a 'border done in a rose color' and was
unimpressed when she was sent 'a dark crimson'.[21] Still, it is clear that a good
colour was both visually appealing and permanent. What use was an exquisite
'pompadour', a silvery-lilac-pink, if it faded?

Whether French grey, brown, green, buff, stone, straw yellow or rose pink, the
precise colour was crucial to the effect in the eyes of Trollope's customers. Moreover, there were quality distinctions to be made within a single colour. As the
Stricklands wrote in 1799, 'We have settled to have the Room done in a plain
french Grey, of the best shade.' Complaints about the wrong colour were common. Miss Crompton, writing from Clapham in July 1801, was 'disappointed in
the effect of the paper he has sent, it being of too blue a tint whereas she had expected it to have a green cast'. A Miss Walvo of Weybridge protested that her new
hall papers 'woud not do' in August 1805 because they failed to match the old:
'hers is a darker grey on a pale grey the paper sent a darker blue on a pale grey
the Border is still more different & she cannot possibly make use of any of them'.
So determined was she to prove her point that she 'pinned to a piece of the paper
the half of the only bit she has remaining of the original of her Hall paper to
prove to Mr Trollope how widely they differ'.[22] Obviously, pigment was the *raison d'être* of the accompanying paint. In July 1800 Lady Rodney of Abesford was
enchanted by Trollope's yellow, which 'she likes so much', requesting patterns to
suit both the paint and the lilac moulding on her doors. A Mrs Simmons had a
nice appreciation of the nuances of hue, requesting a stone colour for the paint
for the entrance and doors, mahogany for the stair rails and French grey for the
paper for the third drawing room, but 'If the Painter could [throw] a little pink
into the stone colour at the same expense it woud be better'.[23]

Choice of colour varied by taste, in dialogue with fashion and, importantly, according to the room and the light. Consumers' awareness of the symbolism of
certain colours is hard to gauge, but there was no universal authority to which
they might refer. In Stuart colour hierarchies derived from heraldry, red was the

principal colour. In conventional symbolism, red was associated with the god Mars, represented fire and was allied with nobility, dignity and state. The state apartments in royal palaces were done in crimson until George IV. Red drapery in paintings signified justice, virtue and defence, according to a ladies' art manual in 1777.[24] Among Trollope's customers, however, there was very little call for red. Perhaps it was a desire for aristocratic panache that led Lord Anson to order white scrolls on a crimson ground for the drawing rooms of his Staffordshire pile in 1803: 'you will be exact in the colour of the Ground that it may be a rich red & to match the bits of tassel I gave you'. With crimson walls and upholstery, the effect approached that of a regal stateroom, matching the other fittings like a 'large fine Engraved and Ornamented steel whole front patent register stove. Top engraved with double Vitruvian scrole & . . . sides engraved with twisted laurel leaves' installed in 1794.[25] But Anson was unique amongst Trollope's customers. No one else ordered red on this scale. In 1802 William Ladler wanted to have his 'Oval Drawing room done in Distemper, the Finest Scarlet Geranium colour' – the only customer in ten years to ask for scarlet.[26] Red was known to absorb the light, requiring costly candle-power to show its beauties, so practicality may have warned off the majority.

Green was associated with Venus and came second in the received colour hierarchy derived from heraldry, but was often thought more pleasing than red as a setting for furniture, and was easier to live with. Green's associations with love and pleasure may have particularly recommended it for bedrooms. In drapery, green signified hope. Paintings in gilt frames were thought to look well against green.[27] Amongst Trollope's correspondents, green was mentioned more than any other colour, requested for bedrooms, parlours, drawing rooms, breakfast rooms, dining rooms and billiard rooms. The therapeutic effects of green were already taken for granted. Mr Pryor of the Foreign Office wanted pea green for his rooms in Whitehall in 1800 on account of his 'eyes being bad'.[28] The pleasantness of green was assumed by Maria Edgeworth in 1798, who imagined a child reflecting: 'I think green is the prettiest of all colours; my father's room is painted green, and it is very cheerful, and I have been very happy in that room; and besides, the grass is green in spring.' And green was the favourite colour of one of literature's mildest heroines – Austen's inoffensive Jane Bennet. 'I like green' was an entirely safe remark for a Regency consumer to make.[29]

Blue came third in traditional colour hierarchies, the colour of Jupiter and the Virgin, signifying pity and sincerity. In drapery, it indicated faith and love.[30] The discovery of Prussian blue in the 1700s hastened its use in paint and dye, and by the 1730s blue had become a feature of fashionable interiors. Amongst Trollope's customers, however, blue paper was less popular than green and even yellow for family rooms, though it was occasionally used for drawing rooms. 'Common blue papers' were used for passages, servants' halls, the insides of cupboards and for under-papering. In grander settings, blue appeared as an accent to grey, yellow, red and even occasionally orange.

Yellow was not mentioned in heraldry and appears to stand outside the formal hierarchies that governed the language of early Georgian interior decoration. Yellow branded cowards, traitors, heretics and Jews in early modern Europe. Yellow drapery signified jealousy, though yellow was the colour of the Greek god Hymen, so it also denoted marriage in some contexts. Yellow showed no contrast to gilt frames, and references to yellow rooms were almost unknown before 1680 and still rare until 1740.[31] Yellow, however, was an exalted colour in imperial China, and the craze for chinoiserie increased its prestige. Yellow was certainly a popular choice by the 1790s amongst Trollope's correspondents, colouring the papers for drawing rooms (in darker hues), bedrooms (in lighter) and dressing rooms. Grey, stone, drab and buff coloured papers were ordered occasionally for bedrooms, but often for halls, stairways and passages. The lighter neutrals were also designed to offset the stronger borders. White papers with dark borders were considered fashionable for drawing rooms. A Warwick customer wanted 'something of a white and dove one shade glazed' for his back parlour in 1805, 'then the black and yellow Bordering wou'd look well'.[32] A touch of lilac appeared in many schemes, while pink was a familiar colour for borders, also appearing regularly with white in Trollope's inevitable trellis papers.

Trollope's leading designs embraced the range of style, from old-fashioned Rococo intricacy to up-to-date Neoclassical simplicity, from garden trellis to floral exotica, from mock stone to Gothic arches (pls 17, 18, 19). Like most manufacturers, the company supplied marbled, plain and glazed coloured papers, and flock. The most frequently cited pattern was the trellis (occasionally 'lattice'), which came in larger and smaller designs, in pink and white, blue and white, green and white, and green and buff. Benjamin Bensfield of Devonshire wanted 'trellice paper and Border of flowers to put on in arches & with a sky Ceiling', for a small room at Bath in June 1806, and later 'trellice Paper for a small Room at my Cottage'. One J. Burgess planned to paper his aunt's room in green and buff trellis, but when the paper was not ready, requested 'five pieces of any paper you think will be pretty for a small parlour . . . let it be either something green or a white sattin paper it should not be a large pattern as the Room is small and low Ceiling'.[33] Trellis was a multivalent design that could imply both Italianate gardens and chinoiserie screens. Nevertheless, it was seen as unpretentious and unaffected, suiting a modest room in town or country, though it may have had a particular affinity with the idea of 'the cottage', a house form that had achieved a remarkable popularity by 1800.

Floral designs included Trollope's geranium, convolvulus and lily, but of these the geranium (almost certainly the pelargonium) outstripped the rest in popularity. Strikingly, all were non-native blooms. Hence one might live in a cramped Georgian house in a rainy town, yet the bold flora of the Americas could still romp across your walls. Leaf and acorn patterns were available for those who preferred the native forest. Intricate patterns, 'full of work', or what we might term 'busy', were still available for those who hankered after the Rococo complexity of the preceding generation. Meanwhile, a pared-down Neoclassicism was reflected in stripes, vertical ribbons, waves and pillars, while the small figures, spots, dots and dashes on lighter grounds found in fashionable dress fabric and embroidery were also mirrored in paper. Rock, stone and brick patterns were requested for staircases. A celebration of inventions of 1797 considered that papers that imitated 'so exactly every variety of marble, porphyry, and other species of stones' were 'among the most elegant hangings of this kind'.[34] Architectural devices included scrolls, Etruscan borders and Gothic arches. Perhaps it was the echo of clerical Perpendicular that led the Reverend Mr Richmond of Freeway, Bedfordshire, to order 'Green and White of a Gothic Pattern with a Particular border made to suit it' in 1806.[35]

Iron convention governed which patterns and colours were most appropriate for different rooms. Trollope's customers abided by the established rule that 'rooms for convenience' and 'rooms for shew' were hung differently.[36] Halls, entrances and passages were often papered in stones and other neutrals, a device to ensure that strong effect was held in reserve for the grander rooms. Simpler patterns suited bedrooms, dressing rooms, attics, garrets, servants' rooms, small parlours, passages and so on, but drawing rooms and dining rooms that saw the most social traffic required impressive papers. Lady Lumm ordered grand crimson and yellow papers for her formal rooms, but expected to economise elsewhere: 'I hope you will put the very cheapest paper in the room joining the hall, and in the Little Room over the Kitchen.' No special requirements for London offices emerge because senior officials at the GPO and such lived in, so any redecoration involved family rooms as well (Mr Freeling of the GPO wanted to 'use the small Room at the end of the passage opposite the board room for a dressing Room'), and thus the office was embraced within a domestic interior, and conformed to the same decorative conventions.[37]

An obsession with propriety and fitness to context suffuses the Trollope letter-books. Paper should be proper for its place and situation. Customers almost invariably specified the rooms for which they were ordering – 'a small bedroom', 'a light north room', and so on – mentioning dominant features such as low ceilings or restricted light and stressing the architectural context – 'a small parsonage' – and the situation – 'in the country'. Large designs were believed to be over-powering and inappropriate in small rooms. MP's wife Lady Charlotte Smith looked for unobtrusive designs for her Chelmsford nursery: 'very Cheap . . . but something neat & genteel & a pattern that does not dazzle the Eyes either in grey blew or yellow as it is a North room which is sunny She likes green'. Rabett of Bramsfield Hall, Suffolk, vetoed anything 'oppressive as its only for papering a breakfast parlour & the pattern would be preferred small'.[38]

A commitment to decorum was shared by the rich and titled, who did not ex-pect magnificence in all their rooms. Sir Samuel Fludyer, son of an immensely rich London merchant, wanted 'patterns of very common papers for Garrets'. Lady Ashburton asked to see patterns for 'servants bedroom paper', and expected her schoolroom and housekeeper's room to be done in the same patterns in 1808. When Sir John Dyke, of Lullingston Castle, Kent, ordered 'patterns of green & white papers with proper borders fit for a common sitting Room in the Coun-try', he was insistent that Trollope 'not send anything that is fine as that will not answer for a room that is very low pitched'. Majestic designs looked absurd out-side grand apartments.[39] Fine paper would not answer in a common room, even if that room belonged to a baronet.

Neatness was a favourite attribute of a wallpaper pattern. Samuel Johnson de-fined neat as 'elegant, but without dignity'. Neatness had been positively associ-ated with wallpaper from the first. Wallpaper was commended in 1699 for making 'the houses of the more ordinary look neat'.[40] For Trollope's consumers, neat papers tended to have small patterns and conveyed a lack of ostentation. William Ellis was an old man who disliked change. He had not had his green dining room in Ware in Hertfordshire redecorated for years, but on recovering from eighteen months of illness, found repairs forced upon him that 'put me quite out of sorts'. Reluctantly, he requested new borders 'not too Expensive about 2¼ or 2½ inches wide neat and not too showey'.[41] Neat papers were found at the cheaper end of the spectrum, but 'cheap and neat' was a world away from 'cheap and nasty' in moral implications. From the cleric who avowed 'I care nothing about fashion if they are neat & clean', to Lady Charlotte Smith's desire for 'something neat & genteel', it is plain that 'neatness' connoted propriety. The Neoclassical vogue ensured that neat could be linked with the modern. In 1798 a William Evans of Wimborne, Dorset, requested an 'assortment of Patterns of Papers the best & most modern for a neat Drawing Room'.[42]

Cheapness was often the deciding factor in an order. Mrs Bonar refused to settle an order in 1799 that she found 'extravagantly dear done'. Landlords in-variably insisted on cheapness in a paper, but private customers often specified that they wanted to see the less expensive patterns, or the common papers, especially for the less formal areas of the house. An eye for a bargain extended to the greater gentry. Mrs Cooke of Ouston, near Doncaster, a member of one of the leading West Riding families, wanted 'some patterns of common papers none new be sent above 4 p yd'. A small group of customers requested old patterns because they had become attached to the familiar, or to make good their worn patches.[43]

Trollope's customers were alert to fashion in interiors. Yet 'fashionable' was an umbrella term, which could mean both a loose conformity to prevailing modes and the more demanding definition of possessing the latest model each season. A handful of customers demanded the *dernier cri*, asking for up-to-the-minute patterns barely dry from the printer. Lord Anson of Shugborough was piqued to hear that Lord Gwydwr had some new French papers at his mansion in Whitehall, and worried that his own choice was passé: 'it has been much in use & will not look so new as I could wish'. Novelty was his sine qua non in a wall covering and he was not to be outdone. But even donnish desires could run to the very latest thing. G. H. Tapley of Merton College, Oxford, wrote in December 1800, ordering 'the most fashionable Paper for my Rooms, with a Border suitable to it, the paper must be light; as the rooms are dark, send it in my name to Mr Cook Upholsterer High St Oxford'.[44] However, an anxious concern not to be too far adrift of fashion motivated many, rather than a craving to set the modes. The Dowager Countess Poulett ordered extra borders for her drawing room, bedroom and dressing room at Lyme Regis, 'As I am told everyone does the corners now'. Some sought reassurance that their choices were fashionable enough. Mrs Burt of Malling, Kent, ingenuously admitted that she 'does not know if the one she has chosen is very fashionable and begs Mr Trollope will send her word whether it is usual to cut out the borders as formerly or whether it is more the custom to leave the edge and for satisfaction sake whether it is tolerably new'.[45] Anxiety about correct behaviour is the cumulative impression of the letter-book, not hedonism.

A vocabulary of beauty was applied to wallpaper. Johnson defined prettiness as beauty without majesty, stateliness, grandeur or dignity. The use of the term ('pretty border suitable to a small room', 'pretty for a small parlour') suggests that prettiness was an attribute of modest, unassuming papers, conveying an impression of charming, graceful, dainty, but unpretentious decoration. 'Smart' was used only once as an adjective and in this instance carried social as well as aesthetic connotations. When Sir John Dyke requested nothing too fine for his common sitting room in the country, what he received was just too ordinary after all. None would do, so he applied again for new patterns in whites, and 'they something of a smarter kind than those he sent'.[46] There was clearly such a thing as too common for a baronet. Beautiful or handsome conveyed something altogether more splendid and assertive. Handsome had a long-established association with wallpaper. The Golden Lyon Inn, in Leeds, advertised bedchambers 'newly hung with handsome papers' in 1763, but inns and later hotels were decorated with bolder patterns than most customers could tolerate every day; surviving examples *in situ* are gorgeous to the point of vulgarity.[47] A strong handsomeness was a quality expected of dining rooms. To Trollope's customers, 'handsome' indicated the grander end of the stocks. Yet there must have been a risk that 'handsome' could be interpreted as flashy, since Guchard, an upholsterer who was a regular customer of Trollope, was careful to specify in 1798 'some patterns of handsome Papers not gaudy' for a London room 17 feet high.[48]

With its associations of over-bright tastelessness, gaudy is rarely a term of praise today. For Samuel Johnson, gaudy could mean pompous and ostentatiously fine. For Austen's Elizabeth Bennet in 1813, part of the appeal of Pemberley lay in the true taste of the furnishings: 'neither gaudy nor uselessly fine; with less of splendor, and more real elegance, than the furniture of Rosings'. There were, however, earlier positive understandings of splendour, colour and show, coexisting with the negative.[49] Nevertheless, none of Trollope's customers used the term with approval; indeed, gaudy epitomised what many sought to avoid. Florid taste and pompous ostentation were the entrenched associations of gaudy by 1800. Mr Thomas Baring sought in 1800 'to chose from the least rich & Gaudy patterns' for his drawing room and bedrooms in the country. Mr Pill returned some patterns that were 'ill done & in very Gaudy Colours & much too small', although which colour combinations might be considered gaudy is unclear: 'I was sure I shoud not like them, unless, they were done in Gold'. Assuredly, there were those who liked a high shine on their domestic fittings. Mr Neave of Hampstead believed his drawing room lacked the necessary burnish. He desired 'to know if the dull Gold on the Border of his Drawing Room cannot be made bright like the Remainder as it looses all its effect'.[50] It was clearly possible for patterns to be too dreary and colours too dingy. Yet even those with a taste for show and a mighty pretty glitter never admitted the word gaudy, though what was splendid, handsome and fine in some eyes was loud and tinsel in others.

Where did this aesthetic vocabulary come from? Most striking is the extent to which wallpaper consumers subscribed to the classical rule of decorum. They were as slavish as polished lords and ladies to the rule that decor should correspond to rank. Hence fine papers in small rooms of families with no fortune would be a flagrant breach of decorum. Sheraton's *Cabinet Dictionary* of 1803 still advised: 'when any gentleman is so vain and ambitious as to order the furnishing of his house in a style superior to his fortune and rank it will be prudent in an upholsterer, by some gentle hints, to direct his choice to a more moderate plan'.[51] Yet even whispers about toning down a scheme were unnecessary amongst Trollope's customers, so deep was the antipathy to indecorous show. Wallpaper shored up social and spatial hierarchies, the innate appreciation of which was a proof of taste.

The opposite of showy excess was neatness. Neatness was an utterly positive quality with many nuances of meaning. Indeed, neat emerges as a Georgian key-word of unexpectedly wide social purchase, which could be applied to towns, houses, objects, personal appearance and even events. Today, the leading mean-ing of neat is tidy, well ordered and trim. The most immediate definition for Georgian consumers, however, was more demandingly architectural. Neat con-veyed a simple elegance of form, finely made and proportioned, free from un-necessary embellishments. Neatness often connoted a spare elegance in keeping with Palladian or Neoclassical architectural ideals. In its emphasis on regularity, proportion and simplicity, neat sat comfortably with classical vocabularies of decorum and harmony.

Neatness was a recognised manner of decoration for social groups or rooms that made claims to taste, but not ostentatious grandeur. Isaac Ware advised as-piring architects in 1756: 'There are apartments in which dignity, others in which neatness, and others in which shew are to be consulted.' Mary Orlebar, of the Bedfordshire gentry, described her ideal country-house retreat in a poem of 1753 as 'small, not elegant, though neat'. In the same decade, a fictional apartment with 'only half a Dozen Cane Chairs, and some Paper Hangings' could never-theless be approved: 'Every thing was neat and elegant; and tho' the Apartment small, it was extremely convenient and well contrived.' Elizabeth Montagu com-mended an elegance that stopped short of grandeur for its character of neat-ness: 'easy chairs & soft couches . . . fine pictures, pretty hangings & a character of neatness make the whole as pleasing a habitation as ever I saw, she enjoys all that riches can give but what appertains to grandeur & magnificence & pomp'.[52] Elegance on a budget and in compact settings should be fittingly neat.

Neat also connoted a regularity of form and well-executed integrity of design in objects. Neat things were well contrived, cleverly put together and smoothly finished. Carpets, stove grates, china, kitchen utensils, prints, upholstery, house carving, tables, chests of drawers, desks, bookcases, looking-glasses, barometers and other furniture were all advertised as 'neat', 'very neat', 'neatly done', 'neatly finished' and 'in the neatest and most modern taste' in the pages of the *Leeds In-telligencer* and *Leeds Mercury*.[53]

Beyond restrained elegance, neatness also demonstrated wholesome cleanli-ness and propriety. Neat wallpaper expressed decency and good housekeeping largely because wallpaper was believed to be clean. Trade manuals warned of insects breeding behind old wall hangings and noxious smells,[54] so fresh papers were an attempt to keep the vermin, grease and nastiness at bay. New paper may even have been the architectural equivalent of spotless personal linen, which even on an unwashed body exemplified inner cleanliness, self-respect and respectability. Neat was used in its more familiar senses of tidy and trim in relation to dress. When deployed by witnesses at the Old Bailey, the leading criminal court in London, neat underscored social credit. The dress of a credible member of the public was invariably 'neat and clean', and trust was extended on that basis.

Neatness could connote either a simple smartness or an elegance stopping short of fashion and extra adornment, or a respectable plainness of attire. Neat radiated a certain moral assertiveness in its very restraint. The Quakers led the most public retreat from finery and show, and so became a byword for sartorial self-control. When Essex yeoman's wife Jane Farrin bespoke a stuff gown for her daughter in the 1750s, she requested a 'neat quakers couler', clarifying 'I would not have very dark nor yet gaudey'.[55] Gaudy was also anathema to John Wesley, who preached the virtues of simplicity to his Methodist followers, though he endorsed the use of dress to reinforce social position. Wesley prohibited any fabrics that were 'gay, glistering or showy', and of 'glaring colour', but urged neatness and cleanliness as a reflection of the inner moral state. For Wesley, neatness and cleanliness in person, clothes and house testified to industry and modesty.[56] Neat, not gaudy expressed the self-righteous restraint of both serious Anglicanism and Protestant dissent.

The opposite of gaudy show, and deeply linked to wholesomeness, cleanliness and decent respectability, neatness had a potentially wide social purchase. Beyond the reach of polite consumerism, neatness embodied an ethical rejection of extravagance. Luxury's 'gaudy visions' were denounced by the imprisoned English republican John Thelwall in 1795, who argued that liberty could take root only in 'virtuous poverty'. Looking back on his happiness in the city lodgings he took with his wife in the 1790s, radical tailor Francis Place concluded: 'our little furniture was good enough for our circumstances and the room was especially neat and clean'. Exuding domestic virtue, 'our neat place' was a fitting home for a self-disciplined radical young couple.[57] Neat, not gaudy had become a badge of sober radicalism.

Decorum contains within it the possibility that decorations would differ for women's and men's rooms. Surprisingly, perhaps, the Trollope letter-books are neutral on what we might call the gendering of interiors. No explicit link was asserted between men and women as a sex and particular styles or colours of wallpaper. There is not a single reference to light, pretty papers to suit the ladies, or bold, handsome patterns that befitted men, though a decorative vocabulary that expressed difference was available. Wall hangings had long been recommended for ladies' rooms, and fanciful Chinese wallpaper seems to have taken hold in ladies' dressing rooms. When Mary Delany stayed at Cornbury in Oxfordshire in 1746, the guest rooms were decorated in a deliberate his and hers idiom. Mr Delany's apartment was 'hung with flowered paper of a grotesque pattern, the colouring lively and the pattern bold and handsome', whereas hers was a fanciful affair 'hung with the finest paper of flowers and all sorts of birds'.[58] Ladies were praised for their skill in creating print rooms, arranging collage on existing papers and freshening up old papers with paint and new borders. 'I have seen great taste exemplified by ladies in this mode of ornamenting apartments', allowed John Pincot, the Hackney colourman, in 1811.[59] In fact, letters and diaries suggest that wallpaper itself could be seen as expressive of femininity, prettiness and *joie de vivre*.

Trollope's customers took for granted a grammar of decorating by situation, which itself implied the sex of the dominant users. They saved their darker colours and assertive patterns for the dining room, a space associated with family dignity and men, while lighter decorations were reserved for drawing rooms, breakfast rooms and parlours, where women congregated. These conventions, however, were neither so fixed nor so complex as the system of rules by which early Victorians decorated, judging by the illustrated orders in the sample book for Cowtan's wallpaper firm. With assertive florals for drawing rooms, delicate small florals for bedrooms, rich flocks for billiard rooms and libraries, grey and brown papers for servants' quarters and pale backgrounds for nurseries, the order books for the 1830s and '40s colour code rooms rigidly by gender, age and position.[60] Victorian decorating is dazzling in its Byzantine variety, but this very complexity can be read as the ultimate articulation of the classical code of decorum – the luxuriant flowering of a plant nursed up most tenderly by the Georgians.

Men and women seem to have shared an aesthetic understanding and vocabulary. Nevertheless, the forthright confidence with which women expressed their preferences in wallpaper is significant, given that we know that men dominated the purchase of luxurious decorative goods such as silver, pictures and substantial china.[61] So although at 21 per cent of Trollope's customers, nominal female consumers of wallpaper were in a minority, their numbers were consistent with those associated with the purchase of other costly decorative items: more than silver, but about the same as paintings and china. Of course, the letter-book itself is not a record of all transactions. In its nature, such a letter-book must overrepresent repeat orders, customers at a distance, those dissatisfied with the orders and those having difficulty paying. The letter-book illuminates female monitoring of the conduct of decorative work in the home, since responsibility for a smooth running of household justified complaint.

> Mrs requests the favour of Mr T to send a Man down on Monday next to rectify the paper in the library for it is impossible to make use of the Room until something is done to it and it being the only Dining Room in the House, the want of it inconveniences Mrs T very much indeed.[62]

Probably the similarities between wallpaper and textiles, long an area of female expertise, empowered women to assert an opinion. Female adeptness at describing textiles is apparent in letters from at least the 1600s. When Mrs Delany described a silk of purple flowers and white feathers 'on a pale deer-coloured figured ground' in 1747 as 'extremely pretty and very modest', she could easily have been describing wallpaper.[63] That the vocabulary used to appreciate wallpaper drew on an older language related to textiles is unsurprising, since wallpaper patterns had so much in common with the silks and chintz that they imitated. 'The preparation of [paper hangings] has a great affinity to the printing of cotton', reported *A History of Inventions and Discoveries* in 1797, 'Artists possess the talent of giving them such a resemblance to striped and flowered silks and cottons that one is apt to be deceived by them on first view.'[64] Trellis featured as much on chintz as on Trollope's wallpaper in the 1790s.

I have used Trollope and Sons' letter-book as a key to the disregarded aesthetics of what might now be termed middle England. In examining the language of the letters, we discover the categories and criteria that informed the ordinary aesthetic judgements of a broadly constituted consumer public. They were not preoccupied with the classical orders that dominate architectural treatises, nor do they exhibit the dense classical allusion that permeates the philosophical debates about taste. What these categories and criteria do draw from those debates is a deep, moralising suspicion of the outward signs of luxury – the rich, the gaudy, the showy. It is striking that almost all Trollope's customers, from the plutocrat to the country parson, shared this suspicion, although the degree of ostentation they were prepared to embrace varied considerably in practice. In these letters the ancient contest between luxury and virtue was re-fought on the terrain of trellis and ribbons in ways that draw on a long-standing set of assumptions about domestic decorum. This language could be generalised beyond wallpaper, to textiles, clothing, furniture, china, even to food.[65] Consumers both male and female, middling and genteel, provincial and cosmopolitan had a clear but flexible vocabulary with which to conceptualise their choices, be they handsome, elegant and beautiful, or unshowy, pretty and neat.

7

THE TRIALS OF
DOMESTIC
DEPENDENCE

IT IS DINNER TIME IN THE HOUSE OF A PROSPEROUS wool merchant in
1720. In the handsome wainscotted dining room, at the head of the table,
enthroned in the best chair, the master is saying grace. He is known for his
modish interest in natural science, but will not neglect his duty, determined to
head his household like another Joshua. Across the polished oak sits his gracious
wife on an elegant cane chair. She presides at the other end of the table and will
shortly carve the beef. Between them sit the children and the two apprentices on
stools, and his sickly sister and her crabbed old aunt. Madam has overseen the
servants cooking in the kitchen, but they are now dismissed, to have a second sitting at the kitchen table. The mistress will dish up the joint herself, serving choice
cuts in order of seniority, a quaint tradition that she observes to show how thoroughly she understands old English customs, despite her personal wealth and
elegant accomplishments (pl. 20).

To see the state in miniature one need only go home. Proverbially, the government of the household revealed the organisation of hierarchical society in
microcosm: husbands were to govern wives, masters and mistresses to rule servants, and parents to discipline children. The years after 1688 saw the acceptance
of new ideas about political authority and social manners, but the household

hierarchy endured regardless. Neither the new political ideas that advocated government by consent, nor the spread of polite protocols, nor the vogue for sensibility in novels and paintings revolutionised the *structures* of authority at home. 'Every family is a little community', as Vicesimus Knox confirmed, 'and who governs it well supports a very noble character, that of the paterfamilias or Patriarch.'[1] Notoriously, Hobbes, Locke and Rousseau did not include every adult individual in their democracy of consent, but rather every male head of household, who was seen to represent the interests of his entourage. The radical Whig Thomas Hollis was a strenuous supporter of the American patriots and an advocate of violent resistance to tyrants, yet he was an exacting master of servants, always lecturing them on their conduct, and they streamed through his bachelor household. Political rebels like John Wilkes and Charles James Fox still assumed that men ruled households, leaving women to organise hot dinners and clean shirts.

The British considered themselves enemies to tyranny, disparaging 'oriental despotism' in foreign families as confirmation of barbarity, but local oppression passed almost unnoticed by political ideas. Mary Astell, however, was wide awake to the contradiction in 1706:

> . . . if Absolute Sovereignty be not necessary in a State, how comes it to be so in Family? Or if in a Family why not in a State? . . . how much soever Arbitrary Power may be dislik'd on a Throne, not *Milton* himself wou'd cry up Liberty to poor *Female Slaves*, or plead for the Lawfulness of Resisting a Private Tyranny.

The blind limitations of male conceptions of liberty could even be the butt of humour. 'Do you not admire these lovers of liberty!', snapped Elizabeth Montagu in 1765, 'I am not sure that Cato did not kick his wife.' Nevertheless, I have yet to encounter a single gentleman musing on whether it might be possible to reconsider his domestic rule in the light of the new political ideas. 'Family life', it was observed in 1779, 'makes Tories of us all . . . see if any Whig wishes to see the beautiful Utopian expansion of power within his own walls.'[2]

Rebellious sons seemed more likely to complain of patriarchal autocracy. The masters of some households 'that are fond of governing by the utmost extremity of their power . . . are no better than domestic Tyrants, and the perfect enemies to peace within doors', reflected John Dunton, a clergyman's son and publisher, in 1705. Father–son power struggles could be the motor of comedy plots, but male tyranny over wives was not a theme pursued by many men in fiction.[3] The 1790s saw a reimagining of authority amongst the avant-garde. Some radical families read the French Revolution as a call for household reformation, and some early nineteenth-century Quakers experimented with models of domestic order – advocating no tyranny over wives, children, servants and even pets. Domestic experiment, however, was a measure and proud boast of advanced radicalism. And even radical families might cling to traditional hierarchies at home, sisters exhibiting a conventional demure deference while brothers debated anti-slavery and republicanism with their cronies.[4]

The conservative majority still understood the household as a hierarchy, which indoor routines and ceremonies reinforced. The comfort of one's bed, the size of one's chair, one's position at the dinner table were all dictated by rank.[5] Household position presupposed the extent of individual control of domestic space, but close quarters generated friction, and struggles over the organisation, decoration or claim to space expressed chronic conflict between family members. The home was celebrated in conduct literature as the stage set for a harmonious hierarchical domesticity, yet this was achieved at the cost of the self-determination of the inferior family members: wives, younger sons, daughters, dependent kin, servants and apprentices all had to accept their place in the chain of command, or brave the consequences. Adult male householders were the principal beneficiaries of this model of government, but households could not run without a proficient female administrator at the helm, and the matron's authority over servants and children was axiomatic. Men and women who fell outside respectable households occupied an even lower rung on the ladder of power.[6] Female tyranny over underlings was common enough. The cantankerous domination of unmarried daughters by elderly mothers was often observed. Governess Agnes Porter (1750–1814?) described one oppressive household in Great Yarmouth in 1797 with unsurprised straightforwardness: 'We have one old lady who is quite extravagant and luxurious with regard to herself, yet refuses a grown-up daughter a little pocket-money, or the least independence in any[thing].'[7] And there were always some female employers who persisted in 'grinding the face of their fellow Christians', as Marthae Taylor, another governess, noted in the 1730s. However, she took the flinty satisfaction that the 'time will come when these haughty ladies who seem to forget that their Dependants are of the same species shall boast of this desparety no more'.[8] In Heaven, the first would be last, and the last first.

Dependence was not a uniquely female experience. Bowing the head to others was a universal performance; even dukes had to grovel at court. Social stability reinforced the social assumption that hierarchy, like Anglicanism, was natural. It was an axiom of Anglican fortitude that it was a Christian's duty to accept the earthly station in which God had placed one: 'he that made us, knows best what's fit for us'.[9] Gentlemen were habituated to institutionalised hierarchy from the moment they left the nursery: the great schools, universities, the Army, the Navy, the Church and the law were all institutions organised into ranks of power and seniority, reifying an unbreakable chain of command. Oxford, for instance, was likened to a hierarchical state, where the different castes (the nobles, gentleman commoners, commoners and scholars, and lowly servitors) had varying privileges, and were compelled to wear different gowns to obviate confusion and fraternisation.[10] The elite obsession with primogeniture meant that birth order was stamped on a boy's consciousness from the glimmering of his very identity. Most younger sons dangled all their lives after the favours of first father and then older brother. Live-in service, apprenticeship and the guilds taught tradesmen that life was a ladder.

Resignation to servitude could be testing. 'Every Station in Life has its *Difficulties*' preached William Brigg to Thomas Stutterd, a Huddersfield bookkeeper and Evangelical, in 1781. 'I must own that being always under servitude and bearing the sharp rebukes of overbearing Persons, are Burthens which do not sit easily upon our Backs.'[11] The Marquis of Halifax expected some inward resistance to authority from his daughters because of 'the natural Love of *Liberty*', but then extinguishing autonomy in girls had been the goal of centuries of training. Marthae Taylor advised an oppressed friend to make a 'vertue of necessity' and gently submit like the reed to the boisterous wind.[12] Women were invariably more constrained than men of the same rank. 'A younger son, you know, must be inured to self-denial and dependence' regrets Colonel Fitzwilliam in *Pride and Prejudice*, warning Miss Elizabeth Bennet that he cannot marry where he likes. Yet self-denial and dependence are still relative, as Elizabeth counters: 'In my opinion the younger son of an Earl can know very little of either. Now, seriously, what have you ever known of self-denial and dependence? When have you ever been prevented from want of money from going wherever you chose, or procuring any thing you had a fancy for?'[13] When James Boswell escaped to the relative anonymity of London in 1763, 'having been so long and so lately under strict family discipline at home', he could not help wondering whether his landlord would tick him off for nocturnal naughtiness, 'Such is the force of custom.' But in practice he had slipped the net, as his bouts of the clap bore rosy witness. Leaving home was an average young man's destiny, if only to board in another, while elite correspondence is sprinkled with bachelors set up in stylish independence at their fathers' expense.[14] Independence was the goal for most men, while for women it would be a fairy-tale achievement.

This chapter recreates the trials of dependence for unmarried women and wives in the upper ranks. What follows is an examination of a series of domestic struggles: all but one being everyday disputes that failed to reach the courts, causing little commotion, apart from local gossip. All arise from the point of view of a household dependant, and all reveal how hard it could be to feel at home amidst the trappings of privilege. The problems of servitude are here exemplified by the journal of the spinster Gertrude Savile. Not that marriage was a guarantee of household autonomy. The letters of Anne Dormer and Margaret, Lady Stanley demonstrate how readily marital friction expressed itself in skirmishes over household space.

Many, if not most, families exploited their unmarried womenfolk, as unpaid housekeepers, nursery maids and sick-nurses, tutors, chaperons, companions and surrogate mothers. Some spinsters were commended for their pains, and drew satisfaction from their value to the family enterprise. Frances Blundell was 'one of the best spokes in the wheel on which our fortunes have turned', acknowledged her brother William.[15] Conversely, a hundred years later in the same county, Ellen Weeton and her widowed mother forwent 'the comforts, and even many of the necessaries of life, to support my brother at Preston' training to be a lawyer, imagining that he 'would repay us when old enough for all these deprivations'. But it was a vain expectation, 'for like all his sex, when he was grown up, he considered what had been done for him was his right; that he owed no gratitude to us, for we were but *female* relatives, and had only done our duty'. Lawyer Weeton declined to offer his sister a home because 'such a kind of family was very unpleasant, causing the most unhappy dissensions'.[16] Some spinsters questioned their lot, but their options for improvement were narrow. 'Should her destination be to remain an inhabitant in her father's house', Priscilla Wakefield intoned, 'cheerfulness, good temper, and obliging resignation of her will to that of others, will be there equally her duty, and her interest'. Eventually, of course, 'it will belong to her to enliven, cheer, to amuse the latter moments of her parent's declining age'.[17] Dependent women were to adapt themselves to the rhythms and priorities of the household. Self-sacrifice on the altar of family was the sentence of the spinster.

Gertrude Savile (1697–1758) was the depressive, portion-less sister of a Nottinghamshire baronet, who found inferiority a sore trial. Her early journals were therapeutic in conception and dense with her complaints, some in code. Her father's early death in 1701, when she was only three, left Gertrude 'a helpless orphan, unprovided for and thrown upon my Brother's bounty'. Savile was awake to the impact of gender and birth order on property and power. Her brother had 'a vast estate and I have nothing'. Without a set allowance, she had to grovel to Sir George for 'every gown, sute of ribbins, pair of gloves, every pin and needle'. Financial dependence ensured inferiority of status, 'treated like a hanger on upon the family', 'subject to affronts', even from her brother's servants. Rufford

Abbey, the Nottinghamshire family seat, was no haven to her: 'I was mightily estrang'd to it. It used to have a more friendly, home air, but now I thought myself a stranger . . . I fancy's the very Walls look'd inhospitably upon me and that everything frown'd upon me for being an Intruder.'[18]

A household headed by a brother was one of the least congenial for an ill-endowed sibling, if the letters and diaries of resentful sisters are anything to go by. Flourishing a little contract theory, Savile argued that she had been born into dependence but had never consented to it. She bridled at 'the baseness of my dependency upon my Brother: neither father nor husband. Nature makes the dependency upon the one, and choice upon the other, easy'. Savile's older sister, Lady Cole, had lived successfully with their brother by choice, but she was a widow of means, who claimed greater consideration. Naively perhaps, Savile imagined that marriage would offer an escape from humiliation, though an abortive flirtation at Bath in 1721 was the nearest she came to courtship. Ineffectually, she even contemplated paid work, claiming that 'if twas possible to get my bread by the meanest and most laborious imployment, I woud without dispute choose it', but there was little likelihood that she would be put to the choice. Such musings were a measure of her bitterness rather than signs of serious strategy.

The state of subjection was henbane to Gertrude Savile. Morbidly insecure with 'a discouraged, dash'd and timmerous temper', Savile was ill equipped to bear her inferiority, never mind make the best of it, hobbled as much by her diffidence as her uncertain fortune. She blamed her insecurities on her disfigured face, cold mother, wretched education and austere upbringing in a joyless house. Savile had even contemplated the sin of suicide, though she regretted making 'such memorandums of resentments', written in 'a passionatt and melancholy fitt', even erasing them in a 'cooler temper'. But when her passionate grief was upon her, Gertrude's only palliative was retreat. 'Entirely confine myself to my room . . . work's chair very hard. That, and my Cat all my pleasure.' Psychological survival rested, in her own estimation, on the possession of a place of refuge. Savile recruited Montaigne in support of her deliberate seclusion, copying out his axiom that a man must not depend for happiness on externals, but must find it in himself through mental retreat: 'We must reserve a back shop, a Withdrawing Room, wholey our own and intirely free within to settle our true Liberty, our principal Solitude and Retreat.'[19] Savile needed a metaphorical and physical sanctuary, a bolthole free from the demands of society, but even amongst the baronetcy, such female closetings were considered unnecessary, if not preposterous. In the Bedfordshire gentry, the Orlebars were worried about a niece who habitually skulked in the chimney corner. Hiding away was unwholesome and inappropriate, a childish fancy that they would not indulge. 'My brother com-

39 Sutton Nicholls, *Golden Square looking East*, 1731, printed engraving. Guildhall Library, London, p5419471. Golden Square was completed in 1707, its houses designed to accommodate gentry.

plained (as I had cause while you was here) that you was rather Gloomy – & fond of keeping away upstairs', Constantia Orlebar remonstrated with young Anne. 'A bad way of mending your spirits . . . you must Brush up.' It was not the aim of domestic training 'to make a *sensitive* plant' of a girl.[20] Women were to participate cheerfully in all the routines of the household.

Eventually, Sir George Savile regularised Gertrude's financial position, fixing her dowry of £3,000 in 1717, and settling her an allowance of £80 a year, and a share in their London house in 1721. When Savile's journal reopens in 1727, all expectation that the 30-year-old spinster would marry had long vanished. Mother and daughter were ensconced together in Sir George Savile's London house in desirable Golden Square, in the throes of redecorating (fig. 39). However, the arrival of Savile's aunt, Mrs Newton, in September challenged their fragile accord. By February 1728 Savile felt displaced in her mother's affections and withdrew in anguish. She ate alone, spent hours on tent work and harpsichord, shrank from company and when obliged to participate in ceremonious family visits, played her part woodenly.[21]

20   Joseph van Aken, *Saying Grace, circa* 1720, oil on canvas. Ashmolean Museum, Oxford, WA1962.17.4.
A virtuous, early eighteenth-century middling household is portrayed thanking the almighty for their
wholesome dinner arranged on pewter and a spotless, well-ironed linen tablecloth. Household goods are few
and simple. The room lacks decorative fixtures. The floor consists of coarse flagstones and the walls are
covered with plain wooden panelling.

21 (above) Cream silk apron (detail) embroidered with English garden flowers by Miss Rossier for Miss Rachel Pain on her marriage to her brother, *circa* 1736. Museum of London 37.178/2. High-quality needlework with an amateur provenance.

22 (right) *Bodice-Coat Flannel the bottom worked*, 1759, flannel embroidered with worsted yarn. London Metropolitan Archives, A/FH/A/9/1/143, Foundling no. 12843. Crude embroidered decoration on the bodice coat left as a token with an infant boy at the London Foundling Hospital.

23   Ribbon embroidery on the inside of the lid of a wooden box decorated on the outside with paper quill work, n.d., Museum of London NN18716. The box contains a set of small interlocking boxes, each covered with a different form of embroidery. It is probably a finished example of the kind of prefabricated kit commercially produced by suppliers like the Temple of Fancy in the early nineteenth century.

24　Workbox, 1808, marquetry in exotic woods. Judges Lodgings Museum, Lancaster, LANMS.2006.8. The box was made by Gillows of Lancaster for Miss Elizabeth Giffard of Nerquis Hall, near Mould, Flintshire, Wales. It is inlaid with a geometric pattern of seventy-two different woods from various parts of the world, including Asia, Europe, the Americas and Australia.

25 *Lady Jane Mathew and her Daughters, circa* 1790, oil on canvas. Yale Center for British Art, New Haven, CT, B1981.25.268. A portrayal of irreproachable female accomplishment. A finely decorated workbox for sewing equipment sits open on the table in the centre.

26 (facing page top) Shellwork vase, 1779–81, probably made at Pelling Place, Old Windsor, Berkshire, by Mrs and Miss Bonnell. Victoria and Albert Museum, London, w.70–1981

27 (facing page bottom) A shell-encrusted surround to a window in the Shell Gallery at A La Ronde, Devon, made by the spinster cousins Jane and Mary Parminter, 1790s. National Trust 113317.

28 (above) Henry Walton, *Sir Robert and Lady Buxton and their Daughter Anne*, *circa* 1786, oil on canvas. Norwich Castle Museum and Art Gallery, NWHCM: 1963.268.9: F. Lady Buxton's tambour frame sits prominently on the table, with her work basket on the shelf below, adding to the elegance of the scene.

29   Settee seat cover, 1728–40, embroidery on canvas in wool and silk, mostly in tent and cross stitch, Victoria and Albert Museum, London, T.473-1970. Adapted from a printed engraving. An example of the kind of figurative tentwork performed by Gertrude Savile.

30   A frieze of feathers in the drawing room at A La Ronde, Devon, made by the spinster cousins Jane and Mary Parminter, using the feathers of game birds and chickens, 1790s. National Trust 146003.

31 Crewelwork bed curtain (detail), 1700–15. Victoria and Albert Museum, London, 353 to I–1907.
An example of the heavy embroidery on hangings deemed old fashioned, even depressing, by the 1790s.

32   Chimneypiece (detail) in the Chinese Room at Claydon House, Buckinghamshire, 1760s. National Trust 66889.

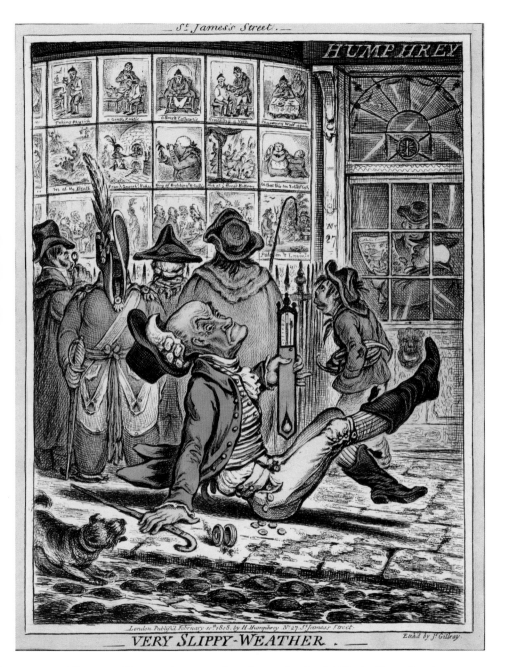

33   James Gillray, *Very Slippy Weather*, 1808, coloured engraving. Lewis Walpole Library, Farmington, CT, 808.2.10.6. An elderly gentleman falls on the pavement outside Mrs Humphrey's print shop in St James's Street, London. Despite holding a barometer, he has not avoided slipping on the ice. The humour lies in the fallibility of scientific instruments and male gullibility.

34　(above) Anon, *A Family Being Served with Tea*, *circa* 1740–5, oil on canvas, Yale Center for British Art B.1981.25.271. An exquisitely dressed older woman presides over a round, three-legged, mahogany tea table. Her porcelain tea set is arranged on a silver tray. On the left, crossing the threshold, a liveried servant brings in a kettle of hot water, the room reflected in its shiny metal.

35　(facing page top) Embroidered casket or workbox, 1671, wood covered with panels of satin, embroidered with coloured silks. Victoria and Albert Museum, London, T.432–1990. Martha Edlin embroidered the coverings for this box, possibly from ready-drawn panels, when she was 11 years old.

36　(facing page bottom) Workbox in the shape of a cottage, 1790–1800, wood veneered with ivory, made in Vizagapatam, India, for the English market. Victoria and Albert Museum, London, W.20–1951. The country cottage, symbolising rustic innocence and domestic retirement, was a popular shape for workboxes, but this Indian-made example also appealed to the taste for exotic materials.

37 An 'elegant bookcase', 1772, mahogany. Judges Lodgings Museum, Lancaster, LANMS.2008.3. Made by Gillows of Lancaster for Mrs Mary Rawlinson, the widow of Thomas Hutton Rawlinson, a Lancaster ironmaster and West Indies merchant. There is nothing recognisably 'feminine' about this piece.

38   Joseph Wright, *Sarah Clayton*, 1769, oil on canvas. Fitchburg Art Museum, Fitchburg, MA. Sarah Clayton, who never married, was an important Liverpool property developer and coal owner. Unusually for a woman, she is shown pointing at a ground plan of the Acropolis in Athens, demonstrating her knowledge of classical architecture.

39   Charlotte Augusta Sneyd, *Drawing Room at Cheverells, Hertfordshire, circa* 1835, watercolour. Keele University Library. A green and pleasant room equipped for the varied pursuits of early nineteenth-century ladies.

Gertrude Savile's complaint was that she had been dislodged in 'a house I was equal Mistress in', struggling for mastery over 'servants I pay wage to', denied her due. 'My Sattisfaction or creditt of no consequence while Servants, Coach and herself are at my Aunt's command.' Henceforward, there was no more 'joyning in house-keeping as formerly'. The women separated into two households under one roof: 'Me, shutt out of the Rooms, with my Aunt and her Maid the chief parts of Mother's separate Family, and the house full of People attending them.' The two sides battled over rights of access to the rooms. When Gertrude heard her mother's servant locking the dining-room door she sent her own servant 'to ask how she durst do it', shouting her protest down the stairs so her mother would hear. In retaliation, Gertrude bespoke a key to open the back parlour, believing her aunt to be storing property there. On Sunday, 1 September: 'Dined in the back parlour. Wondered that I had born to be shut out of it so long.' Ten days later, Gertrude ordered the parlour to be locked against her aunt, and tried to control access to kitchen as well:

> Aunt with her Trade Folks took up the Dining Room; Mother with Stewards (I suppose) took up the Parlor, I (not wisely), as soon as the Parlor was empty, bid Mary to lock it (from my Aunt, not Mother, tho' she locks dores against me without any cause.) . . . I desired Mrs. Mary too, tell her I had lock'd the Parlor dore, because I thought it was fitt I shoud have one room in the house. My angar made me add, that as the Kitchen was in common, I expected none shoud dine there that I [did not] think wellcome, and who had been so saucy to me as Mrs Ann.

Meeting her aunt the same evening going downstairs to dinner sporting 'a malicious insulting smile', Gertrude was goaded into insult, denouncing her aunt as 'an ill-Designing Woman', thereby inciting another shouting match on the stairs, dignity abandoned.[22]

Savile appreciated how 'scandellous to our observing Neighbours' their disputes must appear. Friends reported that 'our Quarrell was the Town talk', 'the subject of discoarse' as far away as Derbyshire. The resolution of these 'domestick affairs' fell to Sir George Savile as head of the family. Gertrude demanded residential independence, but the Saviles insisted on deferential dependence. 'My sentence as to that was to choose to live with Mother with a formall respect and civility, or – Perdition.' Nonetheless, the baronet established Gertrude's entitlement to the coach, proposing a formal system of advance booking the coach in writing. Sir George Savile's temporising counsel was that both mother and daughter 'keep up to form and cerrimony in all things relating to each other'.[23] Propriety restored, the crisis subsided.

This sensible compromise might have ended Savile's quest for emancipation from the family were it not for a twist of fortune worthy of a Victorian novel. Miraculously, in 1730 Savile was left a sizeable property near Newcastle by a cousin. At a stroke, she was delivered from both subordination and dependency. At the deaths of her mother and her sister, the maternal property came into her hands too. At last, at age 40, she became mistress of her own household. At first, she leased a house in Nottinghamshire near Rufford Abbey, the ancestral seat, returning each London season to lodgings in Greek Street. At her brother's death, she established herself permanently in the metropolis, buying her own town house in Great Russell Street, for £240, her last home. Savile had achieved her cherished ambition, so long discountenanced by her family, independence without marriage.

Savile may have been unusually gloomy, but she was hardly unique. The mortification of spinsters in the households of kin can be found from the nobility to the middling. In 1660 Samuel Pepys allowed his sister Paulina to come into his household 'not as a sister but as a servant'; consequently, 'I do not let her sit at table with me', in spatial reinforcement of her inferiority. In 1761, in Horsham in Sussex, the shopkeeper Sarah Hurst protested to her diary: 'My father very angry with me for nothing . . . Oh independence thou greatest blessing this world affords when shall I enjoy thee? Liberty the choicest gift of heaven how I sigh for thee.' While in 1790 Elizabeth Furniss of Bawtry near Doncaster moaned: 'Few people ever met with more cruelty from a father than I have for whilst he made me a Home the frequent unmerited reproaches and Constant ill humours I met with from him made it a Miserable one.'[24] Essentially, Furniss's complaint was the same as Savile's, that a home where one is perpetually made to feel one's inferiority is no home at all.

The shackles of domestic dependence were especially rankling when a parent remarried, introducing an alien authority figure. Living outside the family shelter, yet drawing on family funds, was a luxury given to few unmarried girls. Ann and Mary Martin of Alresford Hall, Essex, managed to extract a separate maintenance from their widowed father when he took a second wife in 1771.[25] But when Lady Caroline and Lady Frances Bruce Brudenell found it too uncomfortable living with their father, the Earl of Ailesbury (1729–1814), and his second wife at Tottenham Park, in Wiltshire, their 'desire to withdraw ourselves' provoked a family crisis and a mild scandal.[26] Most single women lacked the resources to supply a competence; and independence at family expense was a fantastic request. Neither Savile, nor the Martins, nor the Brudenells gave any serious consideration to finding employment as a solution to their woes. The idea was absurd. Even at lower social depths, for every woman desperate enough or brave enough to make shift on their own, there must have been scores who clung on in the households of their natal family or richer relatives, 'lowest and last' as Austen characterised Fanny Price at *Mansfield Park*.[27] Every large house could boast an old woman or two 'who are part of the Old Furniture & have been some years intailed', Elizabeth Robinson observed in 1739.[28]

The lot of an ill-favoured dependant was rarely a happy one. 'Of all the situations in life, that of being humble companion to any lady is the most slavish, the most mortifying, the most disagreeable, of any I ever knew or experienced' reflected Rotherham stonemason's daughter Anne Platt in the 1790s, a position she would never accept even 'if I was reduced to live upon water gruel'.[29] Teaching remained the only significant escape route for spinsters with slender claims to gentility, though to break free of their family of birth they usually had to abase themselves in another. A paradoxical combination of loneliness and an all-pervasive lack of privacy were the price paid for an income; access to a private sitting room was a deal-breaker for some.[30] Nevertheless, degrading employment was still preferable to unpaid subservience for clever women like Platt: 'I well know what ground I stand upon within the family & have no wish or desire to change my present situation to any other title . . . till it may please providence to enable me to keep a little Cott of my own.'[31]

The spinster and the wife were divided by a chasm of status. Upon marriage a woman renounced her legal personality in common law (though she still could make financial claims in equity and ecclesiastical courts), but acquired significant social credit in compensation. A volley of salutations greets the new bride in the humorous *Pleasures of Matrimony* on her first promenade about the neighbourhood, impressing the spinster onlookers: 'Well, thinks the young unmarried Lady, what a surprizing Difference there is between a married Woman and a Maid! Every one respects, treats and honours her.'[32] A wife had a prominent position in the fundamental institution of society, the male-headed household family. Marriage, however, was no shelter from struggle. The household was the anvil on which the marital dynamic was forged, so sparks flew all about. In truth, an ambiguity at the heart of marriage made this more likely.

Patriarchal authority offset by domestic reciprocity was a traditional Christian paradox. Wives were unequivocally subject to their husband's authority, yet they also expected to be partners in the government of the family, and to have its daily management. Wives expected to wield more authority than mere concubines, upper servants, dependent spinsters or honoured guests. Conduct books prated that the management of all things interior fell to the mistress. In popular culture men who meddled with domesticities were disparaged as 'cotqueans', while ballads sniggered at the chaos unleashed by interfering husbands.[33] The courts recognised that women derived authority from their natural position as mistress of their husband's house, and sympathised with deposed wives. The undermining of female authority over ceremonies and servants, provisioning and accounting was often offered as supporting testimony of male abuse when women appealed to the church courts for a separate maintenance. These were seen as aberrant marriages; most men were often only too happy to relinquish the headache of daily management to their wives. Husbands wanted women to be subject, but they also needed them to be responsible to govern.[34]

When a wife went to court, she represented herself as a householder in her own right, not simply the wife of the householder. Analysis of late seventeenth-century church court depositions reveals that married women generally identified themselves, and were identified by other women, as in possession of homes. Men, however, viewed ownership rather differently. Men were less likely to connect women to houses ('the said mistress Jone's husband's house'), tending rather to reinforce their own and other men's authority by downplaying female tenure.[35] Men and women held competing yet coexisting concepts of household government. In successful marriages, a sensible husband gave his wife her head on a long, easy rein. Indeed, if he did not how could she superintend his house to his advantage? Were he fool enough to make a show of his mastery and tighten the reins, he had only himself to blame if she got the bit between her teeth and bridled. In unsuccessful marriages, the ambiguities around household authority made the home the bitterest battleground.

Anne Dormer's difficulties were played out in the closet, chamber, dining room and garden of Rousham House (fig. 40). Anne Dormer (née Cottrell, 1648?–1695) was the devout and strenuously obedient wife of Sir Robert Dormer (1628?–1689) of Rousham in Oxfordshire.[36] An heiress herself, she had married the widower, twenty years her senior, reputedly worth 'several thousand pounds a year', in 1668. She went on to bear him eleven children, of whom eight survived. In 1685, when her surviving letters open, she was mistress of 'at least thirty servants', living in 'the eye of the world', suffering 'the solitude of the country without the quiett'. Anne Dormer's ardently confiding letters to her sister Lady Elizabeth Trumbull reveal a woman struggling to find meaning in a twenty-year marriage to an increasingly tyrannical husband, at the very end of a long road of hope. Now 'a worn out carcase', all spleen and vapours, she had exhausted her youth, looks and health in performing her submission to a Draco. What could be his grounds for anger? She had long endeavoured to 'submit most cheerfully to his absolute dominion over me'. Dormer tried to avoid giving any provocation and hoped the constancy of her forbearance would pacify him: 'I must not exasperate him, for I and my poor children are in his power.' By her own assess-

40   *Rousham, the Seat of Lady Cotterell*, 1823, printed engraving. Private collection. The north front of Rousham House, Oxfordshire, built in the late 1630s. The two wings, the cupola and the crenellation were added by William Kent in the mid-eighteenth century, but the central frontage is otherwise as it was in the late seventeenth century when Anne Dormer lived there.

ment, she was vulnerable because of her diffidence, altogether lacking in the stout self-assurance that might have chastened him. Relinquishing desire, she strove to find self-sufficiency: 'I will concern my self no farther and whether he frowns or smiles it shall be no more to me then the changes of the weather.' Dormer tried to see her appalling marriage as a spiritual test, a reflex shared by other unhappy, but devout, elite wives. She drew some sustenance from the belief that God had ordained this trial for her own spiritual growth, comparing her marriage to the oppression of the Jews in Egypt.[37]

Truly Dormer's marriage was a bondage. Beset by paranoid suspicions and furies, Robert Dormer had ever been a man of strong feelings, driven in courtship by 'such a passion for me that he cod not rest till he had gott me'. In early marriage his possessiveness was such that it was 'two or three years before I could leave to make my father above one visit at a time'. By middle age, his distrust waxed pathological. 'His jealousy is a sort of maddness I think for now I am growne so gray so leane and so hagged that I might justly hope of I might now be trusted in the garden without the feare of anybodyes running away with me.' Anne had no sooner cleared herself of one of his many 'extravagant fancyes' than she was beset by another, constantly 'engaged in a laborious toile to vindicate myself from some strainge suspition'. There is a whiff of the psychopath about Dormer, one minute raging, the next pawing: 'kissing a durty glove of mine and saying he loves me extreamly and then will hang about my neck'. At first, Dormer had hidden his excesses from the neighbours, but latterly even this inhibition had dropped away: 'He railes and reviles me' ever ruder 'when any company is here', thereby flourishing the injustice to observers – 'he doth himself more harm than he doth me'.[38] Nonetheless, the humiliation was so degrading that Anne Dormer resolved to stray beyond the garden no more, reducing Dormer's op-portunities for the exhibition of his tyranny. Robert used to haul Anne about on visits to sustain his 'credit', then cooped her up at home while he went to Lon-don, but far worse was his remaining at home as her gaoler, 'a constant spie he is over me'. His policing was so encompassing that he 'can tell exactly how many [steps] will carry me from my chamber to the garden and if I happen to stopp one minute I am sure to be askt the reason'.[39] He even censored her correspon-dence. Handsome Rousham offered less respite than a cottage: 'A poore woman that lives in a thatched house when shee is ill or weary of her work can step into her Neigh: and have some refres[h]ment but I have none but what I find by thin[k]ing writing and reading.' Her closet was her only sanctuary.[40]

Closet devotions were a fixture in the religious routines of godly women; the diurnal retreat to the closet was a motif of Stuart diaries. The King James Bible suggested that the closet permitted the necessary separation from worldly mat-ters, allowing a proper communion with God: 'When thou prayest, enter into thy closet, and when thou hast shut the door, pray to thy Father which is in se-cret; and thy Father which seeth in secret shall reward thee openly.'[41] Robert Dormer acknowledged some right to closet devotions: 'my closett is a safe shel-ter' noted Anne. Her sister Elizabeth suggested that the closet was the only place she could go to indulge her feelings unobserved, reporting that she used 'to get into [her] closett and cry' when writing to her family. The closet was one thresh-old Robert seemed loath to breach. 'He had been half an hour in the house be-fore I saw him, for being in my closett there I stayed till I heard him pass by the door and say wheres my wife, then I came out and mett him as I always do with a cheerfull face.' Anne, however, could not use the closet for half the year – it was too cold in the winter and too hot in the summer – so then she had 'no resting place'. Patrolling like a gaoler, 'always passing to and fro', Dormer even kicked in the nursery door on the hunt for her – 'broke the doore and made it flie across the roome when he fancied I was there but I was not'. Dormer's extravagant pride 'makes him think a wife cannot be kept too much a slave'.[42]

Dormer had turned the house into a prison for his plaintive wife. His airless bedroom she experienced as a torture chamber – 'that hatefull roome . . . which is so like an oven', 'to stay in it was worss than death'. Even in the spring, she found meagre rest and 'satt every night in a chaire after having beene three or four houres in bed the heat was so extream there'. Her claustrophobia was aggravated by a swarm of objects – 'he begins to clutter up that roome with trinketts as he has done severall others' – redolent of Robert's pathology. When the Trumbulls suggested that Anne sleep in another room, they authorised her flight from that 'hatefull den', but also from the marital bed, to her extravagant relief. By the winter of 1685 she was sleeping 'in that roome next the dining roome', and at last achieving some rest.[43] Nevertheless, Anne Dormer still had no managerial prerogatives. Robert hid their plate she knew not where, and refused to let her open his locked boxes and trunks. Even after his death, Anne still felt like a trespasser: 'going up and down his house and using such things as would scarce suffer me to look upon I am like one haunted with an evil spirit or who has committed some crime'. Her marriage was a 'burden' under which she groaned, a 'nett', and a 'cage'.[44] Rousham was never 'her' house.

Given the extent of Dormer's incarceration, the absence of any reported family intervention is astonishing. The Cottrells and the Trumbulls were politically well connected. Father, sister and brother-in-law all appear to have sympathised with their benighted kinswoman, and the neighbours, at least in Anne's estimation, disparaged Dormer's conduct. Later letters, however, reveal Sir Charles Cottrell concern with the worldly benefits of marrying into the Dormers of Rousham, so perhaps he was too ambitious to risk antagonising Robert. For her part, Anne was determined not to leave her spouse, whatever the provocation, because 'I am tied by a vowe and my duty obliges me to live with him.'[45] Possibly the fact that Robert Dormer inflicted psychological torture, not physical beatings, made his persecution harder for kinfolk to oppose. Anne Dormer was released only by Robert's death in 1689. Unluckily, widowhood was neither tranquil nor independent in Anne's account. Friends believed she had 'cause to rejoice' and imagined she would 'flie out as soon as the cage was broken'. Yet Anne sought only some quiet in her old home. 'It would be insufferable to me to live a life of visiting for now methinks I have done with the world . . . Sweet Retirement is all I covet.'[46] Before she drew breath, however, Sir Charles Cottrell bustled her back to London. There he demanded that she blazon her enhanced status, spending money on 'a coach footman and two maids', engaging in a frenetic round of visiting. Consequently, Anne 'lived beyond [her] fortune', scattering money earmarked for her younger children's portions and any surplus for charity: 'it is torment to me to have so much spent for shew'. Where was the gain, but for keeping up appearances for her father's 'creadit'? Dormer felt as ill equipped as Savile to meet the demands of fashionable society, and saw even less virtue in the attempt.[47] At 42, Dormer still lacked the capacity to determine the shape of her own life: 'I can gett no corner here to rest in.'[48]

The household was an ancient theatre of struggle. Over the eighteenth century, marital conflict would still be played out across kitchens and parlours, bed-chambers and dining rooms. The intensification of domestic sociability, however, made internal arrangements ever more conspicuous to observers, while the fashionable glamour that attached to polite ceremony indoors made quarrelling even more shaming for the participants. Life-threatening cruelty remained the only grounds on which wives could obtain a legal separation in the church courts, but supporting evidence about social isolation, undue confinement and contempt indoors reveals increased expectations of marital courtesy and heterosexual society. The prestige of drawing-room conversation was elevated by the writers of the Scottish Enlightenment. Their histories described how society developed in stages from savagery to civil society and cited the treatment of women as a measure of the advance of civilisation. Furthermore, since communication was the fuel of commercial society, women's suppleness in conversation became seen as a positive talent. The value of domestic company to men was asserted in the periodical literature on politeness, especially in the *Tatler*, *Spectator* and *Guardian*, whose readership extended far beyond liberal coteries to merchants, farmers, shopkeepers, even servants. Pundits agreed that exposure to feminine society moderated men's innate boorishness and brightened their dull pedantry. The polish of female company was crucial to the achievement of modern polite manhood. In the past, men asserted their dominance through violence and brute oppression, whereas the up-to-date gentleman showed his superiority by tempering his authority. He flourished his fashionable modernity and Enlightenment affinities in the choice of a wife who could hold her own in the drawing room.[49]

The husband who could not honour his wife as his companion and hostess now looked like a gothic anachronism. When Lancashire merchant's wife Elizabeth Shackleton was humiliated by her husband in her own parlour in the 1770s ('He is very unmannerly, not much calculated for a matrimonial life'), she recruited the arguments of Addison and Steele to counter his brutish incivility.[50] The frustration of her legitimate rights to social life at home was infuriating to Margaret, Lady Stanley, a bewildering denial by the late eighteenth century. After twenty years 'deeply steeped in bitterness', in 1790 she left her husband, a Cheshire baronet. Lady Stanley penned a long justification to her Welsh mother in May 1790, hoping she could 'reconcile [herself] to the Idea of so desperate a measure' because after two decades of acrimony 'nothing less could procure ease and comfort to my remaining Days'. First among the 'Reasons and circumstances' that precipitated her flight was 'the uncomfortable way in which we have lived' in both London and Cheshire. Lady Stanley insisted on her exhaustive and now exhausted efforts to please: 'For many successive years had I sought and even studied to promote Sir J's satisfaction as far as lay in my power'. Ever submissive to his pleasure, she had been the very pattern of the selfless wife. 'My every Taste and Inclination I sacrificed to his, contending no point however desirable to me and conforming as well as I could in all things (& with chearfulness too) to his humour, different as it was to my own', yet he was never satisfied. He failed to note or value her unvarying 'complaisance' and endless 'endeavour' to 'please or content him'. Instead, Sir John Stanley rewarded her by 'always appearing gloomy reserved dissatisfied & full of Duplicity'. To add insult to injury, 'he never consulted me on any concern respecting either my family, my children or my satisfaction'. Thus he flagrantly refused to honour her position as wife, mother and mistress of his house. The wife of a rich baronet might reasonably expect some social compensations for her icy marriage, yet Sir John Stanley spurned polite company. Social isolation confirmed the domestic doldrums:

> you well know the very inhospitable manner of our house, no friend, no social Guest frequented it, we lived for ourselves and for ourselves alone, and though our Fortune was considerable, we live obscurely, cheerlessly, unbefriended and unbefriending . . .
>
> The situation of our House too, added to the desolateness and disagreeaness of our circumstances, as to remoteness entirely put it out of our power to cultivate evening society, none would forego more convenient and cheerful Haunts, to make dull unprofitable visits to our unconnected and disregarded Family for disregard (not to say contempt) must ever be the consequence of a contracted & inhospitable way of life.

Their loss was therefore societal as well as personal; their credit as junior members of the landed ascendancy was diminished by their failure to cultivate relations with their peers. Thus, 'in the midst therefore of the gay and Social world, we lived in a state of seclusion'. Lady Stanley longed for 'social guests' of her own, but 'Sir J hated society especially at home and still more particularly he disliked Females'. The only social excitement she recollected was 'a few nights within the months of March and April . . . when a few cards brought invitations to Assemblies'. In her years of better health and brighter spirits, she had wanted to give assemblies herself, but 'Sir J had discouraged that project & indeed put it out of my Power, by letting the house remain the best part unfurnish'd nor in fifteen of the years I lived in it could my solicitations prevail on him to do more'. Latterly, when Sir John Stanley had seemed more disposed to refurbishment, Lady Stanley was past caring: 'with Health declined, my spirits broken & my mind disgusted by continual disregards it matter'd to me not', and it would take more than redecoration and a few assemblies to 'amend our circumstances'. Even in London, the very cosmopolis of fashion, Lady Stanley was discouraged from opening the doors of their town house, a perverse prohibition, since the London house was the customary base of social campaign for families with claims to fashion. 'Years and years round had I abided in Grosvenor Place to prevent travelling expenses I had lived there in conformity to his inclination most closely and privately, Guests I never presumed to invite to a Repast, till three or four times the last Spring, & for that I rec a very angry letter.' At length, labouring 'under such Restrictions, & many other aggravating instances of disregard', she became 'weary and disgusted'. She came to think 'that a cabin exempt from the Domination of a man with an ever adverse mind and sullen Brow' were preferable to all the chill amenities of Alderley and Grosvenor Place.[51] Lady Stanley ran away to Lisbon, where she lived in exile, tending her garden, composing her self-justifications and sorrowing.

An extreme statement of the potential tenuousness of a woman's claim to home was the lock-out. Abused wives frequently complained to the judges of the church courts of being turned out of doors, often at night in filthy weather.[52] Denying shelter, however, was commonly seen as an illegitimate abuse of power, disapproved by neighbours and frowned on by the courts. When the aged Mrs Grenville was denied admission to her own house by her husband and son in August 1716, the Buckinghamshire gentry were indignant. Claiming direct descent from the Normans, the Grenvilles were seen as ambition personified.[53] In 1716 they were in the throes of a nasty legal battle, with mother and daughters ranged against father and son. Grenville senior had denied his daughters all income, allowing not 'one farthing sence last Crismus'. In search of justice they had 'delivered some petition to lord chancellor'. Meanwhile, 'Mrs Grenville was advised by her councel to come to Wootton and demand entrans into her home'. The great argument on her side was that 'she is joynt purchaser with her husband in all the estate that has bin boght sence she was married which is between a 11 and 12 hundred a year'. Yet the old lady so dreaded the confrontation that she 'neither eat nor dranke for 2 days before' and persevered only because 'the lawyer told her she must offer to go into her house'. Put to it, Mrs Grenville enlisted a friend, Mrs Egleton, two other supporters and her maid to bolster her courage.

Mrs Egleton 'sate in the coach att the lower gatte', watching while old Mrs Grenville approached the house. Chillingly, 'so soon as they sett eye on her the gattes were all locke up and Mr Grenville stood within and talked to his mother throw the Iron barres and deneyd her coming in'. In a pathetic scene, Mrs Grenville, trembling 'without the gate', asked to see her husband, only to be told by her son that 'it was not his fathers plesure to see her', and that he refused to enquire further. A shocked onlooker 'told me they never saw anything like Mr Grenville' for arrogance, and that it 'would have trobled anybody to see how the poor old Lady Looked that had not a heart of stone'. The defeated dowager was forced to retreat to a friend's house, where 'we gott her to eate something there and drinke a glase of water', and later on to Mrs Dormer's, where a bevy of county friends gathered to succour and revive her: 'when the poor old lady was gott amongst her old acquaintances she was very cheerful'. No friend would or could force an entry for her, but everywhere the Grenville heir was censured: 'Sure Mr Grenville has a great dale to answer for to use his mother as he has done.' The neighbours boycotted Wootten, and when the young Mrs Grenville went a visiting, Lady Wharton refused to see her. 'The whole country crys out shame.'[54]

History does not record what happened to the banished Mrs Grenville, but the unmoved daughter-in-law Hester Grenville succeeded triumphantly. Only the next year, Hester Grenville's childless brother, Viscount Cobham, broke the entail on the Stowe estate and named her as heir. By 1749 she had been created Countess Temple in her own right. All of her five sons became MPs; the eldest inherited both Wootten and Stowe; Henry became governor of Barbados; George became prime minister; and the only daughter, Hester, married another prime minister, William Pitt, Earl of Chatham, and gave birth to yet one more statesman, William Pitt the younger. 'Never indeed was family so well provided for during an entire century as the Temple-Grenvilles.'[55] Hester Grenville could afford to scoff in the face of the county's condemnation; perhaps she simply failed to notice their censure. The ruthlessness of the commanding Whig dynasty was common knowledge. An old lady's quavery wish to set foot in her own home was easily crushed beneath the accelerating wheels of their juggernaut.

Hierarchy was the skeleton that structured households, as natural as landscape. We should be careful not to presume that dependence was insufferable, or that rebellion boiled in every conscious underling. The conviction that hierarchy is abnormal is a modern reflex, not a principle of Georgian common sense. Doubtless thousands of grateful, deferential, beguiling or Machiavellian underlings flourished. Victor-Louis Dutens (1730–1812) was a Huguenot émigré and tutor, who lived in a succession of aristocratic households hoping for preferment. Although the role of glorified factotum brought some twinges of resentment, he deplored 'that fatal principle of equality' that had driven the recent French Revolution, and had a delicious appreciation of the compensating luxuries open to him in the households of the great: 'that urbanity, that taste, that elegance of manners and conversation, which were to be found in no other class of men so much as among them'.[56] Dependence had plenty of secondary benefits for the wily, though some hierarchical situations were inherently more unstable than others. Dependants found it easier to acknowledge the superiority of a father and mother than the arrogant self-importance of other kin, while of all others a stepmother's pretensions were the hardest to stomach. To suffer all the authority but to enjoy none of the love of a mother could be excruciating. Flight from the family home was the only way to escape the government of a new mother. The luxurious opportunity to be one's own mistress, however, set up in an independent household and paid for out of family funds, was given to few unmarried girls. Fathers objected on grounds of expense, but also on principle – ungoverned girls were an anathema to patriarchy.

Once married, however, women congratulated themselves on graduation from raw dependency to the office of mistress. When denied their due weight, aggrieved wives were perhaps more outraged than spinsters, blaming their officious husbands and denouncing them as tyrants, while dependent women were more likely to lament their pathetic condition and the indifference of fate. Old maids suspected that it was their lot to be humbled, but wives did not expect to be humiliated. Yet for all the differences between the condition and expectations of matrons and spinsters, there are some common features of their experience of households. Savile and Dormer adopted a similar stance. Both were highly intelligent, questioning, yet diffident women, who at some level felt that a lack of social ease and active courage put them at a disadvantage in domestic politics. Hovering over the writings of both is the fear that something morbidly retreating in their personalities might have accentuated their victimisation. Dormer's father declared as much when he warned 'he that makes himself the sheep the wolf will eate him'.[57] Savile's attempts to assert herself were gauche and often self-defeating, while a certain hesitancy and desire to please weakened Dormer's manoeuvres. Once Anne Dormer was a widow with a jointure, a thicker skin and some persistency might have seen off her father.

On the other hand, both women were assertive on paper, and in their writing they refused to be defined by their oppressors: Savile arguing out her case ad nauseam with brother, mother and aunt, Dormer constructing her husband as a man to be pitied, her cross to bear, a bit player in her own spiritual drama. Both women unrolled their sorrows on paper, using their writing as a confessional, consolation and emotional release, all of which raises the strong possibility that their distraught testimony offers only a partial account of their emotional experience. Once Gertrude Savile started to come into her money, her diary steadily metamorphosed from frantic confession to calmer reportage of routine. Her fairy-tale deliverance from dependence is barely reported. Perhaps, then, the function of their writing was not to capture the totality of their responses, even were that possible. Rather, it served to ease their mental suffering at its height. None of which is to diminish the weight of the yoke under which they writhed, but it is to suggest that in all likelihood there were periods of uneventful routine, or perhaps even modest satisfaction, that they failed to report. Nor does the inevitable partiality of these bitter narratives reduce their validity as evidence of the way that the control of women could be mapped in space. In fact, it was through space that superiors exerted their most suffocating power.

Hierarchy, rank, dependence and independence were the categories used to make sense of the household and an individual's role within it. One's place in the hierarchy of the household was determined by age, gender, birth order and access to personal capital. Household status was expressed spatially; the higher one's position the greater one's access to personal space and power to govern the use of space. The letter, if not the spirit, of the common law enshrined husbands and fathers as monarchs of their domestic kingdoms, Lord Paramount at home. Court cases map out the extremes of patriarchal oppression, in which men can be seen exercising all-encompassing control over women's use of space: imprisoning them, blocking access to certain rooms, driving them from room to room in terror or locking them out altogether. Nevertheless, such comprehensive oppression was manifest only in highly dysfunctional situations of extreme marital violence. Possibly a timeless pathology infects such episodes, but the perpetrators might still argue that they were only exploiting their patriarchal prerogatives to their logical limit. On the other hand, the church courts would not countenance extreme domestic cruelty or the degradation of the mistress. It is evident that adult women expected to have authority over the house keys, and resented the loss of power and prestige that such a denial necessarily entailed.[58] Propertied wives expected to influence the social uses of space, and where this prerogative was repudiated, matrimonial bitterness was the inevitable result. Sir John Stanley dismissed his wife's legitimate expectation of hospitality at home; he refused to redecorate so she could not throw parties, vetoed dinners, discouraged social guests, especially women, and forced seclusion on his dejected wife. By contrast, Robert Dormer cluttered the house with knick-knacks that Anne Dormer despised, intensifying her feelings of suffocation. He forced society on his wife, and then humiliated her before guests. Both women felt they had received less than their due, and that their menfolk were abusing rather than expressing their proper authority. The office of mistress involved recognised privileges, demarcated areas of authority and the right to social life and to social withdrawal.

Life at home pivoted around the comfort of its most powerful members, usually adult men, but not invariably, for elderly mothers could be equally authoritarian. Underlings were not expected to arrange their routines to their own satisfaction. Whatever their shynesses and finer feelings, in the social areas of the house dependent women of the nobility, gentry and middling ranks were expected to submit to the needs, wants and whims of superiors, matching their mood to the company, fulfilling no selfish desires of their own. The Berkshire parson George Woodward and his chatty wife expected their lodger, a farmer's widow, to contribute to their society and enjoyment in 1759, but finding her glum, formal, particular and solitary, eventually showed her the door.[59] Cumulatively, women's testimonies reveal the weight of the burden of compulsory domestic sociability. The toils of civility could be exhausting for everyone, but social gatherings were periods of absolute penance for both Savile and Dormer. Only in the quiet of her own chamber at night might an unmarried woman enjoy some respite from the demands of family, though the curtained bed was not necessarily a haven for a wife. In the day, even for those of high rank, only the closet furnished some solitude and retreat.

Closets were widespread in the houses of the gentry and mercantile elites by the late seventeenth century. The idea that happy marriages involved respect for women's privacy for secular as well as religious purposes was certainly available. In Congreve's *The Way of the World* (1700) Millamant and Mirabell negotiate a pre-nuptial contract about etiquette behind closed doors. Millamant insists on the right to 'dine in my Dressing room when I'm out of Humour, without giving a reason. To have my closet inviolate; to be sole empress of my tea table . . . And lastly, wherever I am, you shall always knock at the door before you come in.'[60] The female right to privacy is aligned with fashionable urban modernity. Old and new ideas of domestic diplomacy are a humorous issue in Henry Fielding's *Tom Jones*. Squire Western's unmarried sister accuses him of cloddish insensitivity when he bursts in unannounced. 'Brother said she I am astonished at your behaviour will you never learn any regard to decorum? Will you still look upon every apartment as your own, or as belonging to your country tenants? Do you think yourself at liberty to invade the privacies of women of condition without the least decency or notice?' Mrs Western's own understanding of domestic facts is actually less than perfect, nevertheless that ladies should enjoy some defence against intrusion is invoked as a mark of civilisation and the squire's ignorance is a further proof of his Tory boorishness.[61]

'What heroine ever yet existed without her own Closet', laughed Fanny Burney.[62] Literary studies have recreated the secular importance of the closet for reading, writing, reflection and the defence of the boundaries of the self; truly 'a workshop of the mind, a laboratory of the soul'. For Richardson's Clarissa Harlowe, a closet was a psychological necessity, the stronghold of her self-command, not a prison. It is worth remembering that Clarissa's closet locked on the inside, and it was for her to decide when to draw the curtain on the internal window.[63] Yet the right to closet time was not universally sanctioned. Deliberate female seclusion for any purpose but prayer could be seen as an absurd affectation, but withdrawal could sometimes be a successful tactic. When Lady Cowper's husband kept interfering in her management, she washed her hands of administration and retreated: 'I will resign the whole to the Management of Sir W and resolve to live quiet in my chamber.' She sat it out for some months, and her patience was eventually rewarded by his appeal that she resume her housekeeping in return for better behaviour.[64]

Christian men tried to observe 'closet duties' too, of course, and some, like the Nonconformist Richard Kay in Lancashire, complained about interruptions, being called out 'to attend Father's business . . . and many Times to joyn with some Workmen or other'. Very occasionally, we find men at bay, using the same tactics as women. One Stuart gentleman was beaten into retreat in his own Hertfordshire house. By repute 'a mild man of kindly disposition', Sir Samuel Grimston of Gorhambury House was shackled to a domineering second wife. Lady Anne Tufton was a termagant. Worn by her scolding, Grimston had a small room built near his billiard room, where he could retreat part of the day with his books. Accessed only by a narrow stairway, 'Mount Pleasant' was his refuge. Similarly, the Lancashire cleric Oliver Heywood remembered how in July 1672 'being in my house, upon some slight occasion, my wife gave out some peevish discontented words, I durst not speak for fear of greaving her but withdrew myself into my study'. Kneeling to pray on a cushion embroidered with the initials of his sweet dead first wife also calmed his nerves, though I suspect not his second wife's temper. Even Proverbs warned 'It is better to dwell in a corner of the housetop, than with a brawling woman in a wide house.'[65]

For all the normality of hierarchy, subordinates felt that some degree of control over space and time, however flimsy, was essential to make a house a home. But households were not arranged for the ease of underlings; and even the scanty comforts of home were apt to vanish in the face of comprehensive domination. Barren of warmth, the scene of petty trials and humiliations, and at worst tyranny and cruelty, 'home' had a ghastly ring to the helpless. The powerless experienced their servitude always and everywhere, snatching moments to themselves, stealing into corners, longing for a neat cottage of their own or even a hut if it were free from dominion. Without a nook of one's own or a place to keep one's mementos there could be no dignity of living. It was quite possible to have a handsome roof over one's head and yet feel homeless. For a house where an inmate has no autonomy at all is a dungeon, however well upholstered. Observers read control of space as an index of independence, purchased by money and replete with power.

8

A NEST OF COMFORTS:
WOMEN ALONE

'CRANFORD IS IN POSSESSION OF THE AMAZONS', begins Elizabeth Gaskell's comic fantasy derived from the Cheshire town of her youth. Her mothering by maiden aunts in Knutsford in the 1820s and '30s furnished a host of anecdotes for her requiem for petticoat government. Cranford is a country town where 'all the holders of houses, above a certain rent are women'. Whether by chance or design, the gentlemen have all evaporated, leaving the spinsters, widows and grass widows in their 'baby house' dwellings, to their sedate evening parties of best dresses, 'wafer bread-and-butter', cards and tea. Cranford is an insular, judgemental, but ultimately supportive feminine society, where all elect not to notice their neighbours' byzantine efforts to keep up appearances already threadbare. At one tea party, a widow sits in state in the upstairs parlour, while her guests 'talked on about household forms and ceremonies' as if the hostess had a bustling army of servants below, 'instead of the one little charity school maiden', who was not strong enough to carry the tea tray unaided. Elegant economy is Cranford's watchword, because the ladies are all stretching small incomes and annuities. Newspapers are spread to save the carpet; an old muslin dress becomes a window blind; old clothes are worn out in the morning before calling time; the tea tray is stashed under the sofa for lack of space.

The lengths the old ladies go to may be absurd, but Gaskell does not sneer at the campaign to hold forms and community together. The women are living hoards of local memory; homes are drenched in a richer past; possessions are worse for wear; but all turn their best side to the future with dignity and resolve. The sorority is parochial and snobbish, but also selfless and gallant, suffused with that charity that suffereth long, and is kind. Gaskell lends a bitter sweet regret to their toils and faded hopes – going up in smoke like so many love letters and sad ribbons consigned to the fire. Unspoken longing for what might have been surfaces in Miss Matty's recurring dream of the baby girl of two who puts up her face to be kissed at bedtime. So Gaskell smiles indulgently on their brave bonnets and monstrous old brooches – 'some with dog's eyes painted on them; some that were like small picture frames with mausoleums and weeping willows neatly executed in hair inside; some again with miniatures of ladies and gentlemen sweetly smiling out of a nest of stiff muslin'. Spinsterhood and widowhood expose all the Cranford ladies to varying degrees of genteel poverty, which they face with imaginative resource and a certain bravery, even self-sufficiency. 'A man, as one of them observed to me once, "is so in the way in the house".'[1]

The history of family and home is usually written from the perspective of married couples. As wife and mistress of a household, a woman was seen to be in her adult prime, her status at its zenith, yet this achievement was hardly universal, nor was the meridian necessarily prolonged. Even the typical marriage lasted only ten years in 1700.[2] Most women spent years as unmarried dependants, since the average age of marriage was around 26 for females before 1750, and almost 25 thereafter, while probably as many as one in five women in Georgian England never married. Moreover, aristocratic spinsterhood ran between 25 per cent and 30 per cent, for, as Jane Austen drily observed, 'there are not so many men of large fortune in the world as there are pretty women to deserve them'.[3] The importance of differentiating between the spinster and the widow has recently been asserted because their standing, opportunities and relationships were quite different.[4] Nowhere was the distinction more apparent than in homes. Widows were fully expected to head their own households, while the independent spinster was at best a curiosity, and at worst a problem.

What follows is a case study of the interiors and objects of middling and genteel spinsters and widows based on letters and account-books. The chapter considers the women's consumer choices and identifies the significant household objects with which they lived. It asks whether the material culture of lone women was distinctive, and compares their objects with those of wives and husbands of the same genteel background. Spinster arrangements are here exemplified by the letters of Mary Hartley (1736–1803), of Winchester and Bath, the middle-aged daughter of a physician, and the account-books of Gertrude Savile (1697–1758), the sister of a Nottinghamshire baronet, and Miss Diana Eyre (1723–1806), an affluent Yorkshire spinster. Post-marital independence is detailed in the accounts of Mrs Martha Dodson (1684–1765) of Cookham in Berkshire, widow of a rich tin-plate man, and a grocer's daughter, Mrs Elizabeth Forth (1765–1837), the York widow of the Reverend Forth. Supplementary material is gathered from sporadic letters – every correspondence network numbered at least one or two lone older females amongst their scribblers.

Without the confirmation of maturity offered by a wedding ceremony, even the adulthood of the life-long single was vague, adding to the old conviction that they ought to be disciplined in suitably authoritarian households like other disorderly youths.[5] Municipal attempts to prohibit single women from setting up home outside a patriarchal household included whipping, incarceration and deportation. Though municipal persecution waned after 1640, the residential options of the single woman remained limited, by poverty, but also powerfully by custom. Even in the late 1600s, only 15 per cent of life-long maids headed, or co-headed, their own households in Southampton, as compared with 86 per cent of widows, Amy Froide discovered. Those spinsters who did live independently were all quite old, had no living parent, and were of higher social status.[6] Richard Wall extrapolates that widows were everywhere more likely to head their own households than spinsters.[7]

My analysis of Yorkshire probate inventories indicates that eighteenth-century widows enjoyed more space than spinsters (Table 1). Failure in a probate inventory to name individual rooms does not provide conclusive proof that the deceased lived in a single chamber. Nevertheless, the disparity between the Yorkshire widows and spinsters in this respect is so great that it strongly suggests spinsters lived in markedly more confined circumstances. This finding is reinforced by the fact that the average value of their possessions was considerably less, and they tended to own a narrower range of goods, tea wares excepted.

Table 1. Rooms in single women's probate inventories, Yorkshire, 1710–11 and 1780–82.[8]

	All	Inventoried by rooms	% inventoried by rooms	Average value of inventory
Widows	52	30	58	£73
Spinsters	7	1	14	£47

Virgins were not expected to enjoy independence. There was no institutional provision in England for women to devote themselves to a single life beyond the family; Protestant maids who tried to live like nuns ran the risk of being thought 'singular and fantastick'. Catholic claustration was regarded with horror. When a Miss Chichester 'resolved on taking the veil' in 1789, her mother was heartbroken and her friends appalled by 'her erring zeal', and renunciation of 'the happiness arising from domestic connections'.[9] Solutions like Mary Astell's religious retirement for unmarried ladies with £500 to offer as dowry, Sarah Scott's artistic sanctuary *Millenium Hall*, and the institution 'in which single women of small or no fortunes might live with all manner of freedom' proposed by Richardson's perfect gentleman Sir Charles Grandison were never more than fantasies.[10] Corporate harassments of spinsters may have ceased, but immersion and domestication in a family household was still considered the only truly respectable option.

It was normal for families to call first on their unmarried maids in a crisis, so it was common for spinsters to be absorbed in the households of kin for long periods, playing surrogate wife to a bereaved brother-in-law, foster mother to nieces and nephews, live-in nurse to an aged parent, housekeeper to a bachelor brother or uncle. The life of the spinster could be one long tour of kin. The protection of the patriarchal roof could also be bought by the family boarder, who paid her kin rent for her one or two rooms. Others tried to keep up appearances in two rooms in lodgings attended by a maid. Dorothy Rudston was described by her friends as 'a Maiden lady', 'a very good [Christ]ian & a Gentlewoman bred'. In 1752 she refused an offer to live with her sister, taking lodgings in Flamborough, in Yorkshire, instead: 'I have one very good room & two small ones within it'; fine rooms in themselves she stressed, 'with Casements in them all, I'm sure you woud be pleasd if you saw them'. The maiden lady clung onto gentility. One room was 'for my maid', while 'the other a pretty Dressing Room which holds all my books the Dressing Table & 4 Chairs'.[11] Dorothy Rudston was self-consciously uncomplaining, but she was regarded by her friends as a pillar of fortitude with much to bear.

The single life was seen as a miserable predicament, not a heroic freedom. No doubt some spinsters spurned wedlock for autonomy, especially if they were rich, but because marriage was the only entrance to adult privilege for women and the social penalties suffered by older maids were severe, probably most were disappointed in their courtships. 'To keep house with ye Man we love must be preferable to any other state, if that love be mutual', opined Miss Elizabeth Munbee of Bury St Edmunds in 1775. 'I fear that will never be my lot', she accurately foretold.[12] The ramifications of isolation in a society built on connection were all encompassing. 'I felt my unprotected, isolated situation most painfully', wailed the married governess Ellen Weeton Stock when estranged from her violent husband and beloved daughter in Lancashire in the 1820s. Without a house, furniture or servant, she felt unable to return hospitality, so was forced to decline most invitations. 'The solitary life I lead, is not from choice; I see no way of avoiding it.'[13]

Under the wretched circumstances it would be unsurprising if lone women clustered together for comfort, protection and economy. The role of urban landlady was itself associated with middle-aged matrons and widows; renting out a back room to another respectable widow could be a financial makeweight. Genteel and middling maids probably gravitated towards other unmarried female kin, and no doubt sought out lodgings known to be congenial to females. Judging by Ludlow (where exceptional sources for the study of household structure survive), landladies were statistically more likely to rent to other women.[14] Scattered fragments suggest that this was a wider phenomenon. Elizabeth Barker, an unmarried member of a rising mercantile clan, lodged in St Saviourgate, York, with her maid in the 1730s, in a town house stuffed 'so full' with respectable lone women. Mrs Bette Moysder had the best lodging, while Mrs Fothergill and her sister were 'in the great chamber', where 'their maid cleans their room & there own furniture make it looks mighty well'.[15] The house in Ipswich where Clara Reeve lodged in the 1790s was known for its independent ladies; an old bachelor clergyman was turned away, 'hearing that females only were admitted'.[16] Widowed mother and unmarried daughters, or a brace of sisters, could be the nucleus of a cost-effective household, or that proverbial solution, a school.[17] Over a lifetime a single woman might easily experience a variety of residential arrangements, from daughter of the house, to commercial lodger, unpaid housekeeper in a family house, to family boarder, to co-tenant with other women, related and unrelated. Home was hardly a static entity for them.

Gertrude Savile was born to the northern quality, but endured years of rankling dependence on her baronet brother, mother and aunt, until abruptly delivered by a surprise legacy in 1730. In July 1737 Savile leased a house for £6 a year, at Farnsfield in Nottinghamshire near Rufford Abbey, the ancestral seat, returning each London season to lodgings in Greek Street, Soho.[18] By her 40s, she was her own mistress at last. Her account-books for 1739 record the improvements made at Farnsfield to make her hard-won resting place her own. An intelligent woman with a developed sense of her own self-importance, Savile had renounced the beau monde with a self-pitying sneer. Critique surfaces in her diaries, reporting 'debauchery in London', and is described even in her embroidery, copying Hogarth's *Harlot's Progress* (published 1732) in silks on chair covers.[19] The account-book reflects this ambivalence about fashion, Janus faced in decorative choices. An old-fashioned purchase was the 8 yards of gilt leather for doors, but Savile was *à la mode* in spending £2 5s. on 60 yards of 'blue & yellow paper to hang my parlour at Farnsfield' with 48 yards of blue and yellow border to set it off. Wallpaper was something of a daring novelty, and the colour yellow still an exotic feature in interior decoration linked to the Orient.[20]

Savile's window curtains were more conventional, made of 'green cheney stuff' – a glossy worsted. Her print buying was up to date and pointed; she acquired eight prints of Hogarth's *Rake's Progress* (published in 1732), and the *Midnight Modern Conversation* (published in 1730–31). The subject matter of the former confirmed her rejection of high society, and the latter her disappointment with men and her horror of conviviality. Savile improved the core pieces of furniture around her, buying a new bedstead, a mahogany bookcase, a mahogany dressing table, an oak chimney board and a new quilting frame for her beloved embroidery. Savile was poised between past and present in her equipment. She laid out more than £2 on nineteen pieces of pewter, which was already an old-fashioned material in 1739, reinforcing tradition by having the Savile arms engraved on each piece. She had a small collection of the necessary for the new hot drinks, a copper tea kettle, a tin coffee pot and a Japan tea board. Nevertheless, her ceramics were not modish. Savile had a handful of delftware (blue and white tin-glazed earthenware in production for more than a century in England), but she recorded no purchases of imported china, or European porcelain, and unusually for a lone female no teapots or tea wares, despite easy access to the choicest examples in London. Probably Savile inherited a battery of equipment from her mother and sister. Moreover, nine months is but a snapshot in a woman's accounting, and may be too short to capture batch purchasing. Account-books of married women and for other loners note the purchase of a new teapot at a rate of one a year, or eighteen months.[21] Yet the absence of even a single new teacup is suggestive, reflecting perhaps Savile's depressiveness and dread of company. Such was her 'miserable infirmity' and her tremblings, even before servants and children, that Savile asked to eat alone when visiting her brother's family. The liveliness and performance of an archetypal tea party were often beyond her constitution.[22] Savile was solitary by choice and morbid affliction. Her ambitious embroidery, print buying, blue and yellow wallpaper and green cheney bespeak a developed appreciation of the visual, and a determination to beautify the first home she could call her own. However, the comparative lack of brand new china and polite silverware – goods other women bought in abundance – suggests that her interiors were just that, a recess from the world, and her material culture not contrived for a social welcome or exhibition.

Diana Eyre was an affluent Yorkshire spinster, who exemplifies the experience of the semi-independent lodger in the 1750s, '60s and '70s in the polite north. She was one of the six children of the gentleman Anthony Eyre, sheriff of Nottingham. His death in 1748 must have triggered the break-up of the paternal household, for by the next year Miss Eyre was living as a boarder in the house of her sister Elizabeth and brother-in-law William Chambers Esq. in Ripon, where she stayed for the rest of her life. The intricacies of her arrangements are revealed by her surviving account-book for the years 1749 to 1777.[23] At its commencement, she was 26, so only just past the average age at marriage, but when it closed she was 54, and had long been an absolute spinster. Miss Eyre retained a male and female servant and her own mare, so she was well attended, enjoying holidays in genteel lodgings in the northern resorts and regular recourse to the sedan chair in Ripon, and was well above the threshold of feminine gentility. She received a £60 annuity from her 'brother Eyre', as well as the interest on a lump sum of £1,700, which amounted to £76 a year.

Diana Eyre's largest outgoings were board and travel. She paid her sister Elizabeth Chambers £1 1s. od. a week for board for herself and her servants. Therefore, her basic yearly outgoings approached at least £54 12s. od., leaving a surplus of £82 for clothes, domestic goods and entertainment. Miss Eyre was a socialite and made a deliberate effort to decorate her rooms to a high mark. She had at least two rooms to herself: 'my room', or 'the yellow room', and her closet. In addition, she had use of the dining room, for which she spent £3 13s. 6d. on a painting for the chimney breast, though whether she shared this room with her in-laws is not revealed. Diana Eyre progressively improved the structure and fixtures of her room with a battery of brass locks, iron bars, new glass for the sash windows, bell pulls, enlarged frogs to an iron fire grate, a new poker, shovel and tongs, new range stones, and paid for a carved moulding for the chimney. These may sound commonplace introductions, but they were just the sort of fittings that the architect John Wood noticed in his account of the improvement in common lodgings in Bath in 1749. Wood found proof of a revolution in interiors in 'the best kind of Brass locks' that adorned substantial oak doors, the installation of 'Marble slabs and even Chimney pieces', and the fact that every chimney had its own furniture 'of a Brass fender with Tongs, Poker and Shovel agreeable to it', as much as in the introduction of painted wainscot and carpets, and the replacement of oak tables and chests with mahogany and walnut.[24]

The family was not without pretensions. Diana's brother bought an estate in Nottinghamshire in 1762, commissioning the architect John Carr of York to remodel his hall. She herself sought metropolitan fashionability, purchasing yellow wallpaper from London in 1763 and a London floor cloth in 1771. These were made of canvas, thickly coated in linseed oil and pigment, the forerunner of Victorian linoleum (fig. 41). Floor cloths were virtually unknown before 1700, but the commonest floor coverings mentioned in London inventories in 1750, and still held their own against domestic carpets, which proliferated after 1750.[25] Diana Eyre bought 27 yards of green moreen in 1754, and another 75 yards of super-fine moreen in 1772, with green tassels, probably for bed and window curtains.[26] 'Moreen' was a sturdy, ribbed and often embossed fabric, which was the leading choice for bed curtains for a hundred years. An ample store of linen would be a customary possession of a maiden housekeeper, the core of an expectant bridal collection and the remnants of her parents' household stores. Miss Eyre had some linens sent from London in 1756, replenished her stock of coarse cloth, Russia cloth and diaper from time to time, and purchased a cotton counterpane and 13 yards of ticking from her sister in 1768, and a feather bed, bolster and three pillows in a sale in 1772. The cotton counterpane is itself a quintessential late Georgian commodity, displacing earlier decorative bed rugs, and common in even cheap furnished lodgings by the 1790s.[27] For an architect like Wood, the improvement of window curtains, bedding and household linens in common lodgings was an especially striking mark of progress.[28]

Miss Eyre also valued wall decorations, buying twelve unspecified pictures, a little gilded frame, a mirror and, rather impressively for a Ripon lodger, a pier glass, a tall mirror designed to sit between two windows and throw more light into the room – another innovation hailed by Wood.[29] Furniture Eyre brought with her included a clock, table, bureau and footstool, but she acquired 'a great chair', a tent stand for fashionable embroidery, a chimney board to screen the fireplace in the summer, a bird cage, a spinet, trays for quadrille, and with utter feminine predictability spent £1 7s. 0d. on a tea table in 1764. Small pieces of equipment included two teapots, a tea waiter, coffee mill, jelly glasses, a knife and fork for her servants, a kitchen knife, 'chiney' soup plates and basins.

With her male and female servant, her secure, prettified room and her commercially stabled mare, Miss Eyre represented a household within a larger household. She seemed to have few responsibilities for running the outer household, though presumably her servants did a portion of the necessary work, and she did pay for some minor improvements to her brother-in-law's rooms, like a brass lock for the parlour door, possibly as a quid pro quo. She bought food and groceries only intermittently, however, and these savour more of personal treats than contributions to the household larder, such as tea, sugar candy, macaroons, barley sugar, treacle, honey and lozenges. Diana Eyre had the protection of her family, but paid for a clear separation of territory, enjoying a polite apartment where she did her embroidery, played the spinet, listened to a caged bird and

41 Trade card for Biggerstaff's & Walsh's Floor-Cloth Warehouse, Islington, n.d. (mid-eighteenth century), printed engraving. British Museum, London, Banks, 30.1. The scenes portrayed around the Rococo cartouche show the making and selling of floor cloths, and a room being decorated.

read plays and trials, novels and improving works from *Sir Charles Grandison* (1753–4) to Tunstall's *Lectures on Natural & Revealed Religion* (1765). Eyre may even have cut a sedate dash with her lustring dresses, muslin aprons and hair curled for the season in Ripon, York and Scarborough. Spinsterhood did not prevent a decorous cultural engagement, while living as a boarder in her sister's home financially benefited herself and her sibling, offering her security and separation.

Mary Hartley suffered a life of chronic pain and limited scope in the 1780s in Bath. She was the middle-aged daughter of the Yorkshire philosopher and practising physician David Hartley (1705–1757) and his second wife, Elizabeth Packer (1713–1778). Though a woman of impeccable connections and accomplishment,

Mary Hartley had not married, probably on account of her feebleness, a lack of health disqualifying women for marriage in the eyes of received opinion. After the death of her mother, she was dependent for all her comforts on her half-brother David Hartley (1732–1813), who was a scientist, MP for Kingston upon Hull and an opponent of the slave trade and the American war. Mary Hartley put up with the retired life of an invalid in genteel lodgings in Winchester and Bath, enduring a series of grotesque minor amputations on her foot and leg, dosed up on laudanum. She was attended by a servant-cum-nurse Ann Toll, who wrote many of her letters. When Mary Hartley wrote herself, she stressed her determination not be a burden on the family finances.[30]

In the spring of 1784 Mary Hartley had her heart set on rooms with a view, so Ann Toll wrote for David Hartley's opinion on a house in Bath, at an annual rent of £70, with three rooms on the first floor. Although 'tis very magnificent', the terms were very fair, 'tis as cheap as a house of 2 rooms on a [floor]'. Notionally, the first-floor lodgings were to be shared with her older brother, with a superior 'apartment' of best room, dressing room and closet reserved for his visits. Miss Hartley's apartment consisted of a dining room, 'very hansom', connecting to a bed chamber, which led into a dressing room, 'so my mistress room have no [re-lation] with the [staircase], nor the noise, nor smell of the house'. Perhaps the nurse was to sleep in the dressing room, to be on hand in the small hours, for Mary was 'in very great pain and very bad nights, her sperrits tis very bad'. The preoccupation with views and the detachment from the traffic on the stairs argue that this was not a lodging the invalid was expected to leave. There are no reports even of trips to the medicinal hot baths, though there are many accounts of mornings in bed whimpering in pain.

For all the incarceration of illness – indeed, perhaps all the more for her captivity – Mary Hartley ensured that her prison was furnished to the standards of gentility. Miss Hartley acquired a spar bedstead and bedding, though she could not afford matching striped window curtains, making old green ones bought on sale do duty instead, to be 'frugal'.[31] Beds and their textile furniture had long been the most expensive single item in the interior. The whole ensemble required huge amounts of cloth: up to 50 yards for a set of bed curtains, valences, covers and window curtains.[32] No wonder Miss Hartley cut some corners. She acquired 'common servants beds' from the family home, and also a tent bedstead, which once the curtains were 'mended and lined with green stuff' would make 'a very comfortabell bed' for her visiting brother. From David Hartley, she requested 'the best carpet from London, if you have no objection as it will fit [my] dining room, which tis long, and narrow, to a bow window, that have a very good look out'. And enquired whether he wanted curtains for his bedroom, or would the inside window shutters be enough? If he could wait, then Mary would hang on for the textile sales. By July Mary had even bought a chariot for her brother for £26, in part exchange for his broken old one. The invalid had done the business, via a male proxy, who reassured her that she had struck 'A very great bargan'.[33]

Mary Hartley was in the vanguard of fashion when it came to her equipment for domestic hospitality, judging by her bills. In 1786, through her brother, Mary Hartley put in an order to the inventive Birmingham manufacturer Matthew Boulton. She ordered tea canisters, and a chocolate pot and coffee pot with matching lamps for heating the drinks, but also soup and sauce ladles for dinners, and bottle labels for port, claret, white wine, Madeira, sherry, hock and Burgundy to the tune of £11 14s. 10d.[34] The apartment was thus equipped for the manly hospitality an MP might offer. From her sick bed, Mary painted a satin fire screen for her brother to present to Queen Charlotte: 'my mistress is only able to paint in bed, of a morning, in the short time between her Breakfast and Mr Wright coming to dress her foot'. Hartley even planned alterations to a green chaise to be sent to Paris in 1784. The invalid also had a full complement of china and household linen, because in 1788 she was ready to loan back to David Hartley any china, 'good table clothes', 'breakfast napkins' and a dozen teaspoons that he needed.[35] For all her seclusion, Hartley was exceedingly well equipped at home.

One special type of furniture, however, is missing from Mary Hartley's sick chamber. Despite her receptiveness to novelty, there is no evidence of engagement with a new category of furnishings, of which she stood in dire need – specialist gear for invalids and the disabled. Adjustable chairs for illustrious invalids had been around since at least the 1500s. Georgian designers started to promote equipment adapted to the needs of immobilised patients from the 1780s. An invalid stool appeared in the sketchbook of the Lancaster furniture maker Gillows & Co. in 1787, and a prototype was published in Hepplewhite's *Cabinet-Maker and Upholsterer's Guide* in 1788, advertised as 'a Gouty Stool; the construction of which, by being so easily raised or lowered at either end, is particularly useful to the afflicted'.[36] In the same year, Gillows sketched an invalid chair on wheels, the forerunner of our wheelchair, known as a 'gouty chair', and the observant Mrs Lybbe Powys noticed 'mechanical easy-chairs for the gouty and infirm' at Merlin's exhibition in London. Bedsteads were also adapted to meet the needs of chronic invalids and injured army and navy officers.[37] Gillows' accounts confirm that specialist furniture was bought by men of the northern local elite by the late 1780s.[38] It is hard to believe that Lancaster enjoyed such innovations before Bath. Surely the spa was the very fountain of comforts for the sick and injured? After all, the 'Bath chair', a chair on wheels for invalids, was devised there by James

Heath in 1750. Perhaps these innovations were too recherché for the Hartleys, but more likely Mary was seen as too far gone to need them. Doubtless mobility was more highly prized in male patients than in female: legless army majors were more demanding than suffering spinsters. Enfeebled, immobile and out of circulation, the middle-aged, invalid spinster still crafted a nest of comforts for herself, and in fine first-floor rooms, good carpet and new-fangled coffee pots asserted, in spite of everything, that she was a woman of consequence, connections and ingenious taste.

Widowhood is the female condition most visible to history. A husband's death ended a woman's 'couverture' in common law, and her full legal personality was restored. Widows held an ambivalent position in the public imagination. On the one hand, the poor widow was a fitting object of charity. It was in the treatment of widows, orphans and aliens that God gauged the moral fibre of his people. On the other, the merry widow represented a potent cocktail of sexual experience, financial independence and personal autonomy. Widows were invariably more respectable than spinsters and, when heads of households, enjoyed a stake in society. Peter Laslett estimates that 12.9 per cent of households were headed by widows, based on a sample of 100 English communities between 1574 and 1821.[39] Widowhood was a condition subject to extreme variations, turning on the widow's age, past employment, assets, dependants, vigour and, crucially, the terms of her husband's will. The young widow with one or two children and a business or farm to maintain might remarry quite quickly. An older mother of many children often inherited only poverty from her spouse and fell to the mercies of the parish. (Erickson finds that one in four men bequeathed debts.[40]) But the clever widow of an improvident husband might in fact be better off without him, since she was now entitled to relief in her own right, and could manage the scanty family purse as she saw fit.[41] A well-endowed widow with minor sons might emerge as a managing matriarch. Widows of middling wealth proved the most likely to remarry, while richer widows appeared unwilling to run the gauntlet again and poorer widows were rarely offered the opportunity.[42] An unhappy wife left a modest independence might find widowhood a release and eschew the bit and bridle thereafter. In 1724, aged only 24, Mary Pendarves was freed from a penitential marriage; thereafter she refused numerous offers of marriage. 'My fortune . . . was very mediocre but it was *at my own command*.' She was a full 43 when she risked the halter again, and at her second widowhood, aged 68 in 1768, resolved to move to Bath to set up independently once more. 'I think it very proper Mrs Delany should have a house of her own', judged her supportive friend the Duchess of Portland, and regretted only that Mrs Delany had sold her own London house the better to pay her husband's legal fees: 'How vexatious that it is gone!'[43]

The living situation of his widow was one of the crucial issues that a husband tried to secure in his will – she could be left the entire house and holding for life, or house room with her children in possession, or a separate dwelling altogether – though arrangements varied regionally and with the age of the children. Having a resident mother-in-law was a fact of village life in early modern East Anglia, but widows in Hampshire, Leicestershire and Yorkshire were more likely to retain full possession of the house.[44] Research on eighteenth-century wills is less advanced, but there are still many in which a widow was granted one end of her husband's house, or a set or rooms, or a single room, for her survivorhood, though it was quite possible to operate as a separate household under one roof. Moving in with adult children was seen to be fraught with risk. Warnings about the mistreatment of the aged by their children circulated in print and proverb, not least in restagings of King Lear. The principle of residential independence for the elderly was entrenched from at least the Middle Ages.[45] However, retaining one's autonomy was easier in theory than in practice of course. The association between widowhood, especially lone motherhood, and grim immiseration is strong and persistent, for all the preferential treatment of the Poor Law. Most widows had to scrimp and scrape to get a subsistence together – so much so that Pamela Sharpe believes the true symbol of widowhood was not widows' weeds but the humble mangle.[46]

Gentry and genteel families were better able to sustain a discrete existence for their widows, but even among the wealthy, a dower house in the country or superior lodgings in town were not always forthcoming, and a widow might be expected to share the main family residence with the heir and her daughter-in-law, a situation fraught with complication. Even wealthy widows did not necessarily order house and home to their own satisfaction. Complaints about the drain of the widow's jointure on the inheriting son's estates are common. Tidy Russel, the wife of a sea captain, pitied in 1758 the mother of a friend who was an obstacle to her son's ambitions, despite being 'a very easy creature in the house'. The widow

> lives at the family seat which the son is much discontented at, as he thinks the estate suffers by having an old woman living on it, and he wants to live at it himself and be making alterations, as he has a wife and family . . . Therefore tho' he has no discord with the mother and sister, yet he would like to be as it were disburthened of them.

That 'as it were' carries the coolness of Tidy's unexpressed critique. When Tidy herself was widowed in 1765 she was relieved to rent a house to herself in the West End of London, with an interesting lookout on the fashionable throng: 'Tis a very cheerful situation, which I stand in great need of yet, for my spirits are very indifferent'. She offered chocolate to visitors who came to watch the royal traffic.[47] Widows desired both independence and society.

The women most likely to leave an architectural mark and shape an interior to their personal taste were widows. Rich dowagers with pretensions often saved their glitter for London, as a courtesy to their daughter-in-law, the new mistress of the ancestral pile. Rich widows are invariably to the fore among the minority of female consumers listed in surviving ledgers for the luxury and consumer trades. Glamorous noble widows might project themselves in paintings, surrounded by their progeny, but with the dead husband still present in a portrait in the background, an ingenious device that asserted the survival of patriarchal structures, the endurance of the marriage bond even in death, and perhaps the continuity of the blood in the person of the sons.[48] Chastity was an essential condition of virtuous widowhood, as was loyalty to the memory of the dead, but an inflexible retirement or nun-like renunciation of worldly goods was not demanded by propriety. Staged with decorum, widowhood was a dignified condition in Georgian England, and if combined with prosperity could be a period of unique independence and self-expression.

The considerable comforts of a rich widowhood are priced in the account-book of Martha Dodson, widow of John Dodson, 'Tin man to his Majesty's Yards belonging to the Navy', and High Sheriff of Berkshire (1716).[49] John Dodson built a new house on land that he bought for £4,404 in 1703 in Cookham in Berkshire, where he settled with his new wife and two daughters from his first marriage. The Dodsons had two more daughters together. At his death in 1730, the tin man left land and properties in Maidenhead and Cookham, a house in the Minories in London and at least five leasehold properties in east London. The accounts begin in June 1746, when Mrs Dodson was 62, and already sixteen years a widow, and span the last nineteen years of her life, ending in 1765, three months before her death aged 81. The accounts breathe affluence and respectability, cumulatively revealing dignified old age pleasing herself.[50] Dodson was very old by Georgian standards, but atypically affluent and independent, with the money, access and propensity to engage with fashion in interiors.

Mrs Dodson lived on at the Great House in Cookham, having no son to displace her, and though she may have contracted the household in the immediate aftermath of her husband's death, her steady spending on furnishings does not argue for any retrenchment thereafter. Under the terms of her husband's will, she enjoyed an income of £100 a year, a Navy pension, plus the 3 per cent interest on the £2,000 plus she had invested in reduced bank annuity stock. Consequently, unlike most women of even the provincial lesser gentry, she had the wherewithal to partake of a London season, albeit one based in the City of London, not the court or the West End. For a full six months every year, from December to June, the widow and her maid lived in lodgings in and around New Bow Lane in the City. She sent her goods by barge up and down the Thames and was attended by her maid. In the 1750s six months' rent and meals cost her £24 3s. Only when she reached 78, in 1762, did Dodson leave off sojourning in the metropolis. There was a seasonal rhythm to her spending. Typically, the widow acquired her new goods in London in the winter and spring, and in the late summer and autumn installed them. In the autumn, she spent money on maintaining the fabric of the Great House and garden – tiling the parlour chimney, adding new bolts and locks, straightening the fire grates, mending furniture. In London, Mrs Dodson spent time with her daughter and grandson, enjoyed decorous public entertainments and had the nation's best-stocked shops practically on her doorstep, from which she bought china, textiles and, to a lesser extent, furniture.

Mrs Dodson kept abreast of the new trends in interior decoration, dabbling particularly in Rococo. Nearby Cheapside was where she patronised the linen draper, hosier, haberdasher and goldsmith. However, for some products she was more particular. Mrs Dodson went at least once to Carr's in Ludgate Hill, a leading mercers that supplied the royal family and fashionable gentlewomen. Mrs Dodson bought 'yellow silk for cushings' in 1748, replaced chair covers in the best parlour in 1754, spent £3 5s. od. on green moreen window curtains and a Wilton bed carpet – an up-to-date choice since the British carpet industry was still in its infancy in the 1750s. Wilton, Axminster and Kidderminster were centres of the emergent industry, capitalising on the taste for the oriental, by imitating 'Turkey carpets', knotted and tufted in the oriental manner. In placing a carpet in her bedroom, however, Mrs Dodson was typical of early adopters of floor coverings in London, who warmed the floors of their intimate rooms before more utilitarian or formal areas.[51] Mrs Dodson had a cloth bed made in 1752, for £10 16s., and in 1758 commissioned an even more impressive mahogany bed covered in 30 yards of Irish linen and 33 yards of glazed chintz from Michael Bradshaw, a fashionable upholsterer in Budge Row. The widow had an appetite for renovation even in her late 70s. In 1748 she had her chamber fitted out with wallpaper and borders from a Mrs Ravenhill, costing £1 19s. 6d. The next year she had a new border pasted up in her dressing room. In 1753 new paper was tacked up in the hall. In June 1758 Mrs Dodson spent almost £2 on '7 pieces of chint paper' and '2 pieces of Dutch tile pattern', perhaps for what style magazines today call a feature wall. In 1760, aged 76, she had the dressing room repapered in full. Dodson bought some smaller Rococo furniture, such as a scallop mahogany hand board for 10s. 6d., and two mahogany brackets for the parlour chimney to display her best china.

Mrs Dodson had a weakness for porcelain knick-knacks, which could be had for shillings. In 1753 she bought two little china dogs for 2s. 6d., as well as Rococo drolleries like '3 china vine leaves for pickles'. The next year she indulged herself with a 'china nun and one frier'. Her most consistent purchases, however, were tea wares. She bought a teapot nearly every year: a brown teapot in 1747, a red teapot in 1748, an unspecified teapot in 1749, another red china teapot in 1750, a white Bow china teapot in 1753, a white china teapot and stand, and yet another little red teapot in 1754, a blue and white china teapot in 1758 and another in 1759, and a blue and white Worcester teapot and a little Japan teapot in 1761. None of them cost more than 4s., and most cost around 1s. 6d. Dodson bought none of the exquisite Chelsea china, associated with the fashionable nobility, but confined herself to the less expensive brands like Worcester and Bow, while her red teapots may have been sturdy Staffordshire stoneware. The Bow warehouse in Cornhill in the City, which opened in 1753 for both retail and wholesale customers, was but streets from her lodgings, while Worcester porcelain was distributed to retailers from the nearby Aldersgate warehouse, where the stock could be examined. Though Bow produced some gilt fancy wares and figures, its staple was plainer china, strengthened with bone ash for regular service – 'a more ordinary sort of ware for common uses'. In the 1750s, when Dodson was buying, the firm was at its commercial peak, producing blue and white painted wares. Worcester's stock in trade was practical, keenly priced, but well-made common ware, discreetly decorated with print, paint and moulding. Their china was reinforced with soap rock for resilience, prized for 'great tenacity' in the midst of hot water. The city widow's taste for Bow and Worcester confirms the hypothesis that these serviceable wares appealed especially to the prosperous middle ranks.[52] Dodson was loyal to her old stomping ground in the city where affordable novelties were not far to seek. Until she was 77, her London season was synonymous with the purchase of a new teapot, usually towards the end of her stay, to take back to Berkshire. Age did not wither her relish for the city, or dim her eye for the new and choice if it could be had at the right price.

Mary Cooke was the youngest daughter of Anthony Eyre, a sheriff of Nottingham, and sister of Diana Eyre of Ripon, one of our spinster accountants. Mary married the Doncaster gentleman Anthony Cooke of Owston, sixteen years her senior, in 1752. After only eleven years of marriage, he died aged 52 in 1763, leaving her with an estate to manage and two small children to raise. At 37 Mrs Cooke might have married again, but like the eternally faithful widow of male fantasy, she consecrated herself to safeguarding her son's inheritance, and to raising her daughter Nancy to marry well. With a rent roll worth £832 a year in 1764, plenty of money flowed through her account-book. Mary Cooke's accounting differs from that of her sister, Miss Eyre, in that she recorded the management of the Owston estate as executor, not just her own personal expenditure. Like gentleman accountants, Cooke recorded sums spent on the farm, stable, livestock, dues, taxes and annuities, building and repairs to the properties. In practice, Cooke managed like a man, but with one major addition. Like a married female accountant, she was responsible for the clothes, health, education and entertainment of the children, for whom she kept additional separate account-books.[53] Widow Cooke merged the accounting of husband and wife. The right hand paid for the surveying of the estate, a bay roan mare called Silver Tail, a gun and repairs to the chariot, while the left bought three dozen shirt buttons and cotton stockings for young Bryan Cooke at Eton. As custodian of Owston and its contents, as well as a house in Leeds, Mrs Cooke was already the steward of a full inventory of household goods. An 'inventory of plate at Owston in Mrs Cooke's possession in 1763' runs to 231 individual pieces, from little forks and teaspoons, to salvers, candlesticks, coffee pot, kettle, lamp and stand. 'The plate belonged to Anthony Cooke Esq. and is now in my possession', the widow confirmed.[54] She frequently recorded purchasing pieces of Sheffield plate (silver-coated copper), and spent £8 18s. 6d. on 'Mahogany Goods' for her son's room at Eton in 1771. In her late 50s, in 1783, Mary Cooke considered rebuilding Owston Hall, opening discussions with a local architect, William Whitelock, which came to nothing.[55]

Mrs Cooke was the managing matriarch of a very rich Yorkshire family, describing herself as 'in possession' of costly household goods; but technically most of these were not her own to bequeath at the point when she wrote her will. Cooke epitomises what Sandra Cavallo has seen as the paradox of matrimonial experience of domestic things: that the household goods that surrounded wives were seen as part of the property that the husband had already earmarked in his will for his male heirs. The widow may have been custodian of the chattels, but they were not hers to bequeath. Italian widows transmitted only a narrowly circumscribed set of personal items (trousseau linens, underwear, clothes, jewellery, her own plate, a devotional picture), not necessarily because they were more attached to individual objects than men, but rather because these were the only goods wives could legitimately claim as their own possessions. Hence one tactical response was to invest heavily in personal accoutrements, as a store of value that remained under female control.[56] When Mrs Cooke wrote her last testament in a letter to her son, Bryan Cooke, in 1784, the handover of substantial property had been resolved long before: 'As I find my Circumstances less than I expected I don't think it worth while to make a formal will.'

Mrs Cooke named her son executor and bequeathed to him all her real and personal estate, with the exception of some special bequests of furniture and accoutrements. In consequence, her will resembles that of genteel women of much less independence, and itemises only a constellation of objects associated with comfort and female accomplishment. The reward to her maid for nursing her was to be 'the yellow stuff bed Feather Bed, Bolster, two pillows and 3 Blankets with my old white Coarse Cotton Counterpain . . . also the yellow stuff for the two window curtains & the yellow stuff that covers the three Chairs in that room as it is the same stuff as the Bed & it may be useful to her to repair'. Small objects were bestowed on female relatives. The London-bought medicine box and sewing tackle she left to her daughter. Her workbox, a gift from her son, and 'workbag of Miss Hatfield's painting', plus 'a fan Mr Drummond gave me that you brought from abroad', she wanted to go to any future Mrs Cooke of Owston. Her watch, pocket-book, all her bracelets and polished steel netting vice, her silver inkwell from London and the rest off her fans she bequeathed to her granddaughter, Mary Ann Warde.[57] In her will, Mrs Cooke's reduced objectscape finally resembled that of her spinster sister, conjuring two rooms of polite accoutrements.

With utter propriety, Cooke desired to be buried at Owston beside her husband. 'You know I have always wished to be private in my life time,' she reminded her son, 'and I very particularly wish to be laid in my Grave with the greatest privacy.' Cooke asked to be attended only by the steward and by her upper maid in a chaise, and to be met by 'six of the poorest women in Owston', who would bear the pall 'dressed in their oldest Cloaths, not to have any appearance of show', in return for half a guinea apiece. Such rituals had their own conventions, associated particularly with women with a reputation for charity.[58] A triumphant steward, Mrs Cooke prepared to meet her maker with grave panache.

Elizabeth Forth was the daughter of a York grocer, Robert Woodhouse. In 1791 she married the Reverend John Forth, Fellow of Jesus College, Cambridge, and agent to Lord Carlisle at Castle Howard. In 1792 John Forth was appointed domestic chaplain to Lord Carlisle and through him gained the curacy of Hovingham in 1796. The Forths lived for three years at Slingsby, then, in 1794, moved to 'the best part of the house at Ganthorpe', both of which were within four miles of Castle Howard. The couple lived in comfort and modern style. The house at Slingsby had eight family rooms, back and fore staircases, two rooms for male and female servants, a meal chamber, butler's pantry, dairy and three kitchens. The house at Ganthorpe had eleven family rooms, four garrets and two kitchens. Even the manservant's garret had a four-poster bed with blue china drapes, and a half-tester with green drapes, and the maid's garret a four-poster bed with green china fabric. The Forths' bedroom had 'a four posted Bedstead with a mahogany fluted Poles and Green Morene furniture' with matching moreen window curtains, as deployed by Mrs Dodson on her bed at Cookham. Many of their fixtures were novel inventions – like a 'Mahogany biddet', a 'Patent shower bath in the closet from London cost £2:14:8', and a 'patent water closet purchased of Mr Croft of York for £10.10.0' in the hall. Beside the usual mahogany dining, tea, card and dressing tables, glasses, screens and stands, they had examples of the newly introduced cabinet work: a gentleman's travelling writing box, a mahogany dumb waiter and a cellaret (a drinks cabinet), as well as 'a mahogany sofa (to lay on)', and in the drawing room 'three mahogany small sofas fitted under the window with canvas bottoms & white furniture'.

Beyond their own purchases and wedding gifts, the Forths inherited a duplicate set of furnishings from Mrs Forth's mother, and a host of plate from Mr Forth's father. The rich grocer's widow bequeathed her daughter an array of fancy table silver and china, expensive linens, curtains, Wilton carpets (three for bedsides), stair carpets and another houseful of mahogany. Furniture from her mother listed in the inventory of 1806 includes fourteen mahogany chairs for the dining room, mahogany chests of drawers lined with cedar, a dressing table, a mahogany bed made up with chintz and a cotton counterpane, a 'mahogany easy chair with casters covered with old fashioned brocaded silk' and a 'mahogany night chair, with black hair bottom'. As the repository of their parents' effects, the Forths ended up with three japanned tea kitchens (decorated tea urn) with heater, one theirs and one each from dead mother and father. Mrs Forth's cupboards were stuffed with the treasures of her dead friends and relatives, like 'a row of large amber beads 35 in number belonging to Mrs Forth's Mother's Mother' and 'A handsome ring with the late Mr Alderman Woodhouse's Hair set round with Diamond Sparks, (cost 11 guineas)' left by Mrs Woodhouse. The history and association of these objects are etched in the family inventory:

I large silver sauce boat marked EW which belonged to Mrs Forth's mother, the gift of Mrs Williamson, Widow of Mrs J Uncle; 1 small silver cream or sauce boat marked R E W – which belonged to the same & the gift of the same; One silver soup ladle the gift of Mrs Wright; 1 Compleat set of white and Gold tea China the Gift of Mrs Woodhouse; 1 set of foreign China with 6 Coffee Cups the gift of Mrs Silburn (Given to Mrs Berber for her son by Mrs Forth); 2 Foreign Blue and White China tea pots and one Cream pot one of the tea pots and Cream Pot the gift of Mrs Woodhouse and the other Tea pot the Gift of Mrs Wright (1 tea pot broke).[59]

The personal inventory details what an account-book has no interest in, a dense landscape of inherited objects and gifts, all still identified with the original owner. Georgian objects haunted the nineteenth-century home. A dead woman's teaspoons carried her memory into the next century.

Even before her marriage, Elizabeth Forth was practised in the art of keeping accounts,[60] and she shared the task with her husband. In the earliest surviving account-book, both hands are present, Mrs Forth seeming to amend her husband's entries. Mr Forth died in 1816, aged 52. By 1821 Mrs Forth was back in York, almost certainly at a house at Blake Street that she had inherited from her mother and eventually bequeathed to her daughter Caroline. The double-fronted town house faced Burlington's Egyptian assembly rooms. It was well appointed with dining room, drawing room, small front sitting room and a back lodging room on the ground floor, as well as three more lodging rooms upstairs.[61] Mrs Forth was now a widow of 56 with two adolescent children, Frederick and Caroline, both away at boarding school. Any major refurbishment was already complete, though Forth noted in March: 'finished making and altering the late pantry into an upstairs scullery for to be more convenient as I wish my servants to cook upstairs & not in the cellar kitchen as they have done before'.[62]

Widow Forth's account-book notes thirty-eight purchases of household goods in the year 1821–2, all small commissions, the most expensive items being silver tableware. She spent £15 at Busbee and Co., on silver table forks, butter ladles and dessert forks, as well as on '4 plated candlesticks as a present to Mr & Mrs Timm for their attention to Frederick at his school', and a further £3 9s. 6d. on knives and forks from a Mr Joseph Wood. Her next most costly purchases were 'a Coloured Table Cover' for £1 12s., from Mess. W. & Swann and a rosewood workbox 'for my own use'. Ceramics were the only other category of goods that reached such sums. Mrs Forth paid £1 'for a set of China White & gold 12 handled cups & saucers tea pot slop & sugar bason & 2 plates & cream pot'. And she also laid out £1 on 'a Set of 12 Cups & Saucers Red & White Slop Bason & Sugar Do one plate & cream pot & tea pot' – a deal of money to hand over to 'a man who came to the Door'. Of all the lone women discussed here, Elizabeth Forth bore the strongest resemblance in her accounting to the wives Mrs Grimes, Mrs Cotton and Mrs Arderne, especially in the money laid out on children. Clothing, educating, entertaining and polishing the two Forth offspring account for 31 per cent of all transactions listed in the account-book for 1821. Seventeen transactions were for the tools and materials for decorative crafts. Mrs Forth sewed, but her teenage daughter was also expected to net, sketch, paint in oils and watercolours, make collages and screens, as befitted the polite schoolgirl.[63] Elizabeth Forth was a matron of manifest gentility and even some aristocratic connections, who expected to dine well, to entertain and to stage her daughter in the handsome town house in York.

The six women studied here divide roughly as Georgian convention and modern scholarship would expect – the widows were all householders, while of the spinsters only Savile headed her own household, though she too was a tenant. All three spinsters were provincial lodgers, though Savile, the highest-born, rented an entire house, while Eyre and her two servants boarded with kin, whereas Hartley and her nurse took a floor of a house amidst strangers. By contrast, the three widows enjoyed a house of their own, Dodson maintaining the mansion her tinplate man had built in Cookham, Cooke augmenting the estate at Owston, and Forth withdrawing to a York town house she had inherited from her mother. All six women could make material choices without much reference, if any, to male preferences. Savile in the 1730s, Dodson in the 1740s and '50s, and Eyre in the 1760s all brightened their homes with wallpaper, a feature associated with the dressing rooms and personal sitting rooms of stylish wives. For all her reclusiveness, Savile was at the cutting edge of fashion with her blue and yellow wallpaper. The Orient illuminated her Nottinghamshire lodgings. Savile, Dodson and Hartley invested large sums in new beds; Eyre improved hers; and the Forths inherited a showroom's worth of mahogany. Green cheney window curtains were acquired by Savile, green stuff bed curtains by Hartley, green moreen curtains by Eyre, green moreen window curtains and glazed chintz bed curtains by Dodson, and green moreen again by the Forths for their double bed. These were conventional and persistent choices, young wives being advised to make the same purchases in 1825: 'Moreen is very serviceable, and is well suited to cold situations: it requires no lining, and, therefore is less expensive than chintz though not so pretty.'[64] Floor cloths, bedside rugs or carpets were enjoyed by all the women but Savile, though this may be a function of period. The floors are still bare in many of the conversation pieces of the northern painter Arthur Devis in the 1740s. The adoption of floor coverings is an aspect of a major reorientation in interior decoration, whereby textiles (in the form of hangings) left the walls, and took their modern place on the floor and beside the windows.

Tablewares, especially the varied paraphernalia for hot drinks, were indispensable props in the reception of visitors, seen as the excitement and solace of female existence. Even the disabled Mary Hartley, who wore out her days in her striped bed, much of the time drugged or whimpering, ordered new-fangled apparatus for hot drinks from Matthew Boulton of Soho, Birmingham. Miss Hartley expected to entertain her brother and his friends, as well as a wide female acquaintance on the *piano nobile* of Belvedere House. Even the elderly Mrs Dodson (and by Georgian standards she was antique) bought a new teapot in London every year. The comparative lack of china and polite silverware in Savile's account is significant, almost certainly an expression of her claustration. Unlike all the other women discussed here, Savile's material culture was not orientated outwards for exhibition or hospitality. There is no material evidence that her home was a backdrop to a public social life. Not that tea wares were the exclusive possession of women. Mrs Forth acquired a japanned tea kitchen, silver teapot, coffee pot, milk jug, sugar tongs and teaspoons from her deceased father-in-law. The equipment for domestic sociability was more significant for women, however, because they could not entertain at the coffee house or carouse at the inn without catastrophic loss of caste.[65]

A combination of society and separation, company and autonomy produced a bearable existence for lone women. This blend was infinitely more likely in towns, where distances were short, networks of acquaintance dense and inexpensive hospitality feasible. In 1795 Mrs Elizabeth Poole was a widow boarding in 'neat comfortable rooms' on the High Street in Yarmouth who nevertheless longed to return to the company of Norwich, 'to recover an intimacy with half a dozen families'. Poole enquired after some 'small retired rooms' in 'an agreeable private family' for herself and unpaid companion, from which base she hoped to re-establish her acquaintance, though intending to 'confine myself to Morning visits' for reasons of economy.[66] It was certainly easier to sustain a cheerful social life in town, without being put to the cost of pony and trap, or expensive dinners. Some towns look especially congenial. The new Grosvenor Estate in Mayfair drew single women like bees to honey, especially those recently bereaved, though royal mistresses and estranged wives were attracted too. More than half of all ratepayers between 1720 and 1760 were single women. Lucy, the Dowager Duchess of Rutland lived alone, but within a five-minute walk of a married son, a married daughter, a widowed daughter and a married grandson.[67] Travelogues noticed conventicles of ladies in the county towns and the spas. Streets of independent women have been found in Ludlow, Bridgnorth, Shrewsbury and Chichester. Preston was said to be 'remarkable for old maids' of middling fortunes in the 1750s; Lichfield was dominated by widows and spinsters in 1776 (fig. 42).[68] Georgian Bath was a reputed market for marriageable widows, and became a famous place of permanent residence and retirement for older women. By 1851, 10,767 spinsters called Bath home, to only 4,057 bachelors. Similarly, there were 3,980 widows in the city to only 1,086 widowers. No wonder all and sundry claimed to have an aunt in Bath![69]

The lone women bought small decorative objects for their homes, and in this they resembled wives of the same background (see pls 8 and 9). My comparison

42   George Woodward, *A Nottingham Card Party*, 1797, etching. British Museum, London, 1872,0112.168. Four elderly women and four parsons sit at a long table playing cards. The etching illustrated Woodward's *Eccentric Excursions* (London, 1796), which claimed that Nottingham was famous for its old maids.

of the accounting of gentry husband and wives revealed that while major re-building was invariably listed under 'his' expenditure, small decorative purchases clustered in the distaff account. Similarly on the very rare occasions when an inventory survives from both before and after the death of a husband, an expansion of decorative delftware and teaware is discernable.[70] Savile was a print buyer and embroiderer, acquiring a new quilting frame in 1739, while Diana Eyre also bought pictures, a mirror and a pier glass, as well as a tent stand for fashionable embroidery. In her taste for porcelain knick-knacks, the aged Mrs Dodson was most like the married accountants Mrs Grimes, Mrs Arderne and Mrs Cotton.[71] Mrs Forth was smothered with decorative heirlooms, but still could not resist new china in 1821. She also put a premium on craft accomplishments, buying in steady supplies of art materials for her adolescent daughter, and a new rosewood workbox for herself. Even Mrs Cooke, the most powerful of all the lone women here, cherished her medicine box, workbox, workbag, steel netting vice and silver inkwell and bequeathed them all to female kin.[72]

All three spinsters lived on a narrower domestic compass than wives of the same background. Spinsters and widows alike favoured a good bed, warm green bed curtains, bright wallpaper, mahogany tea tables, china ornaments for the chimney and the accoutrements of craft accomplishment – pretty enough in exotic woods to be left about for all to see. These furnishings were sufficient to generate cheerful comfort and summon up a modest stylishness in compact surroundings. The impression of elegance could be contrived with a handful of careful choices. Mrs Montagu advised a spirited but impecunious widow 'determined to keep her freedom and enter not more into wedlock's bonds', on decorating her 'small lodging' with 'economy' in 1750. She recommended furnishing 'in the present fashion of some cheap paper and ornaments of Chelsea china or the manufacture of Bow, which makes a room look neat and furnished. They are not so sumptuous as my mighty Pagodas of China or nodding Madarins', but the effect was similar.[73] In their way, the bedrooms and parlours of the lone women were cheaper miniatures of the jewel-like closets, dressing rooms and private sitting rooms that noble women and courtiers created for their treasures. Moreover, the parlours of widows and old maidens contained the same workboxes and knick-knackery as the drawing rooms, parlours and breakfast rooms of prosperous wives. The chamber of a maiden lady might resemble a dainty land of rose water and lavender, with its prettiness and interminable embroidery, improving tracts and teapots, but it could not be a *terra incognita* to any gentleman who had a wife. Nevertheless, because our maiden lady was of all women least likely to be a householder, she had to be poised to collect her things together and move on, nesting in a corner of someone else's house. Continuity and familiarity lay in the tea tray, the ornaments and the linens, not in bricks and mortar. Like the proverbial snail who carried shelter on her own back, the comfort of home inhered in what she could take with her.

9

WHAT WOMEN MADE

RCHITECTURE, FIXTURES AND FURNITURE CREATED ONLY the frame-work of an interior on which settled a layer of objects crafted by women. Hand-wrought hangings, screens, bed curtains, cot covers, chair seats, stools, pictures, frames and boxes clothed the noble, genteel and middling interior, the very fabric of home. History, however, has been unimpressed by women's efforts. They are a source of disappointment: neither useful, nor truly art. Even positive discussions have not characterised women's productions in ways that would commend them to modern sympathies. John Fowler and John Cornforth attribute to fashionable ladies 'that indefinable thing called the English Style and also much of the charm of the English country house as well'. Their discussion, however, is off-puttingly entitled 'Ladies' Amusements' and the conclusion is quaint.[1] The call for fresh research is not couched in terms contrived to rouse a new generation: 'It is odd that no-one has written a book about ladies' work in the British Isles. It would combine charming and amazing things in an unexpected variety of mediums.'[2] Feminist art historians have also been ambivalent, concerned that 'in embracing activities like flower painting or quilt making as women's separate but equal artistic heritage, we risk reinforcing the hierarchy of values in art history and art practice that has worked to marginalise these activities as craft'.[3]

The domestic context of female decorative work has guaranteed its low prestige. A founding legend of women's history narrates the withdrawal of middling and privileged women from productive work and their relegation to a separate sphere of home as a consequence of industrial capitalism.[4] Despite consistent debunking, this story still underpins much British art history, architectural history and design history scholarship. Notwithstanding the newer interpretations of the affluent home as a site of administrative expertise rather than a cage, handicrafts are still seen as the perfection of pointlessness. Interpretation is still haunted by Thorstein Veblen's satire of the ladies of the leisure class, in 1890s New York, for whom taste was simply an exhibition of conspicuous leisure demonstrating a husband's earning power. Be warned, sneers Germaine Greer, if you insist on viewing Delany's flower collages at the British Museum 'you could end up profoundly depressed by yet more evidence that, for centuries, women have been kept busy wasting their time'.[5] For Ann Bermingham, the rise of accomplishments like fancy sewing, new crafts and watercolours 'went along with the domestic confinement of women and the increasing tendency to transform the home into an aestheticised space of commodity display'.[6] Accomplishments were an exhibitionary strategy in the polite marriage market, a subliminal form of advertising in the drawing room. The construction in manuals and advertisements of the lady as artistic beautifier of the home promoted female cultural authority over matters of taste and aesthetics, but this was an expression of losses in other areas of life.[7] In short, women decorated the doll's house, to the applause of the new economic man.

Scholarly understanding of the function of women's decorative practices has been over-determined by the negative interpretation of handicraft that emerged in the bubbling debate on 'accomplishments' in Georgian print, though denigration was only one theme of a contradictory debate. In fact, the traditional interpretation of female craftwork was highly positive. After all, it was the Almighty who ordered the curtains of the tabernacle to be richly embroidered. Repeated recourse to biblical authority is the striking feature of most male examinations of appropriate domestic expression for women, especially the description of the virtuous woman of Proverbs 13. Her price above rubies, she was indefatigable in the organisation of the household and creative in making 'coverings of tapestry' to the credit of her husband 'when he sitteth among the elders of the land'. Those who endorsed Proverbs extended from the arch-Tory Sir Robert Filmer 'In Praise of the Virtuous Wife', in the 1640s, to the staunch Whig Richard Steele in his frequently reprinted *Guardian*, first published in 1714.[8] They included both the Hertfordshire farmer William Ellis in his doggedly practical *Country Housewife's Family Companion*, published in 1750, and the fashionable London preacher the

Reverend James Fordyce, whose genteel *Sermons to Young Women* first appeared in 1766 and ran to twelve editions by 1800.[9] Filmer was clear that the virtuous wife should not only manage but also beautify the marital home: 'Ornament is twofold. First in herself, then in her husband. For herself she adornes the familye and her person, for her house she makes carpets.'[10] Fordyce, writing more than a century later, agreed: 'The furniture of her house is noble . . . She is not ignorant of what belongs to her rank; and she supports it with a magnificence so much the more conspicuous for being principally her own handy-work.'[11] The honour of female decoration was ancient and venerable.

When handicrafts were also invoked in the Georgian educational debate on 'accomplishments', there was no unanimity even on what counted as an accomplishment, never mind on whether they should be promoted, tolerated or banned. No word was more 'abused, misunderstood, or misapplied, than the term accomplishments', concluded Hannah More.[12] The positive definition of accomplishment was a faculty attained by study and practice that completed or perfected a person for society, adding delicacy of taste and elegance of manners to accuracy of knowledge and correctness of thought. Critics, however, debased 'accomplishments', using it as a shorthand for 'superficial acquirements' that pretended to complete an education that did not exist. By the 1790s accomplishments had become a hook on which to hang an attack on current female education and femininity for feminist critics and educational reformers, both radical and Tory.

The proper balance between useful and ornamental accomplishments was hotly debated. Conservative writers drawing on the Old Testament liked to see the traditional skills deployed for the sake of men, family and household, though signs of extreme virtuosity for public exhibition could be worrying, suggesting the neglect of mundane employments. By contrast, the enlightened found the parade of traditional housewifely skills a rather medieval pose for modern women with claims to intellect. Sarah Pennington thought ostentatious housewifery absurd in the higher ranks. Embroidery could be a pretty amusement, especially small compositions, but monster projects that could not be completed without assistance were a hypocritical extravagance: 'Whole Apartments have been seen thus ornamented by the supposed Work of a Lady who, perhaps, never shaded two Leaves in the artificial Forest'.[13] Similarly, Hester Chapone was unimpressed by women who broadcast their ability to make puddings but could not rise to more intellectual arts. What conversation was possible with a woman 'whose ideas hardly ever wandered beyond the limits either of the kitchen or a dressing room'?[14] Accomplishments that signalled wider intellectual horizons were certainly more becoming than baking and sewing in families of fortune.

Conversely, it was the very ornamentalism of female arts that was enraging for the likes of Mary Wollstonecraft and Hannah More. Obsolete ornamental accomplishments would be one of the first things swept away by Wollstonecraft in her revolution in female manners, for they exemplified everything that was dire about modern female education. If women spent their girlhood 'rigidly nailed to their chair to twist lappets and knot ribbands' they had no opportunity to develop either their rational or their physical capacities, and instead they simply presented themselves like beribboned poodles for the applause of men. Hannah More deplored Wollstonecraft's politics, but shared much of her critique of exhibitionism. It was hardly the mission of education 'to make women of fashion dancers, singers, players, painters, actresses, sculptors, gilders, varnishers, engravers and embroiderers'. Particularly disastrous was the spread of this 'phrenzy of accomplishments' beyond the ladies of rank and fortune to 'the middle orders', the daughters of curates, tradesmen and farmers, a contagion that undermined women's usefulness as it fed their pretensions, raging 'downward with increasing and destructive violence'. Edgeworth deduced that accomplishments had lost much of their social value 'since they have become common'.[15]

Fancy works played a totemic role in the commentary on the social impact of enclosure, symptomatic of the decay of homespun virtue in the farmhouse. Instead of 'dishing butter, feeding poultry, or curing bacon', farmers' daughters studied 'dress, attitudes, novels, French, and music, while the fine ladies their mothers sit lounging in parlours adorned with the fiddle faddle fancy works of their fashionable daughters'.[16]

This heated commentary served a seething debate on female education, the faults of aristocracy and the impact of commercialisation. These were contradictory polemics, not a comprehensive appraisal of craft. There was no consensus about which were the virtuous accomplishments, or the intrinsic value of an embroidery or a shellwork vase. Besides, the force of the attack was not on amateur arts and crafts in themselves, but in so far as they were vehicles for meretricious show. As Cohen has argued, 'it was not accomplishments *per se* that provoked the indignation of moralists and educationists', it was their public display. As Hannah More clarified, the prudent mother 'will be more careful to have the talents of her daughter *cultivated* than *exhibited*'.[17] By implication, crafts undertaken modestly and privately, as an extension of family duty and for the pleasure of close kin, escaped censure, and indeed were creditable, as they long had been. A bird's-eye view over the centuries would spot the decline of spinning in the homes of the gentry and yeomanry and the rise of retail provision. It would not, however, reveal a late flowering of female decorative work coinciding with the acceleration in Enclosure Acts. The ornamental sewing of virtuous Tudor housewives had accompanied their spinning for domestic use; it did not supersede it. Ornamental accomplishments did not disqualify women from household management, and when married to the duty of life and pursued with moderation, were entirely honourable. Hence a conduct book penned by an anonymous grandmother in 1808 defended 'ornamental acquirements' when grafted on the useful, not least 'because many of the most highly accomplished women are remarkable for retirement'.[18] It was the manner, not the matter, that was at issue when women sat down at their worktables.

The vociferous debate about amateur handicraft argues for its centrality to Georgian culture and suggests that a reassessment is overdue. The vitality of female decoration is evidenced in letters, diaries and travelogues, surviving objects in museum and country house collections, even in criminal records, and in the business records of the commercial and educational culture that supported craft. Handicrafts were inescapable amongst the nobility and gentry, and in professional, manufacturing and mercantile families with pretensions to politeness. The most modest female decorators uncovered here were an unmarried sister of a Rotherham stonemason, an Essex farmer's daughter, landladies' daughters and the illegitimate daughter of a Horsham tailor, but craftwork shaded into that everyday sewing that was socially ubiquitous. The miscellany of anonymous and authored craftwork in local and national museums indicates the geographical spread of domestic accomplishment, though, unsurprisingly, where crafted objects can be linked to individuals their makers are often privileged. The survival of decorative work argues at the very least that families valued women's objects enough to preserve them for posterity. In some families they were revered like relics. Nevertheless, the boundary between amateur decoration and professional work is notoriously hard to chart, especially below the ranks of the polite. Superior needlework is assumed to be professional by curators unless there is powerful evidence of amateur provenance (pl. 21).

Surviving objects may give the impression that amateur crafting was the preserve of the polite, but this is a misreading. Occasional detailed private inventories register art tools and sewing kit as unremarkable possessions amongst the middling. The Manchester spinster Jenny Scholes, who died in 1768 aged 22, left an array of tackle for accomplishments: fifteen painting pots, nine brushes, eleven bobbins, a knitting sheath and cotton for knitting, a knotting shuttle, netting silk and cat gut, brass thimbles, beads and wire, seventeen artificial flowers, and 'a few patterns for working'. Jenny, however, was the niece of a wool merchant and a modest heiress. By way of context, my survey of eighty single women's wills and inventories in the diocese of York from the 1710s and '80s uncovers only one woman with sewing equipment, and she was also middling. The widow

Charlotte Bingley, sister-in-law of a surgeon, kept a quilting frame in her back chamber in Rotherham in 1780, valued at 2s.[19] The fact, however, that handicraft equipment – pins and needles, thread, sewing frames – was so inexpensive put it beneath the notice of the appraisers. More modest decorators can be glimpsed occasionally. The architect James Wood remembered that in common lodgings in Bath in the 1720s the fustian beds were flowered in worsteds by matrons, daughters and maids 'to give the Beds a gaudy look'. Tailor's daughter Sarah Hurst used to embroider for herself as well as local ladies in and around Horsham in the 1760s. Joseph Woodward, a London joiner, had a framed sampler stolen from his parlour, which adjoined the workshop, at Red-Lyon Court in 1750.[20] The extent to which the impoverished adorned their homes is very hard to judge, though a poignant intimation survives in the scraps of fabric that mothers left with their abandoned infants at the gates of the London Foundling Hospital, many of which were simply embroidered with the baby's name or a motif, and from which we might infer a poorer woman's desire, however futile, to ornament domestic life (pl. 22).[21]

For every celebrated female amateur there was an army of women for whom craft skills furnished a livelihood, as teachers, tutors, educational authors and occasionally exhibitors. Plain sewing was demanded of female servants, the largest single occupational category for women. The archetypal labouring woman was the seamstress; millinery and mantua making the quintessentially feminine businesses.[22] Decorative arts were already an inescapable feature of the curricula of commercial schools for girls by the 1600s. These served the expanding middling ranks by the 1700s. Rebecca Weekes's inventory documents the school that she and Rebecca Bell operated in the second-floor front room of Weekes's two-storey house in Deptford in south-east London in the 1730s. Handicrafts were displayed throughout, from the coat of arms in 'phillagree' hung in her best chamber, to the flower piece in shellwork, ornamental embroidery and the image of 'Qn Anne in her Robes in Phillagree in a frame' in her schoolroom.[23] Handicrafts also lent themselves to a domestic education, although the history of female tutors is elusive. Elizabeth Mason told the West Riding Quarter sessions in 1738 that she had turned itinerant teacher after the death of her husband, a Bristol baker, and had 'travelled up and down the country selling drafts or [patterns] for flowering, and teaching young ladies to draw figures for flowering'.[24] The *Leeds Mercury* advertised in the 1730s and '40s that Mary England taught 'tent-work, white-work, marking and plain-work' at the Charity School in Wakefield, and was able to copy any drawing whatsoever onto cloth for embroidery, for chairs, firescreens, stools or pictures – 'she having drawn for several gentlewomen in the town and country'.[25] The widow Mrs Hannah Robertson (1724–

INTERIOR of S. & J. FULLER'S TEMPLE of FANCY, 34, RATHBONE PLACE.

43   *Interior of S. & J. Fuller's Temple of Fancy, 34 Rathbone Place*, London, *circa* 1820, printed engraving. British Museum, London, Heal 100.31.

1800) made her living practising and teaching handicrafts in Edinburgh, York, Manchester, London and finally Northampton in the 1770s and '80s. She recommended a wide craft knowledge as a hedge against adversity. Any woman capable of gilding, japanning and making gum flowers 'will always find employment amongst people of fashion, and especially in towns of trade and commerce'.[26] Rotherham governess Anne Platt taught varied fancy work and embroidery in the 1790s to the children of Sir John Eden of Durham, and for her own relaxation made tent-stitch carpets and decorated boxes with dried flowers.[27] All of which fragments reveal only the tip of the infrastructure that supported domestic ornament but imply the scale of its ramifications.

We can also gauge something of the scope of amateur work from the vigour of the commercial culture it spawned. Embroidery kits and printed patterns were available from at least the Renaissance. Practical how-to manuals proliferated in the 1700s explaining a medley of 'curious' crafts from casting pictures in isinglass to making artificial coral for grottoes.[28] Hannah Robertson claimed her school-cum-shop was 'the first of the kind in London . . . for various works of fancy' in the 1780s, but by the 1800s great metropolitan emporia bestrode the applied arts such as Ackerman's Repository of Art on the Strand and the Temple of Fancy on Rathbone Place (fig. 43). Both promised an Aladdin's cave of art materials and prefabricated kits, contrived both to feed and inflame the demand for amateur art and craft (pl. 23).[29] Cabinetmakers were quick to grasp the commercial opportunities of polite craft. New equipment was targeted at the elegant craftswoman, such as the tambour table that swivelled on a pillar, the better for a lady 'to execute needlework by', while the ladies' workbox lent itself to exquisite craftsmanship (pls 24 and 25). The upholsterer James Brown of St Paul's Churchyard, London, had a steady trade in ladies' paraphernalia. In 1785 he furnished Mrs Bacon Foster of Church Street, Kensington, with a satinwood inlaid workbox costing £1 11s. 6d. and 'a square tambour frame on a claw to turn on a ball, coverd with baize, quite plain'.[30] Frames, boxes and specialised worktables had all become recognised pieces of domestic furniture, corresponding in their wood and finishes to the other furnishings in the room (such as tea trays, card tables and backgammon boxes), endorsing the status of handicrafts and advertising that there was a polite but domesticated lady in the house (fig. 44).

How should we account for the popularity of domestic decoration? The needle was an archetypally female instrument, so forged in femininity that, like the distaff and the spinning wheel, it could stand as an emblem for woman herself. Tailoring was a masculine trade, but no male householder expected to do his own plain sewing. Only sailors at sea and soldiers in barracks and on campaign sewed for themselves. Outside the tailor's workshop, a gift for fancy sewing could imperil a man's sexual identity and male amateur embroiderers were as rare as dodos. In Henry Fielding's *History of Amelia*, Mrs Bennet asks 'where's the harm in a woman's having learning as well as man?', to which the doctor answers 'Where is the harm in a man being a fine performer with a needle as well as a woman? And yet answer me honestly would you greatly chose to marry a man with a thimble on his finger?'[31] Needlework had a long-standing appeal for conservative commentators because it was an indoor sedentary activity that enforced passive stillness and implied patient service. If a girl was sewing, she could not be gossiping abroad, or writing, or even surreptitiously reading novels. Nor was she idly lounging. Sewing was used as a tool for the inculcation of uncomplaining femininity in girls, with set tasks from pin cushions, to samplers, to mirror frames, to caskets, leading them through a repertoire of stitches, and training them in acceptance of the idea that life was an odyssey of toil and subordination. In fact, embroidery was so implicated in traditional femininity that the repudiation of sewing was almost axiomatic for feminist rebels and remains so for many to this day.

While the seamstress's hands were busy, however, who was to say that her mind was not flying free? For Roszika Parker, embroidery offered covert power and pleasure for women 'while being indissolubly linked to their powerlessness'.

44   *The Fair Lady Working Tambour*, 1764, mezzotint. Lewis Walpole Library, Farmington, CT, 764.0.11. An exquisitely dressed young woman works with a hook at a small, wooden tambour frame designed to sit at her knee. A Chinese vase and a Chinese figure stand on a chest behind her.

Embroidery cultivated submissive femininity in women, but women could exploit embroidery to find radical expression. Some published patterns were spurned by the embroiderers: Delilah, Salome and Jezebel were ignored in favour of heroines who showed courage to save their people. Ruth Geuter's analysis of 700 pieces of Stuart embroidery confirms that the most compelling biblical role models were the brave petitioners Esther and Deborah. Esther interceding on behalf of the Jews was an especially suggestive image for any persecuted minority, be it Puritan or Royalist, or perhaps even Jacobite under the Hanoverian supremacy.[32] The subjects of Georgian embroidery have not been so systematically analysed, but the changes are striking. Observation and representation of the natural world became ever more de rigueur, although 'nature' could mean an Arcadian pastoral of milkmaids and shepherdesses, a farmyard in Merry England, a scientific interest in botany or a rural genre picture copied from the likes of Thomas Gainsborough, Francis Wheatley and George Morland. There were few embroidered heroines to match the fire of the murderous Jael with her tent peg; nevertheless, the ubiquitous mourning pictures of the late eighteenth century foregrounded the grieving widow, not the dear departed, so even the Neoclassical way of death could be manipulated in silks to give women central billing.[33] Indubitably, women could use embroidery to interrogate and negotiate the constraints of femininity. Both task and declaration, the significance of ornamental needlework was paradoxical.

The high value placed upon women's handicraft in biblical and patriarchal exegesis gave reason enough for the godly or the cynical to decorate the home. Dead wives were eulogised not only for making garments for the poor, but also for 'rich needleworkes' that adorned the house and parish church.[34] Fashionable morality endorsed female sewing too. Samuel Richardson's radiant Protestant heroine Clarissa Harlowe was the embodiment of conduct-book perfection, admired by her friends as much for her fine needlework, letter writing, serious reading and music as for her moral self-containment. When her obnoxious family removed her drawings and the pieces once 'shown to everybody for the magnifying of her dainty fingerworks' in order to punish her, they revealed themselves philistine as well as mercenary.[35] Only villains, it seems, failed to honour female artistry. The stamp of royal approval was also unequivocal. All princesses embroidered. The blameless Queen Charlotte practised, admired and was *known* to admire ladies' work, receiving an array of crafted gifts from loyal subjects.[36] Even on the eve of the French Revolution, royal matrons still picked out their virtue in embroidery silks. Embroidery's ancient association with elevated rank persevered.

Decorative projects, needlework especially, demonstrated female duty. It was not an occupation that all women pursued with pleasure, and a declared preference for the pen over the needle was not uncommon, but even highly educated women felt compelled to some performance.[37] Chance remarks bespeak the pride that men could take in the work of wives and daughters, though whether they liked the objects themselves, admired the artistry or relished the acquiescent humility and feminine service they could be seen to embody is not clear. A Northumberland curate listed needlework, along with piety, beauty and money, as assets in a potential bride in 1722. Her dowry included 'materials for a room, that is hangings, bed, window curtains and a dozen chairs, all her own work', proving that she was 'frugal' and 'most laborious' as well as rich. For the Winchester attorney William Porter, his daughter's 'necessary accomplishments' were expressive of 'learning joined with virtue', and he praised her for her industry in 1742.[38] Women used craft to perform their propriety and servitude to men, sometimes acting a role with cynicism or weary compliance, but also with determination. An elaborate waistcoat was crafted as a wedding gift in the 1770s by Mary Martin, an Essex gentlewoman of commanding presence. In the daytime she oversaw her fiancé's London business, but at night she laboured on her offering: 'I now Rise up Master & go to Bed Dame.' The waistcoat, like the engagement, was years in the making: 'I am sure it will not be done this year, which will vex me very much for I believe it will be tolerably Pretty & ye shape will be so Old Fashion'd by next Summer that it will not be fit for you to Wear.'[39] The never-ending project is ambiguous, both a declaration of wifeliness and perhaps a covert protest about the delays. Possibly Mary was another Penelope, as determined to stage her loyalty as to stay the course. Equally, it remains possible to read female crafting as a simple and sincere exercise in affection. Only a heart of stone would deny that a baby's name embroidered on a quilt was a gesture of tenderness.

Enlightenment ideas and the fashionable spread of polite science added another layer of meaning to the ornamental arts. The rise of shellwork, argues Katherine Sharpe, expresses three crucial features of Georgian taste: a lightly borne but pervasive patrician appreciation of classical myth and symbol; the mid-century vogue for Rococo; and the enthusiasm for a polite natural science (pls 26 and 27). The shell was a classical motif, associated with the sea, unsurprisingly, and Aphrodite. The feminine connotations were reinforced through shellwork grottoes revived in sixteenth-century Italy, which were associated with nymphs and goddesses. The shell was also one of the principal emblems of the Rococo, while the 'Rocaille' denoted the shells, pebbles and rough, rocky materials used in the creation of artificial caves. Shells fascinated: inside was ingenious geometry appealing to reason, but outside fantastic irregularity, as if nature had run riot. Shellwork existed within a scientific culture of collecting, classifying and ordering inspired by the system of the Swedish scientist Carl Linnaeus.

There were some male practitioners of shellwork, famously Alexander Pope (1688–1744), who wrote about shell grottoes and built one of the first in Britain, which connected his house at Twickenham to a shell temple, and Thomas Goldney (1696–1768), a Quaker banker and bachelor, who created a Rococo extravaganza in shells at Goldney Hall near Bristol, beginning in 1737. Shellwork, however, tended to be seen as quintessentially feminine in its fancy, epitomising female facility with natural forms. Shellwork was at its fashionable zenith at mid-century. Five factors spelled the decline of shellwork as an ultra-fashionable enthusiasm: plummeting shell prices, the democratisation of amateur collecting, the creeping institutionalisation of natural history study, the proliferation of handbooks for shellwork made easy, and the rise of the seaside excursion, which made shells accessible and mundane.[40] At its peak, shellwork, like floral embroidery and botanical drawing, sat easily with scientific classification and cabinets of curiosity, a domestic performance that signalled modern intellectual horizons, an expression of polite natural science as at home in the drawing room as in the laboratory. As a guide to reproducing flowers in either drawings or needlework maintained, 'The labour of the hand must second and support that of the Brain.'[41] Crafting in natural objects and floral illustration might look dainty and esoteric to us, but to the Georgians these pieces signalled an engagement in the publicly aware life.

The expression of great artistic talent fired the creation of decorative domestic projects for some unusual individuals. Mary Delany (1700–1788) combined a diverse art practice with voluminous opinionated correspondence. She was an exceptionally well-connected, twice-widowed and financially independent gentlewoman, so the range of her crafts offers a map of the possible. She wrote and illustrated a novel; designed furniture; painted; spun wool; made shellwork, featherwork, silhouettes; invented the entirely new art of paper collage; and was an embroiderer of great artistry, designing her own compositions and relishing painterly effects in embroidery silks. Delany was celebrated for her botanical accuracy, her artistic power and her versatility. A devout Anglican, she had a deep reverence for nature, and saw the hand of God in the faultlessness of natural forms: 'The beauties of *shells* are as *infinite as of flowers*', the examination of which inevitably 'enlarges a field of wonder that leads one insensibly to the great Director and Author of these wonders'.[42] Her crafts could be read as a strengthening of her faith. However, not all crafts were equal. The art of japanning (imitating Japanese lacquer using shellac), for instance, 'put me in mind of the fine ladies of our age – it delighted my eyes, but gave no pleasure to my understanding'. Delany occasionally doubted the moral worth of her recreations, worrying in letters that she was frittering away her time 'with amusements of no real estimation', and compared her storeroom unfavourably with her sister's: 'Mine fits only an idle mind that wants amusement; yours serves either to supply your hospitable table, or gives cordial and healing medicines to the poor and the sick.' Celebrity provoked some soul-searching: 'when people commend any of my performances I feel a consciousness that my time might have been better employed'. Yet these remarks partake more of conventional humility than real misgivings, akin to likening herself to the lily of the valley that nodded fetchingly in the shade: 'as if ashamed to be looked at, not conscious how much it deserves it'.[43] For Kim Sloan, Delany and her peers represent a distinctive culture; unusually well educated, supported by liberal menfolk and connected at court, they occupied their time industriously and innocently, and displayed that they were of liberal taste.[44] In the diversity of her artistic practice, and the intellectual concerns they referenced, Delany offers a distaff version of gentlemanly virtuosity.

Delany did not, however, arise *sui generis* before an astonished public. Horace Walpole celebrated thirty-one ladies of his acquaintance (including Delany) for their artistic skills in everything from modelling in wax, terracotta, marble and amber to copying paintings in silk, watercolours, oils and in miniature.[45] A versatile ingenuity was an ornament of gentility. 'Curious' was one of the keywords of Georgian taste, and a curiosity was a conversation piece designed to raise the wonder, admiration and comment of visitors. Crafted objects provoked compliments, and descriptions of them padded out many a letter. Young gentlemen, from the prim and proper to the republican and licentious, admitted to an admiration for hand-wrought masterpieces, and went out of their way for a viewing.[46] Women's ornaments, 'so very pretty and curious', personified the studied inventiveness so appreciated by the polite gaze.

It is highly unlikely that artistic genius was given to the majority of amateur craftswomen. For the unpretentious, crafts were an unassuming recreation and mediocre performance. The vivacious Mary Warde of Squerryes Court, Kent, was every inch the modish Miss of the 1740s: 'I have been very busy all this summer at a piece of shellwork', she boasted to a shyer northern cousin in 1743, 'It is a very fashionable Employment & a great amusement, & a fancy like yours would display itself to as much advantage as on a *yellow petticoat*.'[47] One suspects that if shellwork had not been 'a very fashionable Employment' Warde's fancy would have lain dormant.

The innocuous appeal of craftwork as a remedy for boredom should not be underestimated. A major defence of accomplishments from both traditionalists and liberals was essentially negative – that they kept women occupied and so stopped them getting up to anything worse. The soul-destroying tedium of life at home was taken for granted. Wettenhall Wilkes preached in 1740 that women should always be usefully or blamelessly employed, to tolerate 'the desert of wild empty wastes', and leave no vacancy whatsoever for idle or dangerous thoughts.[48] Similarly, Dr Gregory believed that innocent pastimes helped women suffer 'the many solitary hours [they] must necessarily pass at home', and discouraged gadding about.[49] With more sympathy Hester Chapone recommended accomplishments for 'filling up agreeably those intervals of time, which too often hang heavily on the hands of a woman, if her lot be cast in a retired situation'.[50] Maria Edgeworth also accepted accomplishments as 'resources against ennui', but argued that since 'women are peculiarly restrained in their situation, and in their employments, by the customs of society' this was no mean benefit. Illusionless, Edgeworth concluded: 'every sedentary occupation must be valuable to those who are to lead sedentary lives'.[51] Accomplishments were supports to sanity.

Bearing the monotony of provincial routine with a smile, not a shriek, demanded all one's inner resources. A noblewoman's account of a wet day in Worcestershire in the 1780s would be familiar to many genteel girls:

> Rising in a morning fidgeting to *Mama*, reading the *newspaper* doing a *bit of work*, then reading again, then changing my cap and what you call cleaning myself, then dining tete a tete with Mrs Fitz then adjourning to the pigging chamber there take my *shuttle* & *knot* till tea time . . . then make the tea, then do another bit of work, which is sprigging a little muslin, then at 8 o clock Miss goes to the land of Nod, then I take my book which is Fieldings *Amelia* and work my lungs till ten, when we satisfy our inwards for the remainder of the night, then *chat a while*, and at eleven go to bed, this is the life of Hester Lyttleton, you'll own it is decently dull.[52]

The deadliness of boring company, however, was often even harder to bear than loneliness. Women whose families pretended to politeness had little choice but to submit to visiting. Fancy sewing was one of the few activities that could be performed in company without reproach. Thomas Jefferson stressed this advantage when writing to his daughter Martha at school in Paris in 1787: 'In dull company and in dull weather, for instance, it is ill-manners to read, it is ill-manners to leave them; no card playing there among genteel people – that is abandoned to blackguards. The needle is then a valuable resource.'[53] Sewing could offer women an aloof self-possession in the midst of clamour. When the Chutes of The Vyne, in Hampshire, saw the tenants on rent day in the early nineteenth century, the ladies of the family were expected to grace the proceedings. 'Each tenant came in by turns, called farmer so and so, talked and grumbled, whilst Aunt C and myself worked.'[54] Doubtless their needlework demonstrated a venerable housewifery to the tenantry, as befitted an old-fashioned, hospitable coun-try family, but it also helped the women endure a long evening of patronage. Similarly, Anna Larpent's sewing enabled her to contain her irritation at her friv-olous guests. 'Mrs Webb, & Mrs Lake chattered here an hour, ribbands, gauzes, this, that, flip, flap. I worked.'[55]

Not all crafts were equally portable, or equal to the gaze of guests. Plain-work, especially the mundane mending of shifts and shirts, fell to most middling women and underclothes could hardly be flourished before visitors, especially those of the opposite sex. However, any woman could be discovered at her tambour stand without a blush (pl. 28). The cleaner crafts gave women something to do in the parlour when they had no choice but to display their company manners.

The pursuit of recreations was a widely recognised antidote to ennui, which, left unchecked, could bring on 'melancholia', a dread malady that threatened the sin of self-murder. The depressive spinster Gertrude Savile used her needlework as occupational therapy in the 1730s. A resentful dependant, excruciatingly shy, gauche and sour, Savile found almost her only relief in needlework: 'My tent is my most elligant Divertion, and all I shall ever be fitt for . . . I stair'd out of the win-dow a little. Tent till dark.' Needlework dignified and justified solitude, but Sav-ile also saw it as one of the few means available to quieten her own torturous inner monologue: 'Sat Oct 26 tent 2 hours Morn (which I knew was most parni-cious). But better than sitt still and let my own mellancholly thoughts lead me to madness).' Drawing her own designs and copying from prints, Savile worked pockets, made patch-work and tent-work screens, chair covers and backs. She feared the intermission between projects: 'Tis a misfortune I have done my Screen. I can't live so much alone without that sort of work'. An ongoing task was a psy-chological necessity. Perhaps she apprehended that a life measured out in wool was no life, but she firmly believed that she was unfit for all but seclusion. Look-ing back on 1728 she concluded: 'Seldom went out . . . I begun a Tent Work Screen; finished it in about 5 months. Besides I know not what I did to keep me from Madness.'[56] Savile's furious needle held both insanity and society at bay (pl. 29).

Even women of manifest calm used needlework as an anodyne. In 1797, when Anna Larpent heard that her niece had died aged only 24, leaving two infants, she 'worked all evening, for my Mind was too disturbed to read and there is a mo-notony in X stitch and a cheerfulness in forming the various shades that soothes my mind'.[57] Decorative work played a role in long illnesses and convalescence. Mary Hartley was a very feeble young woman, who lived in lodgings in Win-chester and Bath in the 1780s with her servant-cum-nurse. Confined to bed with a gangrenous foot in 1784, and suffering a terrifying series of minor amputa-tions, Mary painted a satin fire screen for her brother, an MP, to present to the queen. The gesture was one of the few open to her: 'in the oeconomical way in which I live, spending as little as I can, in every article, I cannot well afford to make presents'.[58] The screen was adorned in pain, and wrought in sad, often drugged, imprisonment. The view from the window was Mary's chief entrée to the world. At least her work might go to court, even if she herself could barely leave the house.

There are copious examples, however, of the strong social context of craft for many women. When Birmingham Unitarian Catherine Hutton went out to dinner in 1779 she regretted having left her half-finished muslin apron at home: 'Miss Greaves and Miss Boothy both worked at their netting and embroidery, while I was an idle spectator, as I had brought no work with me.'[59] Needlework married well with reading aloud in female companies.[60] Collaborative projects were common. When Delany visited Mrs Vesey in 1751, she 'had a whim to have Indian figures and flowers cut out and oiled, to be transparent, and pasted on her dressing-room window in imitation of painting on glass . . . we go again next Friday to finish what we began last week'. Delany designed and advised on the projects of her wide acquaintance, the 'mosaick pattern with cloth work round, will be prettier than the flower pattern for your window-curtains. Have you put up your shell-work over the chimney, and painted it? and how does it look?' The aristocrat Lady Frances Brudenell, daughter of the Earl of Ailesbury, was still gratified in the 1790s to be asked to assist Lady Devonshire in 'working furniture for one of her rooms in Hanover square'.[61] The frequency with which handicrafts were given as gifts suggests both the prestige wrought upon them and the power they had to connect women. From the nobility to the yeomanry, grandmothers wore their granddaughters' work and boasted of their ingenuity.[62] Appreciation of a personal production is a leitmotif of female correspondence.

Craftwork was particularly associated with female sociability, female communities and often female retirement. Elizabeth Montagu (1718–1800) was celebrated for her championing of learned sociability. Widow of one of the richest men in England, Montagu used her vast coal fortune to rebuild her country seat Sandleford Priory near Newbury in 1781 and to build Montagu House, now 22 Portman Square, London. Famously, she commissioned a room for her featherart creations, inspired by the example of the Duchess of Portland.[63] The featherwork screens depicted flora and fauna in every shade, composed of feathers 'from ye gaudy peacock to ye solemn raven' supplied by friends. The screens were ten years in the making, overseen by Montagu's forewoman, Betty Tull. A work of gorgeous exuberance, even the queen and her daughters paid homage.[64]

In pointed contrast, Montagu's retiring sister Sarah Scott, scarred by smallpox and a disastrous short-lived marriage, lived in relative seclusion in rented accommodation outside Bath in the 1750s. Yet she too fostered female community, but on a plainer scale than her sister, and with a greater emphasis on local charity. With her companion, the sickly Barbara Montagu, Scott also crafted decorative compositions from natural forms. But instead of exotic peacock feathers and rare nautilus shells, the couple drew on materials that cost nothing, and performed the work themselves. They made elaborate frames from 'gilded cones corn acorns poppy heads & various evergreens with flowers & leaves in lead & some fruit in pipe makers clay'.[65] Betty Rizzo argues that the sisters developed two rival versions of community, and that their differing crafts were one expression of the contrast. Scott's own community could be read as a critique of her sister's, centring as it did on the poor, not the grand, on self-abasement, not showing off.[66] While Montagu spent a fortune on her exotic screens, Scott and Lady Barbara gleaned from nature's autumnal bounty. In Scott's *Millenium Hall* (1762), a didactic idealisation of female community, the inmates of the model school learned woodcarving, engraving, turnery, perspective, drawing and painting, as well as harpsichord, embroidery and plain sewing. Consequently, the women were able to raise the drooping spirits of a poor widow they had befriended by decorating her house and making little pieces of furniture 'very pretty and curious'. They hung papers, framed drawings in shellwork and covered her plain cabinets with dried seaweed landscapes. For the widowed mother of five, the house so 'prettily adorned', with its neat little flower garden, represented the revival of hope.[67] Here women's ornaments expressed decorative frugality befitting self-effacing and charitable femininity, but also gave heart at home when brightness was most wanting.

A riot of craftwork was characteristic of exclusively female interiors. The link between female design and craft was clear to the observant Londoner Anna Larpent on her polite travels in the 1790s. She was impressed by the 'very neat square house' belonging to a Mrs Hardinge in Kent, thinking it 'compact & pretty', but

> what renders it more interesting is that Mrs H built it herself without an architect, with Country workmen. Almost sat by to see it done. It is furnished with needlework – drawing – furniture painted up by ye Miss Hardinges with great taste & ingenuity – Made of oughts & ends – yet really with Effect as well as Economy – the walls coloured by themselves.[68]

Thrift and ingenuity in decoration are here the hallmarks of a virtuous female taste. Deliberate attempts at separatist female living – at Plas Newydd, the Gothicised 'low roofed cot' of the loving ladies of Llangollen, Wales, and A La Ronde, the sixteen-sided Devon home of the Parminter cousins – were characterised by a rampant culture of flamboyant ornamentation, suggesting both virtuous consecration to a domestic cloister of curiosities and a luxuriant exfloreation of femininity (pl. 30).

Craft projects could be a shared interest for some couples. A bizarre Lincolnshire vicarage and garden contained much ingenious craft by the lady of the house, Mrs Holland, but Mr Holland was credited with the grotesque excavations in the garden. Indeed, the scale and dominance of the fabulous decoration and landscaping bespeaks a *folie à deux*. Vicar's son John Furnis Ogle encountered the thatched Gothic vicarage near Louth, in the Lincolnshire Wolds, in 1800. Inside, the vicarage was 'furnished in a gothic stile' with an assortment of fittings created from natural materials from boughs and bones, to flints and moss, and in imitation of other natural forms: 'The Drawing room is a pattern of industry & ingenuity the walls are in a great part cover'd with raised leaves of white paste bark both the pasteboard & the leaves of Mrs Holland's own making.' The porch to the garden 'is paved with polish'd flints lined with moss', while the roof is 'made chiefly of strong paper in imitation of large rocks'. The porch contained two caged turtledoves and two corner chairs 'made of the boughs & roots of trees in their material state'. The garden offered a series of cloisters built of wood complete with bark and moss, lined with fir apples and 'paved with small polish'd flints & the knuckle of sheeps bones', leading to a chair made from whale bones. Beyond the shrubbery was a little wood-covered hermitage, containing seats and a set of Shakespeare's works.[69] Craftwork was rarely so grotesque or all encompassing, but it was an esteemed feature of most polite and middling homes.

Domestic crafts were prestigious, multivalent and eloquent – we have simply lost the power to read them. A misreading of the polemical attack on accomplishments has over-determined the way historians have approached the subject. The tale of a decline in useful domestic work in the gaudy face of fashionable accomplishments was but one line of discursive attack. How far the sneering about the emptiness of accomplishments tempered the practice and domestic reception of craft seems doubtful. It is unlikely that More and Wollstonecraft had more ideological purchase than the Old Testament. Sewing furnishings for church remained a crucial expression of Anglicanism. Female decoration of the home retained a moral allure. Indeed, were it not so, it is hard to imagine the placid Queen Charlotte devoting herself to decorative work in the 1790s, or the devout Anna Larpent pursuing art and craft as an expression of her high-minded educational domesticity, neither a challenge to family business nor empty trivia.[70] For the rank and file, women's crafts remained a fitting crown to a righteous domestic life. The sensible wife shone as much in the part of 'prudent domestic Wife' as in the role of accomplished lady 'in her Boudoir surrounded by her various collection of shells, feathers, and paintings of her own performance'.[71] The key to success lay in being seen to balance housewifery and accomplishment.

It was possible to use crafts to signal *both* wide Enlightenment horizons and dutiful conservatism. Decoration by hand was so fundamentally and pervasively female that in some ways it lay beyond politics. Needlework was a useful device for the subversion of male authority of whatever complexion in Jane Collier's satirical manual *The Art of Ingeniously Tormenting* (1753). If a husband was a reactionary old dog and demanded a domesticated wife and 'that old-fashioned female employment the needle . . .', Collier advised: 'tell him that every woman of spirit ought to hate and despise a man who would insist on his wife being a family drudge, and declare that you would not submit to be a cook and a seamstress to any man.' But were he a modern progressive who longed to share his love of literature with a well-educated partner, a wife could still out-manoeuvre him: 'if you have any needle-work in your hands, you may be so busy in cutting-out, and measuring one part with another, that it will plainly appear to your husband, that you mind not one word he reads'.[72] Needlework was a universal weapon deployed on any battlefield.

The years 1680 to 1830 saw a transformation in domestic crafts. The early dominance of needlework was challenged, though never superseded, by the fashion for shellwork, silhouette, collage and the like ('Everybody is mad about Japan work' reported Delany in 1729), but also towards 1800 by craft kits, sketching, watercolours and domestic music. ('The present fashionable fancy works are painting Screens, Boxes, tables & c', reported Anne Platt in 1793.) Needlework itself was hardly an inert form – biblical themes in stump work and large tree of life designs in worsteds gave way to tent-work tapestries and exquisite silk embroidery in brilliant colours, which were themselves superseded by tambour work and white on white Neoclassical pieces (fig. 45). Shifting vogues were obvious to practitioners, stamping older crafts as passé. 'One is seldom partial, I think, to ladies work of this kind', concluded Mrs Lybbe Powys on the hangings in a Buckinghamshire mansion made by the late mistress, 'as it generally carries the date of the age it was perform'd in.' Likewise, Lady Fane's Thameside rock and shell grotto was celebrated in the 1720s, but by the 1790s it had fallen into ruin, 'disowned by an improved and purer taste'.[73]

As in other aspects of interior design, the literal didacticism of the Stuarts was superseded by the polite aesthetic preoccupations of the Georgians. Visual lessons in genealogy, allegiance, politics, religion and morality gave way to allusive designs and light mythological subjects. Certain forms came to be seen as archaic, bathed in a glow of nostalgia or depression, depending on perspective. Predictably, Joseph Addison's fictional gentleman Roger de Coverly, an early eigh-

45 Design for tambour embroidery for Miss Thrale, 1788, pen and ink on paper. Victoria and Albert Museum, London, E.227-1973. A professionally drawn design for embroidering a muslin apron on a tambour or embroidery frame. The recipient, Miss Thrale, was the 24-year-old daughter of the London brewer Henry Thrale and his wife Hester, the author.

teenth-century admirer of hospitality and tradition, smiled to see 'your Abrahams, your Isaacs, and your Jacobs, as we have them in old pieces of tapistry'. In 1797 a wistful Thomas Gisborne saw a mastery of the 'mysteries of cross-stitch and embroidery', the 'sciences of pickling' and the 'family receipt book' as the measure of female perfection in the 'last age'. Crewelwork and stump work inevitably brought to mind Stuart housewifery, and implied that the makers were industrious countrywomen (pl. 31). An elderly correspondent of the *Spectator* proclaimed her disgust at seeing 'a couple of proud idle flirts sipping their tea, for a whole afternoon, in a room hung round with the indoors of their great grandmother'. On the other hand, hangings were often taken to symbolise woman's lot in yesteryear, and raised a shudder in some observers. Addison was depressed by 'tedious drudgeries in needlework, as were fit only for the Hilpas and the Nilpas that lived before the flood'.[74] Hannah More disliked the objects women fashioned in 1799 (scorning the wax flowers and cut-paper ornaments that allegedly littered the parlours of pretentious farmers' daughters), but allowed that modern productions were at least superior to the 'hangings of hideous tapestry and disfiguring tent stitch', created by 'the good housewives of the last century', who 'wore out their joyless days in adorning the mansion house' in very bad taste.[75] To our eyes crafts might look interchangeable, but to their practitioners there was a world of difference between a Stuart biblical tapestry, a Georgian feather screen, a Neo-classical embroidery and a Regency fancy-work box. Dusty curtains seemed as remote to Regency viewers as featherwork and bone grottoes appear to us.

Female handicrafts were largely amateur, a term coming into use around 1780 to mean someone who practised the arts without regard to payment, though 'amateurish' had not yet acquired the modern pejorative implication of substandard when compared with professional products. Meanwhile, professional artistry became institutionally male. With the return of Angelica Kauffman to the Continent in 1781, and the death of the flower painter Mary Moser in 1819, the Royal Academy became an exclusively masculine institution. Denied access to prestigious art education and discouraged from exhibiting history paintings or nudes from life, women seem to have taken advantage of the burgeoning of new media, to develop what some see as alternative areas of art practice, though never to the same critical acclaim. Cut paper, shellwork or 'any such baubles' were all banned from the Royal Academy (fig. 46). In genres deemed unimportant and decorative, however, such as flower painting, women were free to excel, and some to make a living.[76] It is also important to remember that copying lacked the entirely negative connotations that it would acquire for later generations invested in the idea of individual genius. Indeed, for all the professionalising snobberies of the Royal Academy, there must have been many consumers who preferred decorative flowers and watercolour landscapes to history paintings. Even today, though conceptual and abstract art have greatest prestige, landscapes, portraits and paintings of animals have loyal audiences, and these genres flourish without the benefit of Saatchi gallery and equivalent media fanfare. Doubtless many a provincial gentleman preferred his wife's firescreen and his daughter's pastel of the dogs to any avant-garde history painting or academic tableau.

We should take care not to let our own assumptions about the appeal of high-mark designer furniture over home-made furnishings today colour our assessment of Georgian amateur productions. Professional handwork adorned furnishings of all kinds and skilled amateurs produced decorations of a piece with shop-bought goods and commissions. Delany maintained that 'the ornamental work of gentlewomen ought to be superior to bought work in design and taste, and their plain work the model for their maids'. Handicrafts were

46 Anna-Maria Garthwaite, cut-paper work picture of a country house and deer park with a neighbouring village, 1707, knife-cut cut-paper work, with pin pricking and collage, paper and ink on a vellum backing. Victoria and Albert Museum, London, E.1077–1993. Made when Garthwaite was 17 years old.

pursued by some of the keenest interior decorators. Even as she supervised the reorientation of the interior at Parham House in Sussex in the 1780s, Harriet Bishop was busy working the chairs.[77] Nor did designers sneer. When Chippendale and Haig furnished Sir Edward Knatchbull's newly renovated house in the 1770s, they incorporated his wife's work for the chair covers ('We must send her Ladyship patterns for the needlework which will be Very large'), seeing no incongruity between amateur embroidery and Axminster carpet and India wallpapers.[78] Men valued women's productions highly enough to pay for them to be expensively framed in mahogany, suggesting that husbands appreciated ladies' work far more than modern historians have done. Lord Parker went to court in 1792 sporting an embroidered waistcoat 'being the work of Lady Parker's leisure hours', *The Times* reported.[79] Matrimonial success on exhibition, her ladyship's diligence only accentuated his lordship's masculinity.

The assumed worth of women's ornamental projects suffers by an implied comparison with men's sturdy public employments, yet the practices of noble, gentry and genteel women were not dissimilar to those of English gentlemen who lived quietly on their inheritance pursuing a range of interests: collecting, horticulture, botany, philosophy and literature. Some crafts were occasionally pursued by ladies and gentlemen together, or side by side, like his collecting and her shellwork. It is quite wrong to suppose that privileged women filled their empty lives with decorative nonsense while their menfolk put away such things. Active leisure was ever the mark of the gentleman. Sir William Hamilton embraced an interest in gardening because

> As one passion begins to fail, it is necessary to form another; for the whole art of going through life tolerably in my opinion is to keep oneself eager about anything. The moment one is indifferent on s'ennuie, and that is a misery to which I perceive even kings are often subject.

Consequently, while a Mrs Freeman was commended by Mrs Lybbe Powys for her embroidered furniture, her husband was noted for cases of fossils, shells and ores, 'in which Mr Freeman is curious and has a fine collection'.[80] The sensible were expected to have artistic and cultural resources to draw upon, what might today be termed a cultural hinterland, to help tolerate the doldrums and reverses of existence.

Inevitably, it was the possession of servants that released the time for elaborate craftwork amongst the affluent. Furthermore, it was common for women to design embroidery that they paid professional seamstresses to execute. That said, middling wives routinely ran complex households with a single maid so they could not escape relentless needlework. London schoolmaster's wife Bessy Ramsden was always behind with her mending when her children were young and often sick: 'Her nursery has thrown her so much behind hand with her *Knitting* that I forsooth must be her secretary', wrote her husband in 1764.[81] Moreover, all housewives were tasked with sewing in the evenings as a form of leisure when their other duties were done, though the balance between decorative projects and mundane chores varied with economic pressures. Even so, surviving homemade baby linens, at once utilitarian and exquisitely decorated, caution against an iron distinction between the ornamental indulgences of the rich and the useful work of the poor. If a farmer's wife contrived some embroidery on a winter's eve while a husband snored over his seed catalogues, it would be perverse to read her sampler as a certificate of idleness.

Women's crafts were productions of supreme individuality. Handworks were individual and personal in material, aesthetic, customary and even in legal terms.

Raw materials were worked upon to produce something literally unique, and even shop-bought kits were virtually never assembled in exactly the same way. Drawing and design, selection of colour and adaptation of patterns all manufactured an aesthetic display that was personal. 'My own work' was a routine identification made by female victims of theft. And even among the highest nobility women's craft helped to define and defend personal property against the devouring maw of the estate. Sarah, Duchess of Marlborough's meticulous inventory of the goods at Blenheim, drawn up in 1740 when she was in a property dispute with her grandson, reveals how personal labour on an object could mark it as paraphernalia – those individual accoutrements that could not be swallowed up by the patrimony: 'A white Indian Stitched Bed made with fringe which is the Duchess of Marlboroughs All things belonging to that Furniture the Trusts but all the fringe is the Duchess of Marlbro's own Work & therefore is hers' – as much her own as the valences 'of very rich Embroidery which was made of the Duchess of Marlboroughs Clothes'.[82] The wily duchess used her needle to colonise property and enlarge the territory of her paraphernalia. In placing their manual work upon something, women from high to low stamped it as their very own. And marks of individuality were no mean achievement in the hierarchical household.

Authorised by God, exemplified by Minerva and hallmarked by royalty, women's crafts were never less than respectable (fig. 47). The claim of domestic ornament to righteousness was archaic. Craftwork was a socially acceptable outlet for creative expression. The very process of making could be useful – a therapy for the distracted and a solace for the wounded. Decorative projects offered women a sense of purpose and resulted in a lasting achievement, unlike laundry, cooking, cleaning and the rest. They offered an innocent remedy for the tediousness of domestic life, though it was often the torture of tiresome company that was harder to bear than loneliness. Nevertheless, handicrafts were often supremely social, linking friends, flourishing in female communities, and often a surreal expression of female intellectual retirement.

The accumulation of objects crafted by women composed its own archaeology of domestic life. Predictably, architects and designers preferred women's crafts to be isolated rather than scattered throughout a carefully planned interior. Sheraton advised excluding female ornaments from the dining room and the drawing room, though they could be safely displayed in the less formal tea room or breakfast room, which 'may abound with beaufets, painted chairs, flower-pot stands, hanging book shelves or moving libraries, and the walls may be adorned with landscapes, and pieces of drawings & c'.[83] Upholsterers' ledgers, however, record that women's work was often mounted, glazed and framed, so it could

Employment, circa 1770, mezzotint. Yale Center for British Art, New Haven, CT, B1970.3.1069. In this British mezzotint based on a painting by a Venetian artist, an elegantly dressed woman turning a miniature spinning wheel is interrupted by a splendidly dressed man. The verses suggest the virtuous allure of women's crafts: 'This Intrusion pardon, and suspend your Task; A short suspension is the whole I ask; More Charms attract me than a shape or Face, For Industry to Beauty adds new Grace.' It was, of course, the vacuous display of accomplishments to attract men that so enraged critics like Mary Wollstonecraft and Hannah More.

be exhibited to advantage alongside the best mahogany furniture. In fact, framing needlework could be as significant a part of a picture framer's business as mounting drawings or prints.[84] Moreover, the attention of tourists was often drawn to ladies' work in drawing rooms and sitting rooms as well as bedrooms and dressing rooms, so, in this, the prescriptions of architects and designers were made to be flouted. Between the excitement of furnishing and the repetitions of housework lay the relentless creativity of handicraft. Decorating and enhancing the home was a constant creative project for women. The interior was fashioned just as much by its home-made firescreens and chair covers as by mirrors, tables and chairs. Like Arachne, the flawless weaver, women fabricated the home and built their houses from the inside.

10

A SEX IN THINGS?

A LETTER PUBLISHED IN THE SATIRICAL MAGAZINE *The World* in 1753, purportedly from a tradesman, though in fact by a sporadic poet, caricatured the plight of a man overwhelmed and unmanned by female taste in all its appalling variety, and so gave a lurid catalogue of all the Rococo elements that were ever linked to women. Every piece of furniture is twisted into fanciful form, every room covered with Wilton carpet and bizarrely branching Chelsea china. Indeed, porcelain figures weigh down every chimney piece in the house. The upstairs apartments 'before handsomely wainscoted are now hung with the richest Chinese and Indian paper, where all the powers of fancy are exhausted in a thousand fantastic figures of birds, beasts and fishes which never had existence'. The best chamber is rigged out in white satin ludicrously adorned with a jumble of French flowers, artificial moss, spangles, beads and shells, while the bed itself nestles in an alcove sacred to Cupid, flanked by two twisted pillars encrusted in shellwork. Inevitably, the wife's dressing room is too stuffed with trinkets for adequate description. The walls are decorated with 'looking glass interspersed with pictures made of moss, butterflies and sea-weed', while under a Chinese canopy stands a toilette holding a veritable pharmacopoeia. Petticoat government is already manifest in the decorations, but it is soon fulfilled in practice: 'In short sir, it is become so great a sight that I am no longer master of it, being constantly driven from room, to give opportunity for strangers to admire it.'[1] The conquest of masculinity is complete.

The god of taste that ruled Georgian aesthetics wore antique clothing. Rigid Palladians and self-appointed authorities on architecture tended to type pure classicism as masculine, and diversions from uniformity and proportion as feminine and undisciplined or effeminate and corrupt. The Rococo, Gothic or chinoiserie could all be read as evidence of disorder, while eclecticism was proof of pretension and inadequate understanding of the rules. 'That true Politeness we can only call, Which looks like Jones Fabrick at Whitehall, Where just proportions we, with pleasure see, Tho built by rule, yet from Stiffness free.'[2]

The Rococo was a sinuous threat to the 'manly noble orders', according to the architect Isaac Ware, whose magisterial *Complete Body of Architecture* has been read as a rallying cry 'to recall taste from the S-curve into the path of rectitude'. Ware found French, Chinese and Gothic decoration 'equally mean and frivolous . . . and equally a disgrace to the taste of the proprietor'. Any client 'captivated. . . with foolish fancies' from Paris should be forewarned that 'this is reviving the decorations of the Goths and Vandals'.[3] On the other hand, an equally vigorous Tory tradition associated gentlemen with the good old days of Tudor manors, while women (and their lackeys) were agents of modern fashion in either Neoclassical or Rococo garb. For Smollett's Matthew Bramble, female taste given full reign is preposterous – 'All without is Grecian, and all within Gothic' – and profoundly inhospitable, creating only a 'temple of cold reception'. A similar lament for 'old hospitality . . . kick'd out of doors; and made to give way to taste' underscores the travel diaries of the retired army officer and tax official John Byng in the 1790s. He admired rural simplicity, venerable old mansions, magnificent cathedrals, the treasures of antiquity, libraries, good inns, family fare, comfortable beds and 'very large portraits in the true taste of full wigs & naked bosoms'. He disliked spa towns, scenes of alleged elegance and refinement, Chinese wallpaper, festoon curtains, flesh-coloured stucco, gilding, whimsical carving, modern glazing, ladies' fancy work and anything French – in most of which he saw the triumph of women and the enfeeblement of men.[4]

The battle of wainscot versus marble, or stucco versus rampant wallpaper, however, was a motif of a wider cultural debate in which gender was a weapon but not the central battle. Effeminacy was an easy accusation called on by both severe classicists and old-fashioned die-hards to disparage the nobility of that which they disliked. How far gender differences were made concrete in architecture is very hard to judge, though the idea that women as a group had a single distinctive architectural taste is dubious. The platitude that an entire sex spurned Greece

48   G. Shepherd, 'Hagley Park. Seat of Lord Lyttelton, Worcestershire', from Francis Laird, *A Topographical and Historical Description of the County of Worcester* (London, ?1815). Built between 1754 and 1760.

and Rome for Paris and Cathay awaits proof. A generation before a brick was laid at Lord Burlington's Chiswick House, Lady Wilbraham made notes for the re-building of Weston Park in Shropshire in her translated copy of the first of Pal-ladio's *Four Books of Architecture*. At Hagley Park in Worcestershire in the 1750s, it was Lady Lyttelton who insisted on monumental Palladian for the exterior, while My Lord's preferences were expressed in the lighter French decorations of the principal apartments (fig. 48). The first complete Neoclassical interior in Eng-land at Spencer House (1765–6) was the joint project of the first Earl Spencer and his bride Georgina Poyntz, realised by James 'Athenian' Stuart.[5]

Female beauty could be interpreted in classical terms, while the orders them-selves were internally gendered. The Ionic was construed as feminine: 'the image of a well-proportioned female, not the girl, for the elegance and slenderness of the Corinthian more naturally is brought in for that resemblance, but the woman'.[6] Women swallowed the dominant stylistic prejudices as easily as men. Lady Cowper revealed an entirely conventional appreciation of improvements and horror of Gothic irregularity when she visited her brother at the bishop's house in Durham in 1750. She approved his creation of a good staircase and handsome rooms 'all neatly fitted up & hung with paper', and especially liked Mrs Cowper's dressing room overlooking the garden 'all sash'd & as pleasant as can be', though the rest of the house was 'more gloomy, more lofty, & is for state. The furniture old chiefly Tapestry', which she generally avoided. Downstairs, the old Gothic cellars and kitchen put her in mind of the dungeon 'where they Torture ye Prisoners in ye Inquisition'. Sash windows and wallpaper reflected the wholesomeness and light of Protestant modernity. Nevertheless, there were ladies in every generation noted for their defiant antiquarianism, like Lady Betty Germain at Drayton and the Countess of Hertford at Longleat, well before Horace Walpole pastiched the Gothic at Strawberry Hill.[7]

The antagonism between classicism and its others, though powerful in texts, was muted, or even refused, in many buildings. Most Palladian boxes were enveloped by a naturalistic landscape park, while within there were often pockets of Chinese wallpaper, Indian chintz and Rococo silk that all refused the symmetries and proportions of Rome. Palladian architects lacked a domestic idiom, borrowing components from classical temples and public baths, and bringing external architectural features indoors. Palladio's lack was Rococo's opportunity. Even the bullying classicist Isaac Ware was forced to accommodate the hated French to please Lord Chesterfield, one of his most important clients, for his London palace (1747–52). Though the entrance hall, stairs, library and sitting rooms were classical in decoration, the drawing room and music room were Rococo. Through gritted teeth Ware resigned himself where absolutely necessary to the discreet acceptance and disciplining of French ornaments 'till we have reduced them into a more decent appearance'. Immaculate uniformity was rare in the built environment; the cold discipline of classical formalism seemed to demand its antithesis by way of visual relief. Old houses were themselves a palimpsest of fashions, while new houses could exhibit the full diversity of contemporary style. Claydon House in Buckinghamshire, for instance, rebuilt in the 1760s, had interlinked rooms of exuberant French, Chinese and Gothic decoration, bankrupting Lord Verney (pl. 32).[8] Inevitably, consumers were more promiscuous in their desires than partisan architects wished them to be.

In a world of proliferating styles and objects, consumers and decorators fell back upon the touchstone of decorum for reassurance about the appropriateness of their choices. Lifted root and branch from classical philosophy, decorum stressed the classical aesthetic ideals of order, proportion and harmony. Hence for early Georgian writers decorum found perfect manifestation in Palladian architecture, proportioned according to the golden rules of geometry. Aesthetics, manners and worldview were all of apiece. 'Behaviour is like Architecture', opined James Forrester in the *Polite Philosopher* in 1734, 'the Symmetry of the whole pleases us so much, that we examine not into its Parts.'⁹ As architectural fashions changed over the eighteenth century, and defences of the waving line of beauty and celebrations of the Sublime loosened the hegemony of geometry, decorum as a principle became detached from its straightforward classical manifestation. By 1798 Maria Edgeworth decided that since 'taste is governed by arbitrary and variable laws; the fashions of dress, of decoration, of manner, change from day to day', encouraging an open mind in students was the best policy. 'Show him, and you need go no farther than the Indian skreen, or the Chinese paper in your drawing-room, for the illustration, that the sublime and beautiful vary at Pekin, at London, on Westminster bridge and on the banks of the Ganges.' Though pupils should be carefully 'accustomed to Grecian beauty, and to all the classic forms of grace', they were not to be bigoted in favour of the antique.¹⁰ Nonetheless, the grammar of decorum was deeper than the expression of a passing fashion. It was about status rather than style. In 1803 the designer Thomas Sheraton still urged that surroundings should mirror status: 'particular regard is to be paid to the quality of those who order a house to be furnished'.¹¹ The maintenance of the traditional social and sexual hierarchy was the explicit goal of courtesy writing on decorum, good breeding and politeness. It was these customary distinctions that the tide of luxury threatened to mask and even dissolve.

Given the strong desire for fixed distinctions revealed in print, an expectation that femininity and masculinity be endorsed in appearances and materials is utterly unsurprising. However, the terrain on which these ideas were applied was itself in flux. This chapter explores the associations and ownership of five crucial types of commodity. It is not an encyclopaedia of the Georgian world of goods, but a set of case studies that are strongly suggestive of the propensities and practices of consumers both male and female – scientific objects, kitchenware, tea wares, porcelain ornaments and cabinetwork. Throughout, the discussion asks: how far can we read a sex in things?

Scientific instruments were yoked to masculinity in the Georgian worldview. In a stage play of 1730, the caddish Gainlove rejects Lady Science and marries her daughter instead, because, he insists, 'the Dressing-Room, not the Study, is the Lady's Province and a Woman makes as ridiculous a Figure, poring over Globes, or thro' a Telescope, as a Man would with a Pair of *Preservers* mending Lace'.¹² Nevertheless, the science that instruments radiated was itself most carefully crafted. The breakthroughs of heroic individuals have long constituted the core narrative of the history of science, but recent research has restored the domestic context of scientific endeavour before the laboratory, recreating a world where experiments and housekeeping intertwined. Feminists have revealed the contribution of women's 'kitchen-physick' and technical knowledge in the stillroom to the emergence of early medicine and chemistry, and the deep involvement of the sisters, wives and daughters of the Royal Society men in the sedulous testing that the new science demanded.[13] One less studied consequence of the domestic location of experimental science is the inevitable clutter of equipment that competed for floor space with sofa and dining table. Patricia Fara is suggestive on this point:

> In addition to the sick babies and students, the Desaguliers's cramped house in Westminster must have been overflowing with his apparatus – instruments in various stages of completion, piles of unsold books, and bulky demonstration equipment that included an eight-foot wide centrifugal bellows and a working steam-engine. Desaguliers was particularly proud of his large mechanical planetarium . . .[14]

While Joanna Desaguliers's contribution to the consolidation of Newtonian ideologies is undocumented, that she was beset by the apparatus on her home turf, overwhelming the very furniture of her marriage, is almost certain. How much of the household budget went on engines over curtains remains to be researched. Apparatus may have been far more widely dispersed than the history of interiors has realised. Even Alexander Pope and Samuel Johnson were not averse to dabbling in experimental chemistry at home.

Microscopes, telescopes, air pumps, globes and orreries were not confined to the households of the heroes of science. The vigour of the commercial trade in scientific instruments was one of the wonders of London. The diffusion of scientific instruments as domestic ornaments is one measure of the unfolding of the Enlightenment across polite and middling society. A telescope in the library was the counterpart of the tea table in the parlour. In its celebration of the workings and wonder of God's creation, polite science married easily with Anglican seriousness. The moral respectability, domestic context and large female audience for polite science were all crucial to its fashionability as a practical activity, subject for conversation and component of a domestic education. Polite science may have owed more to politeness than to science, but the fact that it was 'defined and propagated via merchandise', from elaborate showpieces to educational toys, 'contributed in no small measure to its success'.[15]

The barometer, for instance, arose out of experimental philosophy, but was swiftly translated from a specialist instrument into a mass-produced household object. In the 1660s and '70s barometers had been 'confined to the cabinets of the virtuosi', yet by 1680 they had hit the shops, and by 1708 it was claimed that few gentlemen were 'without one of them'. By 1735 they were said to be in common use 'in most houses of figure and distinction'. In London and the provinces, clockmakers, cabinetmakers, opticians and mathematical instrument makers all seized on the manufacture of barometers.[16] Nevertheless, as Jan Golinski explains, even the take-up of barometers is not straightforward evidence of a monolithic, proto-scientific, masculine, consumer desire: 'On the one hand the devices were tokens of virtuosity and philosophical prowess, or refinement and politeness; on the other hand they continued to be associated with gullibility, vulgar superstition and a feminine susceptibility to the lure of fashion.'[17] A means (however temperamental) to predict the weather, and a crafted object, barometers were at once a device and a decoration, representing the fusion of applied science and applied art, bringing an air of philosophy to the inquisitive and their parlours. The barometer was a conversation piece in an era that prized enlightened conversations, but it was also a luxury purchase like any other cabinet, a fitting 'Piece of Ornamental Furniture for a Gentleman's Parlour or Study'. The finest were crafted by leading furniture makers in tropical woods, elaborately carved with scrollwork and floral motifs, and placed in the dining room where they married with the mahogany.[18]

The most domesticated scientific object in Georgian homes was the clock. Inventory studies have charted a startling expansion in the ownership of clocks. Only 9 per cent of households had clocks in 1675, while 34 per cent had one by 1725. The proportion of rich London households listing clocks rose from 56 per cent to 88 per cent in the same years. Ownership varied regionally (especially high in Kent, Lancashire and London), but clocks were not markedly rarer in rural than urban areas, bought as readily by conservative yeomen as by pushing tradesmen.[19] Clocks, however, emerged as the only household goods owned in higher proportion by men than by single women and widows (who had more looking-glasses, table linen, silver, pictures and prints).[20] Research tracking particular households revealed the frequent disappearance of clocks and watches after the death of the husband, but before the death of the widow – hence the suspicion that 'there was something unfeminine in having, or even wanting to have, an accurate knowledge of the time'.[21] Wealth must be at issue here. Long before the rise of the lady's wristwatch, the pocket watch fitted as easily in a woman's capacious pocket as in a man's breeches. Where there was a single watch to a family and a choice was to be made, it might be set aside for a son or a nephew, yet there is no evidence that time keeping was surplus to female requirements. Personal inventories and account-books in noble, gentry, professional and mercantile families blandly record female possession of pocket watches.[22] When a Dorset boy was left 'a very handsome gold watch' in an uncle's will in 1753, it never occurred to his clergyman father to keep female hands off it: 'My poor brother has given our Andrew a present wch you or I must wear till he comes of age and knows what time is and how to spend it', he wrote to his wife. 'I do not know yet . . . whether our kitty shall wear that wch is yours and you take this.'[23] Women were not allergic to time keeping, even while other technologies left them cold. In May 1766 the Countess Shelburne visited a Birmingham watch warehouse, then went on 'to see the making of Guns but neither Lady Louisa or I being much interested about that we left'.[24] The only timepiece in the middling and yeoman house in remote Westmorland was often based in the kitchen. Most recipe books assumed access to a clock and an ability to read it at a glance by 1730.[25] A taboo around female time keeping is implausible.

Nevertheless, the pocket watch was an important accoutrement of independent manhood. Out of 197 people who pawned watches with a York pawnbroker, George Fettes, in 1777 and 1778 there were just eleven women, despite the fact that women pledged more than three-quarters of all the goods he received. The low rate of female ownership was probably a function of cost, and the likelihood that in plebeian marriages they were treated as belonging to the husband. Yet a watch was not indispensable for the work of most workers, with the exception of men who worked on road transport or for the Post Office calibrated to London time. There were some professionals who had real need of a timepiece, like the thrifty Lincolnshire surgeon Matthew Flinders, who finally succumbed to a purchase in 1780 after many years without, for a watch would be 'very convenient especially when I am out at Labours where they have no clock'. Yet few were the men who had such exact requirements. A watch was above all a prestigious piece of male jewellery, often adorned with extra decorative seals. Adult success, enviable affluence and a command of technology were all embodied in a silver watch.[26] Time keeping could claim a link to astronomy and navigation, however landlocked the watch owner.

Scientific instruments charmed Georgian men up and down the hierarchy, underpinned by a hearty maritime subculture befitting the nation that ruled the waves. Models of naval officers using quadrants outside scientific instrument sellers alerted passers-by to the patriotic utility, heroic engineering and unmistakable masculinity of the treasures within.[27] Possession of these instruments reflected a man's fantasy of himself, perhaps; a creature of questing intelligence or buccaneering freedom. To say that a commodity had a manly glamour is not to claim that all men were fascinated. Matthew Boulton thought his masterpiece 'Sidereal' and 'Geographical' clocks failed to find a market in 1773 because England's 'gambling nobility' were insufficiently interested in 'philosophy', which he found 'at a very low ebb in London'. Men were hardly uniform in their tastes, though in spurning a 'scientifical' machine for horseflesh, the milordi were still choosing between two unashamedly masculine consumables.[28] A special interest in technological innovation is absent in the women's account-books studied here, though manifest in those of newly rich men like Abraham Grimes of Warwickshire in the 1780s, who snapped up gadgets still unproved, like a regulator stove, Bramah water closet and Argand lamps, and John Forth, clergyman and agent of Castle Howard, who boasted a 'Patent shower bath in the closet from London' and a 'patent water closet' in the hall of his Yorkshire house in 1800. Even the paranoid Oxfordshire gentleman Robert Dormer 'will talk over a new invention for a tinder box or some such thing from Monday till Satterday'.[29]

Nevertheless, the barometer and the watch caution against any tendency to view men's interest as utilitarian in any simple sense. Georgian watches still lost up to thirty minutes a day; they required much tinkering and were forever going back to the shop to be serviced. 'A watch is always too fast or too slow,' laughed Austen's Miss Crawford, 'I cannot be dictated to by a watch.'[30] Barometers were literally mercurial and of limited predictive power by themselves. Parson Woodforde's barometer seemed to tell him nothing he did not already know about conditions.[31] Experts recommended a whole performance of taking readings, keeping histories and cross-referring to other meteorological data to interpret the meaning of the mercury, procedures that made a nonsense of the early idea that by glancing at the barometer on the way out one would know what to wear for the day. One can only imagine what the daughters of the house were told when they asked their father whether it would be bonnet weather. A glance out of the front door would be more to the purpose than all the paternal logbooks and tapping of the mercury. The satisfactions for owners in projecting a mastery of the science of technology had to outweigh any irritation with the functional shortcomings of the new devices themselves (pl. 33). Truth to tell, the business they entailed was probably the secret of their appeal. As any one who has kept a vintage car on the road would attest, to complain about the inadequacies of the gears is to miss the point, for it is in coaxing a temperamental engine that most of the fulfilment lies. Which all goes to argue that men's treasured objects were no more inherently 'useful' and less 'showy' than were women's. More flatteringly put, the fact that instruments needed endless checking and comparing for them to be of any practical use made them a quintessential expression of Enlightenment science in action.[32]

Necessaries have rarely excited historians in the manner of china, chintz and exotic groceries, despite the fact that the kitchen was at the forefront of technological innovation in Georgian England, the room that of all the house experienced the most change. The advent of the coal-fuelled chimneyed cooking hearth was a hugely significant development in the early modern period. A fireplace in the middle of the room with a roof vent for the smoke to escape was mildly toxic and dangerous – the mark of the hovel by 1750. The nature of the heat source dictated the equipment and the cuisine. Cooking could be done only in vessels standing or hanging in the fire. Round-bottomed cauldrons had been known since the Bronze Age, while tripods and long-legged cauldrons that stood in the ashes are at least medieval in origin, but wrought-iron chains hanging from the rafters were too expensive for most until the boom in iron production in the late eighteenth century. The dominance of puddings in British cuisine is a reflection of the convenience of boiling several dishes at once in a big cauldron on a hearth.

The introduction of a side hearth with chimney transformed safety and atmosphere at home, and allowed a sophistication of cooking techniques, with built-in ovens, side hobs, cranes and mechanical spits. The spread of ovens – the heart of that other monument of British cooking – the pie. Even the humble pie, virtually unknown in Gloucestershire, for instance, in the 1670s but universal by the 1730s) allowed further subtleties like cooking at a slower rate, or keeping food warm, and encouraged the development of the pie. The proliferation of iron cooking pots, kettles and frying pans was facilitated by Abraham Darby's coke-fired blast furnaces (1708) and in-line production (1707). Along with water-powered brass battery, these industrial innovations underpinned the production of cheaper, less toxic, lighter and more versatile cooking vessels.[33] Concurrently, ownership of cauldrons dropped away, though the saucepans that allowed more sophisticated cooking still appeared in only a third of Kent inventories by the 1730s, and a meagre 5 per cent of Cornish.[34] Yet the pan was the leading edge of change. Already in 1686 a Madam Wetnall was able to buy a saucepan, two chafing dishes, a pair of brass tongs, a brass pot, an iron dripping pan, a box iron and a fish plate from a London ironmonger, as well as having a candlestick mended, a saucepan tinned and various irons provided and varnished. By the 1750s pans outnumbered pots by two to one in the repertoire of furnishings from humble London lodgings.[35]

A repercussion of the introduction of chimney, side hearth and stove was the emergence of a separate kitchen (fig. 49). Probate inventories suggest that separate kitchens became increasingly common in middling houses from the 1600s, although their spread was gradual and geographically uneven. In precocious Kent, 40 per cent of such houses recorded kitchens by the 1730s, but in parts of Yorkshire kitchens appear to have become widespread below the level of the gentry only in the later decades of the century.[36] For Nancy Cox, the isolation of cooking, and the rise of the female-dominated kitchen, encouraged the inferiority of homely cookery.[37] The fact, however, that family cooking was performed by women seems enough to limit its prestige. One could argue that specialisation ensured that at least one room in the house was unequivocally a female domain.

Plate I.   Frontispiece to the Compleat English Cook.

Behold, ye Fair, united in this Book
The frugal Housewife, and experienc'd Cook.

49   Kitchen scene, frontispiece to Martha Bradley, *The British Housewife; or, The Cook, Housekeeper's, and Gardiner's Companion* (London, ?1760). A mistress is depicted in command of her servants and her kitchen, where plates and equipment are stored in good order on the walls. A pot and a pan heat on the fire, while a pig roasts on a spit. The caption reads: 'Behold, ye Fair, united in this Book. The frugal Housewife, and experienc'd Cook.'

After all, the fact that studies and chapels are isolated from the clamour of domestic life has only enhanced the status of the practices performed therein. More persuasive is Sarah Pennell's characterisation of the kitchen as the site of female expertise.[38] The diversification of equipment armed and reinforced a female territory indoors, but also demanded more work at home – one all-in cauldron required infinitely less tending than an arsenal of saucepans and frying pans.[39] Richer male householders could take quite an interest in the stove and major kitchen fittings, but the movables fell to women to acquire and maintain.[40]

Despite their utilitarianism, necessaries were still subject to fashion (fig. 50). The English metal trades were supremely inventive in adapting new materials, product innovation, design and decoration, so even pots were apt to date. 'I hope you was not displeased at your copper pot', sea captain's wife Tidy Russel wrote her rector brother in Bedfordshire in 1759, 'for a brass one is now quite out of date. They make none for nobody asks for them.' Advertising and invention had reached such a pitch that 'every utensil almost has now pretensions, very frequently ill founded, to taste', laughed Frederick Robinson in 1778. Necessary was itself a relative term. What Lord Cholmondeley required in 'pewter and necessarys for the look of his consequence' in Nantwich lodgings in 1679 would look like treasure to a yeoman.[41] Nonetheless, necessaries tended to escape the censure that was heaped on exotic luxuries. A *batterie de cuisine* was a mark of decency and efficient housekeeping that resonated to the credit of husband as well as wife. A rank of well-tinned copper pans testified to a housewife's domestic economy in a way a shelf of porcelain figurines never could.

A sensible husband gave his wife carte blanche with the pots and pans, for there was no making bricks without straw. The humorous *Ladies Dictionary* of 1694 assumed that a bachelor with 'insight into the world' would 'know that the best House-wife in nature can never be able to shew her Art, her Education, and her Housewifery upon Bare Walls'. In fact, it was in a husband's self-interest to keep a wife in equipment to ensure that she was 'always industriously employed at home'. It was humiliating for a wife to be so badly equipped that she was always scrounging. '*They that go a borrowing, go a sorrowing says the proverb.*' 'That woman is in an ill Condition that must be forced to send to her neighbours for every Skillet, or Stew pan, or washing Tub she wants.' Ill-equipped, beholden to neighbours, viewed with ill will, her credit will be thrown away, unlike the proud and self-sufficient housewife 'who has all things necessary about her'. All of which was prologue to the proposal that no man should baulk at the cost of a pan. Even if a wife had her eye on utensils 'a little more gay and sumptuous than ordinary', a good husband should support her quest for quality equipment, and embrace her desire to display her status and ingenuity as a housewife, for her reputation would ring across the parish. 'The brightness of the Bosses of her Fire-Irons and the glaring Lustre of her Pewter and Preserving pan, are the Discourse of all her Acquaintance.'[42] While there was a certain sly mockery in the exaggeration, a cool-headed male reader might still infer that lustrous pans that promised a well-ordered larder were infinitely preferable to lustrous low-cut dresses.

Personal advice echoed humorous commentary. When a young courtier, Margaret Blage, married in 1675, she turned to Mary Evelyn, the wife of her spiritual mentor John, for advice 'concerning housekeeping'. The matron's letter of 'Instructions' was seven pages long and systematic. She recommended £197, £40 and £30 be laid out on plate, linen and bedding respectively, but utensils would be much less costly. She categorised by material, suggesting £15 18 s. on pewter, £7 0s. 6d. on copper and brass, £6 15s. on iron, £3 16s. on wood, £2 11s. on glass

50   Trade card of Elwell & Taylor, smiths, ironmongers and braziers, at the Lock and Hinge, in the Haymarket, London, 1750–1800, printed engraving. British Museum, London, Heal 85.99. Hung around the fashionable Rococo cartouche are various items of kitchenware, including both a pot and pans.

and earthenware, and 8s. 6d. on tin. Plate, Evelyn assumed, the couple would 'be always augmenting', so advised selecting 'rather plain then wrought; there being so much lost in change of ye other when ye fashion alters'. Stinting on the tools of the trade would be a false economy: 'ye Total is not considerable if the Particulars be good & substantial, for you will save nothing by slight things'. Mrs Evelyn aimed at a basic armoury, for 'it is almost impossible to tell what may at one time or other bee wanting till you have occasion and so things will multiply and in a little time you will have all complete for your Family and Designs'. She conjured an era of proliferating and untried kitchen tools: 'Curiositys are infinite . . . what is more than useful is Burden & Lumber not Household-stuff.' Even so, the burden of her commentary was the importance of a full battery of specialist equipment to a well-functioning and honourable house. In fact, the document can be read as a curriculum vitae of Evelyn's own skills. She oversaw the buttery, kitchen, pastry, larder, stillroom, dairy, brew-house and laundry, and the produce of the kitchen garden, orchard, beehive, hog sties, dairy and hen house.[43] The proper tools of the trade ensured the competence and confirmed the dignity of the compleat housewife. If a wife was to be another Martha, then she needs must take gleaming copper as her badge of honour.

Chefs were not shy about demanding the new equipment to work their magic: 'a surgeon may as well attempt to make an incision with a pair of sheers, or open a vein with an oyster-knife as for me to pretend to get this dinner without proper tools to do it', complained a commercial cook in 1759, drafted into an unfamiliar kitchen to cater for a party: 'here's neither stew-pan, soup-pot, or any one thing that is useful; there's what they call a frying-pan indeed, but black as my hat, and a handle long enough to obstruct half the passage of the kitchen.' In asserting the importance of instruments to expertise, the male chef aligns himself with a technical profession. Tools were the mechanism and the manifestation of specialist knowledge in all its science and mystery.[44]

Pots and pans were a common female accoutrement in woodcuts. Banged in outraged moral economy at food riots and community-shaming rituals, frying pans and kettles connoted the matron's virtue, though they were also occasionally the woman's weapon, especially in assaults on her domestic turf. Kitchen goods were often incorporated into female paraphernalia, that small constellation of items usually worn on or associated with a woman's body that she could claim as her own personal possessions, despite her lack of property rights in common law. Moreover, utensils were common female bequests to other women.[45] Pots and pans were the orb and sceptre of the housewife, symbolising female domestic responsibility, the office that authorised their public pronouncements, and the bank from which they drew their moral credit.

The cheapness and disposability of objects today, the quantities of our clutter and the cult of purging ourselves of it, make it easy to forget just how long the life of a household object could be, and the extent to which Georgian artefacts were serviced, repaired and carefully husbanded. The accounts of Kent gentlewoman Anne Brockman log the calendar of servicing. In a single year, in 1702, Anne Brockman paid for the mending of pewter, a chafing dish, a wooden dish, a tray, two candlesticks, an iron, the scales and bought a new key to the larder, and had the clock at the buttery door cleaned, and a crystal replaced in her watch. Over the rest of the decade, she had five saucepans tinned, a new leg on her iron pot and skillet, had the jack, brass kettles, a brass pan and a silver snuff pan mended, and sent clocks, spectacles and watch regularly back to the shop. Repairs sit beside purchases in female account-books across the century.[46] Gentlemen's own metal accoutrements (watches, guns, swords and horse millinery) all needed relentless upkeep too. Perhaps men enjoyed the workshop commerce that proper maintenance of tackle entailed. The local saddler was a magnet to John Arderne of Harden. One of the annual bills presented to Arderne in 1739 was from a brazier-cum-ironmonger, recording thirty-two separate transactions, an array of little jobs – tinning the hash pan, mending the saucepan, soldering the coffee pot cover, putting a new handle to the teapot, cleaning the smoke jack and smoothing iron, fixing locks and grinding all manner of scissors, scythes and knives.[47] Although putting a husband's name to the bill may have been a simple convention, many other local bills are unproblematically made out to Mrs Arderne. The bill suggests that keeping up some metalwares was one mundane task a husband could oversee without dishonour. Equally the tinsmith who went door to kitchen door was usually male; indeed a rogue of cheeky, even goaty virility, if tinkers' songs are any guide. 'Go tell the lady of the place I've come to clout her cauldron' as one likely lad offered, while another advertised: 'Work for the tinker, ho! good wives[.] They are lads of mettle. Twere well if you could mend your lives As I can mend a kettle.'[48]

The air of technical knowledge that attached to tools was robust enough to withstand the womanishness of housewifery. Nonetheless, the link between female virtue and well-kept equipment was strongly soldered. The wholesomeness of pots and pans rested on upkeep; copperware was deadly poisonous without it. Seasoned metalware was even likened to a spotless old lady: 'Age itself is not unamiable. While it is yet preserved clean and unsullied: like a piece of metal kept smooth and bright, we look on it with more pleasure than on a new vessel that is cankered with rust.'[49]

If pots and pans dignified female materialism, ornamental tea wares provoked hostility. The tea table has received disproportionate attention in the history of consumerism, though the focus has been narrow and often unquestioning. One influential story sees ornamental femininity staged and perpetuated through the ritual performance of tea drinking; hence the tea table was a disciplinary apparatus fashioning narcissistic behaviour.[50] The tea set has attracted psychoanalytical theorising; the pale delicacy and breast-like plumpness of the porcelain teacup have not gone unremarked. (Though cynics might ask – what are we to make of the spouts?) However, to present the equipment for hot drinks as principally a disciplinary apparatus governing women is to ignore the social reach, varied contexts and differing outcomes of the ceremony. The teapot was not the sole possession of idle, elite women bent on self-exhibition. The teapot on the mantelpiece appears in representations of poorer interiors from at least the 1730s, (see fig. 11), and tea wares have been excavated in the quarters of American slaves of the early 1800s. Servants' demands for a tea allowance were annoying employers in the 1760s. Tea was served on special occasions in a Yorkshire workhouse in the same decade. 'Tea-time' had entered common parlance by the 1780s, as shorthand for that otherwise cheerless interlude between late afternoon and early evening.[51] Tea was a universal habit by 1760.

Working people in possession of teapots can be glimpsed in criminal records in the provinces as well as London. In 1784 a Kendal weaver accused two men of stealing 'a green teapot' off the dresser, the property of his wife. Bachelors did not disdain tea equipment either. On his first day in Cambridge in 1774, future clergyman Sam Turner spent a term's spending money on 'Candlesticks, kettles, china, Tea chest, tea board with a long tail of et ceteras' for his Queens' College rooms, to the chagrin of his Lincolnshire family. A Monmouthshire wood collier who walked to Westmorland in 1790 carried on him 'three blue and white cups and saucers' and 'a brown teapot' when he was beset by robbers on the Kendal road.[52] Teapots were not necessarily fragile in make or exotic in material. Even in London, china was not universal. Of those teapots reported stolen to the Old Bailey in London in the 1750s, fourteen specified the material: three were silver, four pewter, six china and one earthenware. By the 1780s, of twenty-five stolen teapots, seven were silver, ten were china, seven were earthenware and one was tin, while pewter had disappeared. Thefts, however, must over-represent silverware, which was attractive because it was easy to melt down and sell on, and under-represent both china, which was hard to fence, and earthenware, which was hardly worth lifting. Even so, the Old Bailey cases confirm the decline of pewter and the rise of earthenware and expose the social range of ownership, from a nurse with a pewter pot, a wine merchant, shopkeepers and publicans with china teapots, to a portrait painter, musician, japanner, jeweller, gentlewoman and gentleman with costly silver teapots, to a shagreen case maker, shop-

keeper and a lord with earthenware.[53] The fashion for potter
genius with which Josiah Wedgwood conquered the middle m.
ple creamwares.

There is strong evidence that women at all social levels had a
ment in the paraphernalia for domestic ceremonies.[54] Ownershi
was often attributed to the woman of the house. In January 1755 a
was stolen from the Covent Garden dining room of John Filks, a wine   ....ant,
along with seven china teacups and saucers, a china basin and a china sugar dish
– all 'my china', his wife told the Old Bailey.[55] The set was just the thing for a polite tea party, wherein the hostess presided, pouring out a pretty cup of the fra-
grant tonic to each of her visitors, without needing to call on her servants.

The magic of the ritual lay in the fact that tea arrived semi-processed, having been fermented in China. Tea did not need intensive or messy preparation
in the kitchen, or complex cooking implements, but it still required a little drawing room business to bring to perfection. And of that business the hostess was
mistress. All that was required of her servants was to bring in a cistern, urn or
kettle of boiling water and leave (pl. 34). With her locking tea caddy, spirit lamp
and silver kettle, teapot and tea set, the hostess performed a small personal ceremony for each of her guests – actions that epitomised the giving that was at the
heart of hospitality. Tea provided a new opportunity for the mistress of the
house to oblige her visitors by serving them herself, at a time when, according
to Martha Bradley, the old English practice of the wife personally waiting on
guests at dinner was being superseded by the new French fashion of dinner
guests serving themselves.[56] The tea ceremony was endlessly repeatable and versatile. It could be performed as cheerfully in a weaver's kitchen with earthenware pot and a single silver teaspoon as in a noblewoman's dressing room with
elaborate equipage, or a spinster's chamber with a bargain set of creamware.

The tea ceremony was performed for most impromptu visitors to polite
households in the Georgian provinces, and as an accompaniment to business
with milliners and mantua makers, physicians and lawyers. Just as men bought
a round of ale in the tavern, so ladies poured tea in the parlour for social inferi-
ors to lubricate the process of giving orders. It was tea that women were most
likely to serve to parties of women. Moreover, gentlemen had extra-domestic
opportunities for drinking and socialising that were closed to their womenfolk.
Tea loomed larger in women's social lives.[57] If a woman wanted to participate in
the new commerce of female visiting, then a tea set was indispensable. Nor was
the equipment unattainable. Teapots were surprisingly cheap; a serviceable, attractive type could be had for just a shilling. There is hardly a woman's account-
book that is not studded with purchases of teapots.

…a was the catalyst of a momentous reconfiguration of domestic space. A lively trade in formal visits is apparent in London before the arrival of tea in the 1660s, but hot drinks gave focus to an encounter, stimulated the traffic and became synonymous with it. Visits of 'mere Ceremony and Civility' became a crucial expression of urban politeness, 'a Tribute by Custom authorised, by good Manners enjoined'.[58] The formalities involved were notorious. 'How solemn a business the Observance of Punctilios is among the Female Sex, their set visiting Days and all the Peculiarities which belong to them, may well testify', sneered the *Gentleman's Magazine* in 1736. Among 'persons of any fashion', a debt 'in the ceremonial leidger' could result in the issue of 'a Commission of ill Manners' against the negligent 'to the Loss of her Credit and Acquaintance'. Exaggeration is the soul of humour, but double-entry visiting accounts do occasionally appear in women's pocket-books. *The Ladies' Complete Visiting Guide* of 1800 contained a gazetteer 'of all the Fashionable streets at the West end of Town' with a blank register in columns for the methodical recording of visiting cards delivered and received street by street (figs 51 and 52).[59] Without booking a visit in advance by card, it was easy to miss the company, as Mrs Larpent reported in February 1798 in London: 'Drove out to shops and visits and found nobody', or even worse, 'Other visits not let in'.[60]

Men visited too, of course. Politics and business were often advanced in short formal calls or extended domestic receptions; however masculine traffic was dignified by the claim to officiousness and largely escaped satire. In middling and genteel circles, breakfast parties were statistically more likely to be manly affairs, preceding a sporting or business expedition. As a social event, supper was informal, spontaneous, socially diverse and overwhelmingly male. Dinners were exclusive and ceremonious, either mixed sex or mostly male, followed by an interlude of heavy drinking and toasting, from which the lady of the house may have withdrawn. Polite women abhorred extreme drunkenness and complained about tobacco smoke. The rise of tea was paralleled by the spread of fortified wines like Madeira and Port, which themselves inspired a proliferation of domestic paraphernalia from cut glass decanters and silver bottle labels to punch bowls and cellarets. Few women admitted in their diaries and letters to a taste for strong liquor, but it fuelled the homosocial entertainment offered by elite and middling men at home. The bill from the wine merchant certainly loomed large among the receipts handled by Sir John Hynde Cotton, Abraham Grimes and John Arderne. By comparison, tea was a very tame brew.[61]

The tea table was seen as the very headquarters of female opinion, a byword for feminine confederacy, gossip and slander. Early visual depictions present men as worryingly marginal, eavesdropping from the sidelines (fig. 53). Nevertheless,

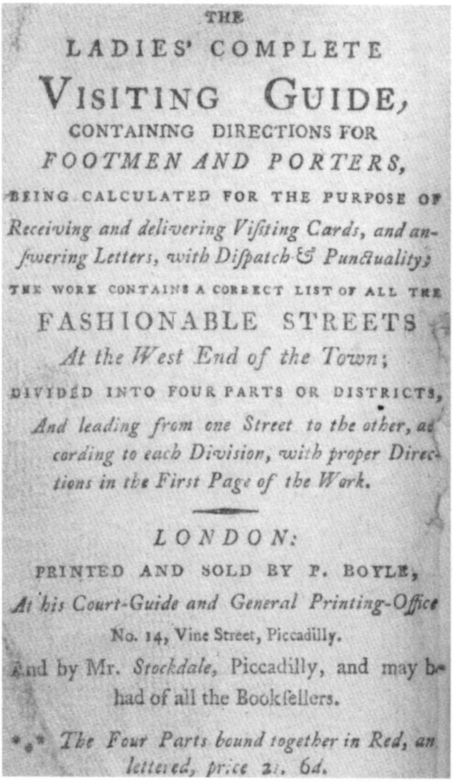
THE

LADIES' COMPLETE

VISITING GUIDE,

CONTAINING DIRECTIONS FOR

FOOTMEN AND PORTERS,

BEING CALCULATED FOR THE PURPOSE OF *Receiving and delivering Viſiting Cards, and anſwering Letters, with Diſpatch & Punctuality;*

THE WORK CONTAINS A CORRECT LIST OF ALL THE

FASHIONABLE STREETS

At the West End of the Town;

DIVIDED INTO FOUR PARTS OR DISTRICTS, *And leading from one Street to the other, according to each Division, with proper Directions in the First Page of the Work.*

LONDON:

PRINTED AND SOLD BY P. BOYLE,

At his Court-Guide and General Printing-Office

No. 14, Vine Street, Piccadilly.

And by Mr. *Stockdale*, Piccadilly, and may be had of all the Bookſellers.

, *The Four Parts bound together in Red, and lettered, price 2s. 6d.*

51 *The Ladies' Complete Visiting Guide* (London, *circa* 1800), title page.

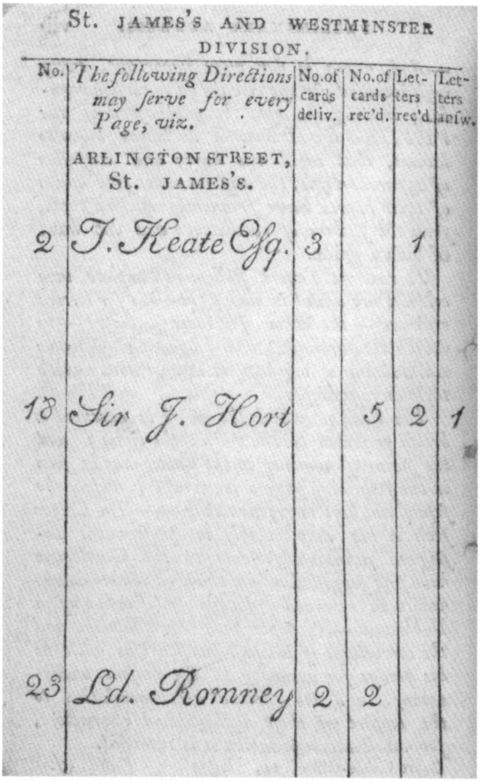
St. JAMES's AND WESTMINSTER DIVISION.

No.	*The following Directions may serve for every Page, viz.*	No. of cards deliv.	No. of cards rec'd.	Letters rec'd.	Letters answ.
	ARLINGTON STREET, St. JAMES's.				
2	T. Keate Esq.	3		1	
18	Sir J. Hort		5	2	1
23	Ld. Romney	2	2		

52 *The Ladies' Complete Visiting Guide* (London, *circa* 1800), a page demonstrating the guide's layout by area and street, with columns for house numbers, householders' names, visiting cards delivered, visiting cards received, letters received and letters answered.

the tea table was a hallmark of female gentility. Searching for a wedding present for his beautiful sister in Philadelphia in 1727, 21-year-old Benjamin Franklin first plumped for a tea table, but on further thought decided a spinning wheel more fitting. The gracious serving of tea may have been appropriate for a 'pretty gentlewoman', but he preferred to support the 'the character of a good housewife'.[62] Many ambitious men, however, saw a well-mannered hostess as an asset; indeed, it was hard to make a convincing social ascent without one. Married men of middling and genteel rank were expected to entertain at home. When John Marsh wed and established himself as a solicitor and amateur composer in Romsey in Hampshire 1774, he spent £250 furnishing the house. Taking posses-

53   *The Tea-Table* (detail), printed engraving, *circa* 1710. Lewis Walpole Library, Farmington, CT, 766.0.37. Five women are shown taking tea around a table in a room with a mirror on the wall and a display of ceramics in an alcove, spied on by two men outside at the open window. The accompanying text and the allegorical figures standing to the left assert that the tea table is a scene of slanderous female gossip.

sion of a town house in Chichester in 1787, a new drawing-room carpet, curtains and chairs for the music room and front parlour allowed the Marshes to 'begin seeing company'.[63] All-female households were also inclined to dress the stage on which the bulk of their social performance rested. Lady Denton would not receive visitors in town in 1706, because she felt the small rooms of her London town house did not mirror her rank.[64] It was the amplification of social life at home that makes sense of a constellation of objects desired by women.

The porcelain ornament has provoked less scholarly excitement than the tea set, though it was no less strongly welded to women in the Georgian imagination. Imported Chinese porcelain was an exquisite prize at European courts in the 1500s, but the expansion of English and Dutch overseas trading companies brought it to the West in commercial quantities only in the 1600s. European production began at Meissen in Saxony, and in France in Saint-Cloud, Vincennes and Mennecy, and later Sèvres, though the secrets of porcelain manufacture eluded the English until the late 1740s, when Chelsea (1747), Bristol (1749), Worcester (1751) and Liverpool (1752) began manufacturing translucent soft-paste wares.[65]

Mary, Princess of Orange commissioned china closets designed by Daniel Marot to show her massed porcelain, and decked out Kensington Palace in a similar style after the Glorious Revolution. Hence she is credited with the British vogue for decorating with porcelain. Orphans' court inventories for London, however, reveal that the wives of the mercantile elite were very early adopters of exotica. Their bedrooms and dressing rooms were often repositories of oriental treasures. In 1666 Lady Noell, had many 'china wares' in her 'study or clossett' in London. Married to a leading member of both the Levant and the East India Companies, her information, access and funds were hard to match. The persistence of female interest surfaces in diaries and letters across the next century. When the Oxfordshire gentlewoman Mrs Lybbe Powys made a special trip to view 'four little rooms fill'd with all sorts of old china fix'd to the walls by three screws' at Blenheim in 1799, her familiarity was revealing of a shared culture of feminine collecting: 'The whole has a pretty effect, but to others might be more amusing than to Lady Hardy and myself, as each of us has most of the same sort.'[66]

Female fondness for porcelain was a theme of Restoration and Augustan literature, from the debauched ornaments in William Wycherley's plays to the clutter on Belinda's dressing table in Pope's *Rape of the Lock*. Critics have noted a similarity between fine ladies and fine porcelain, both prized for smoothness and lustre, but equally fragile and 'despised for the appearance of a crack or flaw'.[67] But porcelain was never the sole possession of women. In fact, men outnumbered women as successful bidders at Chelsea and Derby porcelain sales (sixty-three men to forty-one women). Known customers include virile soldiers like General Conway, hero of three wars, and the Duke of Cumberland, butcher of Culloden, the very last men who one might expect to collect vases (fig. 54). Nevertheless, gentlemen who admitted to a weakness for china regarded it as a slightly female, perhaps even deliciously feminine preoccupation. Horace Walpole liked Chelsea ware himself, but thought the vogue for china figurines was driven by a generic female taste: 'Women of the first quality came home from Chevenix's [a famous trinket shop] laden with dolls and babies, not for their children, but for their housekeeper.' Jonathan Swift sauntered round china shops,

54   *A View of the Mandarine Yacht and Belvedere Belonging to His Royal Highness the Duke of Cumberland at Windsor*, 1753, printed engraving. Royal Collection 700787. 'Butcher' Cumberland had led the British army in its crushing defeat of the Jacobite forces at the battle of Culloden in Scotland in 1746. Even virile soldiers had a weakness for Chinoiserie.

and claimed to 'love it mightily', but he told two female correspondents that when he was at the bookseller 'my finger's itched as yours would do at a china shop'. By 1823 Charles Lamb confessed: 'I have an almost feminine partiality for old china. When I got to see any great house, I inquire for the china closet.'[68] Hence, while a commodity could be typed feminine, it might yet be enjoyed by men, though masculine consumption did not necessarily neuter the metaphorical femininity of the thing consumed. Indeed, a notional femininity may have been one secret of their delight.

The contrast between the patterns of male and female purchasing of china reflects the sexual division of consumption elsewhere. Amongst northern gentry and merchants, while a wife's shopping was predominantly repetitive and mundane, a husband's acquisition was characteristically occasional and impulsive, or expensive and dynastic. Likewise Wedgwood famously lured 'Lords and Dukes' to buy his expensive vases in the antique manner, while ladies came 'in very large shoals together' to purchase useful wares at cash prices. Judith Anderson's analysis of the London day-books of the Derby porcelain business 1786–96 'confirms that the two sexes were buying porcelain related to their respective public roles: women as hostesses, mothers and housekeepers, men as purchasers of status items, gifts, or presents on impulse'. There was a dynamic growth in the number of female retailers buying wholesale Derby, while female customers made up 45 per cent of the private trade by 1789, though they were buying tea sets for around £7 and single replacements for breakages, not prestigious dinner services or vases. Matrimonial compromise is occasionally revealed, as in 1789, when Mr Job Mathews approved the crest on his Derby porcelain, but brought his wife in to decide the shapes.[69]

Furniture design manuals were a key new source of an explicitly gendered language around objects. Thomas Chippendale was the first to publish a catalogue of designs for furniture in 1754, quickly followed by other London cabinetmakers. An attractive catalogue offered range and choice, which inevitably required a taxonomy. The dominant categories were functional and stylistic, but 'lady's' and 'gentleman's' were innovative classifications.[70] The second edition of *Genteel Household Furniture in the Present Taste*, produced by a society of Upholsterers and Cabinet Makers in 1760, included a chinoiserie 'Lady's Desk', 'Ladies' Dressing Stools' and a Rococo 'Lady's Bookcase'.[71] The first edition of Chippendale's genre-forming *Director* in 1754 made no allusions to ladies' or gentlemen's furniture, but by 1762 the third edition advertised a 'Lady's Writing Table and Book Case', and dressing and toilet tables 'for a Lady' (fig. 55). In the same year, the London furniture makers Ince and Mayhew specified pieces for both men and women in their *Universal System of Household Furniture*. 'The Lady's Secretary' had a counterpart in the 'Gentleman's Repository', while the 'Ladies Toiletta' had a 'Gentleman's Dressing Table' for its mate (figs 56 and 57).[72] By 1778 the *Cabinet-Maker's London Book of Prices*, aimed at the trade and flaunting its comprehensiveness, priced an array of specialist furniture for him and for her, from desks and cabinets to dressing chests, firescreens, travelling boxes, dressing stands and tables for tasks. Thomas Sheraton followed the trend in his pattern book of 1793, elaborating upon it in his *Cabinet Dictionary* of 1803, where he imagined the lady's cabinet would be 'used to preserve their trinkets and other curious matters', while 'the cabinets of gentlemen consist in ancient medals, manuscripts and drawing & c.'.[73] Paradoxically, only George Hepplewhite's *Cabinet-Maker and Upholsterer's Guide* published by his widow Alice appears to have bucked the trend and ignored gender as a marketing tool.

The impact of the blossoming of a language of his and hers on the objects themselves, however, should not be over-estimated. Furniture curators often

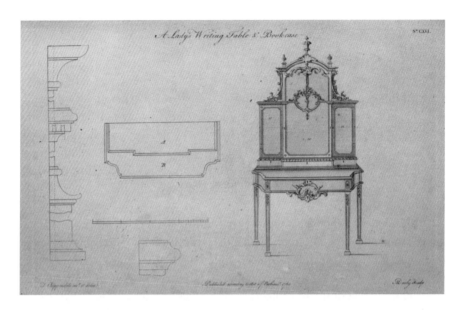

55 'A Lady's Writing Table and Bookcase', Plate 116 in Thomas Chippendale, *The Gentleman and Cabinet Maker's Director* (3rd edn, London, 1762).

see scant difference in the construction, complexity, materials, finish, decorative motifs or style in the pieces aimed at women and men. There is certainly no evidence that Rococo satinwood was aimed at the girls and Neoclassical mahogany at the boys. Only in scale do they differ, men's furniture tending to the massive and imposing, ladies' furniture being typically more petite and compact, which gives the appearance of greater detail.[74] Nevertheless, they made different claims. By 1803 Sheraton's secretaries for ladies were desks 'of a small size, usually with a book shelf in the top part', while the gentleman's secretary was 'intended for standing to write at', and was a substantial piece 'with a cupboard for a pot and slippers' and 'a place for day book, ledger, and journal, for a gentleman's own accounts' (fig. 58).[75] Hence, the furniture presumes that women's writing was a delicate drawing-room performance, while men's business was altogether more official and substantial. Nonetheless, gender was only one classification among several – alongside functional categories and niche specialisms for invalids, nursing mothers, children, the elderly and the itinerant. How far these categories shaped consumers' use of these pieces has not been a subject pursued by furniture historians.

My analysis of unstudied upholders' account-books tests the pervasiveness and appeal of a gendered language of furniture. Probably the earliest known

56 'A Lady's Toiletta', Plate 37 in William Ince and John Mayhew, *The Universal System of Household Furniture* (London, 1762). The corresponding text reads: 'A Ladies Toilet, with Drawers under the Glass; intended either for Japan or burnish'd Gold'.

57 'Bureau Dressing Table', Plate 40 in William Ince and John Mayhew, *The Universal System of Household Furniture* (London, 1762). The corresponding text reads: 'A Gentleman's Dressing Table; the Top is fixt by a Quadrant; the Glass in a Frame; on the Plan is described the Bason, Bottles, Razors, Boxes, etc. at the Ends are Cupboards.'

58 'A Lady's Writing Table. Gentleman's Secretary', Plate 71 in Thomas Sheraton, *The Cabinet Dictionary* (London, 1803).

British upholder's accounts are those of Jonathan Hall of London, whose records cover the years 1701–35.[76] They make no reference whatsoever to furniture entitled a lady's this, or a gentleman's whatnot, but fifty years later those of James Brown in London in the 1780s are warming to the new gimmick. Operating in the heart of London's furniture district, at 29 St Paul's Churchyard, the company served a largely metropolitan, professional and middling clientele, with a sprinkling of provincial gentry, rich merchants and the occasional lesser nobleman. Like other cabinetmakers, Brown offered an extensive service from undertaking, second-hand sales and furniture hire, to repairs and dry-cleaning, wallpaper hanging and pest control – fumigating bug-ridden beds was one of his sidelines. Brown supplied all manner of household textiles from window curtains and carpets to counterpanes, metal fittings like stoves and steel fire grates, an array of furniture in tropical woods, befitting both elite drawing rooms and servants' garrets, and a cornucopia of small domestic objects from tea caddies to cheese trolleys, and even the occasional umbrella. As in all ledgers, named female customers are in a minority. In the order book for 1785, Brown listed 233 customers; of these the sex is unclear for 33 clients designated only by surname, but of the remaining 200 orders only 30 are booked in a woman's name, so nominally women accounted only for barely 15 per cent of the trade. The remaining 168 customers were male (84 per cent), while two orders were made in both men's and women's names. The social status of the consumer is obscure in the majority of entries for 1785 (148/233, 64 per cent), but Brown could boast three lords, eighteen esquires and one sir in that year, with the largest single occupational group being the professions (seventeen lawyers, clerics, army and naval officers), supplemented by provincial merchants and metropolitan tradesmen, like a japanner and a cabinetmaker. Surveying the order books for 1782–91 reveals some flashy clients, such as David Parry, governor of Barbados, among the lawyers and soldiers, but also plenty of London traders – confectioners, china men, lead, coal, brandy and wine merchants, and the proprietors of a girls' boarding school. It was quite possible for men and women to buy furniture linked to their interests, tasks and occupations without recourse to an explicit language of 'lady's' and 'gentleman's'.[77]

The workbox, for instance, was a vintage female object. Needlework, known simply as 'work', was the Ur domestic craft for women, enjoined by God. A sewing box was so archetypally feminine that further specification was redundant. Simple workboxes could be produced in inexpensive woods like pine, but also in fashionable mahogany, rosewood, satinwood and even sandalwood, the choicest examples veneered with ivory, or tortoiseshell, inlaid with marquetry, lacquered or covered in morocco or Russian leather. Stuart workboxes were often decorated with a lady's own stump work (pl. 35). Georgian versions referenced the exotic in their materials and motifs, but boxes in the shape of rustic cottages were also popular, a form that reinforced the domesticity, innocence and old-fashioned virtue of sewing (pl. 36). The ladies' workbox could be said to rival the teapot in its blend of utility, polite display and pleasure to handle; and it was even more inextricably feminine as an object. Like the teapot, a workbox could be had for a shilling or two. So hackneyed were their feminine associations that Jane Austen's Fanny Price had a surfeit in 1814: 'The table between the windows was covered with work-boxes and netting-boxes which had been given her at different times. Principally by Tom.' Fanny took comfort in her old treasures, and loved them as proof of 'kind remembrances', but to the reader they convey a bored lack of interest on the part of the giver.[78] The sympathy of the cousin may be in question, but the irreproachable virtue and unproblematic domesticity of the workbox is not.

There was no law that prevented a widow from buying a camp bed, or a bachelor a sewing box (pl. 37). Nevertheless, there were some customary differences in the patterns of male and female consumption, in so far as names in an order book are a guide. Most of Brown's female customers appeared to be married or widowed. (All but four of the thirty female clients in 1785 claimed the title Mrs.) Occasional women had the wherewithal for large orders, like a Mrs Taylor in 1782 who bought six mahogany chairs, four rout chairs, four carpets, two Pembroke tables, with other accoutrements for handsome dining, but most women tended to commission a single piece like a dressing chest, or items of domestic paraphernalia – tea trays, caddies, tea boards, tea urns, flower-pot stands, bottle stands, bread baskets. Inevitably, men were associated with more of the whole-house commissions, and with larger orders for sets of chairs, beds and sofas, but they too can be seen ordering individual pieces that speak to personal need and entertainment – a backgammon table, a camp shaving stand, a bidet, a music stool. Equally, there were also numerous male orders that seem to imply the interests of a wife and daughters. It was common for gentlemen to commission the mounting of ladies' work – like Richard Charlton, Esq., who paid £6 16s. 6d. for '1 neat mah[ogan]y oval screen Green silk back [to mount] their embroidery front plate glass'.

James Brown had long recognised the perceived domestic functions of women and men, though furniture that met those needs could be categorised by task or use, say a nursing chair or a portable shaving stand, for which gender specification was redundant. By 1782 Brown was exploiting and meeting a taste for furniture tailored to the ladies. Other cabinetmakers offered 'ladies' furniture around the same time.[79] A Mrs Warner commissioned from Brown a 'Ladys dressing case' at a cost of £1 18s. 6d. in May 1782. The next year, he supplied four ladies' dressing cases, three to women and one to a Mr Bright at the Bates Hotel in the Adelphi. By 1787 Brown had widened his so-called ladies' goods to furnish a feminine apartment with designated pieces. A major Leeds woollen merchant, John Denison, Esq., ordered a 'satinwood lady's secretary and bookcase, a satinwood lady's dressing table to suit, a lady's spider table, two spider chamber tables, and a vase dressing glass, tulip band', coming to £29 14s. Some customers were clearly buying for a mixed household. In July 1788 a Mr Richard Parry of Mansell Street bought a shaving stand, two ladies' dressing tables and four netting boxes – evoking a wife and daughters. Some orders support the view that a ladies' object was just one carcass among many. In June 1789 a Mr Kent of Exeter bought 'A pair of handsome inlaid border'd card tables', 'a Pembrook table to match' and 'a very handsome lady's mahogany writing table with Moving top'.

Almost as soon as Brown devised ladies' objects, he began to sell furniture designed for gentlemen. The leading gentleman's object was the shaving and/or dressing table. In 1803 Sheraton suggested that the dressing table could swing either way – 'a table so constructed as to accommodate a gentleman or a lady with

59 'A Gentlemans
Shaving Table', Plate 69
in Thomas Sheraton,
The Cabinet Dictionary
(London, 1803).

convenience for dressing'. The shaving table was 'a piece of furniture fitted up for
a gentleman to dress at, in which there is a glass behind made to rise to any height
. . . They contain a basin to wash in, a cupboard below [fig. 59].'[80] Cleverly, Brown
modified his ladies' prototype in 1783 for a Lawrence Cutler of Love Lane – '1
ladys dressing case with some alterations for a gent 2-5-0'. In July 1783 a Lieutenant General Fawcett of Westminster bought '1 very neat gentlemans shaving
table' with a brace of integral accoutrements. Virtually interchangeable, gentlemen's dressing and shaving tables were commissioned at a rate of one or two a
year thereafter, sometimes alongside other pieces aimed at the man about town,
such as a mahogany drinks case or cellaret.

This sexed terminology was not all conquering. Even among the narrow range
of furniture susceptible to categorisation by sex, it was not necessarily the norm.
Brown supplied plenty of bog-standard desks, tables and chests of drawers. Con-

sumers liked to make multiple uses of things. 'A Mah[ogan]y Desk for Parlour for writings & to use For side board occasionally' was ordered by a china man in St Paul's Churchyard in 1790. Nor should we suppose that female consumers submitted themselves to the discipline of petite ladies' furniture. Requests for adaptations to designs were routine. After all, the *raison d'être* of 'bespoke' was the modification of the design to suit the individual customer.

A gendered language of furniture had begun to spread beyond catalogues to newspaper advertisements placed by upholsterers and furniture makers by the 1790s (Table 2).

Table 2. Gender of addressee in advertisements for goods, shops and entertainments in four editions of *The Times*, 1796.[81]

Type of advertiser	Number of advertisements	No addressee	Female addressee	Male addressee	Addressee not gendered
Entertainment	24	11	0	0	13
Retail	55	19	13	1*	22
All	79	30	13	1*	35
In the retail category above:					
Textiles/fashion	18	2	11	0	5
Furniture	9	5	1	0	3
Health	17	7	1	0	9

* This advertisement, which was addressed to 'Gentlemen', was for the Portugal wine company, which sold Port, Madeira, Sherry and other wines.

Advertisements addressed 'to the Ladies' or 'for the Attention of the Ladies', or including 'ladies' items, tended to be placed by linen drapers, mercers and other dealers in clothing or textiles (which might, of course, include furnishing textiles), while furniture sellers were more sparing in the language of his and hers. Non-gendered categories were more common, as was true in the furniture catalogues, especially the flattering 'to the Nobility and Gentry'. Direct appeal to women was heavily concentrated in the traditionally female domains of fabrics and fashions, while men were hardly identified as addressees at all. Nevertheless, this is a departure, since a gendered language of address is almost non-existent in early eighteenth-century ads.[82] *The Times* commanded a far wider readership than a cabinetmaker's catalogue, and documents the steadily extending reach of gendered advertising. Contemporary advertising is the most potent and exuberant source of ideas about masculinity and femininity in commodities today, the possibilities of which, for good or ill, were germinating in Georgian England. The mightiest rivers have their source in streams.

＊　＊　＊

Commercial expansion and manufacturing innovation hastened the proliferation of new objects, while producers and retailers were in the business of generating new meanings to provoke novel consumer wants. Ancient commodities like linen and cooking pots had an ancient association with the virtuous housewife, though the fertile diversification of linens (associated with new sources of supply and the elaboration of domestic ceremony) and the wonderful proliferation and specialisation of cookwares (caused by a revolution in metallurgy) expanded a traditional terrain. Meanwhile, exotic novelties like tobacco, tea, coffee and chocolate were characterised by the sex of the early adopters and stereotypical users. The femininity or masculinity of certain styles and objects was an evergreen theme of satire. Allusion to an object could be useful as a shorthand for effeminacy, or an easy reference of one of life's fundamental binaries – petticoat versus the breeches, the tea table versus the desk, millinery versus gunsmithery. Some associations, like the femininity, or effeminacy, of French or Chinese decoration had a fanciful life of their own, disconnected from men's and women's stylistic allegiances (see fig. 54). Others like the masculine excitement of scientific instruments were a by-product of a robust maritime culture and the construct of an emerging scientific profession, which defined any female contribution as exceptional and familial. Some associations were inscribed in marketing procedures. Manufacturers were alert to the sex of their best customers. A book of patterns for printed cottons, circulated by a north of England printworks about 1780, assumed a female clientele: 'when any Lady sends for a Sight of the Book, it is entreated she will give Orders that it be Returned immediately'.[83]

Projecting the idea of a distinctive female demand was a ground-breaking departure in the history of marketing. The pioneers were the booksellers and printers who addressed specialist titles to the ladies in the 1600s, while the post-1688 print boom saw the publication of custom-designed ladies' pocket diaries, a proliferation of female manuals of all kinds, the *Female Spectator* in the 1740s and the long-running *Lady's Magazine* from 1770. The leap to objects was made when leading furniture makers started classifying furniture by the sex, age and specialist needs of the implied user in the new printed illustrated catalogues of the 1760s. Of course, sex distinctions in clothes are as old as civilisation, while the idea of furniture suited to female needs is not unprecedented (think of birthing stools), but making difference systematic and concrete by means of word, image and object was a decisive innovation. The rapid diffusion of ladies' and gentlemen's furniture suggests that gender distinctions already resonated powerfully with male and female consumers, but in the extension of the range of differentiated furniture, the projection of the trope by manufacturers thereafter, and its acceptance by consumers, conventional ideas of masculine importance and feminine delicacy were amplified and fixed. In the process, femininity was expressed in a specific and narrowly defined aesthetic register.

Not that the sexes were entirely the tools of the market. It is possible that dainty desks disciplined the women who sat at them to dainty performances, yet ladies' and gentlemen's pieces were often identical in carcass. Old and unisex furniture predominated in most homes and, in any case, people have ever used furniture in ways unanticipated by advertisers or interior designers. Catherine Hutton, the Birmingham Unitarian, was given 'a handsome chest of drawers' by her historian father 'in compensation' for his refusal to send her to boarding school in the 1760s: 'one drawer, by my especial order, being fitted up as a writing desk. This chest *was my own* . . .'.[84] It does not follow that a spindly lady's desk and capacious gent's bureau had occult power to dictate the behaviour of their owners – it takes models, training, practice and compliance to handle props as fashion expected. Objects rely on situated knowledge to work their charms. (After all, as many surgeons found to women's cost, it took more than a pair of forceps and a textbook to deliver an obstructed baby.) Who's to say how many men dashed off letters at a lady's desk? Nevertheless, the diminutive had emerged as a design expression of femininity. His and hers furniture made gender material and visible.

Some clichés of satire were built on solid foundations. Millinery, linens, cottons, tea wares and porcelain figurines were all the focus of special female investment. Many commodities believed to have had a feminine quality, such as tea, china, novels, silks, printed cottons and haberdashery, were not necessarily the preserve of women, but their widespread use by men did not dislodge their feminine connotations. Indeed, a certain feminine allure may have added to their deliciousness for male consumers in private. Equally, commodities researched, selected, acquired and prized by the man of the house, redolent of knowledge and exciting horizons, ambition and dignity, still belonged to the female domain of housekeeping once the dust settled upon them. Even a room seen as proudly masculine in its decoration, say a library, study or dining room, whose mahogany was chosen by a patriarch, still fell to the distaff for polish and daily arrangement (fig. 60).

60   Detail of a bill advertising The Queen's Royal Furniture Gloss, *circa* 1798, printed engraving.
British Museum, London, Banks D2–1281. Two well-dressed women are depicted sitting in a
genteel, but not opulent interior. Their polite conversation turns on the merits of the furniture,
but quickly transmutes into an advertising pitch for furniture polish.

The strongest meanings attached to objects lay with the activities they referenced – diligent housekeeping, lightly worn scientific engagement, feminine sociability and so on. Any negative comment on men's spending on scientific
instruments was mild and affectionate; often, these objects were read in terms of
a laudable interest in natural philosophy or a hearty love of the high seas. Equally,
female pride in necessaries escaped censure too. Base metals did not scream luxury. The output of a Bristol brass furnace was not morally tainted like the har-
vest of a Spitalfields silk loom or a Chinese porcelain kiln. Custom saw the
kitchen as a female department, though diaries and accounts evidence a male
interest in new stoves and a preparedness to help out occasionally with the servicing of metal utensils. The teapot and the ornament were two modest objects
of female desire, yet were often supremely irritating to the conservative gaze.
Surviving account-books confirm that women spent on teapots and ornaments
on their own account, and continued to do so when free of men. Mrs Dodson's
porcelain ornaments of a nun and a friar bespeak the decorous pleasures of affluent widowhood and advanced old age. It is, however, important to remember
how inexpensive decorated earthenware teapots could be – as little as a shilling

– a mite when compared with the hundreds of pounds that could be spent cumulatively on alcohol, or in a single splurge on a horse, carriage, silver plate and dining table. The hysteria in print about a china craze is out of all proportion to the sums involved. Moreover, it was men who were more likely to buy expensive porcelain collectors' items, squandering fortunes, which passed almost unnoticed by caricature. The disproportionate scorn heaped on cheap teapots and sentimental knick-knackery must in the end derive from the new ritual they were seen to inspire and perpetuate, female visiting. 'You are not to suppose that all this profusion of ornament is only to gratify my wife's curiosity', complained an overwhelmed husband in *The World* in 1753, 'it is meant as a preparative to the greatest happiness of life that of seeing company.' Exciting possibilities for entertainment in the genteel and middling family home were hugely significant outcomes of the new world of Georgian goods. To an unprecedented degree, visiting routinely publicised the middling domestic interior, disturbing misanthropic husbands and trembling the balance of power at home. Abusive husbands often tried to stem the tide of female visitors across the threshold. The ritual drew women together, and to some eyes a combination of women will ever be a provocation, at best a waste of time and at worst a coven. The Georgians took for granted a sex in things, further elaborating a vocabulary of gender difference in consumer tastes, material customs and expertise, however much daily experience confused any fixed associations. For some, consumer differences were an attractive manifestation of the fundamental distinctions between women and men. For the old-fashioned, however, an observable link between women and exotica made the advent of the humble teapot evidence of the march of female independence and luxury, latent since Eve's desire for the apple triggered the Fall.

CONCLUSION

'**H**OME IS THE SACRED REFUGE OF OUR LIFE, Secur'd from all approaches but a wife', declaimed one of John Dryden's betrayed characters in 1676.[1] In England, as in other parts of north-western Europe, marriage meant the establishment of a separate household. Weddings ideally marked the transition from household dependent or lodger to independent residence in a house, a graduation that was decisive for the prestige of both women and men. 'Bachelors . . . and Maids when long single, are looked upon as houses long empty, which no-body cares to take', warned Richardson's ideal gentleman Sir Charles Grandison in 1754.[2] It was not necessary to own a house to gain the social status of 'housekeeping', which was seen as proof of adulthood and creditworthiness. Occupation, not ownership, qualified men for the franchise in scot and lot boroughs, while in potwalloper boroughs male lodgers could vote if they rented a separate threshold and hearth. A flourishing household marked life at high tide, just as declining back into boarding rooms signified the ebbing of vigour and importance. The patriarchal household family of master, mistress and children, with servants and perhaps apprentices, remained a universally recognised ideal type, but subaltern forms existed *faute de mieux* – the young lawyer in chambers, the widowed father and children forced on the sympathetic offices of a motherly landlady, a bevy of sisters in a rented house-cum-school, the ageing spinster in two genteel rooms.

Households were ideally patriarchal in structure though cooperative in daily practice, a legal scaffolding and modus operandi well established by 1600. This framework persisted at least until the Married Women's Property Acts of the 1880s, and was substantially undermined only by equal access to divorce, education, employment and banking in the twentieth century. The long drawn-out evacuation of various kinds of live-in service and, from the 1870s, diminishing family size, hollowed out the middle-class home from within. The household remained the pre-eminent machine for living across the eighteenth and nineteenth centuries, promising shelter and safety, meals and laundry. Alternatives existed for some young men and old bachelors (colleges, chambers, barracks and later clubs), but institutional options for women were non-existent before the expansion of women's residential education from the 1860s and the single-girl flats of the 1890s. Within these broad continuities, however, a series of social, economic and intellectual developments redefined some of the core meanings and functions of home for the comfortably off in the Georgian period, which tested the structural certainties of patriarchy. The everyday exposure of middling interiors through the increasingly formalised practice of visiting, the wide currency of the exciting new idea of taste, the affordability of ornamental furnishings and the commercial promotion of feminine artistry at home all publicised the domestic interior, encouraging the idea that even quite modest homes were stages for the display of discernment, manners and marriage. The versatile hostess appreciated in value accordingly.

Hospitality was not a Georgian invention – sociability in the strongholds of the rich must be as old as feasts – but the eighteenth century witnessed an extraordinary escalation of domestic sociability across the genteel and middling ranks with profound implications for architecture and space, manners and gender. The oldest form of socialising at home was encompassed by the medieval ideal of hospitality to strangers and the poor. Hospitality was a Christian obligation entailed on landed wealth, dispensed in the great hall, the most public room of the great house, laid out to symbolise 'the ideal of the integrated but structured community'.[3] A vanished golden age of good old hospitality was often invoked in print in the seventeenth century, but Tudor elites already preferred exclusive dinners to the strain of eating in front of the community, though the great hall remained a proof of lineage, a demonstration of the size of the entourage and a tool of grandeur. By the 1690s the cosmopolitan and courtly ideal of politeness was in the ideological ascendant: the elegant entertainment of a select group of social equals proving more congenial to many cosmopolitan families than traditional largesse and vertical sociability.[4] However, in the provinces, the Georgian gentry staged both old and new forms of hospitality on different occasions and in different rooms of their manors.

As great hall traffic declined, new social demands were most fashionably met in a multiplication of withdrawing rooms (for intimate encounters) and large reception rooms like saloons (for polite parties) and new structural arrangements, such as the circuit of formal rooms around a staircase introduced from the 1720s (for evening assemblies of music, tea, cards and dancing). But internal space was remapped lower down the social hierarchy too. The homes of rich London merchants had double-storey banqueting halls from the late Middle Ages to the seventeenth century. Merchants' houses in late seventeenth-century Bristol still had large double-storey halls bristling with militia armour, coats of arms and old furniture. Yet, by the 1720s halls were becoming obsolete, and arms and armour had disappeared as a form of decoration.[5] Great halls would survive in guilds, colleges and the inns of court – a peculiarity of institutions.

The polite architectural model accommodated a distinctively feminine social life at home. The Bristol architect of a house for a local merchant in 1724 designed a symmetrical house on three floors: 'on the right hand of the vestibule you find a handsome withdrawing room for the mistress of the house to entertain company in, with a private door to the staircase for her servants to bring any thing (without exposing it to people who may be waiting in the vestibule)' (fig. 61).[6] The provision of the withdrawing room is coupled with the socialising of the wife. That women liked specialised rooms of their own for entertainment and withdrawal was common currency by the turn of the eighteenth century. Roger North blamed women's tastes in 1698 for the modern building habit of packing more small rooms into a narrow footprint: 'a dining room, withdrawing room, and perhaps a closet with some new fingle fangle, to tempt her gay ladyship'. Katherine Windham reported with scorn the £150 her besotted son-in-law had laid out on his wife's 'closet & dressing roome' to reconcile her to life in darkest Norfolk in 1707.[7]

The rich and their architects had long drawn a distinction between rooms for 'convenience' and rooms 'for shew'. In vernacular architecture, the transformation from undifferentiated living spaces to compartmentalised interiors made up of specialised rooms is a fundamental shift, with extensive ramifications for behaviour, rituals and relationships, but it was an inconsistent process drawn out over four centuries. Parlours for meeting guests and conversation existed from the Middle Ages. Probably half of all yeoman houses in Kent, a rich and sophisticated county, had a parlour by 1600; these were likely to contain beds in the early 1600s, tea tables and upholstered chairs by the 1700s. Beds, however, could

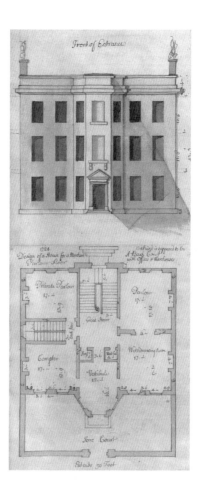

61 *Design of a House for a Merchant*, 1724, ink on paper. Bristol Record Office 33746. Front elevation and ground-floor plan by a Bristol architect of a proposed house for a merchant. The withdrawing room for the mistress of the house to entertain company is at the front on the right.

still be found in the parlour in backward rural Yorkshire and the Midlands around 1800, while north Yorkshire labourers still lived mainly in single-room cottages, unlike their counterparts in the south.[8] Meanwhile, in West Wales, dining rooms were late arrivals even in Georgian gentry manors; meals were eaten in the hall or parlour in the ancient manner and beds could still be found downstairs. In sharp contrast, even ordinary middling families in London were increasingly likely to have a new-fangled parlour at the front of the house, insulated from household traffic, for the entertainment of family and friends in form by the later seventeenth century.[9]

The urban culture of formal visiting, gathering force over the late seventeenth century, but galvanised by tea in the early eighteenth, was potentially much more modest than banqueting. Elaborate visiting rituals were mounted by the nobility – the fountains in front of the Duke of Buckingham's house on the Mall used to play on 'the Dutches's Visiting day' in the 1710s – but a tea set and a handful of chairs sufficed for the urban middling.[10] Unlike feasting, visiting was comparatively cheap to stage; it became a routine, even daily ritual, not an exceptional holiday festival, one that, in the mornings at least, allowed visitor and hostess alike to dress exquisitely, but informally. It could be performed by women alone or en masse. Already in the late seventeenth century, church court records suggest that London women hosted nearly four times more domestic visits than did men. Visitors could be hyperactive. Lady Mary Coke easily made eighteen visits a day in town in May 1767.[11] Hence visiting sanctioned female congregation and exposed the domestic interior to a worrying, and for the middling, unprecedented degree. The invasions involved were legendary. Formal visits are 'but insidious Instructions of a Spy rather than the Good Office of a Neighbour' warned *The Whole Duty of Woman* in 1735. The showy wife of the merchant or shopkeeper was a favourite target of satire, with 'her tea, her card parties, and her dressing-room' spreading the contagion of fashion and scandal. Dudley Ryder found female meetings in Hackney appallingly nosy, if personally secretive. At one breakfast party 'the conversation turned entirely upon the manners, behaviour, way of living, clothes, dress, & c, of their neighbours and though at the same time they were blaming others for prying into the secrets of families and talking about others'.[12] Display of self and surroundings was the alpha and omega of visiting. Joan Kirk, who lived at a tavern in Smithfield, London, in 1684, refused to go out with her vintner husband to call on a cousin, 'saying she had not Cloaths good enough a Visiting'.[13] Hence the prestige of the stage, the props and the hostess that could stand up to the scrutiny of guests.

The importance of contriving domestic space for ceremonies was widely felt. La Rochefoucauld was impressed by the well-kept homes of Suffolk farmers in 1784: 'they are always careful to keep one small sitting-room spotlessly clean and sometimes quite elegant. In this room they receive their guests; the tables and chairs contained in it are of well polished mahogany, the chimney-piece is sometimes of marble but generally of carved wood.'[14] Most homes, however, were too cramped to sustain an unsullied shrine to politeness. Even a metropolitan professional family like the Burneys had no room to entertain when Mrs Burney was ill in August 1792. Upon a visit from Mrs Crewe, 'my father & I both went & sat with her in the coach, as my mother was not well enough for admission into our only Company Room'.[15] Even the northern lesser gentry tended not to keep a pristine temple for guests – dining room, drawing room and parlour were more or less public, more or less formal, according to the time of day, the arrangement of furniture and tableware, the level of ceremony and the status and number of the guests. Props and manners signalled formality, not necessarily the room.[16]

A culture of creative adaptation is exposed in the ingenious advice that a Bedfordshire rector was given on making multiple use of his best room in 1751. The 'scheme for preserving the chamber in its full magnitude' involved 'a handsome sham clothes press, which in the day-time will be a very handsome piece of furniture, and at night the front will turn up and make the tester'. In the morning, the bed could be collapsed and decorated with 'two or three figures, busts or Mrs Williamson's china' and 'there's your large handsome dining room again'.[17] Beds could be concealed in tables, desks, bookcases and cupboards. This metamorphic furniture could be made to a high mark – the London cabinetmaker James Brown had a line in mahogany bureau bedsteads – suggesting a space-strapped market even amongst the rich.[18]

A formal distinction between rooms for convenience and rooms for show was hardly defensible in the vast numbers of urban houses that accommodated either a workshop, a commercial space or live-in tenants, as well as servants and apprentices. Almost half of all houses in London probably contained secondary lodger households. So even immaculate Neo-classical terraces could be internally divided into a warren of separate lodging rooms – which often had to be bedroom and parlour in turn. Most lodgers had to live in one or two chambers, often eating elsewhere, and improvising ceremony with a few tea wares or a decorative bed covering chosen by the landlady.[19] Genteel spinsters and widows often found themselves in commercial lodgings, or withdrawn into a personal cell within the houses of kin. Show involved whisking out the tea table and rearranging the chairs. Temporary set dressing was a Georgian domestic art.

Household management was a pressing subject to the Georgians, often discussed in terms of oeconomy (fig. 62). The word derived from the title of the Greek writer Xenophon's *Oeconomicus*, the most influential classical text on the subject. According to its translator, Richard Bradley,

> The Art of Oeconomy is divided, as Xenophon tells us, between the Men and the Women; the Men have the most dangerous and laborious share of it in the Fields, and without doors, and the Women have the Care and Management of every Business within doors, and to see after the good ordering of whatever is belonging to the House.[20]

But Xenophon also emphasised the need for patriarchal superintendance of household expenditure, management and behaviour. The notion of oeconomy, consequently, could be used to assert either female domestic authority or male

62   *The Good Oeconomists*, 1745, printed engraving. Lewis Walpole Library, Farmington, CT, 745.0.7.

control. The significance of the term's frequent use lies less in what it said about male or female authority in the home, which echoed established practice in its ambiguity, and more in its message that homes must be subjected to systematic, ordered, rational governance. Oeconomy presented household order as critical to the material survival and success of the family and, by extension in the hands of authors like Dudley North, to the well-being of the state.[21] In his *Cottage Economy* (1822), the radical William Cobbett captured the difference between this domestically based notion of what we now call economics and the language he associated with the new political economy of Adam Smith's followers. He insisted: 'the word *Economy*, like a great many others, has, in its application, been very much abused. It is generally used as if it meaned parsimony, stinginess, niggardliness; and, at best, merely the restraining from expending money.' He remained adamant that 'ECONOMY means, *management*, and nothing else; and it is generally applied to the affairs of a house and family, which affairs are an object of the greatest importance, whether as relating to individuals or to a nation.'[22]

The maintenance of order at home was given a near mystical significance in domestic advice books. Order and neatness could be read as expressive of biblical injunctions about the godly household. A sweet-smelling cupboard stacked with crisp linens, a row of gleaming pans and an up-to-date inventory were all emblems of a methodical and therefore virtuous household. Order also sustained classical ideals of decorum whereby everyone and everything was in its proper place. Order was a precondition of respectability and gentility, essential to elevation and progress. It also underscored the health of the inhabitants – fumigating beds and boiling sheets reduced skin diseases and vermin. Catching the itch from soiled linen at an inn was a proverbial risk for travellers. A taste for order was to be inculcated in boys and girls alike by giving them 'convenient places for the preservation and arrangement of their little goods', but general responsibility for tidying fell to girls, who were trained early to be 'Neat and Exact in everything about them', reared to abhor 'anything 'nasty or misplaced', so they instantly detect 'the least Disorder in a house'.[23] A powerful correlation was already forged between household neatness and modesty in women – a correlation clear in the double meaning of disparaging terms like 'slut'. The wholesomeness of the interior was a demonstration of the virtues of the wife.

Mistresses used phrases like 'putting the house in order', 'settling the house', 'regulating the house', 'domestic business' and 'domestic cares' as well as 'domestic oeconomy' to capture the systematic consideration that was their mission. 'Well my dear Mrs Baker I imagine you are enjoying yourself at this time over a high piled fire & have settled your Drawers & looked into the Oconomy of your family', wrote a female friend in the early eighteenth century. The family's contentment rested on the organisation of this Buckinghamshire matron. 'I can guess . . . where abouts the squire is, his dog on one side, his son in front . . . Who is it he envies?'[24] The benefits to men were profound. A Methodist bachelor, Julius Hardy, employed more than thirty people at his Birmingham button works in the 1780s and '90s, but his household was a constant bother. 'How continually has my mind revolved that question: "what step shall I take to obtain a continuance of even orderly management or even good government in the little concerns of my house?" ' Marriage was the proverbial solution: 'To alter my state of life has been suggested again and again.'[25]

A deliberate embrace of domestic mission at personal cost was sometimes articulated. The Londoner Anna Larpent shuttled her family between Marylebone and their suburban retreat near Epsom at the end of the century. On arrival in Surrey in April 1798, having reduced her staff for the summer, she spent a month putting the house in order. First she 'arranged all my accounts, home book, etc. and put all those domestic cares in train here'. Next she made an inventory: 'Family business. Looked over all the crockery and table linen. Spent the morning in preparing it for being thoroughly mended cut some up in short quite a house-wife's day.' As well as 'Sundry odd jobs' and the endless sorting and mending of personal linen, which occupied her 'usefully if not brilliantly', she spent a Saturday 'fully employ'd putting to rights the physic closet'. Finally, Larpent dressed her rooms with flowers and awaited her summer visitors. Larpent was a woman of both wide intellectual horizons and strenuous domesticity, clear-eyed in her attempts to reconcile the two. 'I always employ 4 hours in a week in plain work, etc., both to know how to do it, to keep my mind active in those duties of oe-conomy – and during that time I reflect and digest much of what I study and observe at other times, the mechanism of such work not preventing the action of my mind.'[26]

From garret to basement, middling wives kept their eye on the fixtures and furnishings of the house and orchestrated the relationship of people to domestic objects. London landladies on the witness stand at the Old Bailey showed the reach of their information about their tenants, the habits of household members and the number and nature of objects in the lodging and the family rooms. Characteristically, their knowledge dwarfed that of the male head of household, 'You must ask my wife' being a common response from men on the stand. When a day labourer, James Terry, accused a lodger of stealing from his box in his chamber room in Aldgate in 1793, he seemed at a loss for the details that would back up his prosecution: 'When were they taken? – I cannot say what month; I am no scholar; it was not I that missed them first, it was my wife. How long was it before your wife missed them, did you see them? – The Lord knows that; I cannot say; I was out of the way, I was out at work.' That wives should be 'better acquainted with the things' was an entirely plausible claim at the Old Bailey.[27] The practice of continual inventory taking helped elevate domestic knowledge to an extraordinary level of dignity and competence.

Internal changes at home extended and reinforced the female domain. Our period saw the emergence of separate kitchens in middling houses, but this was an uneven development, well established in wealthy Kent by the second quarter of the eighteenth century, but still materialising in rural Yorkshire at its end. Kitchens represented not just a special room for the business of cooking, but also a space for storing the expanding battery of equipment employed for processing food and drink. It was the female department, men agreed. Meanwhile, an ancient product of female expertise – household linen – was undergoing a huge proliferation and sophistication.[28] Over the *longue durée* an uneven transition from domestic production to retail provision was in train, but effective provisioning still required diligence and discernment in an era before quality control. Household manuals assumed that even the propertied mistress would be involved in relentless grocery shopping: haggling, testing food for quality, spotting adulteration, deciding when to send servants or shop herself. Daughters were schooled to recognise quality and resist sales patter.[29] The complete house-wife became the domestic Chancellor of the Exchequer.

Whether men or women dictated the look of the interior has been open to recent debate. John Cornforth and Charles Saumarez Smith argue that it was in the eighteenth century that interior decoration became a ladies' prerogative, though they disagree slightly on timing – Cornforth plumps for the late 1720s, Saumarez Smith for the 1760s. The art historian Ann Bermingham suggests fe-male cultural authority over domestic aesthetics was fashioned towards the end of the century by the mushrooming commercial culture supporting art and craftwork. Meanwhile, historian of ideas Richard Jones argues that many British writers on Georgian taste came to endow refined women with a distinctive ap-titude for consumer discrimination and tasteful ornamentation, and hence the ability to civilise the promiscuous luxury of commerce.[30]

These precedents barely ruffle the pages of an influential study of Victorian in-teriors by Deborah Cohen which argues that women exercised little or no influ-ence on the look of the home until after the married women's property acts. 'Until at least the 1880s, the business of furnishing was almost entirely a man's world . . . . Woman's sphere may have been the house, but the angel who resided there – without property rights and earning power – had little control over its disposition.'[31] To believe that married women were financially annihilated in everyday practice as well as case law is to read the protests of Victorian feminists as simple description, and to ignore the many exceptions to couverture in com-mon law, and the way even quite ordinary wives manipulated the rival legal ju-risdictions of equity, ecclesiastical law and borough custom to make shift.[32]

Cohen also reduces the look and arrangement of interiors to furniture buy-ing upon marriage, from which she infers female marginality. But the rows of men's names in the ledger of a furniture company represent a black and white commercial convention that masks a colourful universe of gender negotiation. And in any case, heirlooms, wedding presents, second-hand buys, home-made gifts and domestic handicrafts alongside new furniture fabricated the bourgeois interior in all its flouncy mid-Victorian glory. Moreover, the upkeep of interiors and the mending and recycling of objects were central to material experience before built-in obsolescence and cheap mass production. Servicing and repairs were the heartbeat of the business for cabinetmakers and upholsterers. A Victo-rian spinster, Miss Livingstone, employed the local cabinetmaker and uphol-sterer thirteen times over three years in Chichester in the 1840s. Samuel Peat papered her rooms, put up curtains, restuffed the sofa, made a mattress and installed new cupboard doors. In February 1842 he made her coffin. The thrifty middle classes were mindful that there was far more to keeping up appearances than buying spanking new furniture.[33]

At any rate, reading the Victorian interiors literature against the Georgian should at least give pause for thought, for we are hereby offered at least three dates (1725, 1760 and 1890), before which women allegedly exercised no authority over the way interiors were designed, furnished and decorated. Like gender panics and crises of masculinity, it seems victory in the battle of the bed curtains is cropping up everywhere. More helpful in my view is to disentangle the persistent and the newly emergent in the jurisdictions of both women and men.

Energy pulses through some of the women in this book. The likes of Mary Rebow and Anne, Duchess of Grafton stamped themselves upon their surroundings with the same punishing drive that they brought to their relationships. It is easy to imagine them pressing on the doors of Ince and Mayhew until they yielded. Female control over crucial aspects of the interior was based on custom, however, not the vagaries of character. The beautification of the home was a deep-rooted moral obligation. As good husbandry commanded of old: 'woman deck up thyne house'.[34] The conviction that a good wife ornamented the house by her own hand is as old as Proverbs and was endlessly recycled in Georgian and Victorian prints. By 1800 an increasingly sophisticated commercial culture supporting amateur arts and crafts was in the business of persuading affluent women to rejoice in their role as artistic beautifier of the home. The power that women might abuse in consuming for home is manifest in the shrill warnings to husbands of all backgrounds about avoiding expensive brides and the luxuriant satires about unbridled female materialism. A positive version of female authority surfaced in Georgian treatises on taste, which urged virtuous, refined ladies to moderate and domesticate male magnificence and show. Even prime ministers acknowledged female government of taste.[35] An elaborate deference to female preferences characterises some of the most triumphant Georgian design firms, such as Adam, Wedgwood and Boulton. That upholsterers could be caricatured as women's lackeys in the march of fashion ('what would the nice ladies do with them?')[36] reveals the agency that contemporaries ascribed to women. The fact that taste was so ineffable a concept aided its espousal by women, in whom flawless discrimination could be seen as another occult attribute like perfect pitch. There was a strong tendency to view a woman and her decorations as an ensemble, observers moving seamlessly from silk dress, to sofa, to curtains in their descriptions. A minutely detailed interest in interiors was seen as a distinctively female trait. The Bishop of Rochester wrote to Alexander

Pope that *The Arabian Nights* were likely the 'product of some woman's imagination' because of all the 'descriptions of dress, Furniture etc'.[37]

It is not argued here that women asserted their tastes in an incipient bid to cast off the yoke of patriarchal domination, but men who denied the female prerogative could be cast as tyrants. The fact that so many sensible husbands gave their wives a free hand speaks of the benefits to men of successful domesticity. Female ability to engineer a pleasant environment was often admired. The Somerset parson William Holland was impressed by his curate's wife, whom he visited in September 1803: 'She had finished her Drawing Room in very good taste and not expensive. She teaches her daughter Musick and in an excellent stile. In short she is a clever little woman and highly accomplished, both useful and ornamental.'[38] The congeniality of the *mise en scène* is a manifestation of the considerable allure of the wife. A successful marriage would embody, project and celebrate itself in the construction, extension, refurbishment and decoration of the family residence. This was an undertaking in which both husband and wife had substantial social, personal, political and economic investments. A marriage of architecture *and* upholstery, mahogany *and* china, interior decorating bridged a traditional division of gender territories and thus was superlatively matrimonial in its overtones.

Marriage is a union of difference, and the Georgians were alert to gender distinction, which they reinscribed in taste, style, decoration and ornament. The architectural history of interiors notes an increasing specialisation of spaces by sex, with the rise of the masculinised dining room and the femininised drawing room by 1820.[39] An implicit system of rules that assigned the sexes to different rooms in the house is apparent in architectural and design theory. Witness William Marshall's gardening guide in 1785:

> Thus the view from the drawing room should be highly embellished, to correspond with the beauty and elegance within: everything should be *feminine* – elegant – beautiful – such as attunes the mind to politeness and lively conversation. The break-fasting room should have more masculine objects in view: wood, water and an extended country for the eye to roam over: such as allures us imperceptibly to the ride or the chace.[40]

The recommendations of experts, however, represented a counsel of perfection, a fantasy that even the gentry would find hard to fulfil in totality. Nevertheless, architectural good manners were followed where funds allowed. The letters to the wallpaper firm Trollope and Sons bespeak a slavish commitment to the rules of decorum when it came to decorating front rooms and back stairs, handsome dining rooms and small family parlours. Occasional sales catalogues and personal inventories also suggest conformity to decorative convention, and the assignation of 'masculine' and 'feminine' objects to the rooms most associated with their principal or imagined users.[41] The existence of a familiar taxonomy that characterised rooms by gender and organised objects according to the sex of the user must be a strong possibility.

Educational literature advised that young gentlemen should be raised to understand architectural and landscape improvements, while girls were trained to give order, colour and texture indoors. Meeting the great landscape architect Capability Brown in 1767, Josiah Wedgwood 'told him that my Life was devoted to the service of the Ladys as his was to that of the Noblemen & Gent[lemen]'.[42] Men were associated with classical geometry and women with its sinuous and irregular alternatives; in gardening, the male imagination encompassed the landscape park while the female eye fell on flowers; in furnishings, men were seen to buy silver and mahogany, while women had a discriminating appreciation of textiles and ceramics. All these distinctions reinforced the supreme conviction that only men comprehended structure, while women like magpies merely grasped details, a hierarchical dualism that is with us to this day in the snobberies of the male-dominated architectural profession and the critical disparagement of the feminised world of interiors. The fact that individuals occasionally broke with convention, does not disprove the existence of rules; indeed, the pleasure of transgression depends upon them. The gratifications of landscape design for Lady Luxborough lay at least in part in violating customary boundaries. 'This is my own plan, and I am all over embroidered with dust and mortar daily; But should prefer it to embroidery of another kind [pl. 38].'[43]

In Georgian decorating, masculinity was allied with the discipline of formal grandeur, while rooms associated with femininity allowed more informality in behaviour and thus more experiment in ornament. From the 1600s the cabinets of the rich were exquisite laboratories of taste, but playful schemes, exotic motifs and lighter designs of decorative fluency were extended to dressing rooms by the 1740s, and ladies' drawing rooms, breakfast rooms and parlours by the end of the century (pl. 39). Obviously, dressing rooms and drawing rooms were enjoyed by probably only 1–2 per cent of the population, but yellow wallpaper and lacquered tea boards were to be found in the middling parlour, and in the lodging rooms of spinsters stretching an income to keep up appearances. When a Yorkshire farm servant and thief Jane Boys spent her loot on a japanned tea board in 1793, she was appropriating the pleasures enjoyed by the wives of East India Company directors a century before.[44] The spirit of the feminine convention was as vivid for the poor lodger with her cheap decorated teapot as for the duchess in her chinoiserie dressing room. The grammar of decoration was not so rigid and intricate as it would become for the nineteenth-century middle class, but its logic was the seed from which Victorian complexity sprang.

A universe of difference could be read in things. In *A Modern Dissertation on a Certain Necessary Piece of Household Furniture* (1752), toilet humour exploits the ramifications of decorum as a means of understanding artefacts and society. The 'general utility' of chamber pots was inarguable, for '*All* Persons of both Sexes'. But the 'Make of these useful implements' varied across the country, petite in the metropolis 'tending rather to the fashion of a pipkin', but larger and deeper in the regions. The material differed as much as the form:

> The most costly sort are those that are cast in silver, and used by persons of the first rank. Those that are esteemed the neatest and chiefly intended for the fair sex are wrought in China adorned with Trees, or set of with a Variety of birds, beasts and fishes. Those which are composed of white Earth and neatly glazed are generally used by the Middling sort of people . . . the most Inferior sort are those which carry the ordinary Colours on their Outside, which the common People claim as their sole Property.

The joke inheres in the fertility of Georgian commerce and the *reductio ad absurdum* of knowing one's place. But chamber pots did indeed come in all these varieties. Even the unpretentious piss pot flaunted the era's material innovations (white salt-glazed stoneware, naturalistic motifs on delftware and porcelain), exemplifying the burgeoning possibilities for design differentiation by gender, wealth and rank (fig. 63; see also fig. 10).[45]

Countless new goods taken up first by rich merchants found their way down the social hierarchy in cheaper forms. There was some resistance to fashion on grounds of ideology and temperament; some Quakers, Methodists and Radicals disdained the tinsel of the times. 'In household goods the warm, the strong, the durable, ought always to be kept in view', recommended William Cobbett in 1822 to his labouring supporters. 'Things of this sort ought to last several life-times.'[46] Yet the hectoring itself confirms that unseemly weakness for novelty was rife. Inventories reveal that sizeable minorities of Yorkshire labourers and weavers possessed clocks and looking-glasses by the late eighteenth century.[47] To reduce this diffusion to envy and emulation would be facile. It seems unlikely that a mirror had precisely the same associations and impact in a Pennine hovel as in a city mansion. Inevitably, the poor were more likely to value household objects as assets to be pawned or sold in lean times. Nevertheless, the dominant language for evaluating interiors and objects was widely spoken. Magnificence was the privilege of nobility or the pretension of upstarts, while the restrained ele-

63   *A St Giles's Beauty*, 1784, mezzotint. British Museum, London, 1873,0712.812. A cheerful prostitute portrayed in a dingy lodging room in St Giles, London, furnished with a fold-up bed. Even in this cheap lodging, the walls are decorated with a trellis-pattern wallpaper or stencil, while a decorated chamber pot on the floor serves to display flowers.

gance known as neatness suited the middling and genteel. The decency pursued by the respectable working poor was neat and clean.

The French might reign over the luxury trades – they were 'the whipped cream of Europe' according to Voltaire – but English manufactures had a sturdy efficiency befitting the solid worth and affluence of the ordinary and middle market, rather than 'the Magnificence of Palaces, or the Cabinets of Princes'. In consequence of which, claimed Josiah Tucker, 'the *English* . . . have better Conveniences in their Houses, and affect to have more in Quantity of clean, neat Furniture, and a greater variety (such as Carpets, Screens, Window Curtains, Chamber Bells, polished Brass Locks, Fenders etc., etc. Things hardly known Abroad among Persons of such a Rank) than are to be found in any other country of *Europe, Holland* excepted'. Domestic neatness was the proud boast of Europe's leading commercial society.[48]

The rich man in his castle, the poor man at his gate – homes or the lack of them materialised one's place in the social hierarchy. Mansion or parsonage, lodging or hovel, homes nonetheless shared a metaphorical association with the body and the self. The perimeter of 'the private house' represented a sacred frontier in law, everyday practice and folklore, but there was no guarantee of seclusion over the threshold. Living hugger-mugger with strangers robbed the internally divided urban terrace of any refinement of privacy as we understand it. Less than a fifth of the population lived in towns in 1700, but more than half of the population was urban by 1851. Galloping urbanisation drove the proliferation of sub-divided terraced houses, which demanded a new lexicon to describe the layers of the warren – an older vocabulary of front and back chambers gave way to the more flexible terminology of levels: 'two pair stairs room', 'three pair stairs room and closet'. Inmates, however, still toiled to erect their own internal thresholds and maintain some separation of functions as a proof of independent status. The occupation of a two-up two-down terraced house became a reasonable ambition for the Victorian working-class family. A self-contained double-storey terrace became the English housing norm – Newcastle flats and West Riding back-to-backs being the iconic exceptions.[49]

Meanwhile, the houses of the middling and the manors of the greater gentry and nobility remained complex hierarchies, arranged for the comfort and convenience of senior members, an organisation that could leave even privileged underlings feeling destitute. 'Home! Why do I call it Home? I have no Home', despaired the portionless spinster Gertrude Savile at the gates of Rufford Hall in 1721. It was through space that superiors exerted their most smothering power. Georgian houses open to the public, arranged and empty of life, can give a misleading impression of gracious living and lavish personal space for inmates. The spread of small closets for withdrawal can be read as architectural responses to the racket and wearying publicity of life at home, while ingenious secret drawers were an exquisite solution to the prying of servants, visitors and other members of the household.

Personal privacy was in short supply, even in the midst of luxury, especially for non-inheriting children, dependent kin and, most of all, servants. Maids and menservants often had the run of the house for the purposes of their labour, but their own time and room were strictly controlled, as the copious rules for servants testify at length. Noble households flattered themselves on near military discipline in the ranks, frequently issuing 'a body of laws for the good government' of the servile. At Tottenham Park in Wiltshire, 'strict decorum' was demanded of the indoor servants, who had to observe a curfew of ten in the summer and nine in the winter.[50] But even more modest householders aspired to minute surveillance. Grocer's daughter and clergyman's wife Elizabeth Forth was typical in denying her two maids light in the garret of her Yorkshire house in 1792 for fear of fire, insisting that they 'snuff their candle before they go upstairs & never to work or sew in their bed room by candle light or they will lose their places'.[51] Not that the propertied women enjoyed much breathing space either. Even Maria Edgeworth, the daughter of a Protestant gentleman and prominent Irish landlord, had to share a bedroom with siblings for most of her adult life. Lacking a room, the emergent individuality of genteel and middling girls could be expressed in a desk or workbox of their own.

Of all women, the spinster was the least likely to be a householder and most likely to be itinerant. After she left the family home in her early 20s, the lace trader Hester Pinney lodged at thirty-four different addresses over fifty-eight years in London, dying in 1739.[52] Spinsters had to be ready to pack up their things and move on, insinuating themselves into another household as circumstances demanded. Any permanence lay with her chattels, the tea set and bed curtains, not in a static residence. The comfort of home inhered in her movables. Meanwhile, without a house, room, or even bed of their own, the young working poor had to rely on a locking box as their one sacrosanct compartment. Some spatial autonomy and personal props were understood to be basic to the preservation of self-respect in Georgian England. A veil of privacy was a fundamental decency. Homelessness was rightly understood to be an appalling plight and a cannon shot to the defences of the spirit. Yet home was no less significant an idea for being a memory, or ultimately a hopeless goal and an ever receding illusion.

NOTES

Introduction

1 Virginia Woolf, *A Room of One's Own* (1929), 70–71.

2 On the field, see Amanda Vickery, 'Golden Age to Separate Spheres: A Review of the Categories and Chronology of English Women's History', *Historical Journal*, 36/2 (1993), 383–414. For recent studies that still rely on a tale of female incarceration in the domestic sphere, see Marie-Claire Royer-Daney, 'The Representation of Housework in the Eighteenth-century Women's Press', in *The Invisible Woman: Aspects of Women's Work in Eighteenth-century Britain*, ed. Isabelle Baudino, Jacques Carré and Cécile Révauger (Aldershot, 2005), 27–36; Ann Bermingham, *Learning to Draw: Studies in the Cultural History of a Polite and Useful Art* (New Haven and London, 2000), 183, 186; and Michael McKeon, *The Secret History of Domesticity: Public, Private and the Division of Knowledge* (Baltimore, 2005). On men, see Alexandra Shepard and Karen Harvey, 'What Have Historians Done with Masculinity?', *Journal of British Studies*, 44 (2005), 274–80.

3 For the evolution of debate on the family, see Lawrence Stone, *The Family, Sex and Marriage in England, 1500–1800* (London, 1977); Randolph Trumbach, *The Rise of the Egalitarian Family: Aristocratic Kinship and Domestic Relations in Eighteenth-century England* (New York, 1978); Susan Moller Okin, 'Women and the Making of the Sentimental Family', *Philosophy and Public Affairs*, 11 (1981), 65–88; Margaret Hunt, *The Middling Sort: Commerce, Gender and the Family in England, 1680–1780* (Berkeley, CA, 1996); Amanda Vickery, *The Gentleman's Daughter: Women's Lives in Georgian England* (New Haven and London, 1998); Naomi Tadmor, *Family and Friends in Eighteenth-century England: Household, Kinship and Patronage* (Cambridge, 2000); Helen Berry and Elizabeth Foys-

ter (eds), *The Family in Early Modern England* (Cambridge, 2007). A spatial turn in family history is latent, however. See Jennifer Melville, 'The Use and Organisation of Domestic Space in Late Seventeenth-century London' (PH.D thesis, Cambridge, 1999); Elizabeth Foyster, *Marital Violence: An English Family History, 1660–1857* (Cambridge, 2005); Amanda Flather, *Gender and Space in Early Modern England* (Woodbridge, 2007).

4   Lorna Weatherill, *Consumer Behaviour and Material Culture in Britain, 1660–1760* (London, 1988); Carole Shammas, *The Pre-industrial Consumer in England and America* (Oxford, 1990); Mark Overton et al., *Production and Consumption in English Households, 1600–1750* (London and New York, 2004).

5   Two rare studies that wrestle with this problem are Jan de Vries, 'Between Purchasing Power and the World of Goods: Understanding the Household Economy in Early Modern Europe', in *Consumption and the World of Goods: Consumption and Society in the Seventeenth and Eighteenth Centuries*, ed. J. Brewer and R. Porter (London, 1993), 85–132, and S. Bowden and A. Offner, 'The Technological Revolution That Never Was: Gender, Class and the Diffusion of Household Appliances in Interwar England', in *The Sex of Things: Gender and Consumption in Historical Perspective*, ed. V. de Grazia and E. Furlough (Berkeley, CA, 1996), 244–74.

6   Classics in the field include Peter Thornton, *Authentic Decor: The Domestic Interior, 1620–1920* (London, 1984); Charles Saumarez Smith, *Eighteenth-century Decoration: Design and the Domestic Interior in England* (London, 1993); Eileen Harris, *The Genius of Robert Adam: His Interiors* (New Haven, 2001); John Cornforth, *Early Georgian Interiors* (New Haven and London, 2004). A pioneering attempt to bridge architectural and social history is Mark Girouard, *Life in the English Country House* [1978] (Harmondsworth, 1980), while feminist architectural history also seeks to link buildings and behaviour: Alice T. Friedman, *House and Household in Elizabethan England: Wollaton Hall and the Willoughby Family* (Chicago, 1989).

7   George Dickie, *The Century of Taste: The Philosophical Odyssey of Taste in the Eighteenth Century* (New York and Oxford, 1996).

8   William Whately, *A Care-cloth; or, A Treatise of the Cumbers and Troubles of Marriage* (1624), sigs A6–A6v, cited in Alan Mcfarlane, *The Origins of English Individualism* (Oxford, 1978), 75. See the age of marriage table in E. A. Wrigley and R. S. Schofield, *The Population History of England, 1541–1871: A Reconstruction* (Cambridge, MA, 1981), 255. These are broad means, within which there was variation by rank, occupation and locality.

9   C. G. Carus, *The King of Saxony's Journey through England and Scotland in the Year 1844*, 32–3 and Von Archenholz, *A Picture of England*, II, 45–6, cited in Paul Langford, *Englishness Identified: Manners and Character, 1650–1850* (Oxford, 2000), 105–6.

10   Susan Amussen, *An Ordered Society: Gender and Class in Early Modern England* (Oxford, 1988); Gordon Schochet, *The Authoritarian Family and Political Attitudes in Seventeenth-century England: Patriarchalism in Political Thought* (New Brunswick, 1988).

11   Okin, 'Women and the Making of the Sentimental Family'; Tadmor, *Family and Friends*, ch. 1 and 2.

12   Rachel Garrard, 'English Probate Inventories and their Use in Studying the Significance of the Domestic Interior, 1570–1700', *A. A. G. Bijdragen*, 23 (1980), 55–77; Melville, 'The Use and Organisation of Domestic Space'; Flather, *Gender and Space*.

13   Exact national data is lacking before the first national survey, *circa* 1938. Daunton, however, calculated that one in ten houses were owner-occupied in Victorian Cardiff, from a painstaking analysis of every ratepayer in the city: Martin Daunton, 'House Ownership from Rate Books', *Urban History*, 3 (1976), 21–7. His subsequent research tended to

confirm this figure, though there were some exceptional areas like the South Wales coal-field, where miners used clubs to build their own houses. M. J. Daunton, *House and Home in the Victorian City: Working-class Housing, 1850–1914* (London, 1983). There is even debate about the extent of working-class owner occupation after the interwar building boom: M. Swenarton and S. Taylor, 'The Scale and Nature of the Growth of Owner-Occupation in Britain between the Wars', *Economic History Review*, 38 (1985), 373–92. In the absence of comparable sources for Georgian England, precise figure are elusive, but there is no compelling evidence for higher rates of owner occupation.

14   R. G. Thorne (ed.), *The House of Commons, 1790–1820*, 5 vols (London, 1986), i, 21–42, 357–63; Zoë Dyndor, 'The Political Culture of Elections in Northampton, 1768–1868' (PhD in progress); Matthew McCormack, *The Independent Man: Citizenship and Gender Politics in Georgian England* (Manchester, 2006).

15   *The Batchelor's Directory: Being a Treatise of the Excellence of Marriage* (1694), 47.

16   *The Ladies Advocate; or, An Apology for Matrimony in Answer to the Batchelor's Monitor* (1741), 1.

17   Joshua 24:15.

18   Donald Gibson, *A Parson in the Vale of the White Horse: George Woodward's Letters from East Hendred, 1753–1761* (Gloucester, 1982), 90.

19   Sara Mendelson and Patricia Crawford, *Women in Early Modern England, 1550–1720* (Oxford, 1998); Laura Gowing, *Domestic Dangers: Women, Words and Sex in Early Modern London* (Oxford, 1996).

20   Peter Earle, *A City Full of People: Men and Women of London, 1650–1750* (London, 1994), 167.

21   Keith Wrightson, *English Society, 1580–1680* (London, 1982), 104.

22   Rotherham Public Library, Platt Microfilm, f. 26.

23   Linda Pollock, 'Teach Her to Live under Obedience: The Making of Women in the Upper Ranks of Early Modern England', *Continuity and Change*, 4 (1989), 231–58; Ingrid Tague, *Women of Quality: Accepting and Contesting Ideals of Femininity in England, 1690–1760* (Woodbridge, Suffolk, 2002), 97–132.

24   Church court depositions evidence the delegation of household authority in seventeenth-century London and Essex: Melville, 'The Use and Organisation of Domestic Space', 199, Flather, *Gender and Space*, 39–74.

25   Somerset Record Office, DD/SF/4515/48 (January 1695), Mary Clarke to Edward Clarke, London; DD/SF/4515/35 (31 August 1694), same to same.

26   National Archives of Scotland, GD 18/4811 (24 July 1756), Robert Adam, Rome, to Jamie Adam.

27   A. F. J. Brown, *Essex People, 1750–1900* (Chelmsford, 1972), 121; Hampshire Record Office, 44M69/F7/3/3 (13 July 1756), Richard Jervoise to Anne Jervoise; R. Trappes-Lomax, *The Diary and Letter-book of the Reverend Thomas Brockbank, 1671–1709*, Chetham Society, 89 (Manchester, 1930), 256.

28   Keele University Library, SC 1/5 (1766), Mr Walter Baghot to Mr and Mrs Sneyd.

29   Chippendale, Haig & Co. to Sir Edward Knatchbull, 7 May 1773, and 23 June 1778. Cited in Bernard Denvir, *The Eighteenth Century: Art, Design and Society, 1689–1789* (London, 1983), 207–9.

30   John Styles, 'Clothing the North: The Supply of Non-Elite Clothing in the Eighteenth-century North of England', *Textile History*, 25 (1994), 139–66; M. Spufford, *The Great Reclothing of Rural England: Petty Chapmen and their Wares* (London, 1995).

31   Overton et al., *Production and Consumption in English Households*, passim.

32 Gibson, *A Parson in the Vale of the White Horse*, 44.

33 Peter Clark, *British Clubs and Societies, 1580–1800: The Origins of an Associational World* (Oxford, 2001), 190; L. Troide (ed.), *The Early Journals and Letters of Fanny Burney*, 4 vols (Oxford, 1988), I, 83–4; Huntington Library, HM 31201/2: Mrs Larpent's diary, 1796–8.

34 John Clayton, *The Snares of Prosperity To Which Is Added An Essay on Visiting* (1789), 34, 36–7; Charles Burnaby, *The Ladies Visiting Day* (1701), 5; British Library, Add. MS 72516, D'ED C13, f. 213 (10 December 1689), Anne Dormer to Lady Trumbull.

35 Hampshire Record Office, 44M69/F8/1/3 (13 December 1757), Richard Jervoise, Britford, to Tristram Jervoise; Marilyn Butler, *Maria Edgeworth: A Literary Biography* (Oxford, 1972), 226.

36 Berkshire Record Office, D'EZ 12/1 & 2, Account and memorandum book of Edward Belson, distiller, 1707–10; Lincoln Cathedral Library, Diary and account-book of Matthew Flinders, 1775–84, f. 67.

37 Lemuel Gulliver, *The Pleasures and Felicity of Marriage* (1745).

38 *The Universal Spectator. By Henry Stonecastle*, 4 vols (1747), III, 46–7.

39 Anthony Ashley Cooper, 3rd Earl of Shaftesbury, *Characteristics of Men, Manners, Opinions, Times, etc.*, 3 vols (1790), I, 269.

40 *The Polite Companion*, 2 vols (Birmingham, 1749), I, 116.

41 Robert W. Jones, *Gender and the Formation of Taste in Eighteenth-century Britain* (Cambridge, 1998).

42 Cited in B. S. Allen, *Tides in English Taste, 1619–1800* (New York, 1958), 107.

43 See A. Moore (ed.), *Norfolk and the Grand Tour* ([Norwich], 1985); G. Jackson-Stops (ed.), *The Treasure Houses of Great Britain* (New Haven and London, 1985); L. Stone and J. Fawtier Stone, *An Open Elite? England, 1540–1880* (abridged edn, Oxford, 1986), 230; A. Tinniswood, *A History of Country House Visiting* (Oxford, 1989); Shropshire Record Office, 5492/2, Journal of Thomas Brocas, 13 February 1805.

44 K. E. Farrer (ed.), *Correspondence of Josiah Wedgwood*, 3 vols (London, 1903–6), I, 150; Johanna Dahn, 'Active, Social and Temperate: A Construction of Taste with Special Reference to Katherine Plymley (1758–1829)' (PH.D. thesis, University of Wales, Aberystwyth, 2000).

45 Isaac Ware, *A Complete Body of Architecture*, 2 vols (1756); George Coleman, *The Connoisseur. By Mr Town*, 2 vols (1755–6), I, 388; Thomas D'Urfey, *The Old Mode and the New* (1703), 15.

46 Thomas Chippendale, *Gentleman and Cabinet-Maker's Director* (3rd edn, 1762), pls 51, 'A Dressing-Table for a Lady', and 116, 'A Writing-Table and Bookcase for a Lady'.

47 Louisa Collins, 'Women, Writing and Furniture, 1750–1800' (MA dissertation in the History of Design, V&A/RCA, 2005).

48 Margaret J. M. Ezell, *The Patriarch's Wife: Literary Evidence and the History of the Family* (Chapel Hill, 1987), 187; *The Guardian*, 2 vols (6th edn, 1734), II, 325–7; James Fordyce, *Sermons to Young Women*, 2 vols (1766), I, 97–104, 100–01.

49 Maria Edgeworth and Richard Lovell Edgeworth, *Essays on Practical Education*, 2 vols [1798] (3rd edn, 1811), II, 185.

50 Rudolph Ackermann, 'Observations on Fancy Work', *Repository of the Arts, Literature and Commerce* (March 1810), 193.

51 *The Life of William Hutton* [1816] (Oxford, 1998), 3.

52 Beinecke Library, Osborne shelves, C 236, Marthae Taylor letter-book.

53 Edward Hall (ed.), *Miss Weeton: Journal of a Governess*, 2 vols (London, 1939), II, 331, 353, 379.

54 Mary Chandler, *Description of Bath: A Poem* (3rd edn, 1736), 65–7.

55 Rotherham Public Library, Platt Microfilm, f. 155 (*circa* 1795), Anne Platt, Windlestone, to Elizabeth Platt; Chester and Cheshire Record Office, DSA 1 (19 May 1790), Margaret, Lady Stanley to Mrs Owen, Old Burlington Street.

Chapter 1   Thresholds and Boundaries at Home

1 This fiction is a composite based on repeated details in Old Bailey Proceedings online: *www.oldbaileyonline.org* (accessed 15 January 2008).

2 Philippe Ariès, 'Introduction', in *A History of Private Life*, III: *Passions of the Renaissance*, ed. Roger Chartier (Cambridge, MA, 1989), 3–8; Michelle Perrot, 'At Home', in *A History of Private Life*, IV: *From the Fires of Revolution to the Great War*, ed. Perrot (Cambridge, MA, 1990), 342; Linda Pollock, 'Living on the Stage of the World: The Concept of Privacy Among the Elite of Early Modern England', in *Rethinking Social History: English Society, 1570–1920, and its Interpretation*, ed. Adrian Wilson (Manchester, 1993), 89; Elizabeth Foyster, *Marital Violence: An English Family History, 1660–1857* (Cambridge, 2005); Joanne Bailey, *Unquiet Lives: Marriage and Marriage Breakdown in England, 1660–1800* (Cambridge, 2003).

3 Amanda Vickery, 'Golden Age to Separate Spheres: A Review of the Categories and Chronology of English Women's History', *Historical Journal*, 36/2 (1993), 383–414; John Brewer, 'This, That and the Other: Public, Social and Private in the Seventeenth and Eighteenth Centuries', in *Shifting the Boundaries: Transformation of the Languages of Public and Private in the Eighteenth Century*, ed. Dario Castiglione and Lesley Sharpe (Exeter, 1995), 1–21; Lawrence E. Klein, 'Gender and the Public/Private Distinction in the Eighteenth Century', *Eighteenth-century Studies*, 29/1 (1995), 97–109; Amanda Vickery, *The Gentleman's Daughter: Women's Lives in Georgian England* (New Haven and London, 1998), 288–94; Joanna Innes, 'The Rise of the Concept of the "Public Sphere" in British Historical Writing' (unpublished paper); Jürgen Habermas, *The Structural Transformation of the Public Sphere: An Inquiry into a Category of Bourgeois Society*, trans. Thomas Burger (Cambridge, MA, 1989).

4 Mark Girouard, *Life in the English Country House* [1978] (Harmondsworth, 1980), 138; L. Stone and J. Fawtier Stone, *An Open Elite? England, 1540–1880* (abridged edn, Oxford, 1986), 243–6; Christoph Heyl, 'We are Not at Home: Protecting Domestic Privacy in Post-Fire Middle-class London', *London Journal*, 27 (2002), 29; and Heyl, *A Passion for Privacy: Untersuchungen zur Geneseder Bürgerlichen Privatsphäre in London, 1660–1800* (Munich, 2004); Tim Meldrum, *Domestic Service and Gender, 1660–1750: Life and Work in the London Household* (Harlow, 2000), 77–8, 80, 82.

5 E. A. Wrigley, 'A Simple Model of London's Importance in Changing English Society and Economy, 1650–1750', in *Towns in Societies: Essays in Economic History and Historical Sociology*, ed. P. Abrams and E. A. Wrigley (Cambridge, 1978), 215–43.

6 John Summerson, *Georgian London* [1945] (London, 1988), ch. 2; Peter Guillery, *The Small House in Eighteenth-century London* (New Haven and London, 2004), 1–2, 18–19; Dan Cruikshank and Neil Burton, *Life in the Georgian City* (London, 1990), 60; Miles Ogborn, *Spaces of Modernity: London's Geographies, 1680–1780* (New York and London, 1998).

7 Old Bailey Proceedings (hereafter OBP), 23 February 1785, Robert Roberts, William Blann (t17850223–22); OBP, 2 February 1795, John Bruce (t17850112–14); OBP, 29 June

1785, John Godfrey (t17850629–84); OBP, 14 December 1785, Thomas Ballard (t17851214–16); OBP, 29 June 1785, Martin Taylor, Elizabeth Taylor (t17850629–67); OBP, 6 April 1785, James Boston (t17850406–70); OBP, 14 September 1785, Amos Rowsel (t17850914–15).

8   *Oxford English Dictionary*, s.v. 'privacy': '2a private or retired places, 4a private matter, a secret, 4b the private parts, see also 2b a secret place, 3b keeping a secret, reticence, 5 intimacy, confidential relations; the state of being privy to some act'.

9   James Ayres, *Domestic Interiors: The British Tradition, 1500–1850* (New Haven and London, 2003), 2, 69; Robert Blair St George, *Conversing by Signs: Poetics of Implication in Colonial New England* (Chapel Hill, 1998), 184–8; E. Cohen and T. Cohen, 'Open and Shut: The Social Meaning of the Sixteenth-century Roman House', *Studies in the Decorative Arts*, 9/2, (2001), 61–82.

10 John Brand, *Observations on Popular Antiquities: Chiefly Illustrating the Origin of our Vulgar Customs, Ceremonies and Superstitions*, revised edn, ed. Henry Elllis, 2 vols (1813), II, 379; E. P. Thompson, 'Rough Music', in his *Customs in Common* (New York and London, 1991), 467–531.

11 Heyl, *A Passion for Privacy*, 15; *A Foreign View of England in 1725–1729: The Letters of Monsieur César de Saussure to his Family*, ed. and trans. Madame Van Muyden [1902] (London, 1995), 98; Pierre Jean de Grosley, *A Tour to London; or, New Observations on England and its Inhabitants*, trans. Thomas Nugent, 3 vols (Dublin, 1772), II, 79; Meldrum, *Domestic Service and Gender*, 69; Laura Gowing, *Domestic Dangers: Women, Words and Sex in Early Modern London* (Oxford, 1996), 98. The street has its own chroniclers: P. J. Corfield, 'Walking the City Streets: The Urban Odyssey in Eighteenth-century England', *Journal of Urban History*, 16 (1990), 132–74; Tim Hitchcock and Heather Shore (eds), *The Streets of London: From the Great Fire to the Great Stink* (London, 2003); M. J. Power, 'The Social Topography of Restoration London', in *London, 1500–1700: The Making of the Metropolis*, ed. A. L. Beier and Roger Finlay (London, 1986), 209–12.

12 The English jurist Sir Edward Coke (1552–1634) was quoted as saying 'For a man's house is his castle, *et domus sua cuique tutissimum refugium*: for where shall a man be safe, if it be not in his house?': Sir Edward Coke, *The Third Part of the Institutes of the Laws of England* (1644), 101.

13 Richard Burn, *The Justice of the Peace* [1755], 4 vols (16th edn, 1788), II, 'House', 614–15.

14 Burn, *Justice of the Peace*. See also Sir John Baker, *The Oxford History of the Laws of England, 1483–1558* (Oxford, 2003), ch. 9; Jennifer Melville, 'The Use and Organisation of Domestic Space in Late Seventeenth-century London' (PH.D thesis, Cambridge, 1999), 121–5.

15 A. Roger Ekirch, *At Day's Close: Night in Times Past* (New York, 2005), 91; Sir John Fielding, *Thieving Detected* (1777), 9; OBP, 6 April 1785, James Hayward (t17850406–25); Robert Southey, *Letters from England by Don Manuel Alvarez Espriella*, 3 vols (1807), II, 156.

16 Cynthia Wall, 'At Shakespeare's Head, Over Against Catherine Street in the Strand: Forms of Address in London Streets', in *The Streets of London*, ed. Hitchcock and Shore, 10–26.

17 Burn, *Justice of the Peace*, I, 'Burglary', 285; OBP, 20 February 1793, William Lacy (t17930220–1); OBP, 20 February 1793, Alexander Elder (t17930220–61); OBP, 25 February 1789, William Hunter (t17890225–4); Tim Hitchcock, 'You Bitches . . . Die and be Damned: Gender, Authority and the Mob in St Martin's Round House Disaster of 1742', in *The Streets of London*, ed. Hitchcock and Shore, 69; *Low Life; or, One Half of the World Knows Not How the Other Half Live* (3rd edn, 1764), 102.

18 Courts, however, could use their discretion over which offence to indict a young de-

fendant with, since burglars always received harsher sentences and fewer pardons: Peter King, *Crime, Justice and Discretion in England, 1740–1820* (Oxford, 2000), 174.

19   OBP, 15 September 1784, Sarah Hall (t17840915–77).

20   On the Poll Tax, see Craig Spence, *London in the 1690s: A Social Atlas* (London, 2000), 90. On lodgers, see S. J. Wright, 'Sojourners and Lodgers in a Provincial Town: The Evidence from Eighteenth-century Ludlow', *Urban History*, 17 (1990), 14–35; John Styles, 'Lodging at the Old Bailey: Lodgings and their Furnishing in Eighteenth-century London', in *Gender, Taste and Material Culture in Britain and North America*, ed. John Styles and Amanda Vickery (New Haven, 2006), 61–80; Margaret Ponsonby, *Stories from Home: English Domestic Interiors, 1750–1850* (Aldershot, 2007), ch. 5; Joe McEwan and Pamela Sharpe, ' "It Buys me Freedom": Genteel Lodging in Late Seventeenth and Eighteenth-century London', *Parergon*, 24 (2007), 139–61; Melville, 'Use and Organisation of Domestic Space', 19, 127.

21   John Beattie, *Policing and Punishment in London, 1660–1750: Urban Crime and the Limits of Terror* (Oxford, 2000), 20, 23, 35.

22   Melville, 'Use and Organisation of Domestic Space', 127.

23   James Peller Malcolm, *Anecdotes of the Manners and Customs of London during the Eighteenth Century* (1808), 484; Francis Grose, *The Olio* (1796), 74, 75.

24   Malcolm, *Anecdotes*, 485.

25   Locking of lodging rooms. Old Bailey cases brought under the theft from lodgings Act of 1691 (3 Will. & M., c. 9); OBP, 1750–59 and 1790–99.

	locked	unlocked	nil	all
1750s + 1790s	68	22	175	265
1750s	18	5	120	143
1790s	50	17	55	122

26   OBP, 23 February 1785, Rose Fitzpatrick (t17850223–21); OBP, 6 April 1785, Elizabeth Stubbs (t17850406–19).

27   OBP, 11 January 1753, Elizabeth Jones (t17530111–23); OBP, 17 September 1794, Ann Gunby (t17940917–98).

28   OBP, 11 July 1750, Mary Brown, James Brown (t17590711–8); OBP, 4 April 1779, Esther Marklin and Elizabeth Cox (t17790404–14).

29   OBP, 6 December 1752, Sarah, wife of Edward White (t17521206–1); OBP, 26 June 1793, John Smith Burnel (t17930626–2); OBP, 8 December 1794, Telemachus Hopefull (t17941208–16); OBP, 28 February 1759, Mary Harris (t17590228–13); OBP, 26 May 1757, Ann, wife of John Tompson (t17570526–6); OBP, 6 September 1753, Ann Humphreys (t17530906–10).

30   Melville, 'Use and Organisation of Domestic Space', 135, 223; Meldrum, *Domestic Service and Gender*, 79–80; Amanda Flather, *Gender and Space in Early Modern England* (Woodbridge, Suffolk, 2007); Rachel Garrard, 'Probate Inventories and their Use', in *Probate Inventories*, ed. Ad Van der Woude and Anton Schuurman (Utrecht, 1980). Bed sharing may even have increased over time: see Ursula Priestley and P. J. Corfield, 'Rooms and Room Use in Norwich Housing, 1580–1730', *Post Medieval Archaeology*, 16 (1982).

31   OBP, 9 April 1746, William Askew (t17460409–29); OBP, 6 April 1785, James Jones (t17850406–14); OBP, 5 September 1833, Henry Smith (t18330905–130).

32   Melville, 'Use and Organisation of Domestic Space', 115, 135, 137, 158.

33 OBP, 5 September 1833, Henry Smith (t18330905–130); OBP, 27 February 1751, Mary, the wife of Henry Pearson (t17510227–47); OBP, 11 September 1793, Daniel Macarthy (t17930911–67); OBP, 13 April 1791, William Cardwell (t17910413–31); OBP, 6 April 1785, William Harding (t17850406–27).

34 Carolyn Sargeantson, 'Looking at Furniture Inside Out', in *Furnishing the Eighteenth Century*, ed. K. Norberg and D. Goodman (Abingdon, 2007), 205–36.

35 OBP, 5 December 1810, William Britton (t18101205–34); OBP, 10 September 1823, James Clark, Gilbert Downes (t18230910–10); OBP, 17 September 1817, John Bond (t18170917–1); OBP, 16 October 1834, Jemima Fuller (t18341016–9); OBP, 1 July 1801, Catherine Ford (t18010701–77).

36 Hampshire Record Office, IM 44 10/11 (31 January 1786), Viscountess Wallingford to directors of the Bank of England, order to deliver a trunk deposited in the vaults.

37 OBP, 20 May 1795, Alice Burroughs (t17950520–34).

38 OBP, 2 May 1753, David Barkley (t17530502–28); OBP, 24 April 1754, Thomas Rose (t17540424–66); OBP, Elizabeth Ford, 15 September 1790 (t17900915–49).

39 OBP, 29 June 1785, John Godfrey (t17850629–84).

40 OBP, 21 February 1787, William Droyre (t 17870221–29).

41 Robert Latham and William Matthews (eds), *The Diary of Samuel Pepys* (London, 1972), VII, 367, 336; William Matthews (ed.), *The Diary of Dudley Ryder, 1715–1716* (London, 1939), 132.

42 Brynmor Jones Library, DDX/60/3, 1788–97: vol. 3, 1788; Ekirch, *At Day's Close*, 92–7.

43 Doncaster Archives, DD.DC.H6/1, Diana Eyre's account-book, 1749–77; Derbyshire Record Office, D 231 M/F203 (5 October 1758), M. Cole to Mary Okeover. Leases often itemised the door furniture: Hertfordshire Record Office, 71886 (March 1785), Lease of house in Harpenden to Major General Prescott.

44 David Ogborne, *The Merry Midnight Mistake; or, Comfortable Conclusion* (Chelmsford, 1765), 34.

45 The National Archives, C 114/182: Chancery Masters' Exhibits, account-book of a London ironmonger, 1684–6.

46 Joseph Bramah, *A Dissertation on the Construction of Locks* ([1785]), 2; Noel Currer-Briggs, *Contemporary Observations on the Security from the Chubb Collectanea, 1818–1968* (London, [1968?]), 1; F. J. Manning (ed.), *The Williamson Letters, 1748–1765* (Streatley, 1954), 116.

47 Melville, 'Use and Organisation of Domestic Space', 178–80, 199; Flather, *Gender and Space*, 46–7.

48 OBP, 8 April 1719, Elizabeth Batchet (t17190408–8).

49 John Wood, *An Essay towards a Description of Bath*, 2 vols (2nd edn, 1749), 298.

50 Seth Denbo, 'What's in a Pocket?', Pockets of History Symposium, Victoria and Albert Museum, 29 September 2006; Foundling Museum, London.

51 Wetenhall Wilkes, *A Letter of Genteel and Moral Advice to a Young Lady* (Dublin, 1740), 120; Lancashire Record Office, DDB/81/33A (1778), f. 15; Shropshire Record Office, 5492/1, Journals of Thomas Brocas, 1785–1815 (21 April 1786); OBP, 23 February 1785, Jane Beach (t17850223–118).

52 Manning (ed.), *Williamson Letters*, 43.

53 An Account of Lot Cavanagh, 13 April 1743, Ordinary of Newgate's Account: cited in Peter Linebaugh, *The London Hanged: Crime and Civil Society in the Eighteenth Century* (2nd edn, London, 2006), 292.

54 Wright, 'Sojourners and Lodgers in a Provincial Town', 14–35.

55 Personal communication from Stana Nenadic.

56 Museum of London, Medieval Gallery. Georgian satire, however, suggested that the possessions of the dying were rifled by nurses and watchers in the London infirmaries: *Low Life*, 96.

57 Tobias Smollett, *The Adventures of Roderick Random* [1748] (Oxford, 1999), 209.

58 Sir Frederick Morton Eden, *The State of the Poor*, 3 vols (1797), II, 329.

59 F. M. Cowe (ed.), *Wimbledon Vestry Minutes, 1736, 1743–1788*, Surrey Record Society, xxv (Guildford, 1964), 29 January 1775.

Chapter 2   Men Alone: How Bachelors Lived

1 Francis Galton, *Record of Family Faculties* (1884), 38.

2 Lincoln Cathedral Library, Diary and account-book of Matthew Flinders, 1775–84, ff. 3v, 18v, 22v, 31, 61v, 63.

3 Lincoln Cathedral Library, Flinders, ff. 63, 64, 66, 67, 68.

4 Lincolnshire Archives, 15/3/3, Diaries of Benjamin Smith, solicitor, 17 August 1817, 2 December 1817, 7 May 1818, 4 July 1819, 31 December 1819; 15/3/4, 27 November 1820.

5 For reviews of the field, see John Tosh and Michael Roper (eds), *Manful Assertions: Masculinities in Britain since 1800* (Abingdon, 1991); John Tosh, 'What Should Historians do with Masculinity? Reflections on Nineteenth-century Britain', *History Workshop Journal*, 38 (1994), 179–202; Tim Hitchcock and Michèle Cohen (eds), *English Masculinities, 1660–1800* (Harlow, 1999), 1–22; Martin Francis, 'The Domestication of the Male? Recent Research on Nineteenth- and Twentieth-century British Masculinity', *Historical Journal*, 45/3 (2002), 637–52; Alexandra Shepard and Karen Harvey, 'What Have Historians Done with Masculinity?:Reflections on Five Centuries of British History, *circa* 1500–1950', *Journal of British Studies*, 44 (2005), 274–80.

6 Shepard and Harvey, 'What Have Historians Done with Masculinity?'; Alexandra Shepard, 'From Anxious Patriarchs to Refined Gentlemen? Manhood in Britain, *circa* 1500–1700', *Journal of British Studies*, 44 (2005), 281–95, especially 285.

7 Amanda Vickery, *The Gentleman's Daughter: Women's Lives in Georgian England* (New Haven and London, 1998), 287; Jeremy Gregory, 'Homo Religiosus: Masculinity and Religion in the Long Eighteenth Century', in *English Masculinities*, ed. Hitchcock and Cohen, 85–110.

8 Margaret Hunt, 'Wife Beating, Domesticity and Women's Independence in Eighteenth-century London', *Gender and History*, 4 (1992), 10–33; Hannah Barker, 'Soul, Purse and Family: Masculinity among the Non-Elites of Eighteenth-century Provincial England', *Social History*, 33/1 (2008), 12–35; Lawrence Klein, 'Politeness for Plebes: Consumption and Social Identity in Early Eighteenth-century England', in *The Consumption of Culture, 1660–1800: Image, Object, Text*, ed. J. Brewer and A. Bermingham (London, 1995), 362–82; Philip Carter, 'James Boswell's Manliness', in *English Masculinities*, ed. Hitchcock and Cohen, 111–30.

9 *Oxford English Dictionary*, s.v. 'Domestic'.

10 Shropshire Record Office, 112/24/4/1, 1763–1806, Richard Partridge's personal diary; Herefordshire Record Office, AS 594/101 (1740), Charles Bennet of Bosbury, 'His book'; Nottinghamshire Archives, DD/1517/45, Diary of John Jowett, 1789.

11 Sara Mendelson, 'Stuart Women's Diaries and Occasional Memoirs', in *Women in English Society*, ed. Mary Prior (London, 1985), 181–201; Michael Mascuch, *The Origins of the*

Individualist Self: Autobiography and Self-Identity in England, 1591–1791 (Cambridge, 1997), ch. 4; John Locke, *A New and Easie Method of making Common-place Books* (1706); John Brewer, *Pleasures of the Imagination: English Culture in the Eighteenth Century* (London, 1997), ch. 2.

12 West Yorkshire Archive Service, Calderdale, SH 3/AB/9, Jonathan Hall of Elland.

13 Brynmor Jones Library, DOG/9/1, John Ogle's pocket diary.

14 Shropshire Record Office, D3651/B/30/7/1/1, Diary of Thomas Jeffreys, surgeon of Shrewsbury, 1797.

15 Glamorgan Record Office, D/DX 223/1, Diary of the Revd David Jones of Llangan, 1807. Equally scanty are Glamorgan Record Office, D/D c f/1–9, Diaries of John Carne, Clerk, 1762–90, and Nottinghamshire Archives, DD/SK 217/1–26, Diaries and accounts of Robert Lowe Esq., 1793–1822.

16 Herefordshire Record Office, G2/IV/J/4/1, Diary of John Biddulph, 25 December 1778; Brian Robins (ed.), *The John Marsh Journals: The Life and Times of a Gentleman Composer, 1752–1828* (Stuyvesant, NY, 1998), 128.

17 Jane Hamlett, 'Materialising Gender: Identity and Middle-Class Domestic Interiors, 1850–1910' (PH.D thesis, London, 2005), 38.

18 Margaret Ponsonby, *Stories from Home: English Domestic Interiors 1750–1850* (Aldershot, 2007), 64–7.

19 For varied contracts, see Glamorgan Record Office, D/D c f/1, Diary of John Carne, Clerk, 9 January 1762; Shropshire Record Office, D3651/B/30/7/1/1, Diary of Thomas Jeffreys, 1797.

20 See Table 1, in John Styles, 'Lodging at the Old Bailey: Lodging and their Furnishing in Eighteenth-century London', in *Gender, Taste and Material Culture in Britain and North America*, ed. Styles and Amanda Vickery (New Haven, 2006), 61–80.

21 Sarah Pennell, ' "Great Quantities of Gooseberry Pye and Baked Clod of Beef": Victualling and Eating Out in Early Modern London', in *Londinopolis: Essays in the Cultural and Social History of Early Modern London*, ed. Paul Griffiths and Mark S. R. Jenner (Manchester, 2000), 228–59; A. L. Beier, 'Engine of Manufacture: The Trades of London', in *London, 1500–1700: The Making of the Metropolis*, ed. Beier and Roger Finlay (London, 1986), 147–8; Peter Earle, 'The Female Labour Market in London in the Late Seventeenth and Early Eighteenth Centuries', *Economic History Review*, 2nd series, 42 (1989), 338–9; Clyve Jones, 'The London Life of a Peer in the Reign of Queen Anne: A Case Study from Lord Ossulston's Diary', *London Journal*, 16 (1992), 145, 148.

22 John Beresford, *Memoirs of an Eighteenth-century Footman* (London, 1928), 174; Robert Southey, *Letters from England by Don Manuel Alvarez Espriella*, 3 vols (1807), I, 67; Francis Grose, *The Olio* (1793), 207.

23 Johnson cited in M. Dorothy George, *London Life in the Eighteenth Century* (Harmondsworth, 1965), 103. On clubland, see Amy Milne-Smith, 'A Flight to Domesticity?: Making a Home in the Gentlemen's Clubs of London, 1880–1914', *Journal of British Studies*, 45 (2006), 796–818, which draws on Howard Chudacoff, *The Age of the Bachelor: Creating an American Subculture* (Princeton, 1999).

24 William Matthews (ed.), *The Diary of Dudley Ryder, 1715–1716* (London, 1939), 276, 35, 61, 196, 57.

25 *Dictionary of National Biography*, Dudley Ryder.

26 Matthews (ed.), *Diary of Dudley Ryder*, 45.

27 Ralph Houlbrooke, *English Family Life, 1576–1716* (Oxford, 1988), 47–51; Margaret Hunt, *The Middling Sort: Commerce, Gender and the Family in England, 1680–1780* (Berkeley,

CA, 1996), 4, 191, 230, 244, 222; Philip Carter, *Men and the Emergence of Polite Society in Britain, 1660–1800* (Harlow, 2001), 164–74.

28 Matthews (ed.), *Diary of Dudley Ryder*, 151, 195, 184, 131, 66, 119.

29 Matthews (ed.), *Diary of Dudley Ryder*, 133, 134, 121, 126, 152, 104, 109.

30 Matthews (ed.), *Diary of Dudley Ryder*, 203, 177, 163, 251–2, 326–7.

31 Matthews (ed.), *Diary of Dudley Ryder*, 126, 57, 85, 135, 70, 124, 117, 279.

32 Matthews (ed.), *Diary of Dudley Ryder*, 132, 166, 111, 232–3, 274, 224, 309–10, 335–6, 76, 310, 177.

33 Chester and Cheshire Record Office, DDX 597/2, Diaries of John Egerton; *Alumni Oxoniensis*.

34 Chester and Cheshire Record Office, DDX 597/2, Diaries of John Egerton, 24 March 1823, 31 March 1823, 15 June 1823, 26 March 1823, 15 June 1823, 18 May 1823, 13 June 1823, 19 July 1823, 23 July 1823, 12 June 1824, 21 June 1824, 2 April 1823, 23 October 1823, 5 May 1824, 1 April 1823.

35 Chester and Cheshire Record Office, DDX 597/2, 3 October 1823, 7 October 1823, 9 March 1824, 11 March 1824, 30 January 1824.

36 Chester and Cheshire Record Office, DDX 597/2, 23 October 1823, 24 October 1823, 9 August 1823, 19 August 1823, 14 May 1823.

37 Chester and Cheshire Record Office, DDX 597/2, 1 July 1823, 3 July 1824, 24 August 1824, 27 September 1824, 31 July 1823.

38 Chester and Cheshire Record Office, DDX 597/2, 5 April 1823, 13 June 1823, 6 May 1824, 11 May 1824, 3 December 1824.

39 Anthony Trollope, *An Autobiography* (Oxford, 1999), 22, 27.

40 Anthony Trollope, *The Small House at Allington* [1864] (Harmondsworth, 2005), 75, 159.

41 Anthony Trollope, *The Eustace Diamonds* [1873] (Harmondsworth, 1986), 156, 158, 200, 201. Greystock debated with his friend Herriot whether married men were happier than bachelors. They concluded that marriage guaranteed 'morality in life and enlarged affections' but also 'short commons and unpaid bills' (259).

42 For example, Mr Maule and his vain widower father in Anthony Trollope, *Phineas Redux* [1874] (Oxford, 1986), 187–8; Trollope, *Eustace Diamonds*, 259.

43 The excruciations of debt in genteel families are elaborated in Anthony Trollope's *Framley Parsonage* [1860] (Harmondsworth, 1985) and *Last Chronicle of Barset* [1867] (Harmondsworth, 2006).

44 Trollope, *Autobiography*, 27.

45 Anthony Trollope, 'Usurers and Clerks in Public Offices', *Pall Mall Gazette* (23 March 1865), 2.

46 Trollope, *Autobiography*, 41, 39, 35.

47 Trollope, *Autobiography*, 39, 36–7, 53.

48 Anne Hillman, *The Rake's Diary: The Journal of George Hilton* (Kendal, 1994), 13, 45, 78, 61.

49 Hillman, *Rake's Diary*, 41, 71, 44, 63, 41.

50 Hillman, *Rake's Diary*, 69, 28, 31.

51 Susan Neave and David Neave (eds), *The Diary of a Yorkshire Gentleman: John Courtney of Beverley, 1759–1768* (Otley, 2001), 48, 57, 22.

52 Neave and Neave (eds), *Diary of a Yorkshire Gentleman*, 38, 53–4, 64, 69, 72, 87–8, 119, 138.

53 Neave and Neave (eds), *Diary of a Yorkshire Gentleman*, 147–8.

54 Basil Cozens-Hardy (ed.), *The Diary of Sylas Neville, 1767–1788* (London and New York, 1950), 124, 94, 143–4, xii; Kathleen Wilson, *The Sense of the People* (Cambridge, 1995), 220.

55 Cozens-Hardy (ed.), *Diary of Sylas Neville*, 68, 116, 82, 87, 94, 7, 28, 29, 69, 70.

56   Cozens-Hardy (ed.), *Diary of Sylas Neville*, 69, 6, 7, 4, 11, 5, 71.

57   Cozens-Hardy (ed.), *Diary of Sylas Neville*, 87, 182, 126.

58   Cozens-Hardy (ed.), *Diary of Sylas Neville*, 44, 81, 88, 85–6.

59   Cozens-Hardy (ed.), *Diary of Sylas Neville*, 89, 83, 87, 94, 87, 152, 311, 312, xiv.

60   E. A. J. Johnson, *Predecessors of Adam Smith* (London, 1937), 253; *The Women's Advocate, or the Baudy Batchelor Out in his Calculation* (London, 1729), 6.

61   Samuel Richardson, *Sir Charles Grandison* [1754] (Oxford, 1986), 428.

62   Alexandra Shepard, 'Manhood, Credit and Patriarchy in Early Modern England, c. 1580–1640', *Past & Present*, 167 (2000), 82–6.

63   Cozens-Hardy (ed.), *Diary of Sylas Neville*, 85–6.

64   Brynmor Jones Library, DDX/60/3, Diaries of John Courtney, 1788–97, vol. 3, 26 June 1790.

65   Chester and Cheshire Record Office, DDX 597/4, Accounts of John Egerton, 1837; DDX 597/7, list of charities.

66   See Helen Berry and Elizabeth Foyster, 'Childless Men in Early Modern England', in their *The Family in Early Modern England* (Cambridge, 2007), 368–424; Kathleen Wilson, 'Empire, Trade and Politics in Mid-Hanoverian Britain: The Case of Admiral Vernon', *Past & Present*, 121 (1988), 74–109; Karen Harvey, *Reading Sex* (Cambridge, 2004), 111–20, 133–9.

67   Robin Reilly, *Josiah Wedgwood, 1730–1795* (London, 1992), 35.

68   Madame de Staël, *Corinna; or, Italy*, 3 vols (1807), I, 285–6.

69   Lincolnshire Archives, 15/3/3, Smith diary, preface and 2 December 1817.

70   Brynmor Jones Library, DOG8/6 (24 ?November 1779), John Ogle, Hunsigore, to Miss Furniss, Pontefract. Lincolnshire Archives, 15/3/11, Smith diary, 11 March 1850, 13 May 1850.

71   V. Knox, *Essays Moral and Literary*, 2 vols (1782), I, 325.

72   Cited in David Flaherty, *Privacy in Colonial New England* (Charlottesville, 1967), 72.

73   Cited in Marilyn Butler, *Maria Edgeworth: A Literary Biography* (Oxford, 1972), 36.

74   Gloucestershire Archives, PE 98, Autobiography of Thomas Hittingford, 1783–1855.

75   Alexandra Shepard, *Meanings of Manhood in Early Modern England* (Oxford, 2003); K. McClelland, 'Masculinity and the Representative Artisan in England, 1850–1900', in *Manful Assertions: Masculinity in Britain since 1800*, ed. M. Roper and J. Tosh (London, 1991), 83.

Chapter 3   Setting up Home

1   Jane Austen, *Northanger Abbey* [1818] (Oxford, 2003), 156–7.

2   Jane Austen, *Sense and Sensibility* [1811] (Oxford, 2004), 51–3, 146.

3   Jane Austen, *Pride and Prejudice* [1813] (Oxford, 2004), 186, 189.

4   Jane Austen, *Persuasion* [1818] (Oxford, 2004), 34, 37.

5   Austen, *Sense and Sensibility*, 22–3.

6   Jane Austen, *Mansfield Park* [1814] (Oxford, 2004), 38, 194, 332.

7   Austen, *Sense and Sensibility*, 52–3, 146, 284–5. See also Alan Savidge, *The Parsonage in England: Its History and Architecture* (London, 1964).

8   Austen, *Pride and Prejudice*, 94, 96, 121, 129, 165.

9   Austen, *Mansfield Park*, 32.

10   Austen, *Sense and Sensibility*, 271.

11   Austen, *Persuasion*, 24. And even better: 'A lady, without a family, was the very best pre-
     server of furniture in the world.'
12   Austen, *Pride and Prejudice*, 186.
13   Austen, *Northanger Abbey*, 157.
14   Lorna Weatherill (ed.), *The Account Book of Richard Latham, 1724–1767* (Oxford, 1990),
     xxvii.
15   Amanda Vickery, *The Gentleman's Daughter: Women's Lives in Georgian England* (New
     Haven and London, 1998).
16   Centre for Buckinghamshire Studies, D/X 1069/2/22 (n.d.), Ann Baker to her father
     Daniel Baker.
17   Guildhall Library, MS 11021, vol. 1, f. 65 (12 May 1747), George Gibbs, Exeter, to Ann Vic-
     ary, Bristol; f. 43 (*circa* 1747), same to same.
18   Guildhall Library, MS 11021, vol. 1, f. 73 (6 August 1747), George Gibbs, Exeter, to Ann Vic-
     ary, Bristol; f. 117 (30 June 1777), George Gibbs, Exeter, to Nanny Gibbs.
19   Coventry Archives, PA 1484/77/159 (21 July 1749), Mary Hewitt to James Hewitt; PA
     1484/77/163 (21 July 1749), James Hewitt to Joseph Hewitt.
20   Coventry Archives, PA 1484/77/163 (21 July 1749), James Hewitt to Joseph Hewitt.
21   Coventry Archives, PA 1484/77/165 (29 July 1749), Mary Hewitt, [?Coventry], to James
     Hewitt.
22   Essex Record Office, Colchester, C47, vol. 1, 75 (7 November 1770), Mary Martin to
     I. M. Rebow; 19 (13 August 1768), 58 (5 September 1770), same to same.
23   Essex Record Office, Colchester, C47, vol. 2, 221 (16 June 1772), Mary Martin to I. M.
     Rebow; vol. 3, 6 (3 March 1770), 6–7 (3 March 1770); vol. 1, 33 (8 March 1770); vol. 2, 238
     (23 June 1772); vol. 1, 217–18 (12 June 1772), same to same.
24   Essex Record Office, Colchester, C47, vol. 1, 52 (24 August 1770), Mary Martin to I. M.
     Rebow; vol. 1, 41 (30 June 1770); vol. 3, 16 (19 July 1770), same to same.
25   Essex Record Office, Colchester, C47, vol. 1, 42 (30 June 1770), Mary Martin to I. M.
     Rebow; vol. 2, 223 (16 June 1772), 237 (23 June 1772), same to same.
26   Essex Record Office, Colchester, C47, vol. 2, 286 (12 July 1778), Mary Rebow to I. M. Rebow;
     vol. 2, 325 and 273 (10 July 1778), 277 (12 July 1778), 299 (26 July 1778), same to same.
27   Huntington Library, MO 4828, Matthew Robinson-Morris, 2nd Baron Rookery, to
     Elizabeth Robinson.
28   Keele University Library, W/M 28 (1790, Sunday), Josiah Wedgwood, Greek Street.
29   J. Wedgwood and T. Bentley, *A Catalogue of Cameos, Intaglios, Medals, Busts, Small Stat-
     ues, and Bas-reliefs* (2nd edn, 1774), 3. See Neil McKendrick, 'Josiah Wedgwood and the
     Commercialisation of the Potteries', in McKendrick, John Brewer and J. H. Plumb, *The
     Birth of a Consumer Society: The Commercialization of Eighteenth-century England* (Lon-
     don, 1983), 100–45.
30   Eliza Meteyard, *The Life of Josiah Wedgwood*, 2 vols (London, 1865–6), II, 156; Robin
     Reilly, *Josiah Wedgwood, 1730–1795* (London, 1992), 168; Johanna Dahn, 'Active, Social
     and Temperate: A Construction of Taste with Special Reference to Katherine Plymley
     (1758–1829)' (PH.D thesis, Aberystwyth, 2000), ch. 8.
31   Letters quoted in Reilly, *Life of Josiah Wedgwood*, 37, 172–4, 336.
32   Keele University Library, W/M 31 (10 December, 16 November, 15 December, 22 Novem-
     ber, 6 December 1792), Josiah Wedgwood, Etruria and Ludlow, to Elizabeth Allen.
33   Diana O'Hara, *Courtship and Constraint: Rethinking the Making of Marriage in Tudor
     England* (Manchester, 2000); Ingrid Tague, *Women of Quality: Accepting and Contesting
     Ideals of Femininity in England, 1690–1760* (Woodbridge, Suffolk, 2002), 149; Lady

Llanover (ed.), *The Autobiography and Correspondence of Mary Granville, Mrs Delany*, 1st series, 3 vols (London, 1861), 2nd series, 3 vols (London, 1862), 1st series, I, 100–1; II, 211; Lincolnshire Archives, and 5/2/14–21, Burton of Hotham to Dorothy Anderson.

34 Norfolk Record Office, WKC 7/21/14 (1 May 1708), Katherine Windham to Mr Windham, Folbrige [Felbrigg]; Brynmor Jones Library, DDBM/32/7 (24 May 1764), Thomas Wentworth, London, to Diana Bosville; Gloucestershire Archives, D 1799/C11 (5 November 1749), Sophia Blathwayte, Englefield, to William Blathwayte Esq., Dyrham.

35 Robert Lloyd, 'The Cit's Country Box', *The Connoisseur*, 135 (26 August 1756), 233–8.

36 Tobias Smollett, *The Expedition of Humphry Clinker* [1771] (Oxford, 1984), 285–96.

37 C. Bruyn Andrews (ed.), *The Torrington Diaries*, 4 vols (London, 1934), I, 24, 69, 70,

38 Sarah, Lady Cowper's diary, vol. 3, 1706, 215; vol. 1, 1701, 162. See Anne Kugler, *Errant Plagiary: The Life and Writing of Lady Sarah Cowper 1644–1720* (Stanford, CA, 2002).

39 Alice Clark (ed.), *Gleanings from an Old Portfolio*, 3 vols (Edinburgh, 1895–8), II, 39–40.

40 George Savile, *The Lady's New Year Gift* (1688), 74.

41 Austen, *Mansfield Park*, 37.

Chapter 4   His and Hers: Accounting for the Household

1 Charles Jenner, *Town Eclogues* (2nd edn, 1773).

2 Anon., *The Art of Governing a Wife* (1747), 29: 'it is the Husband's Duty to furnish Money, and the wives to govern the Family'. Elizabeth Heyrick, *An Appeal to the Hearts and Consciences of British Women* (Leicester, 1828), 4, 6; Margot Finn, 'Women, Consumption and Couverture in England, c.1760–1860', *Historical Journal*, 39/3 (1996), 703–22.

3 Margot Finn, 'Men's Things: Masculine Consumption in the Consumer Revolution', *Social History*, 25 (2000), 133–55.

4 See D. Kuchta, *The Three Piece Suit and Modern Masculinity: England, 1550–1850* (Berkeley, CA, 2002); C. Breward, *The Hidden Consumer: Masculinities, Fashion and City Life, 1860–1914* (Manchester, 1999); and C. Horwood, *Keeping Up Appearances: Fashion and Class Between the Wars* (Stroud, 2005).

5 Jan de Vries, 'Between Purchasing Power and the World of Goods: Understanding the Household Economy in Early Modern Europe', in *Consumption and the World of Goods: Consumption and Society in the Seventeenth and Eighteenth Centuries*, ed. J. Brewer and R. Porter (London, 1993), 118.

6 S. Pollard, *The Genesis of Modern Management: A Study of the Industrial Revolution in Great Britain* (Cambridge, MA, 1965), 209–49.

7 This is a quote from *Advice to the Women and Maidens of London* (1678), 2. See especially J. Hoppit, *Risk and Failure in English Business, 1700–1800* (Cambridge, 1987).

8 M. Hunt, *The Middling Sort: Commerce, Gender and Family in England, 1680–1780* (Berkeley, CA, 1996), 58; Pollard, *Genesis of Modern Management*, 216.

9 John Dod and Robert Cleaver, *A Godly Forme of Household Government for the Ordering of Private Families* (1612), 168; Richard Steele, *Ladies Library, Written by a Lady*, 3 vols (1714), II, 389.

10 West Sussex Record Office, MS 102 (n.d.), Duchess of Richmond, Goodwood, to the duke, n.d.; Harriet Sampson (ed.), *The Life of Mrs Godolphin* (London and New York, 1939), 227; Frances Harris, *Transformations of Love* (Oxford, 2002), 66–7; British Library, Add. MS 78295, 148 (7 February 1673), George Evelyn to Mary Evelyn, Wootton Surrey; 149 (20 February 1673), same to same.

11 Hampshire Record Office, 44 M69/F10/8/1 (17 October 1798), Eliza Jervoise, Herriard House, to Lieut. Col. Jervoise, Yarmouth; 44 M69/F9/3/3 (1 November 1799), George Purefoy Jervoise, Isle of Wight, to Revd H. Jervoise, Shalstone; 44 M69/F10/8/2 (1 July 1799), Eliza Jervoise, Preston, to Lieut. Col. Jervoise, Isle of Wight; 44 M69/F10/8/4 (8 September 1801), same to same.

12 British Library, Add. MS 62092, Account-book for personal expenses of Margaret Spencer, with her father's notes throughout as auditor.

13 British Library, Add. MS 45208; Add. MS 45204; Add. MS 45210: Anne Brockman's household accounts. See July 1719, f. 59. On William Brockman, see E. Cruikshanks, S. Handley and D. W. Hayton, *The History of Parliament: The House of Commons, 1690–1715* (Cambridge, 2001), 332–5.

14 L. Alcott, *Little Women* [1868] (Harmondsworth, 1989), 282–3, also 280–81.

15 S. P. Walker, 'How to Secure Your Husband's Esteem: Accounting and Private Patriarchy in the British Middle Class Household during the Nineteenth Century', *Accounting, Organizations and Society*, 23/516 (1998), 485–516. Beverly Lemire argues that quantitative thought triumphed over older conceptions of household management by the nineteenth century. See Lemire, *The Business of Everyday Life: Gender, Practice and Social Politics in England, c.1600–1900* (Manchester, 2005), ch. 6.

16 J. Pahl, *Money and Marriage* (Basingstoke, 1989), 67.

17 Leicestershire Record Office, DE 1184/10 (1816?), B. F., Lincoln to William Pratt, Kegworth.

18 Wiltshire Record Office, 1553/69, Personal account-book of William Hunt, 1728–41; British Library, Add. MS 45213, William Brockman, Accompts, 1696–1742.

19 *Lord Chesterfield's Letters to His Son* [1774] (Oxford, 1992), 132–3.

20 P. Cline Cohen, 'Reckoning with Commerce: Numeracy in Eighteenth-century America', in *Consumption and the World of Goods*, ed. Brewer and Porter, 320–34; D. Defoe, *The Complete English Tradesman* (1727), i, Supplement, 31.

21 Sir John Hynde Cotton, a prominent Tory politician who repeatedly sat for the county and borough and was one of the last active English Jacobites; he died in 1752. His son and namesake John Hynde Cotton left the accounts upon which this study is based. In 1791 financial difficulties forced him to transfer control of his lands to his eldest surviving son, Charles, from 1799 an admiral and knight.

22 Cambridgeshire Record Office, 588 DR/A 38, Account-book of Sir John Hynde Cotton, 1760–67.

23 Household accounts of Abraham Grimes, Esq., of Coton House, Warwickshire, 1781–8. Private Collection.

24 In December 1788 Mrs Grimes paid for £5 worth of shirt fabric for her husband, cambric for ruffles and muslin for nine neckcloths. Other rare references to Mrs Grimes's own consumption in the miscellaneous account include dress silk, white calico for curtains, washing bills, toys and sewing equipment, as well as furniture.

25 Chester and Cheshire Record Office, DAR/B/14, Household and personal accounts of Sarah Arderne, 1741–52.

26 It was the shoe bill that tormented the Latham family of Lancashire smallholders when their children were young; see John Styles, *The Dress of the People: Everyday Fashion in Eighteenth-century England* (New Haven, 2007), 233–5.

27 An earlier account-book of the Cottons confirms the disproportionate cost of nursery washing: Cambridgeshire Record Office, 588 DR/A 33, Account-book of Sir John Hynde Cotton, 1756–8. The house washing bill for 29 May to 6 June 1757 was £1 2s. 0d., while the washing bill for the nursery was four times that amount: £4 18s. 0d.

28 Diaper is an unbleached linen with a diamond pattern on it, from which we get the term 'diapers'.

29 Chester and Cheshire Record Office, DAR/C/20, Vouchers to account, Harden Hall, 1744–5.

30 Chester and Cheshire Record Office, DAR/I/21, The Booke of Accounts, Harden Estate, 1726–52, records the gifts of money that John Arderne senior gave to his son. Sarah and John seem to have lived as permanent guests within the household of Mr Arderne senior, for there is no evidence of basic household provisioning, though they did pay their own servants.

31 Of that, children's clothes amounted to £39.

32 R. Campbell, *The London Tradesman* [1747] (New York, 1969), 207.

33 C. Bruyn Andrews (ed.), *The Torrington Diaries*, 4 vols (London, 1934), I, 91–2.

34 See Cambridgeshire Record Office, 588 DR/A 26, Personal account-book of Sir John Hynde Cotton, unfoliated. See entries for 1745.

35 Even conservative writers imagined that ladies would supervise the plain sewing of others: J. Gregory, *A Father's Legacy to His Daughter* (1774), 2.

36 C. H. Beale (ed.), *Reminiscences of a Gentlewoman of the Last Century: Letters of Catherine Hutton* (Birmingham, 1891), 7.

37 Lancashire Record Office, DDGr C3 (3 March 1788), Thomas Greene, Gray's Inn, to P. Bradley, Slyne; DDB/72/306–7 (1777), E. Shackleton, Alkincoats, to J. and R. Parker, London.

38 Brynmor Jones Library, DOG/8 (12 June 1799), John Ogle, Doncaster, to Mrs Ogle.

39 Coventry Archives, PA 1484/77/163, James Hewitt to Joseph Hewitt, Coventry; National Archives of Scotland, GD 18/4847 (1 February 1758), James Adam, London, to Helen Adam; Dorset Record Office, D/BKL H Hg (1 November 1803), W. J. Bankes, Trinity College, to Margaret Bankes, Westminster; (17 November 1803), same to same.

40 Anne Kugler, *Errant Plagiary: The Life and Writing of Lady Sarah Cowper, 1644–1720* (Stanford, CA, 2002), 55

41 Mark Overton et al., *Production and Consumption in English Households, 1600–1750* (London and New York, 2004), 108–11.

42 M. Evans, *Letters of Richard Radcliffe and John James* (Oxford, 1888), 26.

43 On the loathsomeness of laundry, see Caroline Davidson, *Woman's Work is Never Done: History of Housework in the British Isles, 1650–1950* (London, 1982), 136–63.

44 Campbell, *The London Tradesman*, 197.

45 Campbell, *The London Tradesman*, 227. The mantua maker 'must be a sister to the Tailor and like him, must be a perfect Connoisseur of Dress and fashion'.

46 Campbell, *The London Tradesman*, 192.

47 Breward, *Hidden Consumer*, 106–7, 162–5; Horwood, *Keeping Up Appearances*, 77–82. B. Lancaster, *The Department Store: A Social History* (London and New York, 1995).

48 A. Buck, *Dress in Eighteenth-century England* (London, 1979), 52; Campbell, *The London Tradesman*, 207.

49 In one month, Arderne purchased 'one best hunting bridle, one new collar & flap lettered for dog, a backband & links, norzels & straps, mussil & aeany, one collar & two rains, one crupper, one best bridle, one headstall for a martingale, new penneling a saddle, leather & making saddle cloth, mending sirginle & saddle, One curry comb, one strong night collar, two illicit leathers to a martingale, one strap to a rowler, one new 4 strap rowler, three straps to a rowler, mending a rowler, one strap to Cupples & mending a girth, one new pad for behind a sale lined'.

50 *A General Description of All Trades* (1747), 119: 'HORSE-MILLINERS are a sort of Iron-mongers, who chiefly deal in all sorts of Tackling for the Sadlers and Collar-makers Use.'

51 An upholder provided an all-inclusive interior decoration and furnishing service, with an even broader remit than an interior designer today.

52 British Library, Add. MS 48218, f. 125 (14 December 1772), Thomas Robinson, Madrid, Spain, to Theresa Parker; Brian Connell, *Portrait of a Whig Peer: Compiled from the Papers of the Second Viscount Palmerston, 1739–1802* (London, 1957), 346.

53 Birmingham City Archives, MS 3782/16/1, 40 (*circa* March 1776), Matthew Boulton, London, to Nanny Boulton.

54 Lorna Weatherill, *Consumer Behaviour and Material Culture in Britain, 1660–1760* (London, 1988).

55 Jane Collier, *The Art of Ingeniously Tormenting* [1753] (Bristol, 1994), 97–8.

56 Lady Llanover (ed.), *The Autobiography and Correspondence of Mary Granville, Mrs Delany*, 1st series, 3 vols (London, 1861), 2nd series, 3 vols (London, 1862), 1st series, III, 530.

57 *The Housekeeping Book of Susanna Whatman, 1776–1800* (London, 1992), 54.

58 The four most common systems are female management of the couple's entire wage, female management of a housekeeping allowance, joint-pooling and joint management, and independent management arrangements: Pahl, *Money and Marriage*, passim. See also C. Vogler, 'Labour Market Change and Patterns of Financial Allocation within Households', Economic and Social Research Council, *Working Paper*, 12.

59 Daniel Miller, *A Theory of Shopping* (Ithaca, NY, 1998), passim.

60 Claire Walsh, 'Shops, Shopping, Gender and the Art of Decision-Making in Early-Modern England', in *Gender, Taste and Material Culture in Britain and North America*, ed. John Styles and Amanda Vickery (New Haven, 2006), 158.

61 Lord Chesterfield's Letters to His Son, 132.

Chapter 5   Rooms at the Top

1 Dorset Record Office, D/BKL H HG (22 August 1811), W. J. Bankes, Kingston Hall, to Margaret Bankes, Westminster; (22 August 1811), same to same.

2 G. E. Mingay, *English Landed Society in the Eighteenth Century* (London, 1963), 20, 21, 26.

3 Richard Wilson and Alan Mackley, *Creating Paradise: The Building of the English Country House, 1660–1880* (London and New York, 2000), 15.

4 I owe this point to Clarissa Campbell Orr.

5 Charles Saumarez Smith, *Eighteenth-century Decoration: Design and the Domestic Interior in England* (London, 1993), 233; John Cornforth, *Early Georgian Interiors* (New Haven and London, 2004), 206.

6 Nicholas Cooper, *Houses of the Gentry, 1480–1680* (New Haven and London, 1999), 33; Anne Laurence, *Women in England, 1500–1760* (London, 1994), 152–4; Molly McClain, *Beaufort: The Duke and His Duchess, 1657–1715* (New Haven, 2001); Rosemary Baird, *Mistress of the House: Great Ladies and Grand Houses* (London, 2004); Julius Bryant, *Mrs Howard: A Woman of Reason, 1688–1727* (London, 1988).

7 The National Archives, C 108/362, London Building Book; Anne Laurence, 'Women Using Building in Seventeenth-century England: A Question of Sources', *Transactions of the Royal Historical Society*, 13 (2003), 293–303.

8 Baird, *Mistress of the House*, 3–4; Kate Retford, 'Patrilineal Portraiture? Gender and Genealogy in the Eighteenth-century Country House', in *Gender, Taste and Material Culture in Britain and North America*, ed. John Styles and Amanda Vickery (New Haven, 2006), 315–44; Alison D. Wall, 'Elizabethan Precept and Feminine Practice: The Thynne Family of Longleat', *History*, 75 (1990), 23–38.

9   Trevor Lummis and Jan Marsh, *The Woman's Domain: Women and the English Country House* (London, 1990), 70–72.

10 Arthur Young, *A Six Week's Tour* (Dublin, 1768), 3.

11 W. S. Lewis (ed.), *Horace Walpole's Correspondence* (London, 1937–), XXXVII, 566.

12 L. Stone and J. Fawtier Stone, *An Open Elite? England, 1540–1880* (Oxford, 1986), 73; J. Cannon, *Aristocratic Century: The Peerage in Eighteenth Century England* (Cambridge, 1987), 137.

13 L. Colley, 'The Female Political Elite in Unreformed Britain' (unpublished paper, Institute of Historical Research, 25 June 1993); Judith Lewis, *Sacred to Female Patriotism: Gender, Class and Politics in Late Georgian Britain* (New York, 2003); Elaine Chalus, *Elite Women in English Political Life, 1754–1790* (Oxford, 2005); Linda Colley, 'The Power Behind the Patronage: The Female Elite of Eighteenth and Nineteenth-century Britain', paper presented at *The Lady Patrons: Women, Culture and Patronage in Britain, 1700–1875*, Victoria and Albert Museum Symposium, 16 July 1994.

14 Wilson and Mackley, *Creating Paradise*, 199–232; C. Saumarez Smith, 'Supply and Demand in English Country House Building, 1660–1740', *Oxford Art Journal*, 11 (1988), 539–87; J. Summerson, 'The Classical Country House in Eighteenth-century England', *Journal of Royal Society of Arts*, 107 (1959), 539–87.

15 Charles Saumarez Smith, *The Building of Castle Howard* (London, 1990); Cornforth, *Early Georgian Interiors*, 150–68; Christopher Christie, *The British Country House in the Eighteenth Century* (Manchester, 2000), 26–97; Linda Colley, 'The English Rococo: Historical Background' and Gervase Jackson Stops, 'Rococo Architecture and Interiors', in *Rococo: Art and Design in Hogarth's England* (London, 1984), 12, 190; B. Wragg, *The Life and Works of John Carr of York* (York, 2000); Carole Fry, 'Spanning the Political Divide: Neo-Palladianism and the Early Eighteenth-century Landscape', *Garden History*, 31/2 (2003), 181.

16 J. Summerson, *Architecture in Britain, 1530–1830* [1953] (Hardmondsworth, 1970), 372–6; B. S. Allen, *Tides in English Taste (1619–1800)*, 2 vols (New York, 1958), II, 40.

17 Helen Clifford, *Silver in London: The Parker and Wakelin Partnership, 1760–1776* (New Haven and London, 2004), 130, 132.

18 Baird, *Mistress of the House*, 6; Stone and Fawtier Stone, *An Open Elite?*, 83; Sarah Dunster, 'Women of the Nottinghamshire Elite, c.1720–1820' (PH.D thesis, Nottingham, 2003), ch. 7; Jane Austen, *Mansfield Park* [1814] (Oxford, 2003), 72.

19 Laurence, *Women in England*, 154; Cornforth, *Early Georgian Interiors*, 217.

20 R. W. Ketton-Cremer, *Felbrigg: The Story of a House* (Ipswich, 1962), 83, 87, 102; *Felbrigg Hall* (London, 1993), 43; Norfolk Record Office, WKC 7/21/14 (5 May 1708), Katherine Windham, Soho house, to Mr Windham, Folbrige; (1 May 1708), same to same.

21 Hannah Greig, 'Leading the Fashion: The Material Culture of London's Beau Monde', in *Gender, Taste and Material Culture*, ed. Styles and Vickery, 293–313; Julie Schlarman, 'The Social Geography of Grosvenor Square: Mapping Gender and Politics, 1720–1760', *London Journal*, 28 (2003), 8–28.

22 Isaac Ware, *A Complete Body of Architecture*, 2 vols (1756), 423.

23 Mark Girouard, *Life in the English Country House* [1978] (Harmondsworth, 1980), 181–212; W. S. Lewis (ed.), *A Selection of the Letters of Horace Walpole*, 2 vols (Oxford, 1926), I, 92; *Walpole's Correspondence*, XXXVII, 438. Baird, *Mistress of the House*, 132–54.

24 M. H. Port, 'West End Palaces: The Aristocratic Town House in London, 1730–1830', *London Journal*, 20 (1995), 17–46; Christopher Sykes, *Private Palaces: Life in the Great London Houses* (London, 1985); John Summerson, *Georgian London* [1945] (London, 1988); Roy Porter, *London: A Social History* (London, 1994).

25 Port, 'West End Palaces', 25; Baird, *Mistress of the House*, 17–18.

26 Ware, *A Complete Body of Architecture*, 469; Thomas Sheraton, *The Cabinet Dictionary* (1803), 194, 201, 217–18.

27 E. P. Thompson, 'Patrician Society, Plebeian Culture', *Journal of Social History* (1974), 382–405.

28 *Walpole's Correspondence*, XXXIV, 240–41.

29 Suffolk Record Office, HA 513/4/72 (20 December 1764), Duchess of Grafton to the Duke of Grafton; HA 513/4/53 (6 November 1764), same to same.

30 Suffolk Record Office, HA 513/4/53 (6 November 1764), Duchess of Grafton to the Duke of Grafton; HA 513/4/51 (n.d.), same to same.

31 Suffolk Record Office, HA 513/4/68 (10 December 1764), Duchess of Grafton to Duke of Grafton; HA 513/4/54 (11 November 1764), Duchess of Grafton, Eslington, to Duke of Grafton, Euston.

32 Suffolk Record Office, HA 513/4/68 (10 December 1764), Duchess of Grafton to Duke of Grafton; HA 513/4/64 (4 December 1764), same to same.

33 Huntington Library, MO 977 (July 1740), William Freind to Elizabeth Robinson; William Darrell, *The Gentleman Instructed in the Conduct of a Virtuous and Happy Life* (6th edn, 1716), 17.

34 Lady Llanover (ed.), *The Autobiography and Correspondence of Mary Granville, Mrs Delany*, 1st series, 3 vols (London, 1861), 2nd series, 3 vols (London, 1862), 1st series, I, 204.

35 Suffolk Record Office, HA 513/4/57 (27 November 1764), Duchess of Grafton, Eslington, to Duke of Grafton.

36 Suffolk Record Office, HA 513/4/61 (29 November 1764), H. S. Conway, London, to the Duke of Grafton.

37 *Town and Country Magazine*, 1 (1769), 115; Suffolk Record Office, HA 513/4/70 (15 December 1764), Duke of Grafton, Wakefield Lodge, to the Duchess of Grafton.

38 *Walpole's Correspondence*, XXXVIII, 473.

39 Greig, 'Leading the Fashion', 303–8; Baird, *Mistress of the House*, 8.

40 Suffolk Record Office, HA 513/4/64 (4 December 1764), Duchess of Grafton, Newton, to Duke of Grafton.

41 Suffolk Record Office, HA 513/4/63 (1 December 1764), Duke of Grafton to [H. S. Conway]; HA 513/4/67 (7 December 1764), same to same.

42 Ingrid Tague, *Women of Quality: Accepting and Contesting Ideals of Femininity in England, 1690–1760* (Woodbridge, Suffolk, 2002), 100, 104.

43 Suffolk Record Office, HA 513/4/57 (27 November 1764), Duchess of Grafton to the Duke of Grafton; HA 513/4/55 (22 November 1764); HA 513/4/67 (7 December 1764), same to same.

44 Suffolk Record Office, HA 513/4/71 (18 December 1764), Duchess of Grafton to the Duke of Grafton; HA 513/4/54 (n.d.); HA 513/4/73 (21 December 1764), same to same.

45 J. A. Home (ed.), *The Letters and Journals of Lady Mary Coke*, 4 vols (Edinburgh, 1889–96), I, 109, 110, 233. See also 134, 165, 174, 190, 205, 206, 229.

46 Suffolk Record Office, HA 513/4/8 (9 September 1768), T. Nuthall to the Duke of Grafton; HA 513/4/89 (14 September 1768); HA 513/4/95 (14 March 1769), same to same; HA 513/4/94 (9 March 1769), Duchess of Grafton, Coombe House, to the Duke of Grafton.

47 Home (ed.), *Letters and Journals of Lady Mary Coke*, III, 52, 58, 110, 140–41, 436. The Duke of Grafton's remarriage was also a surprise, but a union with the serially adulterous prime minister was seen as a great coup for the young bride Lady Mary Wrottesley (ibid., 72).

48 John Ingamells and John Edgecumbe (eds), *The Letters of Sir Joshua Reynolds* (New Haven, 2000), 214–15, 279.

49 Aristotle, *The Ethics of Aristotle: The Nichomachean Ethics*, ed. and trans. J. A. K. Thomson (London, 1953), 99–100; Cooper, *Houses of the Gentry*, 13, 319–22.

50 Michèle Cohen, 'The Grand Tour: Constructing the English Gentleman in Eighteenth-century France', *History of Education*, 21 (1992), 249–50; Wilson and Mackley, *Creating Paradise*, 70; John Towner, 'The Grand Tour: A Key Phase in the History of Tourism', *Annals of Tourism Research*, 12 (1985), 297–333; Colin Platt, *The Great Rebuildings of Tudor and Stuart England: Revolutions in Architectural Taste* (London, 1994), 142.

51 *An Essay on Taste in General* (1731), 55.

52 H. Walpole, *Anecdotes of Painting in England*, 4 vols (3rd edn, 1782), IV, 4; F. Childs, 'Prescriptions for Manners in English Courtesy Literature, 1690–1760' (D.Phil. thesis, Oxford, 1984), 136–7.

53 Jeremy Collier, *Essays upon Several Moral Subjects* (6th edn, 1722), 107.

54 *Walpole's Correspondence*, XXII, 275.

55 Bowood Archives, loose paper, Lady Shelburne's unfinished story of her engagement in 1764.

56 See Shelburne, in *Oxford Dictionary of National Biography*.

57 Maria Perry, *The House in Berkeley Square: A History of the Lansdowne Club* (London, 2003), 64.

58 Cited in Wilson and Mackley, *Creating Paradise*, 102; Home (ed.), *Letters and Journals of Lady Mary Coke*, I, 237.

59 Bowood Archives, Lady Shelburne's diaries, vol. 3 (1766), ff. 135–6; vol. 4 (1768), f. 167; vol. 3 (1766), f. 131; vol. 4 (1768), f. 89.

60 West Sussex Record Office, Acc 8285 4/18 (1783), Hester Hoare, Stourhead, to Harriet Bishop, Parham: 'I have enjoy'd the tranquillity and *snugitude* of our little society excessively.'

61 This was Elizabeth Montagu's verdict on one of her visits to Bulstrode when it was full of guests. Huntington Library, MO 5543 (20 August 1740), Elizabeth Robinson, Bulstrode, to Sarah Robinson.

62 Peter Thornton, *Seventeenth-century Interior Decoration in England, France and Holland* (New Haven, 1978), 296–9; Cornforth, *Early Georgian Interiors*, 209.

63 Bowood Archives, Lady Shelburne's diaries, vol. 2 (1765), ff. 20, 110.

64 Huntington Library, MO 5846 (8 January 1767), Elizabeth Montagu to Sarah Scott.

65 Bowood Archives, Lady Shelburne's diaries, vol. 3 (1766), f. 102; vol. 4 (1768), f. 121; vol. 3 (1767), ff. 153–4; vol. 4 (1768), f. 313.

66 Perry, *The House in Berkeley Square*, 32.

67 Jill Shefrin, 'Governesses to their Children: Royal and Aristocratic Mothers Educating Daughters in the Reign of George III', in *Childhood and Children's Books in Early Modern Europe, 1550–1800*, ed. Andrea Immel and Michael Witmore (London, 2006); Clarissa Campbell Orr, 'Aristocratic Feminisms and the Learned Governess', in *Women, Gender and Enlightenment*, ed. Sarah Knott and Barbara Taylor (Basingstoke, 2005), 315.

68 Bowood Archives, Lady Shelburne's diaries, vol. 2 (1765), ff. 54, 56; vol. 3 (1766), f. 10; vol. 3 (1767), f. 205; vol. 4 (1769), f. 263; vol. 2 (1765), f. 82. On botany, see Ann B. Shteir, *Cultivating Women, Cultivating Science: Flora's Daughters and Botany in England, 1760–1860* (Baltimore, 1996), ch. 2.

69 Bowood Archives, Lady Shelburne's diaries, vol. 2 (1765), ff. 44, 109; vol. 3 (1767), f. 237; vol. 4 (1768), f. 175.

70   Irene Q. Brown, 'Domesticity, Feminism and Friendship: Female Aristocratic Culture and Marriage in England, 1660–1760', *Journal of Family History*, 7/4 (1982), 406–22; Clarissa Campbell Orr, 'The Late Hanoverian Court and the Christian Enlightenment', in *Monarchy and Religion*, ed. Michael Schaich (Oxford, 2007), 317–42.

71   Bowood Archives, Lady Shelburne's diaries, vol. 3 (1767), f. 225; vol. 2 (1765), f. 72.

72   Bowood Archives, Lady Shelburne's account-book, August–October 1770.

73   Bowood Archives, Lady Shelburne's diaries, vol. 3 (1766), f. 1; vol. 1 (1765), ff. 10, 13, 15, 16.

74   Lord Edmond Fitzmaurice, *Life of William, Earl of Shelburne*, 2 vols (London, 1875–6), I, 5, 11, 13.

75   *Oxford Dictionary of National Biography*, s.v. Shelburne; Eileen Harris, *The Genius of Robert Adam: His Interiors* (New Haven, 2001), 105.

76   Bowood Archives, Lady Shelburne's diaries, vol. 3 (1766), f. 243.

77   Birmingham City Archives, MS 3782/16/1, 38 (6 March 177?), Matthew Boulton, London, to Ann Boulton.

78   Cornforth, *Early Georgian Interiors*, 206–7.

79   Bowood Archives, Lady Shelburne's diaries, vol. 2 (1765), f. 111; vol. 4 (1769), f. 205; vol. 3 (1766), f. 102; vol. 4 (1768), f. 121.

80   Colin Cunningham, 'An Italian House is My Lady: Some Aspects of the Definition of Women's Role in the Architecture of Robert Adam', in *Femininity and Masculinity in Eighteenth-century Art and Culture*, ed. Gill Perry and Michael Rossington (Manchester, 1994), 75.

81   Wilson and Mackley, *Creating Paradise*, 232; Cornforth, *Early Georgian Interiors*, 8.

82   Wiltshire Record Office, 1300/1283 (17 March 1710), Lady Bruce, Henley Park, to Lord Bruce, London; 1300/1298 (*circa* 1710), same to same.

83   Wiltshire Record Office, 1300/1554 (1781), Lady Ailesbury, re painting and alterations to house in Fulham.

84   Brian Fitzgerald (ed.), *Correspondence of Emily, Duchess of Leinster (1731–1814)*, 3 vols (Dublin, 1949–57), I, 83.

85   Lady Llanover (ed.), *Mrs Delany*, 1st series, II, 319.

86   London Metropolitan Archives, B/TRL/09, f. 303.

87   Doncaster Archives, DD/BW/A, Household account-book, 1743–9; Isabella Wrightson's account-book, 1743 (see entries for 17 November 1743).

88   Wetenhall Wilkes, *A Letter of Genteel and Moral Advice to a Young Lady* (Dublin, 1740), 120; Hester Chapone, *Letters on the Improvement of the Mind*, 2 vols (1835), 93; Lady Sarah Pennington, *An Unfortunate Mother's Advice to Her Absent Daughters* (2nd edn, 1761), 27.

89   Richard Steele, *Ladies Library, Written by a Lady*, 3 vols (1714), II, 385–7.

90   Bowood Archives, Lady Shelburne's diaries, vol. 3 (1766), f. 329

91   Huntington Library, MO 5592 (1740/41), Elizabeth Robinson to Sarah Robinson.

92   Eliza Haywood, *The Female Spectator* [1744–6], 4 vols (1748), III, 154.

93   McClain, *Beaufort*, 117; Ruth M. Larsen, 'Dynastic Domesticity: The Role of Elite Women in the Yorkshire Country House, 1685–1858' (PH.D thesis, York, 2003), ch. 1; Dunster, 'Women of the Nottinghamshire Elite', ch. 4, Lummis and Marsh, *The Woman's Domain*, passim, and Baird, *Mistress of the House*, passim; Tague, *Women of Quality*, 97–132; Jane Austen, *Pride and Prejudice* [1813] (Oxford, 2004), 126, 130; John Fowler and John Cornforth, *English Decoration in the Eighteenth Century* (London, 1974), 255.

94   Lewis Walpole Library, LWL MSS vol. 7, Mary Walpole, Recipes, 1673–1676; Christopher

Ridgeway, 'Isabella, Fourth Countess of Carlisle: No Life by Halves', in *Maids and Mistresses*, ed. Ruth Larsen (York, 2004), 42.

95 Larsen, 'Dynastic Domesticity', 40, 54, 63.

96 Lewis, *Sacred to Female Patriotism*, 100; Huntington Library, MO 4723 (10 August 1742), Elizabeth Montagu, Dover Street, to Mrs Robinson; Tague, *Women of Quality*, 149–50.

97 Chapone, *Letters*, 92.

98 Huntington Library, MO 5596 (1740/41), Elizabeth Robinson, London, to Sarah Robinson.

99 Dunster, 'Women of the Nottinghamshire Elite', ch. 7; Naomi Tadmor, 'Dimensions of Inequality among Siblings in Eighteenth-century English Novels: The Cases of Clarissa and The History of Miss Betsey Thoughtless', *Continuity and Change*, 7/3 (1992), 303–33.

100 Cecil Aspinall-Oglander (ed.), *Admiral's Wife: Being the Life and Letters of the Hon. Mrs Edward Boscawen from 1719 to 1761* (London, 1940), 105.

101 William Shenstone, *Ode to Rural Elegance* (1750), 10–11.

102 Mark Girouard, 'Castle Ward, County Down', *Country Life* (23 and 30 November 1961); Cornforth, *Early Georgian Interiors*, 206.

103 Akiko Shimbo, 'Pattern Books, Showrooms and Furniture Design: Interactions between Producers and Consumers in England, 1754–1851' (ph.D thesis, London, 2007), 211–54; Clifford, *Silver in London*, 52.

104 Anthony Trollope, *The Duke's Children* [1880] (Oxford, 1983), 567.

105 For example, in silverwares, the 'fashion' of the finish on Sheffield plate came to be valued above the intrinsic value of the metal. See Helen Clifford, 'A Commerce with Things: The Value of Precious Metalwork in Early Modern England', in *Consumers and Luxury: Consumer Culture in Europe, 1650–1850*, ed. Maxine Berg and Helen Clifford (Manchester, 1999), 164–5.

Chapter 6   Wallpaper and Taste

1 London Metropolitan Archives, B/TRL/09, Joseph Trollope and Sons, letter-book, f. 107.

2 Edmund Burke, *A Philosophical Enquiry into the Origin of our Ideas of the Sublime and Beautiful* (2nd edn, 1759), 4.

3 R. L. Hills, *Paper Making in Britain, 1488–1988: A Short History* (London, 1988); Gill Saunders, *Wallpaper in Interior Decoration* (London, 2002); E. A. Entwisle, *A Literary History of Wallpaper* (London, 1960); Treve Rosoman, *London Wallpapers: Their Manufacture and Use, 1690–1840* (London, 1992); Charles Oman and Jean Hamilton, *Wallpapers: A History and Illustrated Catalogue of the Collection in the Victoria and Albert Museum* (London, 1982), 17–30; James Ayres, *Domestic Interiors: The British Tradition, 1500–1850* (New Haven and London, 2003), 159.

4 Personal communication Treve Rosoman, English Heritage.

5 For pleasure in the inexpensiveness of wallpaper, see [Henrietta Knight], *Letters Written by the Late Right Honourable Lady Luxborough to William Shenstone Esq.* (London, 1775), 24; A. C. Clark (ed.), *Gleanings from an Old Portfolio*, 3 vols (Edinburgh, 1895), I, 184–5. Some dispute the affordability of wallpaper. Ayres thinks that wallpaper was confined to the first- and second-rate houses in Bath based on provenanced examples in the building of Bath museum: Ayres, *Domestic Interiors*, 165 and 242. Nevertheless, the evidence of the Leeds newspapers, account-books nationwide, and the Trollope letter-

book itself indicate that this is too pessimistic an assessment of the dissemination of paper.

6 The shallow stepmother Mrs Gibson in Elizabeth Gaskell, *Wives and Daughters* [1866] (Oxford, 1991), 189, cannot wait to repaper Molly's room, and thus obliterate the relics of her happier girlhood. Similarly, brash Sergeant Troy in Thomas Hardy, *Far From the Madding Crowd* [1874] (Oxford, 1991), 295, wants to rip out the oak wainscot, and paper in Bathsheba's venerable old farmhouse. Saunders, *Wallpaper in Interior Decoration*, 7.

7 Museum of London, Account-book of Mrs Martha Dodson, 1746–1765.

8 W. S. Lewis (ed.), *Horace Walpole's Correspondence* (London, 1937–), IX, 23–4.

9 See John Styles, 'Involuntary Consumers? The Eighteenth-century Servant and her Clothes', *Textile History*, 33/1 (2002), 14.

10 Thomas Sheraton, 'Paper Hangings', in *The Cabinet Dictionary* (1803), 281.

11 E.g., London Metropolitan Archives, B/TRL/09, ff. 254, 266, 290, 451, 323.

12 British Museum, Trade card for James Wheeley's Paper Hanging Warehouse, *circa* 1754.

13 This is Gill Saunders's conclusion based on the V&A, though more modest examples are preserved by English Heritage and the Whitworth Museum, Manchester.

14 V&A, Word and Image, E 1864–1946 96.a.3, Cowtan order books.

15 London Metropolitan Archives, B/TRL/09, ff. 246–7.

16 British Museum, Trade card for Wheeley's.

17 London Metropolitan Archives, B/TRL/09, ff. 137, 141.

18 London Metropolitan Archives, B/TRL/09, ff. 232–3.

19 Matching schemes were favoured in Paris too: Annik Pardailhe-Galabrun, *The Birth of Intimacy: Privacy and Domestic Life in Early Modern Paris* (Cambridge, 1991), 172.

20 See John Gage, *Colour in Turner, Poetry and Truth* (London, 1969); S. Lowengard, 'Colours and Colour Making in the Eighteenth Century', in *Consumers and Luxury: Consumer Culture in Europe, 1650–1850*, ed. Maxine Berg and Helen Clifford (Manchester, 1999), 103–17; Ian Bristow, *Architectural Colour in British Interiors, 1615–1840* (New Haven and London, 1996).

21 London Metropolitan Archives, B/TRL/09, f. 423.

22 London Metropolitan Archives, B/TRL/09, ff. 91, 195–6, 332.

23 London Metropolitan Archives, B/TRL/09, ff. 155–6, 298.

24 John Cornforth, *Early Georgian Interiors* (New Haven and London, 2004), 119; Hannah Robertson, *The Young Ladies School of Art* (4th edn, York, 1777), 25.

25 London Metropolitan Archives, B/TRL/09, f. 261; Staffordshire Record Office, D1240/1–10, Thomas Anson's vouchers.

26 London Metropolitan Archives, B/TRL/09, f. 235.

27 Robertson, *Young Ladies School of Art*, 25; Mary Delany had her 'English room' painted 'a sort of olive . . . for the sake of my pictures' in 1744: Lady Llanover (ed.), *The Autobiography and Correspondence of Mary Granville, Mrs Delany*, 1st series, 3 vols (London, 1861), 2nd series, 3 vols (London, 1862), 1st series, II, 330. At Luton Hoo, thirty years later, Lady Mary Coke noted: 'Almost all the rooms are hung with light green plain papers, which shews the pictures to great advantage': J. A. Home (ed.), *The Letters and Journals of Lady Mary Coke*, 4 vols (Edinburgh, 1889–96), IV, 390. Green was still the fashionable backdrop for pictures amongst Trollope's clients: London Metropolitan Archives, B/TRL/09, f. 324.

28 London Metropolitan Archives, B/TRL/09, f. 163.

29 Maria Edgeworth and Richard Lovell Edgeworth, *Essays on Practical Education*, 2 vols

[1798] (3rd edn, 1811), II, 283. This was remarked by Austen in a letter to her sister in May 1813. See Deirdre Le Faye, *Jane Austen's Letters* (3rd edn, Oxford, 1995), 211. The French agreed. Red and green were predominant in Parisian decoration and upholstery under Louis XIV and Louis XV, but green increasingly became seen as the more congenial colour, Pardailhe-Galabrun, *Birth of Intimacy*, 171. She points out that the *Encyclopédie* described green as just the right mixture of clear and sombre to please and strengthen the sight instead of weakening it or troubling it. It claimed that painters had a green cloth hung near the place where they work, on which to throw their glance from time to time, and to relieve them of the fatigue caused by the brightness of the colours.

30   Robertson, *Young Ladies School of Art*, 25.
31   Robertson, *Young Ladies School of Art*, 25; Cornforth, *Early Georgian Interiors*, 121; *Brewer's Dictionary of Phrase and Fable* (1990), 256.
32   London Metropolitan Archives, B/TRL/09, f. 326.
33   London Metropolitan Archives, B/TRL/09, ff. 366, 356–7.
34   Johann Beckmann, *A History of Inventions and Discoveries* (1797), 160.
35   London Metropolitan Archives, B/TRL/09, f. 350.
36   London Metropolitan Archives, B/TRL/09, f. 50; Isaac Ware, *A Complete Body of Architecture*, 2 vols (1756), 432.
37   London Metropolitan Archives, B/TRL/09, ff. 232–3, 85.
38   London Metropolitan Archives, B/TRL/09, ff. 266, 311.
39   London Metropolitan Archives, B/TRL/09, ff. 256, 450, 452.
40   John Houghton, *Collection for Improvement of Husbandry and Trade*, no. 356; cited in Entwisle, *A Literary History of Wallpaper*, 13.
41   London Metropolitan Archives, B/TRL/09, f. 367.
42   London Metropolitan Archives, B/TRL/09, ff. 107, 21
43   London Metropolitan Archives, B/TRL/09, ff. 262, 213, 344–5 and 128.
44   London Metropolitan Archives, B/TRL/09, ff. 246–7, 172.
45   London Metropolitan Archives, B/TRL/09, ff. 123, 296.
46   London Metropolitan Archives, B/TRL/09, f. 453.
47   *Leeds Intelligencer*, 22 March 1763; Saunders, *Wallpaper in Interior Decoration*, 18. On the gorgeous almost tawdry papers found in a Cambridge inn, see Colin Cunningham, 'Taste of a Tavern Keeper', *Country Life* (24 November 1994), 54–5.
48   Ware, *A Complete Body of Architecture*, 431; London Metropolitan Archives, B/TRL/09, f. 64.
49   Samuel Johnson, *A Dictionary of the English Language*, 2 vols (2nd edn, 1755–6), I: 'Gaudy'; Jane Austen, *Pride and Prejudice* [1813] (Oxford, 2004), 186. Gaudy had no negative meaning for Isaac Ware in 1756; see *A Complete Body of Architecture*, 469.
50   London Metropolitan Archives, B/TRL/09, ff. 137, 43, 122.
51   Thomas Sheraton, *The Cabinet Dictionary* (1803), 215–16.
52   Ware, *A Complete Body of Architecture*, 469; James Collett-White, *Bedfordshire Historical Miscellany*, Publications of the Bedfordshire Historical Record Society, 72 (Bedford, 1993), 136; Huntington Library, MO 5737 (28 September 1753), Elizabeth Montagu, Sandleford, to Sarah Scott.
53   E.g., *Leeds Intelligencer*, 3 May 1763.
54   John Pincot, *Treatise on the Practical Part of Coach & House Painting* (1811), 6, 19.
55   Essex Record Office, Chelmsford, D/DZg 33 (n.d.), Jane Farrin to Mrs Mary White.
56   John Wesley, 'Thoughts Upon Dress' [*circa* 1788], in *The Works of the Rev. John Wesley* (n. d.). XI, 477. Edwina Ehrman, *Dressed Neat and Plain: The Clothing of John Wesley and his Teaching on Dress* (London, 2003). Samuel Wesley, the father of John Wesley, pon-

tificated: 'style is the dress of thought; a modest dress. Neat but not gaudy, will true critics please'; Samuel Wesley, *An Epistle to a Friend, concerning Poetry* (1700).

57 John Thelwall, *Poems Written in Close Confinement in the Tower and Newgate under a Charge of High Treason* (1795), 3; Mary Thale (ed.), *The Autobiography of Francis Place (1771–1854)* (Cambridge, 1972), 124–5.

58 Lady Llanover (ed.), *Mrs Delany*, 1st series, II, 441.

59 Ware, *A Complete Body of Architecture*, 470; Cornforth, *Early Georgian Interiors*, 208; Pincot, *Treatise*, 20.

60 V&A, Word and Image, E1864–1946 96.a.3, Cowtan order books; Saunders, *Wallpaper in Interior Decoration*, 16.

61 Helen Clifford, *Silver in London: The Parker and Wakelin Partnership, 1760–1776* (New Haven and London, 2004), 138.

62 London Metropolitan Archives, B/TRL/09, f. 86. See also ff. 11, 249.

63 Lady Llanover (ed.), *Mrs Delany*, 1st series, II, 447.

64 Beckmann, *A History of Inventions and Discoveries*, 160.

65 English cookery books often described dishes as 'pretty' or 'elegant'; see Hilary Young, *English Porcelain, 1745–95: Its Makers, Design, Marketing and Consumption* (London, 1999), 182.

Chapter 7 *The Trials of Domestic Dependence*

1 *The Works of Vicesimus Knox*, 7 vols (1824), I, 182.

2 Susan Moller Okin, *Women in Western Political Thought* (London, 1980), 249; Caroline Robbins, 'The Strenuous Whig: Thomas Hollis of Lincoln's Inn', *William and Mary Quarterly*, 3rd series, 7/3 (1950), 421; *London Magazine* (1779), 178; Paul Langford, 'Thomas Day and the Politics of Sentiment', *Journal of Imperial and Commonwealth History*, 12/2 (1984), 57–79; Mary Astell, *Some Reflections upon Marriage* (3rd edn, 1706), preface, 27; Huntington Library, MO 5829 (25 October 1765), Elizabeth Montagu to Sarah Scott; Paul Langford, *Public Life and the Propertied Englishman, 1689–1798* (Oxford, 1991), 502.

3 *Life and Errors of John Dunton*, 2 vols (1818), I, 310; Betty Rizzo, *Companions without Vows: Relationships among Eighteenth-century British Women* (Athens, GA, 1994), 11.

4 Kathryn Gleadle, 'British Women and Radical Politics in the Late Nonconformist Enlightenment, c.1780–1830', in *Women, Privilege and Power*, ed. A. Vickery (Stanford, CA, 2001), 123–51; and Gleadle, 'Opinions Deliver'd in Conversation: Conversation, Politics and Gender in the Late Eighteenth Century', in *Civil Society in British History*, ed. José Harris (Oxford, 2003), 61–78.

5 Rachel Garrard, 'English Probate Inventories and their Use in Studying the Significance of the Domestic Interior, 1500–1700', *A.A.G Bijdragen*, 23 (1980), 53–77.

6 Alexandra Shepard, *Meanings of Manhood in Early Modern England* (Oxford, 2003), 3.

7 Joanna Martin (ed.), *A Governess in the Age of Jane Austen: The Journals and Letters of Agnes Porter* (London and Rio Grande, OH, 1998), 35.

8 Beinecke Library, Yale, Osborne shelves, C 236, Marthae Taylor letter-book.

9 Beinecke Library, Yale, Osborne shelves, C 236, Marthae Taylor letter-book.

10 G. Midgley, *University Life in Eighteenth-century Oxford* (New Haven and London, 1996), 1–2; *Gentleman's Magazine*, LXVIII/1 (1798), note 282.

11 Huntington Library, Stutterd letters (23 November 1781), William Brigg to Thomas Stutterd.

12 George Savile, *The Lady's New Year's Gift; or, Advice to a Daughter* (London, 1688), 3; Beinecke Library, Osborne shelves, c 236, Marthae Taylor letter-book.

13 Jane Austen, *Pride and Prejudice* [1813] (Oxford, 2004), 141.

14 F. A. Pottle, *Boswell's London Journal, 1762–1763* (New York, 1950), 220; Brynmor Jones Library, DDBM/32/7 (6 December 1757), Thomas Wentworth, Thorp, to Diana Bosville.

15 Margaret Blundell (ed.), *Cavalier: Letters of William Blundell to his Friends, 1620–1698* (London, 1933), 287.

16 Edward Hall (ed.), *Miss Weeton: Journal of a Governess, 1811–1825*, 2 vols (London, 1939), I, 23, 37.

17 Priscilla Wakefield, *Reflections in the Present Condition of the Female Sex with Suggestions for its Improvement* (1798), 37.

18 Alan Saville (ed.), *Secret Comment: The Diaries of Gertrude Savile, 1721–1757* (Kingsbridge, 1997), 14, 18.

19 Saville (ed.), *Secret Comment*, 11, 14, 15, 11, 1, 16, 22.

20 Bedfordshire Record Office, OR 2071/408, Constantia Orlebar to Anne Orlebar.

21 Saville (ed.), *Secret Comment*, 191, 54, 47, 89, 104–5, 106.

22 Saville (ed.), *Secret Comment*, 120, 134, 118, 128, 133, 134, 135–6.

23 Saville (ed.), *Secret Comment*, 136, 139, 151, 169–70.

24 Susan C. Djabri (ed.), *The Diaries of Sarah Hurst, 1759–1762* (Horsham, 2003), 170; Pepys, *Diary*, I, 288; II, 232; Brynmore Jones Library, DOG/8 (23 April 1790), Elizabeth Furniss, Bawtry, to Mrs Ogle, Wetherby; DOG/8 (12 April 1792), same to same. See also the unhappy Kate Mordaunt in Elizabeth Hamilton, *The Mordaunts: An Eighteenth Century Family* (London, 1965), 15, 19; the disregarded Verney daughters in Susan Whyman, *Sociability and Power in Late Stuart England: The Cultural World of the Verneys, 1660–1720* (Oxford, 1999); and the deferential Katherine Plymley in Gleadle, 'Opinions Deliver'd in Conversation'.

25 Essex Record Office, Colchester, c47, vol. 1, 88 ('Thursday night'), Mary Martin to I. M. Rebow; 92 (8 January 1771), same to same.

26 Wiltshire Record Office, 1300/1390 (30 March 1793), Caroline and Frances Brudenell to Earl of Ailesbury, Tottenham Park.

27 Jane Austen, *Mansfield Park* [1814] (Oxford, 2004), 173.

28 Huntington Library, MO 283 (10 October 1739), Elizabeth Robinson, Horton, to Duchess of Portland.

29 Rotherham Public Library, Platt Microfilm, f. 155 (*circa* 1795), Anne Platt, Windlestone, to Elizabeth Platt.

30 Martin (ed.), *A Governess in the Age of Jane Austen*, 43.

31 Rotherham Public Library, Platt Microfilm, f. 155 (*circa* 1795), Anne Platt, Windlestone, to Elizabeth Platt.

32 Lemuel Gulliver, *Pleasures of Matrimony* (2nd edn, 1745), 16–17.

33 Margot Todd, 'Humanists, Puritans and the Spiritualized Household', *Church History*, 49 (1980), 18–34; K. M. Davies, 'Continuity and Change in Literary Advice on Marriage', in *Marriage and Society: Studies in the Social History of Marriage*, ed. R. B. Outhwaite (London, 1981), 58–80; Sara Mendelson and Patricia Crawford, *Women in Early Modern England, 1550–1720* (Oxford, 1998), 205.

34 Linda Pollock, 'Teach Her to Live under Obedience: The Making of Women in the Upper Ranks of Early Modern England', *Continuity and Change*, 4 (1989), 231–58; Ingrid Tague, *Women of Quality* (Woodbridge, 2002), 97–132; Elizabeth Foyster, *Marital Violence: An English Family History, 1660–1857* (Cambridge, 2004), 52–3.

35 Jennifer Melville, 'The Use and Organization of Domestic Space in Late Seventeenth-century London' (PH.D thesis, Cambridge, 1999), 106.

36 M. E. O'Connor, 'Dormer, Anne (1648?–1695)', *Dictionary of National Biography* (Oxford, 2004).

37 British Library, Add. MS 72516, Trumbull Papers, D/ED C13, f. 177 (5 April), Anne Dormer to Lady Trumbull; f. 159 (28 August), f. 174 (10 March), ff. 180–81 (20 July), f. 193 (3 November), same to same; S. Mendelson, *The Mental World of Stuart Women* (Brighton, 1987), 101–10.

38 British Library, Add. MS 72516, Trumbull Papers, D/ED C13, f. 210 (n.d.), Anne Dormer to Lady Trumbull; f. 211 (24 October), f. 193 (3 November), f. 195 (29 November), f. 165 (22 June), same to same.

39 British Library, Add. MS 72516, Trumbull Papers, D/ED C13, f. 186 (28 September), Anne Dormer to Lady Trumbull; f. 195 (29 November), f. 172 (6 March), f. 192 (3 November), same to same.

40 British Library, Add. MS 72516, Trumbull Papers, D/ED C13, f. 172 (6 March), Anne Dormer to Lady Trumbull; ff. 176–7 (5 April), f. 159 (28 August), same to same.

41 Sara Mendelson, 'Stuart Women's Diaries and Occasional Memoirs', in *Women in English Society, 1500–1800*, ed. Mary Prior (London, 1985), 199; and Ann Laurence, 'The Closet Disclosed: The Ambiguous Privacy of Women's Closets in Seventeenth-century England', forthcoming; Matthew 6:6.

42 British Library, Add. MS 72516, Trumbull Papers, D/ED C13, f. 159 (28 August), Anne Dormer to Lady Trumbull; f. 161 (30 May), f. 186 (28 September), f. 192 (3 November), f. 165 (22 June), f. 190 (n.d.), same to same.

43 British Library, Add. MS 72516, Trumbull Papers, D/ED C13, f. 192 (3 November), Anne Dormer to Lady Trumbull.

44 British Library, Add. MS 72516, Trumbull Papers, D/ED C13, f. 202 (25 July 1689), Anne Dormer to Lady Trumbull; f. 174 (10 March), f. 169 (4 February), same to same.

45 British Library, Add. MS 72516, Trumbull Papers, D/ED C13, f. 170 (4 February), Anne Dormer to Lady Trumbull.

46 British Library, Add. MS 72516, Trumbull Papers, D/ED C13, f. 202 (25 July 1689), Anne Dormer to Lady Trumbull; f. 204 (12 August 1689), same to same.

47 British Library, Add. MS 72516, Trumbull Papers, D/ED C13, f. 215 (22 January 1689), Anne Dormer to Lady Trumbull; f. 213 (10 December 1689), f. 206 (8 August 1689), f. 219 (n.d.), same to same.

48 British Library, Add. MS 72516, Trumbull Papers, D/ED C13, f. 215 (22 January 1689), Anne Dormer to Lady Trumbull; f. 220 (n.d.), f. 213 (10 December 1689), same to same.

49 See Barbara Taylor and Sarah Knott (eds), *Women, Gender and Enlightenment* (Basingstoke, 2005).

50 Amanda Vickery, *The Gentleman's Daughter: Women's Lives in Georgian England* (New Haven and London, 1998), 220–2.

51 Chester and Cheshire Record Office, DSA 1 (19 May 1790), Margaret, Lady Stanley to Mrs Owen, Old Burlington Street.

52 Mendelson and Crawford, *Women in Early Modern England*, 211.

53 John Martin Robinson, *Temples of Delight: Stowe Landscape Gardens* (London, 1990), 40.

54 Centre for Buckinghamshire Studies, D/X 1069/2/9 (11 August 1716), L. Egleton to Martha Baker.

55 Robinson, *Temples of Delight*, 40.

56 Cited in Clarissa Campbell Orr, 'Queen Charlotte as Patron: Some Intellectual and Social Contexts', *Court Historian*, 6/3 (December 2001), 198.

57 British Library, Add. MS 72516, Trumbull Papers, D/ED C13, f. 180 (20 July), Anne Dormer to Lady Trumbull.

58 Melville, 'The Use and Organization of Domestic Space', 188–90; Elizabeth Foyster, 'At the Limits of Liberty: Married Women and Confinement in Eighteenth-century England', *Continuity and Change*, 17/1 (2002), 39–62.

59 Donald Gibson, *A Parson in the Vale of the White Horse: George Woodward's Letters from East Hendred, 1753–1761* (Gloucester, 1982), 121–2, 124.

60 William Congreve, *The Way of the World* (1700), scene 1.

61 Henry Fielding, *Tom Jones* [1749] (Oxford, 1996).

62 Kate Chisholm, *Fanny Burney: Her Life* (London, 1998), xx.

63 Emma Clery, *The Feminization Debate in Eighteenth-Century England: Literature, Commerce and Luxury* (Basingstoke, 2004), 132–3; Cynthia Wall, 'A Geography of Georgian Narrative Space', in *Georgian Geographies: Essays on Spaces, Place and Landscape in the Eighteenth Century*, ed. Miles Ogborn and Charles W. J. Withers (Manchester and New York, 2004), 114–29; Karen Lipsedge, ' "Enter into thy Closet": Women, Closet Culture and the Eighteenth-century English Novel', and Robert St George, 'Reading Spaces in Eighteenth-century New England', in *Gender, Taste and Material Culture in Britain and North America*, ed. John Styles and Amanda Vickery (New Haven, 2006), 81–105, 107–22.

64 Anne Kugler, 'Constructing Wifely Identity: Prescription and Practice in the Life of Lady Sarah Cowper', *Journal of British Studies*, 40 (2001), 291–323.

65 W. Brockbank and F. Kenworthy (eds), *The Diary of Richard Kay, 1716–51* (Manchester, 1968), 22; see also 9, 13, 15, 18, 20, 21, 24, 25, 26, 137; J. H. Turner, *The Rev. Oliver Heywood BA, 1630–1702: His Autobiography*, 4 vols (1881–5), I, 302, 309; III, 112. J. T. Cliffe, *The World of the Country House in Seventeenth-century England* (New Haven and London, 1999), 77; Proverbs 24:24.

Chapter 8   A Nest of Comforts: Women Alone

1 Elizabeth Gaskell, *Cranford* [1853] (Oxford, 1972), 1, 3, 7, 74.

2 This is the estimate of Peter Earle based on depositions in the church courts in the years 1695–1725 in *A City Full of People: Men and Women of London, 1650–1750* (London, 1994), 162. See Richard Wall, 'Women Alone in English Society', *Annales de Demographie Historique*, 141 (1981), 303–17.

3 T. H. Hollingsworth, 'The Demography of the British Peerage', *Population Studies*, 8, supplement (1964); Jane Austen, *Mansfield Park* [1814] (Oxford, 2003), 3.

4 Amy M. Froide, *Never Married: Single Women in Early Modern England* (Oxford, 2005), 2.

5 Olwen Hufton, 'Women without Men: Widows and Spinsters in Britain and France in the Eighteenth Century', *Journal of Family History*, 9 (1984), 355; Paul Griffith, *Youth and Authority: Formative Experiences in England, 1560–1640* (Oxford, 1996); Froide, *Never Married*, 20.

6 Froide, *Never Married*, 22–3.

7 Wall, 'Women Alone in English Society', *passim*.

8 Borthwick Institute for Archives, University of York, Exchequer and Prerogative Courts of York, wills, 1710–11 and 1780–82, Ainsty, Doncaster, Pontefract and York deaneries.

9 This was John Evelyn's fear for Margaret Godolphin when she was pondering a life of religious celibacy in 1676: F. Harris, *Transformations of Love: The Friendship of John Eve-*

lyn and Margaret Godolphin (Oxford, 2002), 173. For Miss Chichester's dreadful decision, see Berkshire Record Office, D/ESV (B), F 11/5 (*circa* March 1789), Arabella Clayfield to Miss Tinney, London. Only a small number went to convents abroad: Claire Walker, *Gender and Politics in Early Modern Europe: English Convents in France and the Low Countries* (New York, 2003).

10 Mary Astell, *A Serious Proposal to the Ladies* (1694); Samuel Richardson, *Sir Charles Grandison*, 7 vols (1753–4), IV, 355; Sarah Scott, *Millenium Hall* (1762).

11 Brynmor Jones Library, DOG/8/3 (1752), Dorothy Rudston, Flamborough, to Barbara Wilkinson.

12 Norfolk Record Office, BOL 2/139/6 Bury (16 February 1775), Elizabeth Munbee to Elizabeth Reading.

13 Edward Hall (ed.), *Miss Weeton: Journal of a Governess, 1811–1825*, 2 vols (London, 1939), II, 331–2, 353, 379, 398.

14 Hufton, 'Women without Men', 361; Leonore Davidoff, 'The Separation of Home and Work? Landladies and Lodgers in Nineteenth- and Twentieth-century England', in *Fit Work for Women*, ed. Sandra Burman (London, 1979), 64–97; Jane Humphries, 'Female Headed Households in Early Industrial Britain: The Vanguard of the Proletariat', *Labour History Review*, 63/1 (1998), 39; Susan Wright, 'Sojourners and Lodgers in a Provincial Town: The Evidence from eighteenth-century Ludlow', *Urban History*, 17 (1990), 14–35, especially 26.

15 West Yorkshire Archive Service, Leeds, Thorp Arch, 13/1 (26 October 1739), Elizabeth Barker, York, to Mrs Gossip.

16 Norfolk Record Office, BOL 2/59/16 (9 December 1797), Mrs Clara Reeve, Ipswich, to Mrs Peach.

17 Centre for Buckinghamshire Studies, D/X 1069/2/45 (n.d.), 'The afflicted condition of Mrs Alice Beckett'; York City Archives, 54.42a (22 February 1799), Lease, Revd J. Forth at Ganthorpe, to Jane, Ann, Elizabeth and Frances Royds of York, spinsters.

18 Marjorie Penn (ed.), *Account Books of Gertrude Savile, 1736–1758*, Thoroton Society Record Series, XXIV, 'Nottinghamshire Miscellany', No. 4 (Nottingham, 1967), 100–44.

19 Alan Saville (ed.), *Secret Comment: The Diaries of Gertrude Savile, 1721–1757* (Kingsbridge, 1997), 234, 238.

20 East India merchants and court nobility first adopted yellow bedroom schemes around 1700, but they were rare before 1740; Clare Browne, 'Silk Damask Bed Furnishings in the Early Eighteenth Century', and David Mitchell, 'Colour Preference in English Furnishings', both forthcoming.

21 See Arderne, Grimes and Cotton accounts above, ch. 4.

22 Saville (ed.), *Secret Comment*, 351.

23 Doncaster Archives, DD.DC.H6/1, Diana Eyre's account-book, 1749–77.

24 John Wood, *An Essay towards a Description of Bath*, 2 vols (2nd edn, 1749), II, preface.

25 Sophie Sarin, 'The Floor Cloth and Other Floor Coverings in the London Domestic Interior, 1700–1800', *Journal of Design History*, 18 (2005), 133–145.

26 Doncaster Archives, DD.DC.H6/17, Diana Eyre's Bills.

27 John Styles, 'Lodging at the Old Bailey: Lodgings and their Furnishing in Eighteenth-century London', in *Gender, Taste and Material Culture in Britain and North America*, ed. Styles and Amanda Vickery (New Haven, 2006), 61–80; Adrienne Hood, 'The Material World of Cloth: Production and Use in Eighteenth-century Rural Pennsylvania', *William and Mary Quarterly*, 53/1 (1996), 62.

28 Wood, *An Essay towards a Description of Bath*, preface; Natalie Rothstein and Santina M.

Levey, 'Furnishings, *c.*1500–1780', in *The Cambridge History of Western Textiles*, ed. David Jenkins, 2 vols (Cambridge, 2003), I, 631–58.

29 Wood, *An Essay towards a Description of Bath*, preface.

30 Berkshire Record Office, mf 688, D/EHY F112 /16 (14 December 1781), Mary Hartley to W. H. Hartley.

31 Berkshire Record Office, mf 688, D/EHY F100/1/63, 78, 70, 73, 79, 71 (May–June 1784), Ann Toll, Bath, to David Hartley, ledgers, 1782–91.

32 Hood's calculations based on relatively prosperous households in Pennsylvania, in 'The Material World of Cloth', 48–50.

33 Berkshire Record Office, mf 688, D/EHY F100/1/79, 71, 73, 86 (May–July 1784), Ann Toll, Bath, to David Hartley.

34 Berkshire Record Office, mf 689, A10/1–2 (27 April 1786), Bills of David Hartley.

35 Berkshire Record Office, mf 688, DD/EHY F100/2/52, 94 (1784, 1788), Ann Toll, Bath, to David Hartley.

36 Alice Hepplewhite, *Cabinet-Maker and Upholsterer's Guide* (1788), 3, pl. 15; Peter Thornton, *Seventeenth-century Interior Decoration in England, France and Holland* (New Haven, 1978), 196–201; Akiko Shimbo, 'Pattern Books, Showrooms and Furniture Design: Interactions between Producers and Consumers in England, 1754–1851' (Ph.D thesis, London, 2007), 154–63, and Frances Collard, *Regency Furniture* (Woodbridge, Suffolk, 1985), 22–3.

37 Akiko Shimbo, 'Pattern Books', 156; Emily Climenson (ed.), *Passages from the Diaries of Mrs Philip Lybbe Powys* (London, 1899), 232.

38 Akiko Shimbo, 'Pattern Books', 160, 162.

39 P. Laslett, 'Mean Household Size in England since the Sixteenth Century', in *Household and Family in Past Time*, ed. Laslett and R. Wall (Cambridge, 1972), 147.

40 Amy Erickson, *Women and Property in Early Modern England* (London, 1993), 200.

41 Pamela Sharpe, 'Survival Strategies and Stories: Poor Widows and Widowers in Early Industrial England', in *Widowhood in Medieval and Early Modern Europe*, ed. Sandra Cavallo and Lyndan Warner (Harlow, 1999), 221.

42 See V. Brodsky, 'Widows in Late Elizabethan London: Remarriage, Economic Opportunity and Family Orientations', in *The World We Have Gained: Histories of Population and Social Structure*, ed. L. Bonfield, R. M. Smith and K. Wrightson (Oxford, 1986); Barbara Todd, 'The Remarrying Widow: A Stereotype Reconsidered', in *Women in English Society, 1500–1800*, ed. Mary Prior (London, 1985); Jeremy Boulton, 'London Widowhood Revisited: The Decline of Female Remarriage in the Seventeenth and Eighteenth Centuries', *Continuity and Change*, 5 (1990), 323–55; Barbara Todd, 'Demographic Determinism and Female Agency: The Remarrying Widow Reconsidered . . . Again', *Continuity and Change*, 9 (1994), 421–50; S. J. Wright, 'The Elderly and Bereaved in Eighteenth-century Ludlow', in *Life, Death and Elderly: Historical Perspectives*, ed. Margaret Pelling and Richard Smith (London, 1991), 102–33.

43 Lady Llanover (ed.), *The Autobiography and Correspondence of Mary Granville, Mrs Delany*, 1st series, 3 vols (London, 1861), 2nd series, 3 vols (London, 1862), 1st series, I, 109; 2nd series, I, 146.

44 Erickson, *Women and Property*, 164–5, 163. Margaret Spufford, *Contrasting Communities: English Villagers in the Sixteenth and Seventeenth Centuries* (Cambridge, 1974), 113, 115, 163

45 Susanna Ottaway, *The Decline of Life: Old Age in Eighteenth-century England* (Cambridge, 2004), 122.

46 Sharpe, 'Survival Strategies and Stories', 237; Humphries, 'Female Headed Households'.

47 F. J. Manning (ed.), *The Williamson Letters, 1748–1765* (Streatley, 1954), 136.

48 Kate Retford, *The Art of Domestic Life: Family Portraiture in Eighteenth-century England* (New Haven, 2006), 106–7.

49 Museum of London, Martha Dodson's Account-book, 1746–65.

50 Edwina Ehrman, 'Dressing Well in Old Age: The Clothing Accounts of Martha Dodson, 1746–1765', *Costume*, 40 (2006), 28–38.

51 Sarin, 'The Floor Cloth and Other Floor Coverings', 133–45.

52 Hilary Young, *English Porcelain, 1745–95: Its Makers, Design, Marketing and Consumption* (London, 1999), 162, 164, 180, 197, 198.

53 See pp. 113–22

54 Doncaster Archives, DD.DC.H2/1/1 (1763), 'Inventory of plate at Owston in Mrs Cooke's possession'.

55 Doncaster Archives, DD.DC.H1/1/1 (17 February 1783), William Whitelock, Brotherton, to Mrs Cooke, Hatfield; H1/1/2, Letters of William Lindley, architect at Doncaster, to Bryan Cooke; A. Taylor, 'William Lindley of Doncaster', *Georgian Group Journal*, [4] (1994), 30–42.

56 Sandra Cavallo, 'What Did Women Transmit?: Ownership and Control of Household Goods and Personal Effects in Early Modern Italy', in *Gender and Material Culture in Historical Perspective*, ed. Moira Donald and Linda Hurcombe (Basingstoke, 2000), 38–53.

57 Doncaster Archives, DD.DC.H7/1/3 (22 March 1784), Mary Cooke to Bryan Cooke, her will.

58 W. S. Lewis and R. M. Williams (eds), *Private Charity in England, 1747–1757* (New Haven, 1938), 41, 103–5.

59 York City Archives, 54: 1 (1796–1806), Household inventory of Revd John Forth and Mrs Elizabeth Forth at Slingsby and Ganthorpe.

60 York City Archives, 54: 21 (1787), Expenses incurred by Miss Woodhouse.

61 York City Archives, 54: 41B (1797), Inventory of the fixtures at Blake Street, York.

62 York City Archives, 54: 9 (1821–2), Housekeeping account-book of Mrs Elizabeth Forth.

63 York City Archives, 54: 9 (1821–2), Housekeeping account-book of Mrs Elizabeth Forth.

64 Mrs William Parkes, *Domestic Duties; or, Instructions to Young Married Ladies on the Management of their Households* (1825), 204.

65 Amanda Vickery, *The Gentleman's Daughter: Women's Lives in Georgian England* (New Haven and London, 1998), 208.

66 Norfolk Record Office, BOL 2/59/13 (1795), Elizabeth Poole to Mrs Peach, Norwich.

67 H. J. Habakkuk, *Marriage, Debt and the Estates Systems: English Landownership, 1650–1950* (Oxford, 1994), 291; W. S. Lewis (ed.), *Horace Walpole's Correspondence* (London, 1974), XXXVII, 269–70; Julie Schlarman, 'The Social Geography of Grosvenor Square: Mapping Gender and Politics, 1720–1760', *London Journal*, 28 (2003), 18.

68 J. J. Cartwright (ed.), *The Travels through England of Dr Richard Pococke*, 2 vols, Camden Society (London, 1888–9), II, 12; Mark Girouard, *The English Town: A History of Urban Life* (New Haven and London, 1990), 103, 115; Wright, 'Sojourners and Lodgers in a Provincial Town', 14–35; Margaret Ponsonby, *Stories from Home: English Domestic Interiors, 1750–1850* (Aldershot, 2007), 138–9.

69 Ponsonby, *Stories from Home*, 134.

70 Peter Borsay, *The English Urban Renaissance: Culture and Society in the Provincial Town, 1660–1770* (Oxford, 1989), 243–8; R. S. Neale, *Bath: A Social History, 1680–1850* (London, 1981), 276.

71   See p. 126.

72   Doncaster Archives, DD.DC.H7/1/3 (22 March 1784), Mary Cooke to Bryan Cooke, her will.

73   Emily Climenson (ed.), *Elizabeth Montagu: The Queen of the Blue-Stockings: Her Correspondence from 1720 to 1761*, 2 vols (London, 1906), I, 271.

Chapter 9   What Women Made

1   John Fowler and John Cornforth, *English Decoration in the Eighteenth Century* (London, 1974), 253.

2   John Cornforth, 'Gentle Preoccupations', *Country Life* (4 February 1991), 38–41.

3   Ann Bermingham, *Learning to Draw: Studies in the Cultural History of a Polite and Useful Art* (New Haven and London, 2000), 224, 202; Linda Nochlin, 'Why Have There Been No Great Women Artists?', *Women, Art and Power and Other Essays* (New York, 1988), 145–76; Griselda Pollock and Rosika Parker, *Old Mistresses: Women, Art and Ideology* (New York, 1981), 58–9. For more positive assessments, see Marcia Pointon, *Strategies for Showing: Women, Possession and Representation in English Visual Culture, 1665–1800* (Oxford, 1997), and Therese O'Malley and Amy Meyers (eds), *The Art of Natural History: Illustrated Treatises and Botanical Paintings, 1400–1850* (Washington, DC, 2008).

4   Alice Clark, *Working Life of Women in the Seventeenth Century* (London, 1919); M. George, 'From Goodwife to Mistress: The Transformation of the Female in Bourgeois Culture', *Science and Society*, 37 (1973), 6; Ivy Pinchbeck, *Women Workers and the Industrial Revolution* (London, 1930), 33–40, 303–5.

5   Thorstein Veblen, *Theory of the Leisure Class* (1890); Germaine Greer, 'Making Pictures from Strips of Cloth Isn't Art at All', *The Guardian*, 13 August 2007.

6   Ann Bermingham, 'Elegant Females and Gentlemen Connoisseurs: The Commerce in Culture and Self-Image in Eighteenth-century England', in *The Consumption of Culture, 1660–1800, Image, Object, Text*, ed. J. Brewer and A. Bermingham (London, 1995), 509.

7   Bermingham, *Learning to Draw*, 183, 186.

8   Margaret J. M. Ezell, *The Patriarch's Wife: Literary Evidence and the History of the Family* (Chapel Hill, 1987), 187; *The Guardian*, 2 vols (6th edn, 1734), II, 325–7.

9   William Ellis, *The Country Housewife's Family Companion* (1750), viii; James Fordyce, *Sermons to Young Women*, 2 vols (6th edn, 1766), I, 97–104.

10   Ezell, *The Patriarch's Wife*, 187.

11   Fordyce, *Sermons to Young Women*, I, 100–1.

12   Hannah More, *Strictures on the Modern System of Female Education*, 2 vols [1799] (1811), I, 111, 73; Michèle Cohen, *Fashioning Masculinity: National Identity and Language in the Eighteenth Century* (London and New York, 1996), 65.

13   Sarah Pennington, *An Unfortunate Mother's Advice to her Daughters* (2nd edn, 1761), 40–41.

14   Hester Chapone, *Letters on the Improvement of the Mind*, 2 vols (1835), II, 62.

15   Mary Wollstonecraft, *Thoughts on the Education of Daughters* (1787), 25–7; More, *Strictures*, I, 105, 106, 6; Maria Edgeworth and Richard Lovell Edgeworth, *Essays on Practical Education*, 2 vols [1798] (3rd edn, 1811), II, 184.

16   *Gentleman's Magazine* (1801), 587–9.

17   Hannah More, *Essays on Various Subjects* (1778), 131. Michèle Cohen, *Fashioning Masculinity*, 65.

18   Anon., *Advice from a Lady to Her Granddaughters* (1808), 61.

19   Borthwick Institute for Archives, York University, Exchequer and Prerogative Courts of York, wills, Doncaster, 1780, Charlotte Bingley.

20   John Wood, *An Essay towards a Description of Bath*, 2 vols (2nd edn, 1749), II, preface; Susan C. Djabri (ed.), *The Diaries of Sarah Hurst, 1759–1762* (Horsham, 2003), xxiv; Old Bailey Proceedings, December 1750, John Richardson (t17501205-42).

21   John Styles, *The Dress of the People: Everyday Fashion in Eighteenth-century England* (New Haven, 2007), ch. 7.

22   Peter Earle, 'The Female Labour Market in London in the Late Seventeenth and Early Eighteenth Centuries', *Economic History Review*, 2nd series, 42 (1989), 328–52; N. J. Phillips, *Women in Business, 1700–1850* (Woodbridge, Suffolk, 2006); Sue Wright, 'Churmaids, Huswfes and Hucksters: The Employment of Women in Tudor and Stuart Salisbury', in *Women and Work in Pre-industrial England*, ed. L. Duffin (London, 1985), 100–21.

23   Hannah Woolley, *The Gentlewoman's Companion; or, A Guide to the Female Sex* (1675), 7; Susan Skedd, 'Women Teachers and the Expansion of Girls' Schooling in England, c.1760–1820', in *Gender in Eighteenth-century England*, ed. Hannah Barker and Elaine Chalus (London, 1997), 101–25; Dorothy Gardiner, *English Girlhood at School: A Study of Women's Education through Twelve Centuries* (Oxford, 1929); Edwina Ehrman, *Judith Hayle: The Judith Hayle Samplers* (n.p., 2007); The National Archives, 29/215, PROB 3, Inventory for Rebecca Weekes.

24   West Yorkshire Archive Service, Wakefield, QS 1/77/9, West Riding Quarter Sessions Rolls, 1738.

25   *Leeds Mercury*, 10 October 1738, 2 August 1743.

26   Hannah Robertson, *The Young Ladies School of Art* (4th edn, York, 1777), ix.

27   Rotherham Public Library, Platt Microfilm (1 January 1793), Anne Platt, Windlestone, to Elisabeth Platt, Rotherham

28   Robertson, *The Young Ladies School of Art*; John Stalker and George Parker, *Treatise of Japanning and Varnishing* (1688); Mrs Artlove, *The Art of Japanning, Varnishing, Polishing and Gilding* (1730); *Arts Companion; or, A New Assistant for the Ingenious* (1749); A. Heckle, *The Florist; or, An Extensive and Curious Collection of Flowers: For the Imitation of Young Ladies, either in Drawing or in Needlework* (1759); George Brookshaw, *A New Treatise on Flower Painting; or, Every Lady Her Own Drawing Master* (1797); B. F. Gandee, *The Artist; or, Young Ladies Instructor in Ornamental Painting, Drawing, etc.* (1835).

29   *The Life of Mrs Robertson* (Derby, 1791), 40; Rudolph Ackerman, 'Observations on Fancy Work as Affording an Agreeable Occupation for Ladies', *Repository of the Arts, Literature and Commerce* (March 1810), 192–3; Bermingham, *Learning to Draw*, 138–40.

30   Thomas Sheraton, *The Cabinet Dictionary* (1803), 316; The National Archives, C107/109, James Brown, 29 St Paul's Churchyard, London, upholsterer ledgers, 1782–91.

31   Henry Fielding, *History of Amelia* [1751] (New York, 1837), 414.

32   Rozsika Parker, *The Subversive Stitch: Embroidery and the Making of the Feminine* (London, 1983), 10, 98, 117–46; Ruth Geuter, 'Women and Embroidery in Seventeenth-century Britain: The Social, Religious and Political Meanings of Domestic Needlework' (PH.D thesis, Aberystwyth, 1997); Ruth Geuter, 'Reconstructing the Context of Seventeenth-century English Figurative Embroideries', in *Gender and Material Culture in Historical Perspective*, ed. Moira Donald and Linda Hurcombe (Basingstoke, 2000), 97–111.

33 Parker, *Subversive Stitch*, 117–46.

34 Ezell, *The Patriarch's Wife*, 187.

35 Samuel Richardson, *Clarissa; or, The History of a Young Lady* (1747–8).

36 Royal Archives, Queen Charlotte's Diaries, 26 August 1789, 11 September 1789, 15 September 1789. I thank Edwina Ehrman for these references.

37 'Rest of morning occupation breaking brains over Worke, or relieving them with harpsichord' sighed Marchioness Grey in 1745: Ann Buck, *Dress in Eighteenth-century England* (London, 1979), 203. Charlotte Orlebar complained: 'I have but little time at present for the *pen*; which is much greater favourite of mine then the *Needle*', but her daughter and her sister had 'a genius for Working': Bedfordshire Record Office, OR 2071/404 (31 August 1788), Charlotte Orlebar, Hinwick House, to Constantia Orlebar.

38 *Six North Country Diaries*, Publications of the Surtees Society, CXVIII (Durham, 1910), 164–5; Hampshire Record Office, IM 44 36/1/1 (18 May 1742), William Porter, Winchester, to Mary Porter.

39 Essex Record Office, Colchester, C47 (23 June 1772), Mary Martin to Isaac Rebow.

40 Katherine Sharpe, 'Conchology and Creativity: The Rise of Shellwork in Eighteenth-century England' (MA dissertation in the History of Design, V&A/RCA, 1995).

41 Heckle, *The Florist*, 2.

42 Lady Llanover (ed.), *The Autobiography and Correspondence of Mary Granville, Mrs Delany*, 1st series, 3 vols (London, 1861), 2nd series, 3 vols (London, 1862), 1st series, I, 485.

43 Lady Llanover (ed.), *Mrs Delany*, 1st series, I, 227, 344–5; II, 601.

44 Kim Sloan, *'A Noble Art': Amateur Artists and Drawing Masters, c.1600–1800* (London, 2000), 46.

45 Horace Walpole, 'Ladies and Gentlemen Distinguished by their Artistic Talents', in *Anecdotes of Painting in England*, 5 vols (New Haven, 1937), V, 228–40

46 John Rylands Library, R 93692 (1770), Dorothy Richardson's journal, ff. 23, 32; Basil Cozens-Hardy (ed.), *The Diary of Sylas Neville, 1767–1788* (London and New York, 1950), 68, 116; Susan Neave and David Neave (eds), *The Diary of a Yorkshire Gentleman: John Courtney of Beverley, 1759–1768* (Otley, 2001), 52.

47 West Yorkshire Archive Service, Bradford, Sp St 6/1/50 (17 August 1743), M. Warde, Squerryes, to Mrs Stanhope; see also John Rylands Library, R 93692 (1770), Dorothy Richardson's journal.

48 Wettenhall Wilkes, *A Letter of Genteel and Moral Advice to a Young Lady* (Dublin, 1740), 182.

49 John Gregory, *A Father's Legacy to his Daughters* (1774), 51–2.

50 Chapone, *Letters on the Improvement of the Mind*, II, 118.

51 Edgeworth and Edgeworth, *Essays on Practical Education*, I, 522–3.

52 West Sussex Record Office, Acc 8285, 4/100 (n.d.), Hester Lyttleton, Hagley, to Harriet Bishop, Parham.

53 Cited in Parker, *Subversive Stitch*, 136.

54 Trevor Lummis and Jan Marsh, *The Woman's Domain: Women and the English Country House* (London, 1990), 105.

55 Huntington Library, HM 31201, Mrs Larpent's diary, 1790–95, facing f. 23.

56 Alan Saville (ed.), *Secret Comment: The Diaries of Gertrude Savile, 1721–1757* (Kingsbridge, 1997), 107, 112, 114, 154.

57 Huntington Library, HM 31201/2, Mrs Larpent's diary, 1796–8, f. 149 (12 June 1797).

58 Berkshire Record Office, D/EHY F100/2/28 (12 October 1784), Mary Hartley, Bath, to W. H. Hartley; D/EHY F112/16 (14 December 1781), Mary Hartley to W. H. Hartley, Winchester.

59 C. H. Beale (ed.), *Reminiscences of a Gentlewoman of the Last Century: Letters of Catherine Hutton* (Birmingham, 1891), 17.

60 *Guardian*, no. 155 (8 September 1713); Huntington Library, HM 31201, Mrs Larpent's diary, vol. 1, 1790–95; facing 154.

61 Lady Llanover (ed.), *Mrs Delany*, 1st series, III, 40; II, 561; Wiltshire Record Office, 1300/3199 (1794), Lady Frances Brudenell, London, to Earl of Ailesbury, Tottenham Park.

62 Essex Record Office, Chelmsford, D/DZg 34 (22 December 1770), Jane Farrin to Poll, Borton; Hampshire Record Office, IM 44/7/34 (1 November 1780), Lady Wallingford to Earl of Banbury, and IM 44/7/43 (22 February 1783), same to same.

63 Huntington Library, MO 264 (3 December 1736), Elizabeth Robinson to Duchess of Portland.

64 Elizabeth Eger, 'Luxury, Industry and Charity: Bluestocking Culture Displayed', in *Luxury in the Eighteenth Century: Debates, Desires and Delectable Goods*, ed. Maxine Berg and Elizabeth Eger (Houndmills, Basingstoke, 2003), 199.

65 Huntington Library, MO 5223 (1752), Sarah Scott to Elizabeth Montagu.

66 Betty Rizzo, 'Two Versions of Community: Montagu and Scott', in *Reconsidering the Bluestockings*, ed. Nicole Pohl and Betty A Schellenberg (San Marino, CA, 2003), 193–214.

67 Sarah Scott, *A Description of Millenium Hall and the Country Adjacent* [1762] (London, 1986), 7, 149.

68 Huntington Library, HM 31201, Mrs Larpent's diary, vol. 1, 1790–95, f. 77.

69 Brynmor Jones Library, DOG8/6 (11 November 1800), John Furnis Ogle, Cambridge, to Mrs Martha Ogle.

70 Huntington Library, HM 31201, Mrs Larpent's diary, vol. 1, 1790–95, f. 14.

71 Lancashire Record Office, DDGr C3 (21 July 1819), S. Tatham, Southall, to Mr and Mrs Bradley, Slyne.

72 Jane Collier, *The Art of Ingeniously Tormenting* [1753] (Bristol, 1994), 123, 124–5.

73 Lady Llanover (ed.), *Mrs Delany*, 1st series, I, 213; Rotherham Public Library, Platt Microfilm (1 January 1793), Anne Platt, Windlestone, to Elisabeth Platt, Rotherham; Emily Climenson (ed.), *Passages from the Diaries of Mrs Philip Lybbe Powys* (London, 1899), 147; William Combes, *An History of the Thames*, 2 vols (1794), I, 228.

74 *The Spectator*, 8 vols (1712–15), V, 56; Thomas Gisborne, *An Enquiry into the Duties of the Female Sex* (1797), 18–19; *Spectator*, VIII, 294; Huntington Library, MO 2277 (8 July 1753), Elizabeth Montagu, Tunbridge Wells, to Edward Montagu.

75 More, *Strictures*, I, 111; *The Complete Works of Hannah More* (1835), I, 130.

76 Sloan, 'A Noble Art', 7, 43, 45, 215; cites Walpole, *Anecdotes of Painting in England*, III, 335–6.

77 Lady Llanover (ed.), *Mrs Delany*, 2nd series, III, 507, 503; West Sussex Record Office, Acc 8285, 4/77 (7 June 1783), Hester Hoare, Adelphi, to Harriet Bishop, Parham.

78 Bernard Denvir, *The Eighteenth Century: Art, Design and Society 1689–1789* (London, 1983), 207–8.

79 *The Times* (Thursday, 19 January 1792), 2; issue 2207; column A.

80 Hamilton is cited in Sloan, 'A Noble Art', 46; Climenson (ed.), *Passages from the Diaries of Mrs Philip Lybbe Powys*, 147.

81 Lancashire Record Office, DDB/72/181 (11 December 1764), W. Ramsden, Charterhouse, to Mrs Parker, Alkincoats.

82 Tessa Murdoch (ed.), *Noble Households: Eighteenth-century Inventories of Great Houses* (Cambridge, 2006), 281 and 277.

83   Sheraton, *Cabinet Dictionary*, 219.

84   The National Archives, c 107/109: James Brown, 29 St Paul's Churchyard, London, up-holsterer. T. Whitewood, a stationer and bookseller at Portsea in Hampshire in the 1780s, advertised 'DRAWINGS, PRINTS AND PIECES OF NEEDLE-WORK, framed and glazed in the neatest Manner'; label attached to the back of framed engraving offered for sale by Grosvenor Prints, London, http://www.grosvenorprints.com, 10 October 2008.

Chapter 10   *A Sex in Things?*

1   Adam Fitz-Adam, *The World*, (Edinburgh, 1776), 227–32 (20 September 1753).

2   James Forrester, *Polite Philosopher* (Dublin, 1734), 25.

3   Isaac Ware, *A Complete Body of Architecture* (London, 1768), 473, 521; B. S. Allen, *Tides in English Taste, 1619–1800*, 2 vols (New York, 1958), II, 112.

4   Tobias Smollett, *The Expedition of Humphry Clinker* [1771] (Oxford, 1984), 285–96; C. Bruyn Andrews (ed.), *The Torrington* Diaries, 4 vols (London, 1934), I, xx.

5   John Cornforth, *Early Georgian Interiors* (New Haven and London, 2004); Rosemary Baird, *Mistress of the House: Great Ladies and Grand Houses* (London, 2004), 47; J. Summerson, *Architecture in Britain, 1530–1830* [1953] (Harmondsworth, 1970), 372–6.

6   Ware, *Complete Body of Architecture*, 176.

7   British Library, Add. MS 75460 (31 August 1750), Sarah Cowper, Durham, to Mrs Poyntz.

8   Ware, *Complete Body of Architecture*, 521; Allen, *Tides in English Taste*, II, 40; National Trust, *Claydon House* (1984).

9   James Forrester, *Polite Philosopher* (Dublin, 1734), 25.

10   Maria Edgeworth and Richard Lovell Edgeworth, *Practical Education*, 2 vols (1798), II, 607–8. On changing ideals, see W. J. Bate, *From Classic to Romantic: Premises of Taste in Eighteenth Century England* (Cambridge, MA, 1946).

11   Thomas Sheraton, *The Cabinet Dictionary* (1803), 215–16.

12   James Miller, *The Humours of Oxford* (Dublin, 1730), 82. For a gloss, see Patricia Fara, *Pandora's Breeches: Women, Science and Power in the Enlightenment* (London, 2004), 11.

13   On the domestic context, see Fara, *Pandora's Breeches*; Londa Schiebinger, *The Mind Has No Sex? Women in the Origins of Modern Science* (Cambridge, MA, 1989); Schiebinger, *Nature's Body: Gender and the Making of Modern Science* (Boston, MA, 1993); Lynette Hunter and Sarah Hutton (eds), *Women, Science and Medicine, 1500–1700: Mothers and Sisters of the Royal Society* (Stroud, 1997).

14   Patricia Fara, *Newton: The Making of a Genius* (London, 2002), 95.

15   Nicholas Goodison, *English Barometers, 1680–1860* (Woodbridge, Suffolk, 1977), 39; Alice N. Walters, 'Conversation Pieces: Science and Politeness in Eighteenth-century England', *History of Science*, 35 (1997), 121–54. See also G. L. E. Turner, 'Scientific Toys', *British Journal for the History of Science*, 20 (1987), 377–98, and 'The London Trade in Scientific Instrument Making in the Eighteenth Century', *Vistas in Astronomy*, 20 (1976), 173–82; James A. Secord, 'Newton in the Nursery: Tom Telescope and the Philosophy of Tops and Balls, 1761–1838', *History of Science*, 23 (1985), 127–51; Simon Schaffer, 'The Consuming Flame: Electrical Showmen and Tory Mystics in the World of Goods', in *Consumption and the World of Goods: Consumption and Society in the Seventeenth and Eighteenth Centuries*, ed. John Brewer and Roy Porter (London, 1993), 489–526.

16   Goodison, *English Barometers*, 30, 32, 39.

17   Jan Golinski, 'Barometers of Change: Meteorological Instruments as Machines of En-

lightenment', in *The Sciences in Enlightened Europe*, ed. William Clark, Jan Golinski and Simon Schaffer (Chicago, 1999), 69–93, especially 72.

18 Edward Saul, *An Historical and Philosophical Account of the Barometer* (1730), 1, 2; Benjamin Martin, *The Young Gentleman and Lady's Philosophy*, 14 vols (1772), I, 324–5; Graham Mclaren, 'The Belhus Barometer: Its Owners and Makers', *Burlington Magazine*, 132/1047 (June 1990), 407–9.

19 Lorna Weatherill, *Consumer Behaviour and Material Culture in Britain, 1660–1760* (London, 1988), 25–8, 31.

20 Lorna Weatherill, 'A Possession of One's Own: Women and Consumer Behaviour in England, 1660–1740', *Journal of British Studies*, 25 (1986), 131–26.

21 Moira Donald, 'The Greatest Necessity for Every Rank of Men: Gender, Clocks and Watches', in *Gender and Material Culture in Historical Perspective*, ed. Moira Donald and Linda Hurcombe (Basingstoke, 2000), 69.

22 The inventory of the Forth family lists three watches, belonging to the clergyman Mr Forth, his wife Mrs Elizabeth Forth, and one inherited from Mrs Forth's mother, the wife of a York grocer. York City Archives, Acc 54: 1.

23 Berkshire Record Office, D/ESV (B) F 31/41 (3 March 1753), J. Pern, Abington, Cambridgeshire, to Kitty Pern, Gillingham, Dorset.

24 Bowood Archives, Lady Shelburne's diaries, vol. 3, f. 61.

25 Sara Pennell, 'Pots and Pans History: The Material Culture of the Kitchen in Early Modern England', *Journal of Design History*, 11 (1998), 201–16, especially 205.

26 John Styles, *The Dress of the People: Everyday Fashion in Eighteenth-century England* (New Haven, 2007), ch. 6.

27 Claire Walsh, 'Shops, Shopping, Gender and the Art of Decision-Making in Early-Modern England', in *Gender, Taste and Material Culture in Britain and North America*, ed. John Styles and Amanda Vickery (New Haven, 2006), 158.

28 Birmingham City Archives, MS 3782/16/1,43, Matthew Boulton, London, to Nanny Boulton.

29 British Library, Add. MS 72516, Trumbull Papers, D/ED C13, f. 186 (28 September), Anne Dormer to Lady Trumbull.

30 Jane Austen, *Mansfield Park* [1814] (Oxford, 2003), 75.

31 J. Beresford, *The Diary of a Country Parson, 1758–1802* (Oxford, 1949), 182.

32 Golinski, 'Barometers of Change', 91.

33 Nancy Cox, ' "A Flesh Pott, or a Brasse Pott or a Pott to Boile in": Changes in Metal and Fuel Technology in the Early Modern Period and the Implications for Cooking', in *Gender and Material Culture*, ed. Donald and Hurcombe, 143–57; David Eveleigh, *Old Cooking Utensils* (Princes Risborough, 1986), 16.

34 Mark Overton et al., *Production and Consumption in English Households, 1600–1750* (London and New York, 2004), 98–100

35 The National Archives, C 114/182: Chancery Masters' Exhibits, Account-book of a London ironmonger, 1684–6; John Styles, 'Lodging at the Old Bailey: Lodgings and their Furnishings in Eighteenth-century London', in *Gender, Taste and Material Culture*, ed. Styles and Vickery, 72, and personal communication.

36 Overton et al., *Production and Consumption in English Households*, 125; D. W. Black, I. H. Goodall and I. R. Pattison, *Houses of the North York Moors* (London, 1987), 90–93.

37 Cox, ' "A Flesh Pott" ', 153.

38 Pennell, 'Pots and Pans History', passim.

39 Overton et al., *Production and Consumption in English Households*, 108.

40 Coventry Archives, PA 1484/77/161 (1749), James Hewitt, Inner Temple, to Joseph Hewitt, Coventry; Lincoln Cathedral Library, Diary and account-book of Matthew Flinders, surgeon, 1775–84.

41 F. J. Manning (ed.), *The Williamson Letters, 1748–1765* (Streatley, 1954), p. 49; Bedfordshire Record Office, L30/14/333/91 (4 May 1778), Frederick Robinson, Whitehall, to Thomas Robinson, Madrid; Chester and Cheshire Record Office, DCH/L/50/15 (19 July 1679), H. L. Cholmeley, Feltham, to Lord Cholmondeley, Cheshire. On advertising, see Karin Dannehl, 'To Families Furnishing Kitchens: Domestic Utensils and their Use in the Eighteenth-century Home', in *Buying for the Home: Shopping for the Domestic from the Seventeenth Century to the Present*, ed. David Hussey and Margaret Ponsonby (Aldershot, 2008), pp. 27–46.

42 *The Ladies Dictionary* (1694), 183–4.

43 Harriet Sampson (ed.), *The Life of Mrs Godolphin* (London and New York, 1939), Appendix B, 227; Frances Harris, *Transformations of Love* (Oxford, 2002), 66–7.

44 William Verral, *A Complete System of Cookery* (London, 1759).

45 Pennell, 'Pots and Pans History', 211.

46 British Library, Add. MS 45208; Lancashire Record Office, DDB/81/33A (1778), f. 195, and DDB/81/37 (1780), ff. 62, 237; York City Archives, Acc 54:6, Housekeeping account for the year 1799, John and Elizabeth Forth.

47 Chester and Cheshire Record Office, DAR/E/81, Vouchers to John Ardene of Harden, 1739–40.

48 'Clout the Caldron', William Thomson (ed.), *Orpheus Caledonius, a Collection of the Best Scotch Songs set to Musick* (2nd edn, London, 1733), 2 vols, II, 58. 'The Tinker's Song', Charles Henry Wilson, *The Myrtle and the Vine; or, Complete Vocal Library; Containing Several Thousands of Plaintive, Sentimental, Humorous and Bacchanalian Songs, Collected from the Muses of England, Ireland and Scotland* (London, 1800), 4 vols, II, 95.

49 James Forrester, *A Present for a Son* (c.1775), 191.

50 B. Kowaleski-Wallace, *Consuming Subjects: Women, Shopping and Business in the Eighteenth Century* (New York, 1997), 19–36.

51 On tea allowances, see Suffolk Record Office, HA 513/4/73 (21 December 1764), Duchess of Grafton to the Duke of Grafton, and Amanda Vickery, *The Gentleman's Daughter: Women's Lives in Georgian England* (New Haven and London, 1998), 142. For tea in the workhouse, see West Yorkshire Archive Service, Kirklees, Mirfield workhouse account-book, 1755–74; 'tea for Amelia Laycock's merry meal' (March 1767). The phrase 'tea-time' was used by a York dealer in old clothes in 1788: The National Archives, ASSI 45/36/2/63–5: Northern Circuit Assize Depositions, York, 1788.

52 The National Archives, ASSI 45/35/1/219–23: Northern Circuit Assize Depositions, Westmorland, 1784; Lincolnshire Archives, TENNYSON 2/4/3 (8 January 1774), Sam Turner, Cambridge, to John Turner; The National Archives, 45/37/1/252: Northern Circuit Assize Depositions, Westmorland, 1790.

53 Based on all cases involving teapots where the material is cited in Old Bailey Proceedings online for the 1750s and '80s: *www.oldbaileyonline.org* (accessed 15 January 2008).

54 Carole Shammas, 'The Domestic Environment in Early Modern England and America', *Journal of Social History*, 14 (1980), 3–24; see appendix.

55 Old Bailey Proceedings, 25 February 1755, Anne Clark (t17550226–1).

56 Martha Bradley, *The British Housewife; or, The Cook, Housekeeper's, and Gardiner's Companion* (London, 1760), 73–4.

57 Vickery, *Gentleman's Daughter*, 208.

58 Lady Sarah Pennington, *An Unfortunate Mother's Advice to Her Absent Daughters* (2nd edn, 1761), 44.

59 Susan Whyman, *Sociability and Power in Late Stuart England: The Cultural World of the Verneys, 1660–1720* (Oxford, 1999), 95; *Gentleman's Magazine* (1736), 390; Essex Record Office, Chelmsford, D/DRU F10 (1769), Anonymous diary of a young girl; Patrick Boyle, *The Ladies' Complete Visiting Guide* (1800), preface.

60 Huntington Library, HM 31201/2, Anna Larpent's diary, 1796–8, ff. 215, 217.

61 Philippa Glanville and Sophie Lee (eds.), *The Art of Drinking* (London, 2007); Karen Harvey, 'Barbarity in a tea-cup? Punch, domesticity and gender in the eighteenth century', *Journal of Design History*, 21 (2008), 205–21; David Hancock, *Oceans of Wine: Madeira and the Emergence of American Trade and Taste* (New Haven and London, 2009); Vickery, *Gentleman's Daughter*, p. 207. For wine merchants' bills, see Chapter Four above. On Boulton's bottle labels for David Hartley, see p. 217.

62 Lancashire Record Office, DDB/72/225 (25 July 1769), W. Ramsden, London, to E. Shackleton, Alkincoats; Carl Van Doren, *Letters of Benjamin Franklin and Jane Mecom* (Princeton, 1950), 35.

63 Brian Robins (ed.), *The John Marsh Journals: The Life and Times of a Gentleman Composer, 1752–1828* (Stuyvesant, NY, 1998), 126, 138, 139, 144, 293, 349, 402.

64 Whyman, *Sociability and Power in Late Stuart England*, 92.

65 Hilary Young, *English Porcelain, 1745–95: Its Makers, Design, Marketing and Consumption* (London, 1999); Sarah Richards, *Eighteenth-century Ceramics: Products for a Civilized Society* (Manchester, 1999).

66 Peter Thornton, *Seventeenth-century Interior Decoration in England, France and Holland* (New Haven, 1978), 250; David Mitchell, 'The Influence of Tartary and the Indies on Social Attitudes and Material Culture in England and France, 1650–1730', in *A Taste for the Exotic: Foreign Influences on Early Eighteenth-century Silk Designs*, ed. Anna Jolly (Riggisberg, 2007), 21; Emily Climenson (ed.), *Passages from the Diaries of Mrs Philip Lybbe Powys* (London, 1899), 331.

67 David Porter, 'A Wanton Chase in a Foreign Place: Hogarth and the Gendering of Exoticism in the Eighteenth-century Interior', in *Furnishing the Eighteenth Century*, ed. Dena Goodman and Kathryn Norberg (New York, 2007), 55.

68 Cited in Young, *English Porcelain*, 192, 190–91.

69 Vickery, *Gentleman's Daughter*, 164–8; Judith Anderson, 'Derby Porcelain and the Early English Fine Ceramic Industry, c.1750–1830' (D.Phil. thesis, Leicester, 2000), 36–40; K. E. Farrer (ed.), *Correspondence of Josiah Wedgwood*, 3 vols (London, 1903–6), I, 151–2.

70 See, for an early example, Thomas Chippendale, *Gentleman and Cabinet-Maker's Director* (3rd edn, 1762), pl. 51, 'A Dressing-Table for a Lady', and pl. 116, 'A Writing-Table and Bookcase for a Lady'.

71 *Genteel Household Furniture in the Present Taste* (1760), pls 11, 53, 54.

72 Wiliam Ince and John Mayhew, *Universal System of Household Furniture* (1762), pls xviii, xxl, xxxvii, xl.

73 Thomas Sheraton, *The Cabinet-Maker and Upholsterer's Drawing Book in Three Parts*, 2 vols (1793–4); Sheraton, *The Cabinet Dictionary*, 115.

74 Louisa Collins, 'Women, Writing and Furniture, 1750–1800' (MA dissertation in the History of Design, V&A/RCA, 2005).

75 Sheraton, *Cabinet-Maker and Upholsterer's Drawing Book*, 397, 405, 409, Sheraton, *Cabinet Dictionary*, 303.

76   West Yorkshire Archive Service, Calderdale, SH 3/AB/8–15, Jonathan Hall of Elland and London, 1701–35.

77   The National Archives, C107/109: James Brown, 29 St Paul's Churchyard, London, upholsterer ledgers, 1782–91.

78   Jane Austen, *Mansfield Park* [1814] (Oxford, 2003), 120.

79   In 1783 Joseph Lewis, a London cabinetmaker, supplied Charlestonian Thomas Hutchinson with 'a ladies dressing table of mahogany': E. Fleming, 'Staples for Genteel Living: The Importation of London Household Furnishings in Charleston During the 1780s', *American Furniture* (1997), 336–7.

80   Sheraton, *Cabinet Dictionary*, 202.

81   *The Times*, 23 January 1796, 23 April 1796, 23 July 1796, 24 October 1796.

82   For the prelude, see R. B. Walker, 'Advertising in London Newspapers, 1650–1750', *Business History*, 15 (1973), 130.

83   *Catalogue of a Loan Exhibition of English Chintz* (London, 1960), 13.

84   C. H. Beale (ed.), *Reminiscences of a Gentlewoman of the Last Century: Letters of Catherine Hutton* (Birmingham, 1891), 4.

Conclusion

1   John Dryden, *Aureng-Zebe* (1676), 23. This example is offered as a definition of home in Samuel Johnson, *A Dictionary of the English Language*, 2 vols (2nd edn, 1755–6), 1: 'Home'.

2   Samuel Richardson, *Sir Charles Grandison* [1754] (Oxford, 1986), 428.

3   Nicholas Cooper, *Houses of the Gentry, 1480–1680* (New Haven and London, 1999), 275.

4   Felicity Heal, *Hospitality in Early Modern England* (Oxford, 1990); Amanda Vickery, *The Gentleman's Daughter: Women's Lives in Georgian England* (New Haven and London, 1998), 195–223.

5   Roger H. Leech, 'The Symbolic Hall: Historical Context and Merchant Culture in the Early Modern City', *Vernacular Architecture*, 31 (2000), 1–10.

6   Colin Platt, *The Great Rebuildings of Tudor and Stuart England: Revolutions in Architectural Taste* (London, 1994), 135–7; John Bold, 'The Design of a House for a Merchant, 1724', *Architectural History*, 33 (1990), 75–82; Leech, 'The Symbolic Hall'.

7   Cited in Platt, *Great Rebuildings*, 136; Norfolk Record Office, WKC 7/21/11 (26 September 1707), Katherine Windham to Ashe Windham.

8   Mark Overton et al., *Production and Consumption in English Households, 1600–1750* (London and New York, 2004), 132; Margaret Ponsonby, *Stories from Home: English Domestic Interiors, 1750–1850* (Aldershot, 2007), 53, 105, 125; D. W. Black, I. H. Goodall and I. R. Pattison, *Houses of the North York Moors* (London, 1987), 92–3; John Tuke, *General View of the Agriculture of the North Riding of Yorkshire* (1794), 80; William Stevenson, *General View of the Agriculture of the County of Dorset* (1812), 84; Abraham Driver and William Driver, *General View of the Agriculture of the County of Hants* (1794), 58.

9   David Howell, *Patriarchs and Parasites: The Gentry of South West Wales* (Cardiff, 1986), 179; F. E. Brown, 'Continuity and Change in the Urban House: Developments in Domestic Space Organization in Seventeenth-century London', *Comparative Studies in Society and History*, 28 (1986), 558–90.

10 Lewis Walpole Library, LWL MSS vol. 70, Observations made by Mrs Percivall when in London, 1713 or 1714.

11   J. A. Home (ed.), *The Letters and Journals of Lady Mary Coke*, 4 vols (Edinburgh, 1889–96), I, 232–3; Melville, 'Use and Organization of Domestic Space', 233–4.

12   *The Whole Duty of Woman* (1735), 62; *London Magazine* (1767), 668; William Matthews (ed.), *The Diary of Dudley Ryder, 1715–1716* (London, 1939), 126.

13   Old Bailey Proceedings, 2 July 1684, Edward Kirk (t16840702–6).

14   Norman Scarfe (ed.), *A Frenchman's Year in Suffolk, 1784: François de la Rochefoucauld*, Suffolk Records Society (Woodbridge, 1998), 203.

15   F. J. Manning (ed.), *The Williamson Letters, 1748–1765* (Streatley, 1954), 8;

16   Vickery, *Gentleman's Daughter*, 195–223.

17   Joyce Hemlow et al. (eds), *The Journals and Letters of Fanny Burney*, 12 vols (Oxford, 1972–84), I, 225.

18   The National Archives, C 107/109: James Brown, 29 St Paul's Churchyard, London, upholsterer, 21 October 1782; M. Dorothy George, *London Life in the Eighteenth Century* (Harmondsworth, 1965), 103.

19   John Styles, 'Lodging at the Old Bailey: Lodgings and their Furnishing in Eighteenth-century London', in *Gender, Taste and Material Culture in Britain and North America*, ed. Styles and Amanda Vickery (New Haven, 2006), 61–80.

20   Richard Bradley, *The Country Housewife and Lady's Director, in the Management of a House, and the Delights and Profits of a Farm* (6th edn, 1732), vii–viii; *The Science of Good Husbandry; or, The Oeconomics of Xenophon*, trans. Richard Bradley (1727).

21   Sarah Pennell, ' "Pots and Pans History": The Material Culture of the Kitchen in Early Modern England', *Journal of Design History*, 11 (1998), 214; Dudley North, *Observations and Advices Oeconomical* (1669), 1–2. For earlier uses of oeconomy, see Craig Muldrew, *The Economy of Obligation: The Culture of Credit and Social Relations in Early Modern England* (Basingstoke, 1998), 158–9. For its application to the plebeian household, see Jonathan White, 'Luxury and Labour: Ideas of Labouring-class Consumption in Eighteenth-century England' (PH.D thesis, University of Warwick, 2001).

22   William Cobbett, *Cottage Economy* (1822), 1–2.

23   Maria Edgeworth and Richard Lovell Edgeworth, *Essays on Practical Education*, 2 vols [1798] (3rd edn, 1811), II, 397; Richard Steele, *Ladies Library, Written by a Lady*, 3 vols (1714), II, 391.

24   Centre for Buckinghamshire Studies, D/X 1069/2/13/1 (15 October, n.y.), Sarah Pratviel, Woodfield, to Mrs Martha Baker.

25   Birmingham City Archives, Transcript of diary of Julius Hardy, button maker, 1788–93, 36.

26   Huntington Library, HM 31201/2, Anna Larpent's diary, 1796–8, ff. 235, 238, 239, 242, 254v, 261v.

27   Old Bailey Proceedings, 11 September 1793, Daniel Macarthy (t17930911–67); 4 December 1793, Susannah Emery (t17931204–48).

28   Overton et al., *Production and Consumption in English Households*, 108–11, 125, 130–31; Black, Goodall and Pattison, *Houses of the North York Moors*, 90–93.

29   Vickery, *Gentleman's Daughter*, 133–4, 147–9, 151, 164–8.

30   John Cornforth, *Early Georgian Interiors* (New Haven and London, 2004), 206; Charles Saumarez Smith, *Eighteenth-century Decoration: Design and the Domestic Interior in England* (London, 1993), 233; Ann Bermingham, *Learning to Draw: Studies in the Cultural History of a Polite and Useful Art* (New Haven and London, 2000), 183, 186; Robert W. Jones, *Gender and the Formation of Taste in Eighteenth-century Britain* (Cambridge, 1998).

31   Deborah Cohen, *Household Gods: The British and their Possessions* (New Haven and London, 2006), 120.

32 Amy Erickson, *Women and Property in Early Modern England* (London, 1993); Nicola Phillips, *Women in Business* (London, 2006), 23–47; Margot Finn, 'Women, Consumption and Couverture in England, c. 1760–1860', *Historical Journal*, 39, 703–22.

33 Margaret Ponsonby, *Stories from Home: English Domestic Interiors, 1750–1850* (Aldershot, 2007), 81–2, but see the whole chapter on 'Recycled Homes', 79–102. For wide coverage see Jane Hamlett, 'Materialising Gender: Identity and Middle-class Domestic Interiors, 1850–1910' (ph.d thesis, London, 2005).

34 Thomas Tusser, *A Hundreth Goode Pointes of Husbandrie* (1557), verse 41, under heading 'Christmas'.

35 Jones, *Gender and the Formation of Taste*; Lord Edmond Fitzmaurice, *Life of William, Earl of Shelburne*, 2 vols (London, 1875–6), 1 [1737–66], 11.

36 *A General Description of All Trades* (1747), 214.

37 Alexander Pope, *Mr Pope's Literary Correspondence*, 5 vols (1735), v, 89.

38 Jack Ayres (ed.), *Paupers and Pig Killers: The Diary of William Holland, a Somerset Parson, 1799–1818* (Stroud, 1984), 87.

39 Juliet Kinchin, 'Interiors: Nineteenth-century Essays on the "Masculine" and "Feminine" Room', in *The Gendered Object*, ed. Pat Kirkham (Manchester, 1996), 12–29.

40 William Marshall, *Planting and Ornamental Gardening* (1785), 616.

41 E.g., Centre for Buckinghamshire Studies, d/x 852/11, Catalogue of the household furniture of John Andrews Baker, Esq., Penn.

42 K. E. Farrer (ed.), *Correspondence of Josiah Wedgwood*, 3 vols (London, 1903–6), 1, 143–4.

43 Henrietta Knight, *Letters Written by the Right Honourable Lady Luxborough to William Shenstone Esq.* (London, 1775), 256.

44 The National Archives, assi 45/38/1/18–23a: Assizes, Northern Circuit Depositions, Yorkshire, 1793, Jane Boys.

45 *A Modern Dissertation on a Certain Necessary Piece of Household Furniture* (1752), 8, 10, 12–13. For all you ever needed to know about chamber pots, see Ivor Noël Hume, 'Through the Looking Glasse; or, The Chamber Pot as a Mirror of its Time', *Ceramics in America* (2003), 138–71.

46 Cobbett, *Cottage Economy*, 197.

47 Borthwick Institute for Archives, University of York, Exchequer and Prerogative Courts of York, wills, 1710–11 and 1780–82, Ainsty, Doncaster, Pontefract and York deaneries.

48 John Leigh, 'Voltaire and the myth of England', in *The Cambridge Companion to Voltaire*, ed. Nicholas Cronk (Cambridge, 2009), 79; Josiah Tucker, *Instructions for Travellers* (London, 1757), 26.

49 M. J. Daunton, *House and Home in the Victorian City: Working-class Housing, 1850–1914* (London, 1983).

50 Huntington Library, stg Misc., Stowe, Directions for the management of servants and for the village sick; stb personal, James Brydges, 1st Duke of Chandos, Instructions for servants at Canons; Wiltshire Record Office, 1300 1500 a & b 1763, Regulations in family at Tottenham Park; and 1300 1488, Instructions for house steward.

51 York City Archives, Acc 54 : 4, 1792, Mrs Forth's Memorandum book.

52 Cited in Joe McEwan and Pamela Sharpe, ' "It Buys Me Freedom": Genteel Lodging in Late Seventeenth and Eighteenth-century London', *Parergon*, 24 (2007), 149.

MANUSCRIPT
COLLECTIONS

International collections

Beinecke Library, Yale University, New Haven, CFT, USA
  Osborne shelves, C 236, Marthae Taylor letter-book

Huntington Library, San Marino, CA, USA
  MO, Montagu collection
    Stutterd letters
  Box 16/1, Hastings accounts
  HM 31201, Diaries of Mrs Anna Larpent, 16 vols, 1790–1830
  STG, Misc., Directions for the management of servants
  STB, Personal, James Brydges, First Duke of Chandos, Housebooks

Lewis Walpole Library, Farmington, CT, USA
  LWL MSS vol. 70, Observations made by Mrs Percivall when in London, 1713 or 1714
  LWL MSS vol. 7, Recipes, 1673–76; Walpole, Mary Burwell, 1655–1711
  LWL MSS vol. 9, Ledger for the Duke of Grafton, 1774

Yale Center for British Art, New Haven, CT, USA
  Clayton family papers re their house in London on Hyde Park Street, 1814–71
  Miles & Edwards and Charles Hindley & Sons, Correspondence, 1832–75

National archives

British Library, London: Manuscripts
Add. 45718, Elizabeth Freke, her book
Add. 72516, Trumbull Papers, D/ED C13, Anne Dormer letters, 1685–8
Add. 75771, Althorp Papers, Notebook compiled by Lady Spencer of tradesmen, n.d.
Add. 45213, William Brockman, Accompts, 1696–1742
Add. 45204–10, Household accompts of Anne, wife of Sir William Brockman, 1700–24
Add. 75460, Althorp Papers, Correspondence of Hon. Mrs Stephen Poyntz and Lady Cowper, 1721–55
Add. 62092, Account-book for personal expenses of Margaret Spencer, with her father's notes throughout as auditor
Add. 78304, Correspondence of George Evelyn II of Wotton

British Museum, London: Department of Prints and Drawings
Heal Trade card collection
Banks Trade Card Collection

National Archives of Scotland, Edinburgh
GD 18/4737–4847, Correspondence of Robert Adam and family, 1755–8

The National Archives, Kew
C 108/362, London Building Book [Matthew Brettingham]
C 114/182, Account-book of a London ironmonger, 1684–6
C 107/164, Inventories of the stock in trade and furniture of Morris Lewin Mogeley, silversmith of Liverpool, 1801–2
C 107/109, Ledgers of James Brown, 29 St Paul's Churchyard, London, upholsterer, 1782–91
C 108/284, Arthur Webb Sale Catalogue, jeweller, 1792
29/215 PROB 3, Inventory for Rebecca Weekes
ASSI 45/35/1/219–23: Assizes, Northern Circuit Depositions
ASSI 45/37/1/252: Assizes, Nortern Circuit Depositions
ASSI 45/38/1/18–23A, Assizes, Northern Circuit Depositions
ASSI 45/36/2/63–5, Assizes, Northern Circuit Depositions

The Royal Archives, Windsor Castle
Queen Charlotte's Diaries

Victoria and Albert Museum, London: Word and Image
E 1864–1946 96.a.3, Cowtan order books

Victoria and Albert Museum, London: National Art Library
86.AA.9–13, Day and delivery books, J. Duppa & Sons, 6 vols, 1797–1822
86.SS.77, Account book of Elizabeth Dodson, 1728–1732

Provincial Archives

Bedfordshire Record Office, Bedford
Or, Orlebar collection
M 10/4, Williamson letters, 1750–95
L 30, Wrest Park papers

Berkshire Record Office, Reading
Mf 688, D/EHY F 83–113, Mary Hartley letters, 1781–4, 1785–7
D/EP 7/139, Transcript of diary of Susannah Stevens, 1795–6
D/ESV (B) F 31, Catherine Pern letters, 1701–75
D/EZ 12/1&2, Account and memorandum book of Edward Belson, distiller, 1707–22
D ESV (B), F 11, Arabella Clayfield letters, 1785–1800
D/EZ 30 F1–2, Diaries of Robert Lee, 1735–7, 1742–4
D/ED F9, 17 A 18, Inventories of furniture, etc., at Esthampstead Park, *circa* 1678
D/EX/1422/1, Diaries of Robert Davidson, jeweller, 1798–1820

Birmingham City Archives
MS 3782, Boulton collection
MS 669002, MS 218, Diary of Julius Hardy, button maker, 1788–93
MS 249, Gough family papers, miscellaneous bills and receipts
MS 397968 and MS 397970, Inventories of Staunton of Longbridge, 1811
MS 397971 [11R20], Household account of John Staunton of Longbridge, 1800–16
MS 1365, Household inventory of Charles Wyatt, St Paul's Square, Birmingham, 1794
MS 59/1, Inventory of William Matthews Green, Lettuce Lane, London, 1792
MS 397971, Household account of John Stanton of Longbridge, 1800–16
MS 1434/10, Inventory of utensils and memorandum of fixtures of Mrs Cooper, Batholomew Street, Birmingham, 1819
MS 331069-70 [11R13], Inventories of household goods of William and Thomas Hutton destroyed in the Birmingham riots of 1791
MS 303600 [11R53], Sale catalogue, contents of Grendon Hall, Warwickshire, 1750

Borthwick Institute for Archives, University of York
Exchequer and Prerogative Courts of York, wills, 1710–11 and 1780–82, Ainsty, Doncaster, Pontefract and York deaneries

Bowood Archives, Wiltshire
Diaries of Lady Shelburne, 1765–70
Lady Shelburne's account-book, Aug–Oct 1770

Brynmor Jones Library, University of Hull
DOG/9/1, John Ogle's pocket diary
DOG/8, Correspondence of Ogle family of Flamborough, 1740s–1830s
DDBM/33/20, Inventory of Lady Osbalderston's plate and linen, 1730
DDBM/33/33, Account for Lady Macdonald's wedding clothes, 1768
DDCA 31/18, Inventory of Mrs Addis's clothes and possessions, 1791

DDFA (3) 9/5, Inventory of goods at Lady Dawes's house at York, 1750

DDMM/2/10, Memorandum by Rosamund Constable re her financial arrangements and household expenses, 1726

DDBH/24/2, Accounts of Mary Robinson, 1675–1703

DDHO/15/2, Account-book and notes of Elizabeth Hotham, 1678–97

DDCB/22/4, Account-book of Sarah Robinson, 1770–75

DDBM/32/7, Thomas Wentworth, letters to Diana Bosville, 1734–83

DDX/60/3, Diaries of John Courtney, 1788–97, vol. 3: 1788–90

DMEV/66/19, 'Account of linen in Mary Dale's custody', 1732

Cambridgeshire Record Office, Cambridge

588 DR/A 26, 29, 30, 31, 33, 38, Account-books of Sir J. H. Cotton, 1745–67

588 DR/A 37, Account-book of Mrs Cotton, 1760–70

588 DR/A 39, Accounts of Elizabeth Cotton, 1766–9

588 DR/A 45, Account-book of Lady Cotton, 1800–11

Centre for Buckinghamshire Studies, Aylesbury

D /X 1277/23, Household account-book of Dorothy Richardson, 1789–95

D /CE, Correspondence of the Clayton family, *circa* 1662–1834

D/X 1069/1/2, Diary of journey of John Baker, 1728

D/X 1069/2/1–155, Correspondence of Baker family, *circa* 1670–*circa* 1765

D/X 852/11, Catalogue of the household furniture of John Andrews Baker, Esq. at Penn, 1769

Chester and Cheshire Record Office

DDX 597/2–5, Diaries and accounts of John Egerton

DDX 597/7, List of charities

DAR, Arderne of Harden account-books, vouchers and commonplace books

DMD/L/2/1, Diaries and accounts of Benjamin Wyatt

DCH/L/50, Cholmondeley of Cholmondeley correspondence

DSA, Stanley correspondence

DLT/D/154, Accounts of Mary Chorley, Draper, *circa* 1820

DMD/L/2, Diary of Sarah Wyatt, 1786

Coventry Archives

PA 1484/77, Correspondence of James Hewitt, 1748–68

Derbyshire Record Office, Matlock

D 231, Okeover of Okeover collection

D 37, Turbett of Ogston collection

WH, Osmaston collection

D 803, Gresley of Drakelow collection

D 5430/8/10, Household account-book, Eyam Hall, 1808–24

Devon Record Office, Exeter

4902z/f1, Account-book of Philip Gell, Esq., 1747–61

2346M/EL–3, Account-books for furnishing of Creedy House, 1820

71/8, Journal of Exeter merchant [Samuel Milford], 1760–74

2741M/FV1-47, Ley family vouchers for expenditure in Exeter and London, 1774–1866

Doncaster Archives

DD.DC.H6/1, Account-book of Mrs Diana Eyre of Ripon, 1749–77

DD.DC.H6/2, Account-book of Mrs Mary Cooke of Owston, 1763–83

DD.DC.H1/1/1–3, Cooke of Owston, plans, letters from architects, estimates, 1783–99

DD.DC.H7/1/3, Mary Cooke to Bryan Cooke, her will, 22 March 1784

DD.DC.H2/, Cooke of Owston inventories, 1763–1822

DD.DD.H17 & 18, Miscellaneous bills of Diana Eyre and Mary Cooke, 1763–78

DD/BW/A/4–15, Account-book of Isabella Wrightson, 1743–83

Dorset Record Office, Dorchester

D/WIB/F 42, Diaries of Sophia Cunningham, 1808–20, 1813–20

D/BKL, Bankes of Kingston Lacey collection

D/PLR/F65, Diary of John Richards of Warmwell, 1692–94

D/87/7, Estimate and specification for building a house at Gillingham for Mrs Helme and Misses Cox, 1783

Essex Record Office, Chelmsford

D/DRU F10, Anonymous diary of a young girl, 1769

D/DZG 33, Correspondence between Mary Farrin and future husband William White, 1744

D/DZG 34, Letters of Jane Farrin, 1760–84

D/DB B7, Bills and receipts of Misses Mary and Matilda Conyers, 1742–69

Essex Record Office, Colchester

C47, Letters of Mary and Isaac Rebow, 1767–79

Glamorgan Record Office, Cardiff

D/DX 223/1, Diary of the Revd David Jones of Llangan, 1807

D/D c f/1–9, Diaries of John Carne, Clerk, 1762–90

D/DX cb 2, Account-book of Elizabeth Martin of Vervil, 1763–4

D/D xei 10/16–34, Letters from Eliza Wilkins of Brecon to her stepmother, 1729–46

D/DX 478/5, Tradesman's receipts of G. Richards of Cardiff, 1802–5

Gloucestershire Archives

PE 98, Autobiography of Thomas Hittingford, 1783–1855

D 1799, Letters and accounts of Blathwayte family of Dyrham Park

D 2685/23, Diary of Elizabeth Watkins, 1771

PA 328/18, Typescript diary of Thomas Pike the younger, 1752–1815

D 149/A33, Accounts of Mrs Elizabeth Phillips of Frampton on Severn and Gloucester, 1781–93

D 610/F8, Household accounts of Mrs Mary Leigh of Broadwell, 1788–91

D 1183, Diary of Margaret Anne Croome of Cirenceseter, 1823, 1829

Guildhall Library, London
MS 14951, 14951/2, Diaries of Elizabeth Tyrell, 1808–11
MS 14 951/3, Diary of Elizabeth Tyrell jnr, 1818
MS 10823/4, Journal of Benjamin Boddington, 1747–91
MS 10883/1, Ledgers of Thomas Handyside and Son, upholsterers, 1807–34
MS 9939, Diaries and accounts of William Mawhood, 1764–90
MS 00205, Diaries of Stephen Monteage, accountant at Southsea House, 1733–64
MS 00433, Architectural sketch and notebooks of Richard Kelsey, architect, *circa* 1791–1837
MS 11021–2, Letters and papers of Gibbs family, merchants, 1744–*circa* 1858
MS 03041:6, Household accounts for Thomas Bowrey, 1699–1714

Hampshire Record Office, Winchester
44M69, Jervoise collection
IM 44, Banbury collection
96M82/P225, Account-book of Mary Medhurst, draper, 1762–80
94M72/F10, Letters of John Bonham Carter to his wife Joanna Maria, 1818–38
94M72/F49–6, Diaries of Lady Joanna Bonham Carter, 1802–66
29M69, Diaries of Emma, schoolgirl at Tangley, 1784

Herefordshire Record Office, Hereford
AS 594/101, Charles Bennet of Bosbury, 'His book', 1740
A 95/3/1–4, Journals of Jane Pateshall, *circa* 1763
C54, Diary of Sarah Ravenhill of Hereford, 1798–1807
F76/1V/547, Diary of Joseph Amphlett, 1789–99
G2/1V/J/1–76, Diary of John Biddulph of Ledbury, 1768–1845
A95/box 36, Inventory of furniture at Allensmore Court, 1790

Hertfordshire Record Office, Hertford
70150–70168, Diaries of Mrs Louisa Arrowsmith, Totteridge Park, 1818–36
86326, Diary of Eliza Hope Stevens, 1820
D/EP/F204, letters of Mary, Countess Cowper, 1720
D/EP/A2, Pin money account of Judith, wife of William Cooper, later first Earl of Cowper, 1685–92
D/EP/A6, Pin money account kept for Henrietta Countess Cowper by Earl Cowper, 1741–8
71886, Lease of house in Harpenden, 1785
AH1732-1858, Accounts re: building and repairs to London house, Francis, Third Duke of Bridgewater, 1796
D/EWO/E38, Fire insurance policies on furniture in Twyford House, 1808–35
68335, Will of Jane Burgess of Totteridge
D/EHX/F25, Sale catalogue of household furniture of late Mrs Sarah Neild of West Street, Hertford, 1819

John Rylands Library, University of Manchester
R 93692, Dorothy Richardson's journals, 5 vols, 1770–75

Keele University Library
  w/m, Wedgwood Moseley collection
  sc, Sneyd collection

Kent Archives Service, East Kent
  ek/u725/5, Catalogue of goods saved from the iris, 1807
  ek/u725/7, Catalogue of goods saved from the George, 1807
  ek/u725/9, Catalogue of goods saved from the Juno, 1812

Lancashire Record Office, Preston
  ddgr, Dawson Greene collection
  ddb, Parker of Browsholme collection

Leicestershire Record Office, Leicester
  de 1184/10, Letters of B. F. Lincoln to William Pratt, Kegworth, *circa* 1816

Lincoln Cathedral Library
  Diary and account-book of Matthew Flinders, surgeon, 1775–84

Lincolnshire Archives, Lincoln
  and 5/2/1, Anderson collection
  tennyson 2/1–5, Correspondence of the Turner family, 1770–97
  Smith 15/3, Diaries of Benjamin Smith, solicitor, 1794–1854

Liverpool City Archives
  920/nic, Correspondence of Nicholson family of merchants, 1715–1828
  920 Par, Correspondence of Parkers, 1760–1811

London Metropolitan Archives
  b/trl/09, Joseph Trollope and Sons, letter-book, 1797–1808

Museum of London
  Account-book of Mrs Martha Dodson, 1746–65

Norfolk Record Office, Norwich
  wkc 7/21/1–40, 404x1, Letters from Katherine Windham to her son Ashe, 1704–28
  bol 2/139, 740x4, Letters from Elizabeth Reading to Elizabeth Munbee, 1773–5
  fel, Account-books and memoranda of Ann Fellowes, 1776–1811
  bol 2/59, Correspondence of Elizabeth Leaths, Mrs Peach, 1780–97

North Yorkshire County Record Office, Northallerton
  mic1230, Account book of Benjamin Agar for the building of his house Brockfield, *circa* 1801

Nottinghamshire Archives, Nottingham
  dd/sk 217/1–26, Diaries and accounts of Robert Lowe Esq., 1793–1822

DD/SR 212/10–11, Diaries of Gertrude Savile, 1721–2, 1737–57
DD/SR A4/45-46, Account books of Gertrude Savile, 1736-58
DD/1517/45, Diary of John Jowett, 1789
DD 1907/1, Daily journal of George Hopkinson, 1780–81
DD/BB 114/46, Typescript of diary of Mrs Margaret Fisher, 1740–1806
DD/CW 8C/5/1–58, Diaries of R. R. Pegge Burnell, 1748–97
DDFJ 11, Foljame collection

Rotherham Public Library
Platt Microfilm, Correspondence of the family of George Platt, architect and mason, 1742–1803

Shropshire Record Office, Shrewsbury
894, 1144, Hanmer of Pentrepant collection
112/24/4/1, Personal diary of Richard Partridge, 1763–1806
D3651/B/30/7/1/1, Diary of Thomas Jeffreys, surgeon, 1797
5492/1–2, Journals of Thomas Brocas, 1785–7, 1804–15
1066/1–37, Diaries of Miss Katherine Plymley, 1791–1827
5399/2, Diary of Mary Langdon, 1750–83

Somerset Record Office, Taunton
DD/SF/4515, Correspondence of Mary Clarke to husband Edward, 1675–1704
DD/FS 5/2, Accounts of Mrs Frances Hamilton, 1797–1800
DD/FS 7/3, Diaries of Mrs Frances Hamilton, 1791–4, 1797–1800

Southwark Local Studies Library, London
A296, Account-books of Ann, Lady Rose of Walworth, 1797–1807

Staffordshire Record Office, Stafford
D1240/1–10, Accounts and vouchers of Thomas Anson of Shugborough

Suffolk Record Office, Bury St Edmunds
HA 513/4/8–95, Correspondence re the separation of the third Duke of Grafton and his first wife, Anne, 1764–5

Surrey Record Centre, Woking
G111/6/16(26a), Itemised bill for paperhanging at Shalford House

Wellcome Library, London, Archives and Manuscripts
PP/HOID, A408, 722, 729, Letters of Thomas Hodgkin re: moving house, 1837

Westminster Public Library, London
Gillows Collection

West Sussex Record Office, Chichester
Goodwood MS 102, Letters of second Duchess of Richmond, 1720–40

Goodwood MS 228, Letters of third Duchess of Richmond, 1792–5
Goodwood MS 349, Letters of fourth Duchess of Richmond, 1799–1842
Acc 8285, Zouch collection
Add. MSS 7462–7514, Diaries of Sophia Trower, 1793–1857
Add. MSS 21, 311, Diaries of Sarah Goodyer, 1803–7
Add. MSS 14861, No. 10, Part of a diary? of Victoria Tripping, 1683–93

West Yorkshire Archive Service, Bradford
Sp St, Spencer Stanhope collection, letters and accounts

West Yorkshire Archive Service, Calderdale
SH 3/AB/8–15, Jonathan Hall of Elland, 1701–35

West Yorkshire Archive Service, Kirklees
WBH/7, Account-books of Susannah Beaumont, 1703–14
Mirfield parish, Mirfield Workhouse account-book, 1755–74

West Yorkshire Archive Service, Leeds
TA, Gossip of Thorp Arch collection
RDP 96/71, Spofforth overseers accounts, 1707–67

West Yorkshire Archive Service, Wakefield
QS 1/77/9, West Riding Quarter Sessions Rolls
WDP 14/15/1–2, Thornhill Township Book

Wigan Record Office, Leigh
EHC, 51/M820, Scarah accounts

Wiltshire Record Office, Swindon
1412, Stourhead bills from Chippendale jnr, 1795–1820
1300, Ailesbury collection, letters, plans, inventories
1553/69, Personal account-book of William Hunt, 1728–41
1742/8112–8113, Personal day cash account books of Paul Methuen, 1760–95

York City Archives
Acc 54, Account-books and inventories of the Forth family, 1778–1825

Primary Source Websites

Old Bailey Proceedings Online: www.oldbaileyonline.org

SELECT

BIBLIOGRAPHY

Printed Primary Sources

Anon., *An Essay on Taste in General* (1731)
—, *A Modern Dissertation on a Certain Necessary Piece of Household Furniture* (1752)
—, *The Accomplished Lady's Delight in Cookery; or, The Complete Servant's Maid's [sic] Guide* (Wolverhampton, [1780?])
—, *The Batchelor's Directory: Being a Treatise of the Excellence of Marriage* (1694)
—, *The Compleat Servant-Maid; or The Young Maiden's Tutor* (London, 1677)
—, *The British Jewel, or Complete Housewife's Best Companion* (London, [1770?])
—, *Forwarn'd, Fore'arm'd; or, The Batchelor's Monitor* (1741)
—, *The Ladies Advocate; or, An Apology for Matrimony in Answer to the Batchelor's Monitor* (1741)
Mrs Artlove, *The Art of Japanning, Varnishing, Polishing and Gilding* (1730)
Cecil Aspinall-Oglander (ed.), *Admiral's Wife: Being the Life and Letters of the Hon. Mrs Edward Boscawen from 1719 to 1761* (London, 1940)
C. H. Beale (ed.), *Reminiscences of a Gentlewoman of the Last Century: Letters of Catherine Hutton* (Birmingham, 1891)
John Beresford, *Memoirs of an Eighteenth-century Footman* (London, 1928)
Patrick Boyle, *The Ladies' Complete Visiting Guide* (1800)
Martha Bradley, *The British Housewife; or, The Cook, Housekeeper's and Gardiner's Companion* (London, 1760)
Richard Bradley, *The Country Housewife and Lady's Director, in the Management of a House, and the Delights and Profits of a Farm* (6th edn, 1732)

—, trans., *The Science of Good Husbandry; or, The Oeconomics of Xenophon* (1727)

Penelope Bradshaw, *The Family Jewel, and Compleat Housewife's Companion; or, The Whole Art of Cooking made Plain and Easy* (7th edn, London, 1754)

Joseph Bramah, *A Dissertation on the Construction of Locks* ([1785])

George Brookshaw, *A New Treatise on Flower Painting; or, Every Lady Her Own Drawing Master* (1797)

C. Bruyn Andrews (ed.), *The Torrington Diaries*, 4 vols (London, 1934)

Edmund Burke, *A Philosophical Enquiry into the Origin of our Ideas of the Sublime and Beautiful* (2nd edn, 1759)

Charles Burnaby, *The Ladies Visiting Day* (1701)

J. Burton, *Lectures on Female Education and Manners* (London, 1793)

R. Campbell, *The London Tradesman* [1747] (New York, 1969)

Mary Chandler, *Description of Bath: A Poem* (3rd edn, 1736)

John Clayton, *The Snares of Prosperity To Which Is Added An Essay on Visiting* (1789)

Emily Climenson (ed.), *Passages from the Diaries of Mrs Philip Lybbe Powys* (London, 1899)

William Cobbett, *Cottage Economy* (1822)

George Coleman, *The Connoisseur. By Mr Town*, 2 vols (London, 1755–6)

Jeremy Collier, *Essays upon Several Moral Subjects* (6th edn, 1722)

F. M. Cowe (ed.), *Wimbledon Vestry Minutes, 1736, 1743–1788*, Surrey Record Society, xxv (Guildford, 1964)

Basil Cozens-Hardy (ed.), *The Diary of Sylas Neville, 1767–1788* (London and New York, 1950)

Susan C. Djabri (ed.), *The Diaries of Sarah Hurst, 1759–1762* (Horsham, 2003)

Sir Frederick Morton Eden, *The State of the Poor*, 3 vols (1797)

William Ellis, *The Country Housewife's Family Companion* (1750)

K. E. Farrer (ed.), *Correspondence of Josiah Wedgwood*, 3 vols (London, 1903–6)

Adam Fitz-Adam, *The World* (Edinburgh, 1776)

Brian Fitzgerald (ed.), *Correspondence of Emily, Duchess of Leinster (1731–1814)*, 3 vols (Dublin, 1949–57)

James Fordyce, *Sermons to Young Women*, 2 vols (6th edn, London, 1766)

B. F. Gandee, *The Artist; or, Young Ladies Instructor in Ornamental Painting, Drawing, etc.* (1835)

Edward Hall (ed.), *Miss Weeton: Journal of a Governess, 1811–1825*, 2 vols (London, 1939)

A. Heckle, *The Florist; or, An Extensive and Curious Collection of Flowers: For the Imitation of Young Ladies, either in Drawing or in Needlework* (1759)

Alice Hepplewhite, *Cabinet-Maker and Upholsterer's Guide* (1788)

Anne Hillman, *The Rake's Diary: The Journal of George Hilton* (Kendal, 1994)

White Kennett, *The Excellent Daughter* (7th ed., London, 1760)

Henrietta Knight, *Letters Written by the Right Honourable Lady Luxborough to William Shenstone Esq.* (London, 1775)

Lady Llanover (ed.), *The Autobiography and Correspondence of Mary Granville, Mrs Delany*, 1st series, 3 vols (London, 1861), 2nd series, 3 vols (London, 1862)

The Life of William Hutton [1816] (Oxford, 1998)

James Peller Malcolm, *Anecdotes of the Manners and Customs of London during the Eighteenth Century* (1808)

F. J. Manning (ed.), *The Williamson Letters, 1748–1765* (Streatley, 1954)

The John Marsh Journals: The Life and Times of a Gentleman Composer, 1752–1828 (Stuyvesant, NY, 1998)

William Marshall, *Planting and Ornamental Gardening* (1785)

William Matthews (ed.), *The Diary of Dudley Ryder, 1715–1716* (London, 1939)

Susan Neave and David Neave (eds), *The Diary of a Yorkshire Gentleman: John Courtney of Beverley, 1759–1768* (Otley, 2001)

John Pincot, *Treatise on the Practical Part of Coach & House Painting* (1811)

F. A. Pottle, *Boswell's London Journal, 1762–1763* (New York, 1950)

Hannah Robertson, *The Young Ladies School of Art* (4th edn, York, 1777)

Alan Saville (ed.), *Secret Comment: The Diaries of Gertrude Savile, 1721–1757* (Kingsbridge, 1997)

Thomas Sheraton, *The Cabinet Dictionary* (1803)

Samuel Stennett, *Discourses on Domestic Duties* (London, 1783)

Mary Thale (ed.), *The Autobiography of Francis Place (1771–1854)* (Cambridge, 1972)

L. Troide (ed.), *The Journals and Letters of Fanny Burney*, 4 vols (Oxford, 1988)

Anthony Trollope, *An Autobiography* (Oxford, 1999)

William Verral, *A Complete System of Cookery* (London, 1759)

Isaac Ware, *A Complete Body of Architecture* (London, 1768)

[Susanna Whatman], *The Housekeeping Book of Susanna Whatman, 1776–1800* (London, 1992)

Hannah Woolley, *The Gentlewoman's Companion; or, A Guide to the Female Sex* (1675)

Secondary Literature

Books

B. S. Allen, *Tides in English Taste, 1619–1800*, 2 vols (New York, 1958)

Susan Amussen, *An Ordered Society: Gender and Class in Early Modern England* (Oxford, 1988)

James Ayres, *Domestic Interiors: The British Tradition, 1500–1850* (New Haven and London, 2003)

Joanne Bailey, *Unquiet Lives: Marriage and Marriage Breakdown in England, 1660–1800* (Cambridge, 2003)

Rosemary Baird, *Mistress of the House: Great Ladies and Grand Houses* (London, 2004)

Toby Barnard, *Making the Grand Figure: Lives and Possessions in Ireland, 1641–1770* (New Haven and London, 2004)

W. J. Bate, *From Classic to Romantic: Premises of Taste in Eighteenth Century England* (Cambridge, MA, 1946)

Maxine Berg, *Luxury and Pleasure in Eighteenth-century Britain* (Oxford, 2005)

D. W. Black, I. H. Goodall and I. R. Pattison, *Houses of the North York Moors* (London, 1987)

Ian Bristow, *Architectural Colour in British Interiors, 1615–1840* (New Haven and London, 1996)

Philip Carter, *Men and the Emergence of Polite Society in Britain, 1660–1800* (Harlow, 2001)

Tita Chico, *Designing Women: The Dressing Room in Eighteenth-Century English Literature and Culture* (Lewisburg, *circa* 2005)

Howard Chudacoff, *The Age of the Bachelor: Creating an American Subculture* (Princeton, 1999)

Helen Clifford, *Silver in London: The Parker and Wakelin Partnership, 1760–1776* (New Haven and London, 2004)

Nicholas Cooper, *Houses of the Gentry, 1480–1680* (New Haven and London, 1999)

John Cornforth, *Early Georgian Interiors* (New Haven and London, 2004)

Dan Cruikshank and Neil Burton, *Life in the Georgian City* (London, 1990)

M. J. Daunton, *House and Home in the Victorian City: Working-class Housing, 1850–1914* (London, 1983)

Bernard Denvir, *The Eighteenth Century: Art, Design and Society, 1689–1789* (London, 1983)

Peter Earle, *A City Full of People: Men and Women of London, 1650–1750* (London, 1994)

A. Roger Ekirch, *At Day's Close: Night in Times Past* (New York, 2005)

Margaret J. M. Ezell, *The Patriarch's Wife: Literary Evidence and the History of the Family* (Chapel Hill, 1987)

David Flaherty, *Privacy in Colonial New England* (Charlottesville, 1967)

Amanda Flather, *Gender and Space in Early Modern England* (Woodbridge, Suffolk, 2007)

Elizabeth Foyster, *Marital Violence: An English Family History, 1660–1857* (Cambridge, 2005)

Alice T. Friedman, *House and Household in Elizabethan England: Wollaton Hall and the Willoughby Family* (Chicago, 1989)

Amy M. Froide, *Never Married: Single Women in Early Modern England* (Oxford, 2005)

Mark Girouard, *Life in the English Country House* [1978] (Harmondsworth, 1980)

Laura Gowing, *Domestic Dangers: Women, Words and Sex in Early Modern London* (Oxford, 1996)

Peter Guillery, *The Small House in Eighteenth-century London* (New Haven and London, 2004)

Eileen Harris, *The Genius of Robert Adam: His Interiors* (New Haven, 2001)

Christoph Heyl, *A Passion for Privacy: Untersuchungen zur Geneseder Bürgerlichen Privatsphäre in London, 1660–1800* (Munich, 2004)

Margaret Hunt, *The Middling Sort: Commerce, Gender and the Family in England, 1680–1780* (Berkeley, CA, 1996)

Robert W. Jones, *Gender and the Formation of Taste in Eighteenth-century Britain* (Cambridge, 1998)

Anne Kugler, *Errant Plagiary: The Life and Writing of Lady Sarah Cowper, 1644–1720* (Stanford, CA, 2002)

Beverly Lemire, *The Business of Everyday Life: Gender, Practice and Social Politics in England, c.1600–1900* (Manchester, 2005)

Trevor Lummis and Jan Marsh, *The Woman's Domain: Women and the English Country House* (London, 1990)

Matthew McCormack, *The Independent Man: Citizenship and Gender Politics in Georgian England* (Manchester, 2006)

Michael Mascuch, *The Origins of the Individualist Self: Autobiography and Self-Identity in England, 1591–1791* (Cambridge, 1997)

Tim Meldrum, *Domestic Service and Gender, 1660–1750: Life and Work in the London Household* (Harlow, 2000)

Sara Mendelson and Patricia Crawford, *Women in Early Modern England, 1550–1720* (Oxford, 1998)

Stana Nenadic, *Lairds and Luxury: Highland Gentry in Eighteenth-century Scotland* (Edinburgh, 2007)

Miles Ogborn, *Spaces of Modernity: London's Geographies, 1680–1780* (New York and London, 1998)

Susanna Ottaway, *The Decline of Life: Old Age in Eighteenth-century England* (Cambridge, 2004)

Mark Overton et al., *Production and Consumption in English Households, 1600–1750* (London and New York, 2004)

Annik Pardailhe-Galabrun, *The Birth of Intimacy: Privacy and Domestic Life in Early Modern Paris* (Cambridge, 1991)

Rozsika Parker, *The Subversive Stitch: Embroidery and the Making of the Feminine* (London, 1983)

Maria Perry, *The House in Berkeley Square: A History of the Lansdowne Club* (London, 2003)

Margaret Ponsonby, *Stories from Home: English Domestic Interiors, 1750–1850* (Aldershot, 2007)

Kate Retford, *The Art of Domestic Life: Family Portraiture in Eighteenth-century England* (New Haven, 2006)

Sarah Richards, *Eighteenth-century Ceramics: Products for a Civilized Society* (Manchester, 1999)

Treve Rosoman, *London Wallpapers: Their Manufacture and Use, 1690–1840* (London, 1992)

Charles Saumarez Smith, *Eighteenth-century Decoration: Design and the Domestic Interior in England* (London, 1993)

Gill Saunders, *Wallpaper in Interior Decoration* (London, 2002)

Gordon Schochet, *The Authoritarian Family and Political Attitudes in Seventeenth-century England: Patriarchalism in Political Thought* (New Brunswick, 1988)

Carole Shammas, *The Pre-industrial Consumer in England and America* (Oxford, 1990)

Alexandra Shepard, *Meanings of Manhood in Early Modern England* (Oxford, 2003)

Ann B. Shteir, *Cultivating Women, Cultivating Science: Flora's Daughters and Botany in England, 1760–1860* (Baltimore, 1996)

Kim Sloan, *'A Noble Art': Amateur Artists and Drawing Masters, c.1600–1800* (London, 2000)

Craig Spence, *London in the 1690s: A Social Atlas* (London, 2000)

L. Stone and J. Fawtier Stone, *An Open Elite? England, 1540–1880* (abridged edn, Oxford, 1986)

John Summerson, *Georgian London* [1945] (London, 1988)

—, *Architecture in Britain, 1530–1830* [1953] (Harmondsworth, 1970)

Christopher Sykes, *Private Palaces: Life in the Great London Houses* (London, 1985)

Naomi Tadmor, *Family and Friends in Eighteenth-century England: Household, Kinship and Patronage* (Cambridge, 2000)

Ingrid Tague, *Women of Quality: Accepting and Contesting Ideals of Femininity in England, 1690–1760* (Woodbridge, Suffolk, 2002)

Peter Thornton, *Seventeenth-century Interior Decoration in England, France and Holland* (New Haven, 1978)

—, *Authentic Decor: The Domestic Interior, 1620–1920* (London, 1984)

Randolph Trumbach, *The Rise of the Egalitarian Family: Aristocratic Kinship and Domestic Relations in Eighteenth-century England* (New York, 1978)

Amanda Vickery, *The Gentleman's Daughter: Women's Lives in Georgian England* (New Haven and London, 1998)

Lorna Weatherill, *Consumer Behaviour and Material Culture in Britain, 1660–1760* (London, 1988)

Susan Whyman, *Sociability and Power in Late Stuart England: The Cultural World of the Verneys, 1660–1720* (Oxford, 1999)

Richard Wilson and Alan Mackley, *Creating Paradise: The Building of the English Country House, 1660–1880* (London and New York, 2000)

Hilary Young, *English Porcelain, 1745–95: Its Makers, Design, Marketing and Consumption* (London, 1999)

Collections of Essays

Isabelle Baudino, Jacques Carré and Cécile Révauger (eds), *The Invisible Woman: Aspects of Women's Work in Eighteenth-century Britain* (Aldershot, 2005)

A. L. Beier and Roger Finlay (eds), *London, 1500–1700: The Making of the Metropolis* (London, 1986)

Maxine Berg and Helen Clifford (eds), *Consumers and Luxury: Consumer Culture in Europe, 1650–1850* (Manchester, 1999)

Maxine Berg and Elizabeth Eger (eds), *Luxury in the Eighteenth Century: Debates, Desires and Delectable Goods* (Houndmills, Basingstoke, 2003)

Helen Berry and Elizabeth Foyster (eds), *The Family in Early Modern England* (Cambridge, 2007)

John Brewer and Roy Porter (eds), *Consumption and the World of Goods: Consumption and Society in the Seventeenth and Eighteenth Centuries* (London, 1993)

Dario Castiglione and Lesley Sharpe (eds), *Shifting the Boundaries: Transformation of the Languages of Public and Private in the Eighteenth Century* (Exeter, 1995)

Roger Chartier (ed.), *A History of Private Life*, III: *Passions of the Renaissance* (Cambridge, MA, 1989)

Moira Donald and Linda Hurcombe (eds), *Gender and Material Culture in Historical Perspective* (Basingstoke, 2000)

V. de Grazia and E. Furlough (eds), *The Sex of Things: Gender and Consumption in Historical Perspective* (Berkeley, CA, 1996)

Tim Hitchcock and Michele Cohen (eds), *English Masculinities, 1660–1800* (Harlow, 1999)

Tim Hitchcock and Heather Shore (eds), *The Streets of London: From the Great Fire to the Great Stink* (London, 2003)

Sarah Knott and Barbara Taylor (eds), *Women, Gender and Enlightenment* (Basingstoke, 2005

Maryanne Kowaleski and P. J. P. Goldberg (eds), *Medieval Domesticity: Home, Housing and Household in Medieval England* (Cambridge, 2009))

Ruth Larsen (ed.), *Maids and Mistresses* (York, 2004)

K. Norberg and D. Goodman (eds), *Furnishing the Eighteenth Century* (Abingdon, 2007)

Michelle Perrot (ed.), *A History of Private Life*, IV: *From the Fires of Revolution to the Great War* (Cambridge, MA, 1990)

Gill Perry and Michael Rossington (eds), *Femininity and Masculinity in Eighteenth-century Art and Culture* (Manchester, 1994)

M. Roper and J. Tosh (eds), *Manful Assertions: Masculinity in Britain since 1800* (London, 1991)

John Styles and Amanda Vickery (eds), *Gender, Taste and Material Culture in Britain and North America* (New Haven, 2006)

Essays and Articles

Hannah Barker, 'Soul, Purse and Family: Masculinity among the Non-Elites of Eighteenth-century Provincial England', *Social History*, 33/1 (2008), 12–35

John Bold, 'Privacy and the Plan', in *English Architecture Public and Private*, ed. John Bold and Edward Chaney (London, 1993), 107–19

P. J. Corfield, 'Walking the City Streets: The Urban Odyssey in Eighteenth-century England', *Journal of Urban History*, 16 (1990), 132–74

Colin Cunningham, 'Taste of a Tavern Keeper', *Country Life* (24 November 1994), 54–5

Peter Earle, 'The Female Labour Market in London in the Late Seventeenth and Early Eighteenth Centuries', *Economic History Review*, 2nd series, 42 (1989), 328–53

Margot Finn, 'Men's Things: Masculine Consumption in the Consumer Revolution', *Social History*, 25/2 (2000), 133–55

—, 'Scenes of Literary Life: The Homes of England', in *The New Cambridge History of English Literature: The Romantic Period*, ed. James Chandler (Cambridge, 2009), 293–313

Martin Francis, 'The Domestication of the Male? Recent Research on Nineteenth- and Twentieth-century British Masculinity', *Historical Journal*, 45/3 (2002), 637–52

Carole Fry, 'Spanning the Political Divide: Neo-Palladianism and the Early Eighteenth-century Landscape', *Garden History*, 31/2 (2003), 180–92

Rachel Garrard, 'English Probate Inventories and their Use in Studying the Significance of the Domestic Interior, 1570–1700', *A.A.G Bijdragen*, 23 (1980), 55–77

Christoph Heyl, 'We Are Not at Home: Protecting Domestic Privacy in Post-Fire Middle-class London', *London Journal*, 27 (2002), 12–33

Lawrence Klein, 'Politeness for Plebes: Consumption and Social Identity in Early Eighteenth-century England', in *The Consumption of Culture, 1660–1800: Image, Object, Text*, ed. J. Brewer and A. Bermingham (London, 1995), 362–82

Amy Milne-Smith, 'A Flight to Domesticity?: Making a Home in the Gentlemen's Clubs of London, 1880–1914', *Journal of British Studies*, 45 (2006), 796–818

Susan Moller Okin, 'Women and the Making of the Sentimental Family', *Philosophy and Public Affairs*, 11 (1981), 65–88

Sarah Pennell, 'Pots and Pans History: The Material Culture of the Kitchen in Early Modern England', *Journal of Design History*, 11 (1998), 201–16

—, 'Consumption and Consumerism in Early Modern England', *Historical Journal*, 42 (1999), 549–64

—, ' "Great Quantities of Gooseberry Pye and Baked Clod of Beef": Victualling and Eating out in Early Modern London', in *Londinopolis: Essays in the Cultural and Social History of Early Modern London*, ed. Paul Griffiths and Mark S. R. Jenner (Manchester, 2000), 228–59

M. H. Port, 'West End Palaces: The Aristocratic Town House in London, 1730–1830', *London Journal*, 20 (1995), 17–46

Sophie Sarin, 'The Floor Cloth and Other Floor Coverings in the London Domestic Interior, 1700–1800', *Journal of Design History*, 18 (2005), 133–45

Julie Schlarman, 'The Social Geography of Grosvenor Square: Mapping Gender and Politics, 1720–1760', *London Journal*, 28 (2003), 8–28

Alexandra Shepard, 'Manhood, Credit and Patriarchy in Early Modern England, c.1580–1640', *Past & Present*, 167 (2000), 75–196

— and Karen Harvey, 'What Have Historians Done with Masculinity?: Reflections on Five Centuries of British History, circa 1500–1950', *Journal of British Studies*, 44 (2005), 274–80

John Styles, 'Involuntary Consumers? The Eighteenth-century Servant and her Clothes', *Textile History*, 33/1 (2002), 9–21

Amanda Vickery, 'Golden Age to Separate Spheres: A Review of the Categories and Chronology of English Women's History', *Historical Journal*, 36/2 (1993), 383–414

Cynthia Wall, 'Gendering Rooms: Domestic Architecture and Literary Acts', *Eighteenth-Century Fiction*, 5 (1993), 360–7

—, 'The English Auction: Narratives of Dismantlings', *Eighteenth-Century Studies*, 31 (1997), 1–25

—, 'At Shakespeare's Head, Over Against Catherine Street in the Strand: Forms of Address in London Streets', in *The Streets of London: From the Great Fire to the Great Stink*, ed. Tim Hitchcock and Heather Shore (London, 2003), 10–26.

Lorna Weatherill, 'A Possession of One's Own: Women and Consumer Behaviour in England, 1660–1740', *Journal of British Studies*, 25 (1986), 131–26

Susan Wright, 'Sojourners and Lodgers in a Provincial Town: The Evidence from Eighteenth-century Ludlow', *Urban History*, 17 (1990), 14–35

E. A. Wrigley, 'A Simple Model of London's Importance in Changing English Society and Economy, 1650–1750', in *Towns in Societies: Essays in Economic History and Historical Sociology*, ed. P. Abrams and E. A. Wrigley (Cambridge, 1978), 215–43

Unpublished Dissertations and Papers

Judith Anderson, 'Derby Porcelain and the Early English Fine Ceramic Industry, c.1750–1830' (D.Phil. thesis, Leicester, 2000)

Fenela Childs, 'Prescriptions for Manners in English Courtesy Literature, 1690–1760' (D.Phil. thesis, Oxford, 1984)

Linda Colley, 'The Female Political Elite in Unreformed Britain' (unpublished paper, Institute of Historical Research, 25 June 1993)

Louisa Collins, 'Women, Writing and Furniture, 1750–1800' (MA dissertation in the History of Design, V&A/RCA, 2005)

Johanna Dahn, 'Active, Social and Temperate: A Construction of Taste with Special Reference to Katherine Plymley (1758–1829)' (ph.d thesis, Aberystwyth, 2000)

Sarah Dunster, 'Women of the Nottinghamshire Elite, c.1720–1820' (ph.d thesis, Nottingham, 2003)

Zoë Dyndor, 'The Political Culture of Elections in Northampton, 1768–1868' (ph.d thesis, in progress)

Ruth Geuter, 'Women and Embroidery in Seventeenth-century Britain: The Social, Religious and Political Meanings of Domestic Needlework' (ph.d thesis, Aberystwyth, 1997)

Jane Hamlett, 'Materialising Gender: Identity and Middle-class Domestic Interiors, 1850–1910' (ph.d thesis, London, 2005)

Ruth M. Larsen, 'Dynastic Domesticity: The Role of Elite Women in the Yorkshire Country House, 1685–1858' (ph.d thesis, York, 2003)

Jennifer Melville, 'The Use and Organization of Domestic Space in Late Seventeenth-century London' (ph.d thesis, Cambridge, 1999)

Katherine Sharpe, 'Conchology and Creativity: The Rise of Shellwork in Eighteenth-century England' (ma dissertation in the History of Design, v&a/rca, 1995)

Akiko Shimbo, 'Pattern Books, Showrooms and Furniture Design: Interactions between Producers and Consumers in England, 1754–1851' (ph.d thesis, London, 2007)

INDEX